The Regional and Urban Policy of the European Union

NEW HORIZONS IN REGIONAL SCIENCE

Series Editor: Philip McCann, *University of Groningen Endowed Chair of Economic Geography, Faculty of Spatial Sciences, University of Groningen, the Netherlands*

Regional science analyses important issues surrounding the growth and development of urban and regional systems and is emerging as a major social science discipline. This series provides an invaluable forum for the publication of high quality scholarly work on urban and regional studies, industrial location economics, transport systems, economic geography and networks.

New Horizons in Regional Science aims to publish the best work by economists, geographers, urban and regional planners and other researchers from throughout the world. It is intended to serve a wide readership including academics, students and policymakers.

Titles in the series include:

The Regional and Urban Policy of the European Union

Cohesion, Results-Orientation and Smart Specialisation

Philip McCann

University of Groningen Endowed Chair of Economic Geography, Faculty of Spatial Sciences, University of Groningen, the Netherlands

NEW HORIZONS IN REGIONAL SCIENCE

Edward Elgar
PUBLISHING

Cheltenham, UK • Northampton, MA, USA

Published by
Edward Elgar Publishing Limited
The Lypiatts
15 Lansdown Road
Cheltenham
Glos GL50 2JA
UK

Edward Elgar Publishing, Inc.
William Pratt House
9 Dewey Court
Northampton
Massachusetts 01060
USA

Paperback edition 2016

A catalogue record for this book
is available from the British Library

Library of Congress Control Number: 2014947220

This book is available electronically in the **Elgar**online
Economics subject collection
DOI 10.4337/9781783479511

ISBN 978 1 78347 950 4 (cased)
ISBN 978 1 78347 952 8 (paperback)
ISBN 978 1 78347 951 1 (eBook)

Typeset by Columns Design XML Ltd, Reading
Printed in Great Britain by Clays Ltd, St Ives plc

To my family

Contents

Preface

The regional and urban development policy of the European Union, or more precisely, EU Cohesion Policy, is currently undergoing many changes. These changes are driven both by the enormous changes in European regions and also by changes in thinking and analysis. The issues raised by these changes touch on fundamental analytical and conceptual matters regarding the nature of regional growth and development processes as well as the case for public policy in this arena. The debates regarding the policy changes cannot be separated from a detailed assessment of the major regional and urban features of the European economy. Moreover, the issues raised by the changes to regional and urban development policy in Europe also span many different academic disciplines and build on many different research methodologies and no single discipline or analytical approach has a monopoly of knowledge. A broad approach is therefore required in order to properly address these issues and while many of the main themes of the book follow an economic geography approach, this book explicitly incorporates insights from a range of different disciplines. As such, in terms of scientific audiences, this book is aimed at all economists, geographers, regional scientists, spatial planners, transportation scientists, sociologists, urban studies researchers, environmental scholars, political scientists and policy-analysts who are interested in regional and urban issues.

In terms of professional audiences the book is aimed principally at two rather different audiences. On the one hand, the book is written for a range of academics, scholars and researchers – working in fields such as economics, geography, environmental sciences, spatial and land-use planning, political science, urban studies, sociology and transportation systems – who are interested in issues of EU regional development but for whom many of the EU regional policy discussions and debates are rather opaque. Many of the EU Cohesion Policy debates and the policy-related publications often presume a great deal of prior knowledge regarding legal, institutional, political and economic issues specific to the policy in question, and it can be quite difficult to find an arena where such a body of both background and core material can be easily accessed in a single volume. This book therefore aims to synthesise these discussions into an accessible and research-relevant format.

On the other hand, this book is written for policy-makers working at EU, national, regional or local governance authorities, who have a reasonably good knowledge of the workings and architecture of the policy but for whom some of the conceptual debates seem to be rather abstruse. Many of these policy-makers have a broad understanding of the day-to-day case for the policy, but tend to be largely unaware of the fierce academic debates regarding the nature of the policy or the arguments about the justifications for or against the policy. In addition, policy-makers are also often unaware of the extent to which these debates both inform and also draw from much wider international and global debates well beyond Europe. These are not just European issues but matters of more general relevance for many parts of the world. Again, this book aims to synthesise these discussions into an accessible and policy-relevant format.

Finally, as well as examining the major regional and urban features of the European economy and then discussing the analytical underpinnings of the current re-design to EU Cohesion Policy, the book also aims to provide a roadmap of the various EU regional and urban data-sources which are available to researchers and policy-makers. There are numerous sources of high quality data on almost all aspects of the regional and urban economies of Europe. Sometimes, however, these are rather fragmented and produced by different institutions and organisations and therefore an overview of where and how to find out what is also an important aspect of this book. Much more is known about regional and urban issues in Europe than many observers realise and basing all policy-related discussions on sound evidence is essential. Indeed, this is one of the fundamental principles of the policy-reform.

ACKNOWLEDGEMENTS

I am very grateful to the following people who have read different draft parts of the book and who provided very detailed feedback, criticism and constructive comments.

Wolfgang Petzold, EU Committee of the Regions
John Bachtler, European Policies Research Centre, University of Strathclyde
Iain Begg, London School of Economics
Luc van den Brande, EU Committee of the Regions

Lewis Dijkstra, European Commission
Veronica Gaffey, European Commission
Mikel Landabaso, European Commission
Karen Maguire, OECD
Joaquim Oliveira-Martins, OECD

Chapters 5 and 6 could not have been written without enormous intellectual help from Raquel Ortega-Argilés, University of Groningen, who co-authored the various scholarly papers on which these two chapters are largely based. Raquel also helped to source and interpret large numbers of technical documents relating to many different aspects addressed by the policy reform process.

Andreas Huck, University of Groningen, kindly proofread the whole text.

I am also heavily indebted to various other people with whom I have discussed the matters discussed in this book in great detail over recent years. Most importantly have been my discussions with Fabrizio Barca, Italian Ministry of Economy and Finance, and Johannes Hahn, EU Commissioner for Regional Policy, alongside whom I worked for 20 out of my 36 months as Special Adviser to the EU Commissioner for Regional Policy.

In addition, I wish to thank: Maria Abreu, University of Cambridge; Dirk Ahner, European Commission; Rudiger Ahrend, OECD; Andrea Bonaccorsi, University of Pisa; Monica Brezzi OECD; Gianni Carbonaro, EIB European Investment Bank; Claire Charbit, OECD; Mario Cervantes OECD; Nicola de Michelis, European Commission; Alessandra Faggian, Ohio State University, USA; Dominique Foray, École Polytecnique Féderale de Lausanne, Switzerland; Enrique Garcilazo OECD; Xavier Goenaga, JRC-IPTS, Seville; Henri de Groot, Free University of Amsterdam; Simona Iammarino, London School of Economics; Eric Marlier CEPS/INSTEAD; Rose Olfert, University of Saskatchewan, Canada; Mark Partridge, Ohio State University USA; Andrés Rodriguez-Pose, London School of Economics; Matthias Ruth, Northeastern University USA; Riccardo Scarpa, Queens University Belfast; William Tompson OECD; Frank Vanclay, University of Groningen; Jouke van Dijk, University of Groningen; Attila Varga, University of Pecs, Hungary; Eric von Breska, European Commission, all of whom have provided me with important intellectual insights relating to different dimensions of the reform process, along with Ronald Hall, Katja Reppel, Elisa Roller, Luisa Sanches and Claus Schultze, all from the European Commission, who provided me with great support and policy-related inputs during my time as Special Adviser.

Disclaimer

I have taken on board advice and insights from these many different people but in the end the material contained in this book reflects entirely my own understanding of these issues. The material contained here therefore does not reflect the views of any sub-national, national, international or European organisations, but reflects my own understanding as a scholar and a policy adviser.

Philip McCann
Special Adviser to the European Commissioner for Regional Policy,
Johannes Hahn, 2010–2013
Chief Scientific Advisor 2013–2014: *Investment for Jobs and Growth – Promoting Development and Good Governance in EU Regions and Cities. Sixth Report on Economic, Social and Territorial Cohesion*

Groningen, the Netherlands
May 2014

1. The backdrop to EU Cohesion Policy debates: Europe 2020 and the post-crisis economy

1.1 INTRODUCTION TO THE BACKDROP TO EU COHESION POLICY DEBATES

One of the flagship policies of the European Union (EU) is 'Cohesion Policy', which is the regional and urban development policy of the European Union. This book aims to explain the role played by EU regional and urban policy, its role within the wider EU system (European Union 2012; Pinder and Usherwood 2007), and also the ideas which underpin the recent reforms to the policy. While there are obviously many local, regional and urban policy initiatives which take place within the national context and which are independent of EU initiatives, it is those local development initiatives which are related in part to EU funding schemes which are the specific focus of this book.

In general, the level of awareness on the part of the public of the role and impacts of EU Cohesion Policy is closely related to the relative scale of EU Cohesion Policy interventions in their own countries (European Commission 2010a). Not surprisingly, therefore, in the richer Northern and Western European nations the overall levels of public awareness of the role and impacts of EU Cohesion Policy are much less than in the lower income countries of Central, Eastern and Southern Europe (ibid.). However, EU Cohesion Policy has for a long time been a key policy of the European Union, and one of its main levers for promoting the development of the EU. Today Cohesion Policy is the single largest policy of the European Union and therefore examining the nature, logic, role, goals, mechanisms, workings, impacts and outcomes of the policy is important in its own right for providing a good understanding of one of the most important activities in the European policy arena.

The key focus of this book, however, is on the reforms to EU Cohesion Policy and understanding the issues raised regarding the required reforms of the policy also allows us to address fundamental questions about the role played by economic geography in growth and development processes, as well as modern thinking regarding economic policy. Many of the issues raised in this book reflect crucial analytical and conceptual issues which are common to all aspects of economic geography and to all development policies operating at the regional, urban or local levels, and in all parts of the world. Some of the ideas which inform these debates have emerged relatively recently in response to new developments in the fields of urban and regional economics and economic geography. However, some of these issues are also based on longstanding traditions, so the intellectual inputs into the policy reform debates reflect a mixture of both old and new arguments. However, it is this particular mixture of old and new arguments which is novel, and renewed intellectual agendas challenge many preconceived approaches and assumptions regarding all aspects of these policies. Of particular interest here is the role which local context plays in questions of policy design. EU Cohesion Policy operates in a highly heterogeneous environment and an awareness of this heterogeneity allows us to examine different development policy arguments in different contexts, but from the standpoint of a single policy logic and architecture. As such, investigating the changes to EU Cohesion Policy opens up a broader set of discussions which are pertinent to wider development policy debates, including that of the European Union.

However, making a case for a policy or a case for its reform also requires a sound understanding of the earlier experience of the policy and the earlier arguments underpinning its existence and design. All current policies and their design are the result of a complex set of earlier issues and discussions, some of which are complementary to each other and some of which may be rather conflicting to each other. This is also the case for EU Cohesion Policy, and in this book we will address these various issues. However, at this stage it is necessary to underline the fact that policies also reflect a political economy process which takes place over time. As such, while many aspects of the policy-reform discussions examined here are relatively recent, the discussions regarding the links between European integration, the impacts on regions and role of policy in this arena, already have a longstanding pedigree based on a well-established tradition. This tradition reflects the different stages of European integration. There are various publications which reflect the geographical and regional aspects of the earlier stages of European economic integration following the establishment of the EU Single Market (Armstrong and Vickerman 1995; Button and Pentecost 1999; Cappelin and Batey 1993; Cheshire and Gordon 1995; Cole and Cole 1993; Delamaide 1994; Fingleton 2003). There is also material which discusses the complexities and heterogeneity of the EU context (Le Galès

2002; Rodriguez-Pose 1998, 2002) as well as different aspects of previous generations of EU Cohesion Policy (Artobolevsky 1997; Bachtler and Turok 1997; Leonardi 2005; Martin 1999; Molle 2007; Vanhove 1999). There are also useful publications which help to position the EU regional and urban debates with respect to North American debates (Summers et al. 1999; Sweet 1999). Finally, there is also a more recent generation of publications which deal with particular issues facing the European regional and urban arena (Bellini and Hilpert 2013; Blokker and Dallago 2009; Faludi 2008; Hall and Pain 2006; Jovanović 2009; Sardadvar 2011; Stierle-Von Schütz et al. 2008; Zientara 2009) and specifically the Cohesion Policy negotiation environment (Bachtler et al. 2013). These publications add a great deal of detail, colour and nuance to the policy-reform discussions, alongside the numerous European Commission and European Union official publications and information tools (DG Regio 2013) referred to in this book.

A good knowledge of this wide-ranging literature offers a broad picture of the integration experience which Europe and its regions have undergone over recent decades, and helps to provide a sound and nuanced understanding of how the current context has been arrived at. This knowledge also helps us to sketch out a likely road-map of how the policy debates and the policy processes may evolve. The ideas and issues referred to in this established regional development literature are constantly referred to throughout this book, and knitted together as far as possible with the newer ideas emerging from a variety of different fields. This is necessary because over recent years there has emerged a wide-ranging debate regarding the role which regional and urban policy plays, can play or should play, in European integration processes and this debate re-engages with both these older and newer issues. The different aspects of these complex debates are discussed in detail throughout this book. However, before we engage in these discussions it is essential to highlight the key influences which heavily shape the backdrop to these discussions.

In order to begin our discussions it is necessary to point out that all of the debates regarding the reforms to European regional and urban policies need to be set against the backdrop of four important influences which both help to foster and also heavily shape these debates. These four influences are: (i) major steps forward in academic thinking about spatial economics, economic geography and development policy; (ii) the diversity and heterogeneity of the European Union context; (iii) shifts in European growth perspectives and the development of the Europe 2020 strategy; and (iv) the geographical impacts of the 2008 global financial crisis. The first of these four issues, namely the advances in thinking about economic geography and spatial economics, are discussed in detail throughout the following chapters of this book, and indeed are the key focus of this book, so they will not be discussed in this chapter. However, before moving on to these discussions it is useful for us to address the other three issues briefly here, so as to provide a sound basis for our subsequent discussions and to properly situate the discussions about the reforms to EU Cohesion Policy.

1.2   THE DIVERSITY AND HETEROGENEITY OF THE EUROPEAN UNION

The European Union (EU) is a diverse economic, social and territorial arena. European Integration is a slow process with important break-points and thresholds defining critical stages. As of 2014 the EU is made up of 28 countries, known as 'member states', comprising what are known as the 'EU-15' mixed economy countries which had joined the EU by 1995, the 'EU-12 accession' countries which had joined from 2004 onwards of which ten were former transition economies plus Malta and Cyprus, and finally Croatia which joined in 2013. The degree of heterogeneity of the European context, and the context in which EU Cohesion Policy operates, can be understood initially simply by considering the national productivity variations within the EU. In 2014, the EU-wide average per capita GDP is just approximately €25,500 (US$34,000[1]), while the national per capita GDP ranges between approximately €11,000 (US$14,000) in Bulgaria and Romania to some €66,000 (US$89,000) in Luxembourg, which is then followed by a group of countries comprising The Netherlands, Denmark, Ireland, Austria, Germany and Sweden, all of whose per capita GDP levels are of the order of approximately €33,000 (US$42,000). A group of EU member states including The Netherlands, Belgium and Denmark, exhibit some of the highest levels of labour productivity per hour in the OECD (OECD 2014). Belgium and Finland have GDP per capita figures around €30,000 (US$40,000) while the UK and France both have per capital GDP levels of the order of €28,000 (US$36,000), followed by Italy €26,000 ($US34,000) and Spain with per capita GDP levels of approximately €24,500 (US$32,000). The rest of the former transition economies exhibit productivity levels of between just over €15,000 (US$20,000) in Latvia to €21,000 (US$28,000) in Slovenia. Finally, in the wake of the 2008 global financial crisis both Portugal and Greece now have GDP per-capita levels approximately of €19,000 (US$26,000) and as such are now between the levels exhibited by the former transition economies of the Czech Republic €20,700

(US$27,500) and Slovenia. What becomes very clear from these figures is that the diversity and inequality within the EU is much greater than that which exists within the USA, Canada, Australasia, Japan or Korea, while at the same time it is much less than that which exists in the BRICS (Brazil, Russia, India, China and South Africa) countries (Iammarino and McCann 2013; McCann 2009; OECD 2011a, b, 2014). The Europe regional system displays features which combine elements from many different parts of the world, but in a manner which is specific to Europe. In particular, the heterogeneity of the EU interregional system is unique, in that within a single integrated market the variation in national and regional per-capita incomes almost exactly reflects the national and regional per-capita income variations evident across the whole of the OECD. Understanding these variations is important in order to ensure a correct positioning of discussions regarding the European interregional context in terms of different parts of the global economy. By setting the EU regional discussions within this comparative context we are better able to ensure that our discussions are properly grounded, in that the EU interregional variations are far greater than are evident in the USA or Canadian context, and equivalent to those evident in the North American context including Mexico.

Allowing for this heterogeneity, the EU is now already a highly integrated economic arena. Most recent estimates suggest that the positive impact of the EU Single Market on national economies with estimates for EU different countries varying between 3–10 per cent of GDP with most estimates being of the order of 5–6 per cent of GDP (BIS 2011; BIS/DFID 2011; Boltho and Eichengreen 2008; CBI 2013). While these numbers may not sound large to some observers and may be less than some optimistic forecasters might have expected, for comparison purposes these percentage changes in GDP are more than comparable to: the contribution of railways to nineteenth-century US economic growth;[2] equivalent to the potential economic growth effects of doubling of the size of a nation's cities;[3] greater than the impacts of Asia's two-and-a-half decades of growth on the Australasian economies;[4] greater than the growth effects of NAFTA[5] which was established a couple of years after the EU Single Market; similar to the growth contribution of Europe's ICT-producing sectors (Timmer et al. 2011) or the growth effects of investments non-ICT-capital on the EU-15 countries over the same period (Timmer et al. 2010; Van Ark et al. 2012);[6] and many times greater than the negative output effects of the 2008 global financial crisis on the overall EU economies (OECD 2014). Viewed in the light of these other impacts, the Single Market effects are clearly very significant.

At the same time, however, economic geography and industrial economics suggest that these impacts will vary markedly across countries and regions within the EU. A sense of the scale of the Single Market effect can be gained from the fact that in the case of The Netherlands the relevant estimates are equivalent to one month's extra salary per annum for Dutch workers,[7] while for the UK these estimates are equivalent to three times the annual contribution of North Sea Oil to the UK economy[8] and similar to the growth contribution of financial services to the UK economy over the period of the Single Market (Aghion et al. 2013). In addition, the full removal of the remaining intra-EU trade barriers, particularly in services, is expected to generate additional benefits[9] of a similar order of magnitude (BIS 2011). As such, the existing benefits of the Single Market integration process are largely consistent with those predicted by the original analytical exercises (Cecchini et al. 1988; Commission of the European Communities 1990; Emerson et al. 1988, 1992), and if the Single Market is fully completed, this would be expected to generate total productivity benefits which are much greater than those which were originally forecast.

Today the integrated arena of the EU economy is characterised by dense cross-border flows of goods, services, people, capital and investment funds. These flows operate within networks of value chains spanning sectors and borders (Timmer et al. 2013) with the value-adding role of different countries changing (Jaegers et al. 2013) as production-related investments moves across borders. However, even allowing for the processes of out-sourcing, off-shoring and production fragmentation all of which are associated with modern globalisation (McCann 2008), it is still the case that the domestic value-added within the EU represents more than 85 per cent of the final value of EU consumer sales and this share is very similar to that which is observed for the USA and Japan (European Union 2013a). The reason is that over the last three decades the majority of these fragmentation processes have been reflected in shifts of value-adding followed by cross-border cross-hauling and re-importing to and from other EU countries, rather than to other parts of the world. This phenomenon of 'global regionalism', whereby neighbouring countries become increasingly integrated in all aspects of their economies, is a well-known outcome of the modern era of globalisation (Rugman 2000), and also reflects similar trends in other parts of the world (McCann 2013). The process of European integration is neither smooth nor a continuously forward-moving process, but rather a process which ebbs and flows. Although over time the process of economic integration has indeed progressed a long way, at the present time the current environment in Europe is very challenging. In particular, the fiscal and monetary issues evident within many of the Eurozone economies raise complex macroeconomic challenges. For the purposes of this book, however, it is not necessary to discuss many of the diverse challenges facing Europe. Rather, it is important to note that in spite of aspects of recent retrenchment in the post-crisis era, most evidence continues to point to increasing long-run international integration (Ghamawat and Altman 2012; MGI 2014; UNCTAD 2012) in Europe and elsewhere.

1.3 THE EUROPE 2020 STRATEGY AND ITS REGIONAL AND URBAN DIMENSIONS

In the case of Europe, any discussions regarding the role of EU Cohesion Policy must necessarily first be positioned against the backdrop of the overall EU policy agenda, which is known as the Europe 2020 strategy. In June 2010 the Council of the European Union approved the Europe 2020 strategy[10] (European Union 2011) and this strategy advocates that public policy should aim to promote smart, sustainable and inclusive growth (European Commission 2010b). The smart growth dimension includes improving the conditions for innovation, research and development and improving education levels; the sustainable growth dimension includes meeting climate change and energy objectives; and the inclusive growth dimension includes promoting employment and promoting social inclusion, in particular through the reduction of poverty (European Commission 2010b). This multidimensional approach is based on a growing awareness that successful and longstanding growth and development processes must necessarily incorporate these three different dimensions and that growth processes which are overly concentrated on only one or two of these development dimensions are unlikely to be viable in the long run. The Europe 2020 strategy of smart, sustainable and inclusive growth also closely mirrors the 2009 OECD 'Global Standard' growth strategy (OECD 2009a) of 'stronger, cleaner and fairer growth'[11] as well as recent international[12] and US thinking[13] leading to the US growth strategy of 'sustainable communities, innovation clusters, revitalizing neighborhoods'.[14] Indeed, these various approaches all reflect a growing consensus that development needs to be environmentally aware,[15] broad-based and inclusive in order to be long-lasting (Berg and Ostry 2011; Ezcurra 2007; Piketty 2014; *The Economist* 2014a) and that modern policy approaches to growth and development also need to consider these broader dimensions of environmental and social sustainability in order to be effective.[16] These ideas have been gradually emerging over the last decade and reflect something of a shift away from the largely sectoral approach of the earlier 'Lisbon Strategy' which was originally launched in 2000 and re-launched in 2005 (João Rodrigues 2009), but whose results were widely viewed as disappointing (Bachtler et al. 2013; European Commission 2010c), including at the regional level (Dijkstra 2010).

The broader multi-dimensional approach to growth and development reflected in the Europe 2020 strategy also raises fundamental issues regarding the nature of growth and development processes at the local and regional levels. In particular, the complementarities and trade-offs between the different smart (stronger), sustainable (cleaner) and inclusive (fairer) growth dimensions differ between regions and localities (OECD 2011a) and these differences pose significant local and regional policy challenges. In the case of the EU these differences are very marked and an acknowledgement of these differences heavily shapes the debates regarding the role played by regions and cities in the long-run growth and development processes of the European Union. Yet, the thinking underpinning the different aspects of the Europe 2020 strategy at the regional level (DG Regio 2008, 2009a,b) as well as at the national and EU-wide levels, also very much pre-dates the 2008 global financial crisis. Over recent years there has emerged a broad-based consensus that EU Cohesion Policy is ideally positioned to play a key role in driving the Europe 2020 agenda. This is in part because Cohesion Policy already seeks to address smart, sustainable and inclusive challenges, and these all have explicitly spatial and local dimensions as also reflected in both OECD (2009a, 2011a) and US policy approaches. However, this consensus has also arisen in response to much reflection and a fundamental intellectual reconsideration of the role and nature of the policy during 2008–2009, as well as a widespread public consultation process.[17]

The *Fifth Cohesion Report on Economic, Social and Territorial Cohesion* (European Commission 2010d) proposed that regional, city and local authorities working in partnership with the both national governments and the EU through Cohesion Policy (European Union 2011) could help to drive many aspects of the Europe 2020 agenda. As we will see in this book, the EU-wide consultation exercise along with the deliberations within the European Commission (2011a), the European Parliaments and the European Council, demonstrates that these ideas were strongly supported across the European Union at many different national, regional, urban and local levels (CoR 2014). In the words of the European Commission President José Manuel Barroso, 'Cohesion Policy is one of the key instruments to realise the Europe 2020 goals. It is the largest EU investment in the real economy and a key pillar of the EU economic policy triangle of fiscal consolidation, structural reforms investment in growth' (European Commission 2014a). However, the idea that local, regional and urban actors implementing actions and interventions at the local, regional or urban scale can help to foster aggregate national growth and development, reflects thinking which has been undertaken again in a wide range of international arenas over a long period including Europe (Padoa-Schioppa et al. 1987), and most recently in particular at the level of the OECD (OECD 2009b, c; 2011a). These debates, however, regarding the nature of growth and development, the role of regions and cities in these development processes, and also the possibilities for modern policy initiatives to foster broad-based growth, have all recently been thrown into sharp relief by the 2008 global financial crisis. The aftermath of the crisis has witnessed dramatically differing fortunes amongst the regions of Europe, faltering progress towards Europe 2020 goals (European Commission 2014b), and a re-ordering or reshaping of regional trajectories.

1.4 THE IMPACTS OF THE 2008 GLOBAL FINANCIAL CRISIS ON THE EU ECONOMIES

The thinking underpinning the different aspects of the Europe 2020 strategy very much pre-date the 2008 global financial crisis, and reflect broader debates regarding the nature of growth and development processes and the role which policy can play in shaping these processes. However, the goals of the Europe 2020 strategy are also very pertinent to the challenges which have arisen in the aftermath of the 2008 global financial crisis (European Commission 2011b), and as such, the 2010 adoption of the strategy was especially timely. Across Europe the complex economic, social and political effects of European economic integration processes are well documented (Addison and Siebert 1997; Baldwin et al. 1999; Bliss and de Macedo 1990; Crafts and Toniolo 1996; Eichengreen 2007; Florio 2011; Jovanović 2005; Kahanec and Zimmerman 2011; Mayhew 1998; Rogowski et al. 2011; Rosamond 2000), as are the impacts on Europe of the global financial crisis, and the future options and challenges facing Europe in this arena are heavily debated (Alesina and Giavazzi 2006; Arestis and Sawyer 2012; Berglund et al. 2009; Fitoussi and Le Cacheux 2010; Marsh 2009; Pisani-Ferry 2014; *The Economist*, 2014b; Vaughan-Whitehead 2013; Zientara 2009). While an exhaustive discussion of these issues is not necessary here, as a preparation for engaging with the material in the following chapters in this book, it is useful to highlight some of the key effects of the global financial crisis which particularly impact on the regional and urban aspects of Europe.

For our purposes here, and drawing directly from the official publications of the European Union, it is useful to highlight four major features of the 2008 global financial crisis and its aftermath on the EU economies, namely: (i) the effects on sectors; (ii) the effects on foreign direct investment (FDI); (iii) the effects on poverty; and (iv) the effects on public finances.

(i)   Although the global financial crisis of 2008 originated in the arenas of finance and insurance, most of its most severe and adverse impacts across the EU have been felt in other sectors, and in particular in the construction sector. While EU-wide output and employment in the finance and insurance sectors had again reached its 2007 levels by 2011, EU-wide gross value added (GVA) and employment in construction had fallen by 3 per cent between 2007 and 2011. In those countries most severely affected by the crisis, these contractions ranged between 6 per cent and 20 per cent, while property prices in these countries fell by 30–50 per cent during this period (European Union 2011).

(ii)   Much of the growth and economic convergence between member states in the two decades prior to the 2008 global financial crisis was associated with massive increases in intra-EU trade and inflows of Foreign Direct Investment (FDI), which spearheaded massive cross-border processes of technological transfer of all forms (World Bank 2012). In the years prior to the 2008 global financial crisis interregional trade in Europe increased rapidly (Thissen et al. 2013). At the same time, the inflows of FDI into EU member states originated both from outside of Europe, but also from within Europe, from other EU member states (McCann 2009). In 2004 some three-quarters of total FDI inflows into EU nations originated from other EU nations with one-quarter originating from outside of the EU. The scale of these inflows relative to national GDP was most marked in the EU-12 countries (MGI 2013), with the ratio of annual FDI inflows to national GDP being of the order of 15–23 per cent in 2005–2007 in Bulgaria, Estonia, Malta and Belgium (European Union 2013b). The cumulative result of these inflows over previous years meant that in 2004 the FDI stocks which originated from inside of the EU accounted for some 60 per cent of total EU FDI stocks, while some 40 per cent of the FDI stocks within the EU originated from outside of the EU (European Union 2013b).

(iii)   At a global scale, however, the major impacts of the 2008 global financial crisis were massive reductions in FDI flows and in some cases actual withdrawals and retrenchment of FDI stocks (Ghamawat and Altman 2012; UNCTAD 2012) and this was also the case within the EU. Europe experienced major falls in both inter-regional and cross-border trade followed by a slow recovery (Thissen et al. 2010), alongside similar falls in FDI. These effects were particularly marked in the case of some EU member states, with FDI flows falling between 2005 and 2007 by the equivalent of 1.5–6 per cent in many EU-12 member states, with Bulgaria experiencing a fall equivalent to 12 per cent of GDP (European Union 2013b). In 2011 the current FDI inflows into EU member states from both within the EU and from outside of the EU were running at some 60 per cent of their pre-crisis levels (European Union 2013b). These changes have been wrought primarily by sharp reductions in intra-EU FDI flows in the aftermath of the 2008 global financial crisis which have been more severe than the reductions in FDI inflows from outside of the EU. This reduction in intra-EU FDI inflows means that the relative size of FDI inflows into EU member states originating from within the EU and those originating from outside of the EU have shifted markedly. FDI inflows from outside of the EU now account for one-third of total FDI inflows into EU member states while two-thirds are still accounted for by inflows from within the EU. These changes in FDI flows have obviously heavily impacted on the distribution and scale of FDI stocks within the EU. By 2011 the FDI stocks within the EU which had originated from within the EU were only just over 50 per cent of total FDI stocks in the EU, while those which had originated from outside of the EU accounted for just under 50 per cent of total European FDI stocks (European Union 2013b). Recent evidence suggests that FDI flows in EU countries from other parts of Europe as well as from outside of Europe are again recovering to pre-crisis levels, and in particular in western Europe (Ernst and Young 2014).

(iv)   The share of the population at risk of poverty or social exclusion has risen in almost every EU member state since 2008, except for Poland and Romania (European Union 2013b). The three major dimensions of this phenomenon are share of the population at risk of poverty, experiencing severe material deprivation, or experiencing very low work intensity. Prior to the 2008 global financial crisis disposable income had been growing rapidly in all countries, but the subsequent falls in disposable income in the wake of the crisis mean that real disposable income in many countries is now no higher than it was prior to 2005 (European Union 2013b), and in some cases no higher than it was prior to 2003. Similarly, the at-risk-of-poverty levels in many countries have again returned to pre-2005 levels, while the share of very low work intensity households is now greater than it was in 2005 in many countries (European Commission 2012).

(v)   Since 2008 the levels of public debt relative to GDP have increased in every EU member state except Sweden (European Union 2013b). At present only four EU-15 countries, namely Sweden, Luxembourg, Finland and Denmark, have public levels below 60 per cent of GDP, while this is also the case for all of the EU-12 countries. However, some of the EU-12 countries with low levels of public debt, such as Estonia, have been severely affected by the crisis. Sub-national government investment as a share of total national public investment has tended to increase in decentralised countries and to decrease in centralised countries, although the long-run OECD-wide trend is towards decentralisation (OECD 2013a). In order to reduce their national debts public investment in many of these countries in productivity-enhancing arenas such as transport infrastructure, education, R&D and innovation-related activities are being cut, such that gross fixed capital formation in 2013 is lower in 18 EU member states than it was in 2011 (European Union 2013b). However, these public expenditure reductions also hide subtle shifts. In particular, a majority of EU member states have shifted towards capital expenditure and away from non-capital expenditure, while also increasing the relative share of sub-national government investments (Dotti and Bubbico 2014). At the same time, since the global financial crisis, the levels of public trust in national governments have fallen in the majority of European countries, and these falls are most notable in those countries facing severe government debt problems (OECD 2013b).

These four key features of the 2008 global financial crisis have led to both the stalling and the acceleration of the processes of European integration, both politically as well as economically. In economic terms the aftermath of the 2008 global financial crisis has in part reversed many of the benefits associated with increasing European economic integration which we have witnessed over the last two decades. However, although all sections of Europe have been adversely affected by the crisis, these effects have not been evenly distributed across Europe, but rather have tended to be concentrated in particular sectors, in particular countries and regions, and amongst particular sections of the population. The fact that the effects of the crisis are unevenly felt threatens the unity of the EU, because the benefits and costs of EU-wide economic integration are perceived differently in different parts of Europe. At the same time, the required urgent responses to the crisis have led to an acceleration of various institutional measures aimed at deepening the union and which are designed to allay future shocks. Many of these measures are unlikely to have taken place in other circumstances, and again, they heavily shape the arena in which EU Cohesion Policy operates.

It is the combination of the new policy thinking provided by the Europe 2020 strategy plus the new policy challenges thrown up by the impacts of the 2008 global financial crisis, which now provide the backdrop to all current debates about the nature and role of EU Cohesion Policy. The Europe 2020 strategy highlights the importance of the multi-dimensional nature of growth and development and the need for policy to be similarly multi-dimensional in its approach. At the same time, the post-crisis economy is one in which the integration processes of Europe are under severe strain, as are the economies of many regions which were previously very buoyant. The new thinking and the new realities together frame all current policy discussions. Although as we will see in this book the discussions regarding the case for regional and urban development policy at the level of the EU largely pre-date both the launch of the Europe 2020 strategy and also the onset of the 2008 global financial crisis, both of these developments have heavily shaped all subsequent discussions regarding the future nature, role and design of EU Cohesion Policy. Importantly, the new thinking and the new post-crisis context together provided an opportunity for fundamental policy reform debates to be aired, and for policies actually to be reformed after a long period of relatively little change.

1.5 THE STRUCTURE AND LOGIC OF THE BOOK

The aim of this book is to examine the various debates surrounding the reforms to EU regional and urban policy, or more specifically EU Cohesion Policy, and to explain the logic which underpins the outcomes of these debates. Any policy agenda, policy framework or policy approach such as Cohesion Policy which has to operate across very diverse environments and to respond to the enormously differing challenges associated with different parts of Europe, automatically faces immense challenges. Yet, these policy challenges are not only related to the range of different issues to be addressed and the range of different contexts in which these issues are situated, but also to intellectual challenges regarding the modern case for these policies and the contemporary role which economic development policy can play in diverse situations. Having sketched out here the major features of Europe's diversity and heterogeneity, the Europe 2020 strategy and also some of the key impacts of the 2008 global financial crisis in Europe, we are now in a position to begin a serious discussion regarding the role, nature and impacts of EU Cohesion Policy.

In order to develop this discussion the structure and logic of the book is organised as follows. In Chapter 2 we begin by discussing the major features of the regional and urban economies of the European Union, comparing them where relevant to their counterparts in the US and elsewhere in order to provide a reference scale. In Chapter 3 we examine the workings and impacts of the policy, and the combination of the material discussed in Chapters 1, 2 and 3 then provides the basis for the policy reform debates examined in Chapter 4. Chapter 4 explains the place-based issues and challenges raised by the Barca (2009) report, and discusses in detail the ensuing EU Cohesion Policy reforms which have been implemented as a result of these debates. In the post-crisis era, of the three Europe 2020 growth dimensions it is the role played by policy in fostering smart growth that is seen as being critical to the recovery of Europe. Therefore Chapter 5 discusses the case for innovation policies being implemented at the level of the region, and this provides the grounding for the discussion of the EU 'smart specialisation' agenda discussed in Chapter 6. The high profile EU smart specialisation agenda has generated a great deal of interest in many countries and regions leading to a widespread level of public awareness of the role which well-designed Cohesion Policy interventions can play in fostering development. Although the smart specialisation approach originally emerged from a slightly different intellectual arena to the place-based issues raised in the Barca (2009) report, as we will see in Chapter 5 the smart specialisation concept dovetails very closely with all of the other thinking underpinning the reform of EU Cohesion Policy. Smart specialisation is widely regarded as being a spearhead of the policy reform agenda and its perceived importance in the new policy approach requires a chapter in its own right. Lastly Chapter 7 offers some final observations and conclusions.

NOTES

1. In US$ at current prices and Purchasing Power Parities (OECD 2014).
2. The estimates of Nobel Laureate Robert Fogel (1964) put this figure at 2.7 per cent of Gross National Product GDP although David (1969) and Donaldson and Hornbeck (2013) put the figure at closer to 5 per cent or above.
3. See Chapter 2 for details.
4. http://www.transtasman-review.productivity.govt.nz/sites/default/files/14-trans-tasman-supplementarye.pdf
5. North American Free Trade Agreement http://www.cfr.org/trade/naftas-economic-impact/p15790
   https://www.fas.org/sgp/crs/row/R42965.pdf
6. See Timmer et al. (2010) Table 5.7 page 175; Van Ark et al. (2012) Table 3.5 page 78.
7. See also:
   http://ec.europa.eu/internal_market/top_layer/historical_overview/background_en.htm
   http://ec.europa.eu/internal_market/publications/docs/20years/achievements-web_en.pdf
   http://www.cpb.nl/publicatie/de-interne-markt-en-de-nederlandse-economie-implicaties-voor-handel-en-economische-groei
   http://nieuwsuur.nl/onderwerp/313318-euro-levert-extra-weeksalaris-op.html
   http://www.dbresearch.com/PROD/DBR_INTERNET_EN-PROD/PROD000000000003228 97/The+Single+European+Market+20+years+onpercent3A+Achievements,+unfulfilled+expectations+percent26+further+potential.pdf
   http://www.kas.de/wf/doc/kas_34913-1522-2-30.pdf?130716135256
8. http://www.oilandgasuk.co.uk/2013-economic-report.cfm
9. http://www.cepii.fr/PDF_PUB/lettre/2011/let316ang.pdf
10. The Europe 2020 strategy was launched with headline targets and seven 'flagship initiatives' being included as part of the strategy, which are aimed at highlighting key themes which Europe needs to urgently address. These relate to innovation, digital economy, the mobility of young people, employment, poverty, resource efficiency and industrial policy. See: http://ec.europa.eu/europe2020/europe-2020-in-a-nutshell/index_en.htm
11. See: http://www.oecd.org/document/10/0,3746,en_2649_201185_42393354_1_1_1_1,00.html
12. As reflected in the 2014 Richard Dimbleby Lecture entitled 'A New Multilateralism for the Twenty First Century' given by the Managing Director of the IMF Christine Lagarde on 03.02.2014 http://www.imf.org/external/np/speeches/2014/020314.htm and also by the reports of the *Commission on Growth and Development* published by the World Bank (2008, 2010a,b) and Stiglitz et al. (2009).
13. National Intelligence Council (NIC) (2012).
14. See:
   http://www.whitehouse.gov/sites/default/files/omb/assets/memoranda_2010/m10-21.pdf
   http://www.whitehouse.gov/blog/2010/06/30/place-based-investments
   http://www.eda.gov/pdf/CEDS_Flyer_Wht_Backround.pdf
   http://yosemite.epa.gov/opa/admpress.nsf/0/75E1F57EB6D0FCEC8525788CA0063A5CB
15. http://report.mitigation2014.org/spm/ipcc_wg3_ar5_summary-for-policymakers_approved.pdf
16. Stiglitz et al. (2009).
   'Monitoring economic performance, quality of life and sustainability' jointly produced by the French 'Conseil d'analyse économique' and the German Council of Economic Experts, December 2010. Available at: http://www.cae.gouv.fr/IMG/pdf/095_ANG.pdf
17. http://ec.europa.eu/regional_policy/consultation/5cr/index_en.cfm

2. The regional and urban economies of the European Union

2.1 INTRODUCTION

Working as a local and regional development policy across multiple different countries, EU Cohesion Policy is probably the largest single development policy in the western world (McCann and Ortega-Argilés 2013a, b). However, relating the insights and lessons derived from the experience of EU Cohesion Policy to wider global arenas, and also vice-versa, needs to be undertaken carefully, because Cohesion Policy operates in a unique and very specific context. It is an integrated development policy which works on the basis of a single overarching legal basis, logic and architecture, which is then adapted to the national context of each EU member state. The backdrop to the policy is both interesting and challenging, and a careful assessment of the effects of Cohesion Policy which is predicated on the specifics of the EU context does indeed provide powerful insights and lessons for other parts of the world. Similarly, as will be seen in this book, the insights and lessons from the wider development agenda in other parts of the world have also heavily influenced the Cohesion Policy reforms. However, in order to make these types of discussions fruitful, they need to be underpinned by a good knowledge of the EU context and also an awareness of the logic, architecture and intended role of the policy.

The European Union is an enormous and also a highly heterogeneous economic environment. The EU economy currently accounts for just over 500 million people representing 7.7 per cent of the global population, an economic output of some €13 trillion (OECD 2011a) accounting for 21 per cent of global output (ESPON 2013), and this economic sphere spans 28 countries, more than 30 different legal systems, some 30 different land market systems, and approximately 40 different languages. As an EU policy, Cohesion Policy has a legal basis which is enshrined in the European Union's Treaties. It has a long history, and its goals, systems and architecture have been adapted and developed at various stages to respond to the changing context of the EU over more than four decades. The nature, role and performance of the policy have been widely discussed in many arenas on numerous occasions, as ought to be the case with what is now the EU's largest policy and the largest expenditure component of the EU's budget. Yet, designing and implementing a development policy which is applicable and appropriate for such a diverse context is a major undertaking, both intellectually as well as practically. The details of the policy logic and architecture along with the evidence regarding its development impacts, as well as the rationale for the reforms to the policy, are all discussed extensively and in depth in the following chapters, and therefore we will not discuss these issues here.

What will be discussed here are the major features of the European urban and regional economic system. EU Cohesion Policy seeks to promote growth and development amongst Europe's regions and cities. However, the major features of the European regional and urban economic system are often rather more complex, heterogeneous and specific than many observers realise and it is essential that these features are clearly outlined in order to ensure that discussions about Cohesion Policy are placed on a sound footing. A good understanding of the EU regional and urban context provides not only the appropriate backdrop to debates about the policy agenda but also a realism regarding the day-to-day context in which the policy operates. Understanding the specific features of the European regional and urban system is essential in order to make sense of many of the activities of EU Cohesion Policy.

2.2 THE CHARACTERISTICS OF THE EU'S REGIONAL AND URBAN ECONOMIC SYSTEM

The EU economy is so large and exhibits so many different characteristics that there is no single preferred way of describing the context in which EU Cohesion Policy operates. A comprehensive assessment of the many features of Europe's regions can be found in the *Sixth Report on Economic, Social and Territorial Cohesion* (European Union 2014), along with its respective earlier predecessor reports. However, for the purposes of this book, we are going to discuss the various features of the EU's regional and urban economic systems from six different perspectives, namely: (1) productivity and economic dynamism; (2) cities and scale; (3) accessibility and connectivity; (4) labour markets, migration and demographics; (5) energy and environment; (6) institutions, governance and quality of life. These six different perspectives allow us to capture the major features of Europe's regions and cities and to understand the high degree of heterogeneity within which EU Cohesion Policy operates. They also provide an appropriate context for us to review the various regional impacts associated with the aftermath of the 2008 Global Financial Crisis, as described in the previous chapter

2.2.1 Productivity and Economic Dynamism

Within the European Union there are large differences between countries (European Commission 2014a) and between regions regarding the levels of labour productivity, defined in terms of gross domestic product (GDP) per capita, and also the associated rewards to this productivity, defined in terms of income per capita. The EU exhibits a core set of regions which exhibit these high levels of productivity. One such set of regions stretches broadly from the South East of the UK across the Low Countries, Northern and Eastern France, via Western and Southern Germany, and into Northern Italy via Austria and Switzerland. These centrally-located regions account for a very large proportion of the total European population, being characterised by many densely populated areas. At the same time, however, there are various other groups of regions within Europe which also exhibit high levels of labour productivity and high levels of income per capita. These include some rather more peripheral regions in the Nordic countries, as well as regions in Ireland, Northern Spain and Southern France. These regions typically exhibit relatively high levels of expenditure (European Union 2011) on research and development (R&D), high levels of innovation (Crescenzi and Rodriguez-Pose 2011; European Commission 2014b), high levels of entrepreneurial activities[1] (European Union 2014) and high levels of human capital (OECD 2013a). In terms of innovation, there is evidence that at the national levels EU member states are slowly gaining some of the ground lost to the USA over the previous two decades. In contrast, at the regional level (European Commission 2014b) the gaps in innovation performance between the leading and lagging regions appear to be increasing. However, this is not a simple urban versus rural story, as the economically dynamic regions leading in innovation (European Commission 2014b) and entrepreneurship (European Union 2014) vary quite significantly in terms of their characteristics, with some dynamic regions being heavily urbanised regions while other dynamic regions are also variously rural regions or those intermediate regions which combine rural with urban areas (OECD 2013a). Some of these regions are very much science-based areas, often related to natural resources or environmental matters (OECD 2012a), while others are dominated by service activities (European Commission 2014b). Europe's highly dynamic, innovative and entrepreneurial regions vary considerably in terms of their characteristics (OECD 2011a, 2013b).

In marked contrast, there are also many regions in Southern, Central and Eastern Europe which exhibit noticeably lower levels of both per capital gross domestic productivity and also income per capita (European Union 2014). Not surprisingly these lower levels of economic dynamism are also associated with lower levels of entrepreneurship (European Union 2014) and innovation (European Commission 2014b). Some of these low innovation and entrepreneurial regions in the EU are urban regions as well as being rural and intermediate regions (European Commission 2014b; European Union 2014). Often, such regions within southern and central Europe are still relatively heavily dependent on older industrial activities and traditional agricultural activities (ESPON 2013) in comparison to urbanised regions in Western and Northern Europe and even in comparison to many economically dynamic inter-mediate or rural regions in Northern or Western Europe. Many of these regions are located in the countries which joined the EU from 2004 onwards after undergoing a transition process from planned to market-based economies, and from communist to democratic societies. A much smaller number of these regions are also located in countries which emerged from military dictatorships in the 1970s and joined the European Community in the 1980s. Each of these regions to some extent bears the adverse legacy effects of these earlier non-democratic govern-ance systems and such legacy effects include the use of outdated technologies, insufficiently updated infrastructure, contaminated land, and institutional and governance systems with limited capacities and capabilities. However, poor performing regions also vary significantly in terms of their characteristics.

Finally, there is a very large group of regions distributed all over Northern, Western, and parts of Southern Europe, which exhibit per capita GDP levels and income per capita levels which are close to the EU average (European Commission 2014b). These regions are also of many different types, including highly urbanised regions, rural regions, and intermediate regions comprising both rural and urban areas, and they also include industrial areas, service industry areas and agricultural areas. They are the largest broad group of regions and also in many ways also the most diverse group of regions.

Although the Northern and Western parts of Europe exhibit most of the highest productivity EU regions while Central, Eastern and Southern Europe exhibit most of the lowest productivity regions, one of the major trends we have observed within Europe over the last two decades is that these gaps have fallen. In economic parlance this is referred to as 'convergence' and the scale of convergence within the EU has been particularly striking (World Bank 2012). However, these convergence trends represent neither a smooth linear nor an all-encompassing process (Quah 1996). Groups of regions often experience similar fortunes which are quite distinct from those of other groupings of regions (Ertur et al. 2006; Neven and Gouyette 1995; Quah 1996;) and these effects are mediated by geography at least as much as by national factors (Overman et al. 2002; Quah 1996). Moreover, the relationships between regional convergence–divergence trends and national development appear to differ between the EU-15 nations and the EU-11 central eastern European member states (Monasteriotis 2014). While sub-national interregional divergence has been more prevalent in the EU-11 than in the EU-15 (ibid.), regional growth rates in the EU-11 have tended to out-perform those in the EU-15 (Thissen et al. 2013a). Furthermore, and rather differently to classical trade theory assumptions, EU regional integration is not necessarily associated with increasing regional specialisation. The evolving patterns of agglomeration, spatial concentration and dispersion are complex (Brülhart and Traeger 2005) but there does appear to be something of a general shift towards sectoral diversification rather than specialisation in many of Europe's cities and regions (Brülhart and Mathys 2008).

During the two decades prior to the advent of the global financial crisis in late 2008 the lower income countries in Europe had generally grown at a faster rate than the higher income countries, such that the EU-wide interregional dispersion of income per capita had also fallen.[2] This process continued annually until the onset of the global financial crisis in 2008, after which the process went into reverse both in terms of per capita GDP and unemployment rates (European Union 2013a). Two out of three EU regions experienced output contractions and one in two regions experienced unemployment increases in the aftermath of the 2008 global financial crisis. Southern and Eastern European regions experienced the greatest adverse shocks of the crisis and the result of this has been that the long-running overall process of EU international convergence has stalled and somewhat reversed at the same time as increasing interregional divergence is also observed (European Union 2013a; World Bank 2012).

Most of the investment capital spurring the economic growth in these lower income countries prior to the crisis of 2008 had flowed from the richer member states (MGI 2013), and this had also been accompanied by the technology transfers embodied in eastward firm relocations (World Bank 2012). Yet, while there were marked but falling differences in per capita GDP and income per capita between the EU's member states in the two decades prior to the 2008 global financial crisis, at the same time this period also witnessed the emergence of increasing differences between regions within the same member state. The majority of EU member states exhibited increasing interregional income inequalities during this period (OECD 2011b) with core city-regions gaining more economic prominence than other regions, and these trends reflected more global patterns (Brakman and van Marrewijk 2013). However, both the levels and the changes in interregional inequality vary markedly between EU member states (OECD 2013a), with some countries experiencing very small and also slowly-growing inequalities while others exhibit large shifts. Moreover, over more recent years there has also been something of a reversal of these shifts within the EU-15 with both intermediate and rural regions playing a greater overall role in economic growth (Dijkstra et al. 2013), and particularly those which are closer to urban centres (OECD 2013c). The result of these trends over the last couple of decades since the late 1980s is that while convergence was observed at the level of member states, at the level of regions convergence across Europe has been slower, and in some cases divergence has been the key feature (Monfort and Nicolini 2000). Interregional convergence has lagged international convergence, and in some cases divergence has actually increased (Brakman and van Marrewijk 2013). This is particularly the case for Central and Eastern European member states where as yet there is little or no evidence of sub-national interregional convergence after 25 years of the market economy (Monasteriotis 2014). In contrast, in the EU-15 countries, the levels of interregional divergence are generally much smaller than those in the Central and Eastern European countries. Moreover, in many of the EU-15 countries the levels of interregional inequality in productivity performance have hardly changed over this period and in at least a third of these countries the levels have actually fallen (Monasteriotis 2014). As a whole, therefore, what we observe is an EU-wide combination of international convergence and slower processes of interregional convergence which recently have also gone into reverse in the aftermath of the 2008 global financial crisis (European Union 2013b). Moreover, many of these European trends are not simply a European phenomenon, but reflect trends observed more generally across a global scale (OECD 2011b).

2.2.2 Cities and Scale

A key principle of urban economics is that in general larger cities exhibit higher per capita productivity levels and higher income per capita (McCann 2013). The reason is basically due to agglomeration economies, or in other words those positive externalities associated with city size. At the same time, another principle which derives from the same urban economic models is that more densely populated location will also exhibit higher per capita productivity levels (McCann 2013). Finally, recent research over the last two decades has tended to emphasise the productivity and growth advantages associated with diversified cities which exhibit many different sectors and activities, rather than special-ised cities which exhibit a smaller number of specific sectors and activities. Following on from these arguments there have been various high profile publications (Florida 2005; Glaeser 2011, 2014; World Bank 2009) arguing not only that urban dynamism is critical for fostering economic and productivity growth, but that the urban role in growth is becoming increasingly important. Nowadays these arguments have gained enormous traction in many international debates and international arenas (MGI 2011, 2012a,b, 2013; OECD 2006; PWC 2012; World Bank 2009).

Earlier evidence from the USA and Asia regarding the urban size–productivity relationships suggested that the elasticities are somewhere between 0.03–0.08 (Rosenthal and Strange 2004), such that a doubling of the city size is associated with a productivity increase of 3–8 per cent, with a mid-point of around 5 per cent. While some research from the USA suggests higher values (Bettencourt 2013; Bettencourt and West 2011, 2014; Davis et al. 2014) a meta-analysis of the range of recent estimates from around the world (de Melo et al. 2009) points to a slightly lower range of 0.02–0.06 (Combes et al. 2008), a result which is consistent with OECD-wide estimates which suggest a range of 0.02–0.05 (OECD 2014a). Productivity estimates associated with density also give similar elasticities of around 0.02–0.06 (Brakman and van Marrewijk 2013; Ciccone 2002; Ciccone and Hall 1996; Duranton 2011; OECD 2014a), implying that a doubling of density is also associated with productivity increases of 2–6 per cent, although recent estimates for Europe suggest slightly higher values of 5–8 per cent for the density–productivity relationships (Brakman et al. 2009; Ciccone 2002). Product-ivity estimates for the geographical size urban area are also in a similar range of 0.05–0.09 (OECD 2014a). Finally, estimates regarding the advantages of urban diversity over specialisation again tend to give elasticities of a similar order of magnitude to those relating to scale and density (Duranton 2011), although these results are often mixed, incon-clusive and very sensitive to the methodology employed (Beaudry and Schiffauerova 2009; de Groot et al. 2009) and the spatial scale of analysis employed (Mameli et al. 2008, 2014).

Even within the same country urban productivity premia are found to vary significantly for cities of the same scale (OECD 2014a), and this suggests that many other productivity-enhancing factors are at play other than simply urban scale or density (ibid.). In addition to the heterogeneity of results regarding urban scale, density, specialisation and diversification, and also working against any positive urban scale effects, are institutional fragmentation effects. The negative elasticities associated with local governance fragmentation are of the order of 0.05–0.06 (ibid.), which implies that for a given city size, having twice the number of local municipalities reduced productivity by 5–6 per cent (ibid.). Moreover, the pooling of governance powers in order to counter these adverse impacts only overcomes the negative fragmentation effects if the resource-pooling is backed up by real policy-implementation powers, regarding for example spatial planning, rather than being just for policy-exchange purposes (ibid.).

These various estimates are derived from many studies around the world. However, in the particular case of the Europe there are also some important aspects of the EU's urban system cities which heavily colour the debates surrounding the relationships between urban scale, productivity and economic growth. Firstly, as a continent Europe is already heavily urbanised and has been so for many decades, although it is not as urbanised as some other continents. In particular, according to the MGI (2011) and United Nations (2012) estimates, Latin America and North America (MGI 2011; UN-Habitat 2012; United Nations 2012) and Australasia (OECD 2013a) are more urbanised than Europe, with close to 80 per cent or more of the population of these areas living in urban areas (United Nations 2012). In the case of Europe, the share of the overall population living in urban areas is 72.9 per cent (ibid.), with just over 27 per cent living in rural areas (United Nations 2012; European Union 2011). According to the UN and MGI (2011) estimates, in aggregate, the share of the population of Europe in urban areas is noticeably less than the global average for industrialised countries of 78 per cent (United Nations 2012). However, this aggregate EU figure of 72.6 per cent hides significant variations, with 77 per cent of the EU-15 population living in urban areas while 62 per cent of the population of the former transition economies of Central and Eastern Europe live in urban areas (MGI 2013).

Other estimates are available from the new OECD (2012a) standardised definition of 'urban' which is based on functional urban areas calculated to allow for dense commuting patterns as well as simply contiguity.[3] This methodology is more advanced than the United Nations estimates which are based on national statistical population registers broken down by administrative area definitions. According to the OECD definition the share of urban dwellers is 69 per cent in the USA and 73 per cent in Canada (OECD 2013a). In Europe the equivalent figure varies between 38 per cent in the Slovak Republic to 83 per cent in Luxembourg, with densely populated countries such as the UK and Netherlands both exhibiting an urban share of 74 per cent, followed by Spain with 69 per cent, France with 65 per cent and Germany with 64 per cent, while those for Ireland, Denmark, Sweden and Finland are 56 per cent, 55 per cent, 53 per cent and 52 per cent (OECD 2013a). The respective figures for Poland, Hungary and the Czech Republic are 55 per cent, 50 per cent and 47 per cent (OECD 2013a).

What we observe from these UN and OECD figures is that broadly the EU-15 countries exhibit urbanisation levels which are consistent with the global average for industrialised countries whereas Central and Eastern Europe are much less urbanised. Indeed, at a smaller spatial scale, parts of Europe such as the Low Countries and the UK exhibit some of the most densely populated regions in the OECD while parts of the Nordic countries exhibit some of the lowest density regions within the OECD (OECD 2013a). Moreover, even the urban population distributions also contain subtle variations. Amongst the EU's urban dwellers, 47 per cent live in large metropolitan areas of over 250,000 while 25 per cent live in small towns and suburbs (European Union 2011). For the USA and Canada for example, close to 80 per cent of the urban population live in cities of more than 200,000 and almost half of the urban population lives in very large cities of more than 1.5 million inhabitants (OECD 2013a). For EU countries, only Greece and Denmark exhibit higher equivalent shares of very large city dwellers. In contrast, many of Europe's richest countries, such as The Netherlands, Norway and Finland, display the lowest equivalent population shares (OECD 2013a). At the same time, the overall contribution to economic output of large metropolitan areas of over 500,000 is relatively smaller in all European countries than in the USA (OECD 2013a). Typically such cities in European countries account for 40–50 per cent of national output, but the metropolitan share of total national output is not closely related to overall national productivity. Many of those European nations with low shares, such as The Netherlands, Norway, Switzerland and Finland, are amongst the richest European nations, while some of the poorer European nations, such as Estonia, Greece and Portugal, exhibit high metropolitan shares of national output (OECD 2013a). Similar arguments also hold for the contributions of metropolitan areas of over 500,000 to national economic growth and to national employment growth (ibid.). Typically, in Europe such large cities account for 40–60 per cent of economic growth and employment growth (ibid.). However, the growth share of capital cities relative to the overall urban growth contribution tends to be higher in central and eastern European countries than in EU-15 countries although in some cases the overall urban growth share is smaller in these countries due to the lower overall levels of urbanisation (OECD 2014b). As such, while cities are clearly very important in national growth processes, the overall relationships in Europe are rather more complex than simply a question of urban scale being a good indicator of national economic performance (OECD 2013a).

Secondly, in the USA the relative productivity advantage of metropolitan areas over rural areas is over 30 per cent (MGI 2011) and this is much higher than the relative productivity advantage of European cities over their hinterland rural regions, which is typically of the order of 10–25 per cent (European Commission 2007).[4] European capital city-regions tend to be the most highly productive areas in Europe (Eurostat 2013). EU cities have higher levels of human capital on average than non-urban areas (European Commission 2007), with 22 member states exhibiting urban–rural university-educated human capital differences of between 10 per cent and 25 per cent, while some capital city regions in some cases exhibit productivity premia of the order of 50 per cent (European Union 2011), most notably in central and eastern European regions (European Union 2011; McCann and Acs 2011). Large metropolitan cities of over 250,000 people exhibit higher numbers of patent applications per capita than small towns, suburbs and non urban areas in almost all EU countries (European Union 2011), with capital metropolitan regions often displaying the highest patent scores along with the highest tertiary education shares and the highest levels of broadband coverage (European Union 2011). However, the heterogeneity of European regions means that per capita differences in patent applications between metropolitan cities and other areas are not large and not nearly as marked as in North America, Asia or Australasia. But again the EU case is also not static, with many changes taking place over time and geography which differ by country and which preclude simple aggregate US–EU comparisons. In particular, the population growth (European Commission 2007) and changes in the relative productivity advantages and over their rural hinterlands 1995–2004 also tended to be greater in geographically more peripheral member states than in the more centrally-located member states (ESPON 2013). On the other hand, however, only just over a quarter of EU cities exhibit employment activity rates higher than their national averages and while two-thirds of cities exhibit unemployment rates higher than their national averages (European Commission 2007).

Thirdly, large cities in Europe on average are far smaller than those in North America, Asia and Latin America (OECD 2006). As of 2010 Europe had 52 cities with populations of over 1 million people (European

Commission 2010). However, the large European cities on average are generally smaller than those in the USA, Latin America and Asia, and more broadly comparable with the major cities in Australasia and Canada (OECD 2006). The result is that 67 per cent of the European urban population resides in urban areas comprising less than 500,000 people and only 9.6 per cent of Europe's population lives in cities with 5 million or more inhabitants (United Nations 2012). This is in contrast with North America where almost half of the urban population lives in very large cities of more than 1.5 million inhabitants (OECD 2013a) and approximately one-fifth of the total population lives in metropolitan regions with populations greater than 5 million (United Nations 2012).

There are arguments to suggest that that the wider prevalence of these smaller cities in Europe may impose a productivity disadvantage on the EU relative to the USA (MGI 2013). Yet, although they are typically much smaller than their US counterparts, outside of the USA many of the world's most productive cities are actually in Europe (McCann and Acs 2011). The majority of the most highly productive cities in Europe are what the OECD refers to as 'medium-sized' cities, ranging between 1 and 4 million inhabitants (OECD 2006), and many of these are also amongst the world's most productive cities (McCann and Acs 2011). In addition, below these medium-sized cities are more than 350 'small' cities (OECD 2006) with populations of between 200,000 and 1 million (European Commission 2007, 2010), and a much larger proportion of the European population is resident in these types of cities than is the case with the North American, Japanese, Korean, Latin American or Australasian economies (United Nation 2012). Cities of over 250,000 inhabitants account for 59 per cent of the EU population and 67 per cent of total EU output (Dijkstra 2009). One effect of these EU urban population distributions is that on average a European industry is geographically more evenly spread than in the US and EU integration has little affected this situation (Midelfahrt-Knarvik and Overman 2002). On the other hand, many of Europe's cities are more densely populated than US cities (European Commission 2007; Wilson et al. 2010) and this is particularly the case for cities in Southern and Eastern Europe (Coutard et al. 2014). If density–productivity effects operate in cities as much of the literature suggests, these may somewhat counter any possible lower scale–productivity effects associated with having smaller cities.

Fourthly, the increased contribution of cities to European output growth is less than in other parts of the world. Prior to the millennium the aggregate population of Europe's urban areas was growing at a rate of 0.35 per cent per annum (European Commission 2007). However, this hides a great deal of variation with one-third of cities growing at above

0.2 per cent per annum, one-third exhibiting stable populations and one-third exhibiting population decline (European Commission 2007). Moreover, EU urban population growth is not necessarily a large city phenomenon. During the rapid growth years since the millennium and prior to the 2008 global financial crisis, the aggregate EU population growth of cities of over 250,000 inhabitants was only 0.5 per cent, and the aggregate EU-wide output growth of these cities was also 0.5 per cent (Dijkstra 2009). Indeed, without Poland the EU-wide output growth of these medium and large size cities was actually zero (ibid.). This contrasts strongly with the experience of the BRICS countries (MGI 2011) and even the US (MGI 2011) where economic growth is dominated by increasing urbanisation.

In general we know that cities grow in response to the movements of people and capital, and the observation that Europe exhibits smaller cities than other parts of the world such as the USA and Asia, which exhibit lower and higher population densities, respectively, is most likely associated with the heterogeneous national-historical institutional aspects of the pan-European economic context. For example, historically, the largely fragmented nature of the European economy in comparison to the vastly more integrated US system has in the past limited many of the potential scale advantages associated with home market effects (Krugman and Venables 1995). Regional multipliers are lower in Europe than in the USA, and this may be due in part to lower scale effects and also lower levels of interregional labour mobility (Van Dijk 2014). Indeed, overcoming the problems associated with international and interregional fragmentation has been a key argument underpinning the creation of the EU Single Market.

Given these general features of the EU urban system and also the types of city productivity estimates which are widely referred to in urban economics, one argument is simply to say that European cities need to grow larger in order for Europe to improve its growth and productivity performance. For some observers these arguments may also be bolstered by the observation that in the wake of the 2008 crisis, for metropolitan regions of over 250,000 people, 74 per cent of small metropolitan regions have exhibited productivity declines relative to their countries, 54 per cent of second-tier metro regions have experienced relatively sharper productivity declines than their countries, while only 30 per cent of capital city regions have suffered in this way (European Union 2013a). However, while larger cities fared better in terms of productivity performance, smaller ones appear to have out-performed larger cities in terms of employment. Slightly more than half of the second-tier metropolitan regions exhibited employment declines greater than their countries or slower employment growth than their countries, while slightly less than half of smaller metropolitan regions did so (European Union 2013b). These rather conflicting outcomes mean that rather than performance being simply a question of urban scale, the overall picture in Europe appears to be that cities have accentuated national performance, with cities spearheading growth in countries which are growing while cities are bearing the brunt of economic decline in countries which are declining (European Union 2013b). Urban scale appears to be a blessing where the economy is performing well and something of a curse where the economy is struggling. Therefore, simple arguments that EU city sizes should increase in order to drive EU productivity growth insufficiently reflect the observed heterogeneity of EU growth experiences. The situation in reality is vastly more complex than this and there are several reasons for this, of which three are particularly pertinent here.

The first reason why urban expansion alone will not of itself solve many of the EU's growth development challenges is that the differences in the levels of per capita productivity and income per capita between regions are not necessarily indicative of differences in growth outcomes. Some of the largest, densest and most highly productive cities in Europe currently exhibit very low or even negative productivity growth (OECD 2009a), and the contribution of large cities to national growth varies enormously across the EU (OECD 2014b). Indeed, while European economic growth during the 1990s was dominated by cities, since the millennium the economic growth of the EU-15 nations during the 2000s has been dominated by predominantly intermediate regions and rural regions (Dijkstra et al. 2013; ESPON 2013). In contrast in Central and Eastern Europe, and in particular in those member states which were formally transition economies, productivity growth has been heavily driven by urbanisation and most sharply focused on their capital city regions (McCann and Acs 2011). While entrepreneurship appears to have some small degree of urban bias (Sternberg 2011) and in particular opportunity-driven entrepreneurship (Bosma and Sternberg 2014), in Europe at least this is not especially associated with large cities.[5] As such, the relationships between cities, city size and economic growth differ markedly across Europe, and there is no single urban growth trajectory which is observable (OECD 2009b). Moreover, the productivity advantages of urban scale and concentration alone appear to attenuate sharply above the per capita income levels consistent with the current levels of Brazil and Bulgaria (Brülhart and Sbergami 2009; Dijkstra 2013). Beyond these income levels the apparent trade-offs between interregional equality and national growth largely disappear, and instead other issues come into play (Brülhart and Sbergami 2009). As almost all

EU regions are above these per capita income levels what we would therefore expect is that other issues are just as important for growth and development as those relating to urbanisation and interregional equality. Indeed, what we observe is that the aggregate economic output of Europe's major cities of over 250,000 inhabitants hardly increased at all during the prosperous years prior to the global financial crisis (Dijkstra 2009), and without Poland the aggregate growth contribution of these cities stayed exactly constant. More recently, the growth contribution of many of these cities has actually fallen (OECD 2011b, 2012e). As such, the simple textbook assumption that very big cities are likely to be the key driving force in the growth of Europe is not at all substantiated by the evidence (Dijkstra 2013).

The second reason why urban expansion will of itself not solve many of the EU's growth and development challenges, and following on from the first point, is that the urban productivity experience and the urban population experiences of different EU countries have also been very different. All EU countries exhibit cities with higher productivity levels than their non-urban or rural hinterland areas (Dijkstra 2009). At the same time, however, the majority of EU countries also contain a group of cities with productivity levels which are lower than their own non-urban or rural hinterland areas. Consequently, many EU member states exhibit both a group of growing cities and also a group of shrinking cities, and many of these shrinking cities are actually very large (Dijkstra et al. 2013; European Union 2013b). In addition, there are also differences across countries in terms of the growth experience of peri-urban regions and hinterland areas (Coutard et al. 2014). The policy challenges associated with dealing with these types of large and declining cities are extremely complex, and even more so given that many of these cases are also in the lower income countries of Central and Eastern Europe (ibid.).

At the same time, the effects of the global financial crisis in Europe appear to be closely linked to the performance of cities. As already mentioned, in countries which have performed reasonably well in the aftermath of the global financial crisis, major cities have played a dominant role in this performance. In contrast, in countries whose economic performance has been poor in the aftermath of the global financial crisis, again it is the cities which have been central to this poor performance. In particular, the collapse in the real estate markets in countries such as Greece, Ireland, Italy, Spain, Portugal and the Baltic countries, has been primarily focused on the property markets of the major urban centres (European Commission 2013). Many of the cities in these countries currently represent the major problems in these economies, because of the adverse market-wide financial impacts on business lending which are associated with the collapse in real estate collateral.

The third reason, as we will see shortly, is that interregional migration within the EU is too small to bring about widescale change, other than in particular global-city regions.

The historical and institutional background context means that the EU's urban reality is far more complex than the standard textbook model. European urban growth is not necessarily an indicator of national economic growth. Nor is it an unambiguous indicator of national productivity levels. While these urbanisation effects have been particularly important in Central and Eastern Europe over the last two decades, there is also increasing evidence that these effects are nowadays attenuating even in many of these regions (ESPON 2013). Therefore, in the European case, policy prescriptions advocating the urban expansion of dominant or capital cities as a direct and principal growth-driver (World Bank 2009) may vary from being rather naïve and over-simplistic to being significantly misplaced (Dijkstra 2013).

2.2.3 Accessibility and Connectivity

Apart from London and Paris there are no very large cities in the top echelons of the EU urban productivity rankings, with the majority of EU urban centres being small and medium-sized cities. The result of these city sizes and distributions is that many of the regions of Europe also exhibit what are often known as 'polycentric' urban systems (Brezzi and Veneri 2014; Hall and Pain 2006), with high frequency interactions of people, knowledge, goods and services taking place between a group of small and medium-scale urban centres, rather than hinterland–core interactions being dominated by a single large urban centre. In network-node terminology, the geography of these polycentric inter-node interactions is more typical of a distributed set of nodes, rather than that of a single dominant node. As we have already seen, neither urban scale, sectoral diversity nor sectoral specialisation provide a clear indicator of urban productivity performance in Europe. This is also the case for urban scale. As such, if neither scale nor diversity provides a clear and unambiguous indicator of urban productivity performance, other factors must also come into play in the European context. Of these, accessibility and connectivity appear to be very important (McCann and Acs 2011), in that they heavily influence regional market potential (European Union 2014).

Accessibility, defined in terms of the ease and ability to access a particular location within a day, varies significantly both in terms of its extent, the sectors concerned, and also in terms of the modes of transport which can be used. The cross-border interregional trade of manufactured products within Europe accounts for an estimated 20 per cent of total manufacturing sales within Europe and is more than twice the equivalent share for agricultural products and five times that of services (Thissen et al. 2013b). On average some 75 per cent of services outputs are sold within the same EU region and an additional 18 per cent within the same country, and only 4 per cent is exported to regions in other EU countries and 3 per cent to the rest of the world (ibid.). Many service activities are knowledge-intensive activities. Knowledge spillovers are constrained by distance (Arita and McCann 2000; Belezon and Shankerman 2013) and they are also likely to be much more prevalent within a daily return travel distance which itself is conditioned on the mode of travel (Arita and McCann 2000). The available evidence suggests that knowledge spillovers are probably more localised in Europe than within the US (Bottazzi and Peri 2003; Criscuolo and Verspagen 2008), with something of the order of 300km appearing to be the likely critical distance within which the vast majority of intra-EU knowledge spillovers occur. The densely populated regions of Northern Europe spanning Northern and Eastern France, the UK, the Low Countries, Germany, Austria and Northern Italy, are all served by dense and fast railway networks which afford daily business trips to very large market areas spanning many of these countries, as well as passenger air transport access to almost all parts of Europe. More geographically peripheral parts of Europe including the Nordic countries, the Iberian peninsula, Western and Southern France, Poland, Hungary, Slovakia and the Czech Republic, all exhibit access within a day-return flight to all parts of Europe, but only limited interregional day-return rail access. Finally the major cities in the most peripheral parts of Southern and Eastern Europe exhibit only limited day-return access, with most intra-EU business trips involving overnight stays. Outside of the cities, hinterland towns in these parts of Europe display very limited accessibility to the rest of Europe.

These differing patterns mean that the most intercontinentally accessible regions of Europe also exhibit the greatest range of options in terms of transport modes and transport routes. Knowledge-intensive activities characterised by high levels of face-to-face contact, and also multinational activities requiring high degrees of international coordination, are all well-served by these dense and varied transportation networks. This is also because the network density means that such regions are largely unaffected by changes in individual transport services or routes (ESPON 2013). At the other end of the spectrum are those regions which display very little accessibility to the rest of Europe. Their economies are largely driven by a local and internal logic, with limited international or interregional face-to-face interactions (McCann 2007). As such, they are also largely unaffected by changes in individual transport modes or routes (ESPON 2013). In between these extreme cases there are many regions which are very dependent on specific and individual transport routes and modes. The economic accessibility of these regions is therefore very sensitive to any disruption or changes to individual transport links, and as such, in many ways these regions are actually those which are the most risky in terms of business investment decisions (ibid.).

A broader concept than accessibility is that of 'connectivity', which derives from sociological thinking regarding the emergence of the so-called global cities (McCann and Acs 2011). The concept of urban connectivity is broader than the concept of accessibility, because as well as accessibility, the dimensions of urban connectivity are also measured in terms of the movements of money, information, ideas, people and cargo through these cities, as well as the discretionary ability to make decisions about each of these issues in particular cities. In these terms, many of Europe's highest productivity cities are also amongst the world's most high-connectivity cities (Iammarino and McCann 2013; McCann and Acs 2011). Of critical importance here appear to be the number of multinational enterprises which are located in cities as these facilitate and mediate the global trade and knowledge-flow linkages between regions (Iammarino and McCann 2013). In particular, it appears that the location patterns of the headquarters and research centre activities of multinationals are critical in determining the knowledge flows between regions (Iammarino and McCann 2013), and across Europe larger metropolitan regions and technologically specialized regions are the 'hotspots' for knowledge-intensive FDI (PBL 2013). Yet, it also appears that neither urban scale, sectoral diversity nor the home-market scale play any systematic or dominant role in determining urban connectivity patterns via these multinational location patterns. Rather, within Europe the structure of the global airline transport systems is crucial (Bel and Fageda 2008; Poelman 2013), and it is this which is most closely related to the distribution of multinational headquarter functions (Bel and Fageda 2008). Many European cities are crucial nodes in the global knowledge networks. However, given that urban scale is only seen to play a limited role in the growth and productivity performance of Europe, much thinking is now currently underway regarding how to better link many of the so-called 'second-tier' cities across Europe in order to help these smaller cities tap into these core knowledge nodes. Some 23 per cent of Europe's cities have potential to build cross-border metropolitan regions by linking up with cities across the border and which are within commuting distance (ESPON 2013). This inter-urban network-building agenda, which is seen by many as an alternative growth-enhancing logic to simply arguing for increased urban scale, is aimed at better facilitating the strengthening of inter-urban and polycentric networks, and underpins much of the 'Connecting Europe' logic discussed in the following chapters. At the other extreme end of the spectrum are those regions which are sparsely populated and geographically remote. Not surprisingly, the majority of these areas are on the edge of Europe, but also there are many rural, coastal and mountain regions which are more centrally-located but which exhibit low population levels and low accessibility (ibid.). Many of these regions still remain largely unconnected with the major trans-Europe transport networks, and the connectivity of these regions is likely to remain very low for the foreseeable future.

2.2.4 Labour Markets, Migration and Demographics

Globalisation and increasing market integration has led to greater income inequality across people and places (Spence 2011) and these processes of polarisation are in part related to the spatial shifts in employment opportunities associated with the reconfiguring of global value-chains (McCann 2008) afforded by technological changes (Autor et al. 2008). However, social inclusion and social exclusion across Europe exhibits many features which cannot be explained solely by either personal characteristics (European Union 2011) or by the reconfiguring of global value-chains, but also depend on the interactions between skills, technologies and consumer demand (Goos et al. 2009). Although the spatial 'sorting' of high skills workers into productivity cities is a key feature shaping urban population skills-distributions (Combes et al. 2008), other factors are also at work. As we have already seen, across Europe many cities exhibit relatively high levels of productivity and exhibit many of the features driving the knowledge economy, and these reflect the dominant and positive aspects of the role played by cities in driving regional and national economies. On the other hand, however, European cities also pose some major societal problems related to social inclusion. Many cities are becoming increasingly polarised in terms of their income distributions and this appears to be just as true for prosperous cities as for struggling cities (Gordon and Kaplanis 2014). Yet the reasons for this polarisation relate to both a re-ordering of local job opportunities across skills-classes and also greater interregional and international labour mobility (ibid.). More developed member states tend to display less inclusive cities, such that the urban dimension of inclusive growth is inversely related to the levels of development (European Union 2011).

Unemployment is higher in urban areas than in non-urban areas in the richer EU member states while the reverse is true in poorer member states, and these patterns have not changed due to the 2008 crisis (European Union 2013b). Severe material deprivation is higher in urban areas than in non-urban areas in eighteen EU member states, low work intensity is higher in cities in fifteen member states, and the at-risk-of-poverty rates are higher in cities in ten member states (European Union 2013b). The result is that European regional differences in the broader dimensions of human development including health and social exclusion do not always follow income levels, with low levels of human development evident in both rich EU regions as well as in poorer regions (Bubbico and Dijkstra 2011). These social exclusion and wellbeing features might on face value be expected to lead to significant migration outflows amongst the relatively disadvantaged urban cohorts to other areas in search of better employment prospects. However, such outflows are unlikely to be widely observed because often those facing such exclusion are already living in prosperous cities and migration to less prosperous cities is unlikely to increase their employment possibilities. Secondly, widespread falls in labour demand, as have been witnessed in the wake of the 2008 global financial crisis, militate against migration in general, as we will see shortly.

Across the European Union, the aftermath of the 2008 global financial crisis has highlighted the major differences evident within European regions in terms of the workings and performance of labour markets and the processes of labour market adjustment. Almost all of the EU member states have experienced adverse shock effects associated with the crisis, with only a small number of countries, most notably Poland and Germany, largely escaping its worst effects. In particular, many parts of Southern and Eastern Europe have experienced severe downturns in employment and activity rates and marked upturns in unemployment rates. These effects have been most evident in the Iberian peninsula, Ireland, Greece and the Baltic States, and to a lesser extent in Italy, Hungary and Slovenia (European Union 2013b). Each of these countries has been attempting to implement labour market reforms in order to help their respective economies better adjust to the adverse shocks, although these reforms are always a slow and difficult process. However, employment–unemployment issues are only one part, albeit a critical part, of a broader set of demographic and labour market issues. Unemployment shocks experienced in many of these countries are very much concentrated among the cohorts of younger people, as well as in particular sectors such as construction and manufacturing (European Union 2013b). While all age cohorts have been affected by the economic crisis, the impacts on young people have been most marked in those countries which have been most severely hit by the crisis. Older cohorts of workers appear to have been relatively better able to maintain their employment status than younger workers have been able to access new employment opportunities (ILO 2012). As a result, many parts of Europe have experienced significant outflows of workers, and in particular younger workers, while other parts of Europe have experienced significant inflows. Over the last decade Germany (ESPON 2013), Ireland and the UK have been a major destination for workers from Poland in particular (OECD 2012b), while large numbers of migrants from countries such as Romania have moved to Spain and Italy. In the wake of the 2008 global financial crisis, however, some of these flows have been largely or partially reversed, and migration flows have increasingly shifted towards the more robust economies in the core of Europe, and most notably Germany (NIESR 2013).

Migration in Europe is generally a pro-cyclical phenomenon, which means that as the global, continental or national economy grows more people move, and conversely as the economy contracts fewer people migrate (McCann 2013). In the European context, international and interregional migration is also largely a disequilibrium phenomenon (Dennett 2014), which means that most migrants seeking work move in response to demand 'pull' factors towards areas of higher wages, higher activity rates and lower unemployment and away from the 'push' factors associated with low wages and low employment opportunities (Fassman et al. 2009; Nijkamp et al. 2012). Many of these migrants exhibit high levels of human capital, and move to new destination regions for periods of several years in order to acquire income, skills and experience. The destination regions targeted by these migrants are often major and economically buoyant cities. However, many of these migrants also have no intention of permanently settling in the destination region. Consistent with the life-cycle-escalator model of migration (Faggian and McCann 2009), large numbers of these younger migrants tend to rent rather than purchase housing in the destination region, with a view to returning to their own home countries and regions once a certain level of income and experience has been acquired. At the same time, a smaller but significant number of European migrants also move for reasons of amenities, and in particular to regions with warmer climates and often lower wages (Cheshire and Magrini 2006). Many of these migration movements are not to major cities, but to smaller towns, rural areas and maritime regions. These migrant cohorts tend to be dominated by older people, many of whom already have high levels of housing equity and who subsequently also purchase real estate in their destination regions in order to enjoy the local natural amenities on a long-term basis. These migration flows are largely unrelated to the local employment conditions, because many of the migrants are already well established financially, and are not moving for employment reasons. In the case of European regions these effects are only really discernable at the intra-national level rather than the EU-wide level (Cheshire and Magrini 2006). This reflects the fact that in general EU labour markets are still very 'sticky' locally and dominated by implicit transnational boundaries (Cheshire and Magrini 2009), except for mobility towards specific global city locations.

In 2006/07 almost 2 million people moved between EU countries, representing 0.4 per cent of the EU population, while 6.5 million moved between NUTS2 regions, representing 1.29 per cent of the population (ESPON 2013). These migration movements were both from and to home countries, and the net effect of these movements is that between 2004 and 2008 the number of EU citizens living outside of their own country increased by 1.5 million per year such that the share of the EU population living in other EU countries increased from 5.1 per cent to 6.2 per cent (European Union 2013a). For the immediate post-crisis years of 2009-2011 the annual cross-border migration flows fell to 0.9 million leading to a share of 6.7 per cent of the EU population living in other EU countries as of 2011 (European Union 2013a). The severe and adverse employment impacts associated with the aftermath of the global financial crisis on young people in particular in Europe's regions is likely to accelerate outflows of these groups to more prosperous regions. These impacts have been most notable in the case of Ireland, the Baltic States and Spain (European Union 2013a). However, the labour outflows from many of the Southern European economies are still remarkably small, and largely dominated by outflows of recent in-migrants rather than new outflows of domestic workers (NIESR 2013). Out-migration as an adjustment strategy is much lower in Europe than in the USA (Storper 2013) and this exit process itself appears to have diminished in the wake of the crisis. The slowdown in international net migration was most marked in those countries which had experienced the greatest inflows during the pre-crisis era, most notably Spain, Portugal, Ireland, the UK and Northern Italy (European Union 2013a,b). Intra-EU migration prior to the 2008 crisis was dominated by outflows from Eastern Europe (NIESR 2013) and massive falls and even reversals in these flows have been associated with contractions in the construction industry in many of the destination countries and regions (European Union 2013a; NIESR 2013). The migration-flow adjustments from Eastern European countries have dwarfed the recent outflows from EU-15 countries. The fact that the labour outflows from many of the countries most severely affected by the crisis are still generally very small is largely explained by the fact that so many EU regions are experiencing economic contractions at the same time. The result of this is that there is a widespread employment-demand reduction across many parts of Europe, and the shrinkage in pan-European migration 'pull' factors militates against outward migration flows even when the 'push' factors are so strong.

The international and interregional flows within the EU have been greatly facilitated by the establishment of the EU Single Market which allows for labour mobility across the EU, either for reasons of employment or also for residential reasons. Yet, the motives for these two different types of migration flows are very different, as are the associated demographics, with the employment-migration flows being dominated by younger people while the amenity-migration flows are dominated by older cohorts. However, these intergenerational differences in mobility and employment experiences also raise broader challenges related to the ability of Europe's regional economies to adjust to different age-related and demographic effects (DG Regio 2008). As medical advances proceed, all of Europe's regions exhibit an ageing population. On the other hand, younger and more highly educated workers tend to be the most geographically mobile groups displaying the highest migration propensities (McCann 2013). Therefore, regions and cities (European Commission 2007) experiencing major inflows of young people, and in particular young and highly educated workers, exhibit a relatively slower ageing process because the inflows of youth alter the population distribution in favour of these younger groups. In contrast, regions experiencing out-migration of workers tend to exhibit more rapidly-ageing populations, because it is the younger groups who dominate these outflows.

These different demographic shifts imply that regions facing worker outflows and more rapidly-ageing populations will require the local provision of relatively more public goods related to welfare and health services than those regions facing population inflows (ESPON DEMIFER 2010). At the same time, those regions displaying population inflows also tend to experience an increasing local economic and fiscal base while those displaying population outflows tend to face a declining local economic and fiscal base. The regions experiencing population inflows therefore tend to exhibit relatively favourable balance between the need for local public services and the ability to finance these services locally. This is also true even for regions exhibiting population inflows of older cohorts for primarily amenity-related reasons, because the local real estate purchases and income-multiplier impacts of such migrants already provide financial injections into the local economy. In contrast, regions facing population decline are highly vulnerable in demographic terms because they face a toxic combination of increasing local public service needs allied with a declining ability to fund such services locally. These regions become increasingly dependent on fiscal redistribution from their own central state, as well as European regional development aid. Indeed, all of the available evidence suggests that Europe's regions now exhibit large differences in their levels of demographic vulnerability (European Commission 2010), with regions in Central and Eastern Europe tending to display higher levels of vulnerability in comparison to those in Western and Northern Europe (ESPON 2013), precisely because of these inter-generational differences in international and interregional mobility (ESPON DEMIFER 2012). Part of these demographic shortfalls could in principle be made up by international migration. Indeed, 49 per cent of immigration into EU countries has originated from outside of the EU while 51 per cent has originated from within the EU. Although both of these flows can contribute to the foreign-born population of a member state, only the former flow affects the foreign-born population of the EU as a whole. However, the migration flows which originated as immigration from outside of the EU have, if anything, tended to mirror and exacerbate the demographic effects of the intra-EU interregional and international migration flows (ESPON 2013). In particular, they closely mirror the employment-migration flows to major capital cities and other large urban areas (ESPON 2013).

2.2.5 Energy and Environment

The environmental challenges facing Europe associated with moving towards the Kyoto targets and also the Europe 2020 agenda are both complex and also rather different in different parts of the continent (EEA 2012a, b). In terms of environmental challenges associated with fostering sustainable growth (OECD 2008, 2012c) there are nowadays a wide a variety of new development policy mechanisms (OECD 2009c) available to help respond to the specifics issues at hand. In particular, regions and localities are increasingly understood as playing a key role in these responses (European Union 2011; OECD 2010a, 2012d, f). At the national level, in the Climate and Energy Package of Europe 2020 the overall European greenhouse gas emissions-reductions goals are to be achieved via the EU Emissions Trading Scheme (ETS) and the 'Effort Sharing Decision' (ESD). The EU as a whole is committed to achieving at least a 20 per cent reduction of greenhouse gas emissions by 2020 compared with 1990 (European Union 2011), and this implies a 21 per cent reduction in activities covered by the ETS compared with 2005 and a 10 per cent reduction in emissions relative to 2005 for those activities

covered by the ESD scheme. For those activities which are not included
in the ETS the ESD establishes binding emissions-reductions agreements
for each member state for the period 2013–2020, using 2005 as the
baseline date (European Union 2011). The types of activities which are
not included in the ETS include transport, buildings, agriculture and
waste (ibid.) and these activities account for some 60 per cent of current
carbon emissions (European Union 2014). Given that richer countries
tend to produce more greenhouse gas emissions than poorer countries,
and also that newly-industrialising countries generally increase their
greenhouse gas emissions rapidly, the logic of the ESD scheme is that the
higher productivity EU nations face absolute emissions-reductions targets
whereas the poorer EU nations face restrictions in the growth of their
emissions. The individual national emissions-reduction targets are closely
related to the levels of development of the member state, as well as
allowing for the existing use of renewables in energy production (European Union 2011).[6] As already mentioned, the types of activities not
included in the European Emissions Trading Scheme ETS and which
instead fall under the heading of the ESD Effort Sharing Decision
scheme include transport, buildings, agriculture and waste (ibid.). The
longstanding experience of Cohesion Policy in each of these arenas
suggests that as a policy it is well placed to respond to these issues
(European Union 2011), although activities and actions under the ESD
cannot be used to substitute for, or to indirectly subside, actions under the
ETS (ibid.).

The issues Europe has faced and continues to face regarding environmental challenges fall into two broad categories, namely the provision
and consumption of energy supplies, and the management and use of
land and water assets (EEA 2010). In terms of energy production and
consumption, as a whole Europe has become increasingly self-sufficient
in the provision of energy and energy services (ESPON 2013), although
this is largely due to the contributions from Norway which produces
more than nine times its own energy needs. In contrast, countries such as
Belgium, Spain, Ireland, Italy and Portugal all have resources to produce
less than one-quarter of their own energy needs while tiny countries such
as Cyprus, Luxembourg and Malta produce less than 2 per cent of their
energy needs (ESPON 2013). The EU-15 countries consume some 50 per
cent more energy per capita than EU-12 countries, which would appear
to make them relatively vulnerable to rising energy prices. However, the
high industrial and manufacturing GVA gross value-added intensity of
EU-12 countries allied with lower GDP per capita levels as well as the
poorer energy conservation levels of their buildings means that the
energy cost associated with producing one extra Euro of output in EU-15

countries is only 30 per cent of the equivalent figure in EU-12 countries. Given their existing industrial specialisation it takes more than three times as much energy inputs in the EU-12 countries to generate an additional Euro of output than in EU-15 countries. As such, the combination of their current industrial structures alongside their lower GDP levels means that these countries are in many ways actually far more vulnerable to rising energy prices, or to increasing volatility-related energy price risks, even though their energy consumption per capita is lower than that of the EU-15 countries (ESPON 2013). Rising energy prices also disproportionately impact adversely on geographically peripheral regions, due to the associated increases in transportation costs. Similarly, regions engaging in energy-intensive production activities are also at risk from what is known as 'carbon leakage' effects, whereby firms may relocate facilities outside of the EU in order to avoid or offset increasing carbon taxes (ESPON 2013). At the same time, rising energy prices offer new opportunities to those regions with energy-provision resources, and this is becoming increasingly important in regions able to take advantage of the possibilities associated with renewable energy sectors (ESPON 2013; OECD 2012a). Many of Europe's regions with the greatest potential capacity for solar-power, wind-power or tidal power are in non-core and more geographically peripheral regions (ESPON 2013; OECD 2012b), and these emerging renewable energy possibilities provide some new opportunities to counter the economic effects associated with peripherality (OECD 2012b). At the same time, new approaches to urban development (OECD 2010a, 2012d) as well as the relationships between rural and urban regions (OECD 2013c) are also providing a variety of local responses within European to these broader environment al challenges.

While the EU represents 7.7 per cent of the global population it also accounts for 9.5 per cent of the world's bio-capacity ability to absorb waste and to produce useful biological materials (ESPON 2013). Yet, even though its bio-capacity is relatively high the EU also accounts for 16 per cent of the global ecological footprint (ibid.). The richer parts of Europe in general have the highest ecological footprints, with lower income countries such as Romania exhibiting ecological footprints which are close to the global average (ibid.). While countries such as Germany have used technology to significantly reduce their ecological impacts (ibid.), in general the high development levels of EU countries also come at a price in terms of climate change and European countries rely on other parts of the world to help mitigate their adverse environmental effects.

The effects of global warming and climate change are also unevenly and differently distributed across Europe (EEA 2010; European Union 2014). Broadly, northern parts of Europe close to the sea will experience the lowest temperature increases but will become wetter, while temperature increases will become progressively greater the further south is the country or region, and the climate will become drier (Coutard et al. 2014; ESPON 2013). Rising sea levels will pose flood-related threats to many of the coastal and low-lying areas of Europe, including areas bordering the Atlantic Ocean, the Baltic Sea, the North Sea, the Black Sea, as well as some Spanish regions bordering the Mediterranean Sea (ESPON 2013). Meanwhile, extreme wind, rain and storm-related threats are likely to be greater in Northern Europe (Coutard et al. 2014). Overall, however, Northern and Western regions of Europe are better-placed to respond to the climate change challenges than more Southern or Eastern regions of Europe (European Union 2014).

Although the climate change effects on natural rural and marine habitats are widely discussed in the popular press, in terms of the performance of the EU's regional economies it is the effects of climate change and rising sea levels on Europe's cities which is especially challenging. Europe has numerous large cities located in coastal and low-lying areas, many of which are immediately adjacent to the sea. Indeed some 70 per cent of Europe's large cities are at elevations of less than ten metres above sea level (ESPON 2013), and the combination of rising sea levels and increasing rainfall means that many of northern Europe's cities will become increasingly vulnerable to flooding (ibid.). Also, inland cities situated on many of Europe's major rivers are also likely to be increasingly vulnerable to climate change (Coutard et al. 2014). At the same time, a combination of rising temperatures and lower rainfall mean that many southern European cities and regions will face increasing challenges associated with water acquisition.

Cities in Southern Europe generally exhibit poorer air quality than those in Northern Europe, although former industrial cities in Western and Northern Europe also often display relatively poor air quality (European Commission 2007, 2010). Urban dwellers use public transportation facilities more intensively than non-urban areas (European Union 2011) although cities in Western Europe generally display lower levels of public transportation usage than those in Central and Eastern Europe (European Commission 2007). Cities also consume lower per capita energy inputs associated with heating systems (European Union 2014). At the same time, at a more local level, the challenges associated with the management of urban land and water assets are becoming increasingly acknowledged. These challenges involve the provision of services associated with land decontamination and conversion activities, wastewater treatment initiatives, waste recycling activities, the provision of cooling and air-conditioning services, and activities aimed at the mitigation of urban pollution and 'heat island' traps associated with dense urban transportation and heating systems (ESPON 2013; European Union 2014). All of these activities pose significant and different environmental challenges in different regions due to differential climate change effects and also due to the differences in the expansion or contraction experiences of particular cities. Urban contraction which associated with widespread urban land dereliction poses environmental challenges every bit as real as those arising from urban sprawl and expansion. Moreover, responding to these various urban environmental challenges appears to be particularly complicated in the case of large coastal cites, in that the waste products of these agglomerations tend to lead to the degradation of both the local marine ecosystem as well as the local land-based ecosystem. Europe has many such cities.

2.2.6 Institutions, Governance and Quality of Life

The quality of public sector governance varies significantly across European countries and also across different dimensions of government performance (Jonker 2012). At the same time, the member states of Europe are also very heterogeneous in terms of their national–regional governance systems. Countries such as the United Kingdom and France are large and highly centralised states while Germany and Spain are large and decentralised states. The Netherlands and Denmark are small and relatively centralised states while Austria and Belgium are small and decentralised states. At the same time, the degree of financial and governance autonomy of Europe's cities varies significantly (European Commission 2007, 2010). The autonomy of the sub-national regions and cities to make public policy decisions across a range of issues therefore varies significantly according to the overall national governance structure. However, over the last two decades there has been a marked increase in global patterns of regional decentralisation and devolution (Rodriguez-Pose and Gill 2003, 2004). This is also the case in many European countries and these shifts towards greater regional decentralisation provide one of the key backdrops to discussions about EU regional and urban policies. We know that governance fragmentation at the urban level is associated with lower productivity-enhancing scale-effects (OECD 2014a). At the same time, as well as differing degrees of governance centralisation or decentralisation across regions and cities, the nature of institutional set-up for delivering regional and local development also varies enormously across countries (OECD 2010b,c). Each of these factors may affect regional performance and also the ability to deliver good development policies.

Across Europe, there are major differences in terms of the share of total public investment and public expenditure which is undertaken at the sub-national level (OECD 2013a, d, e). At the same time, as well as differences in their governance roles, European nations (European Commission 2014; Jonker 2012), regions and cities also display significant differences in terms of the quality of their institutions and governance systems, as well as in terms of the perceived quality of life of their citizens. Nowadays there are performance indicators at the regional level for all EU regions regarding the quality of government (Charron et al. 2012, 2013, 2014). These indicators demonstrate that countries with relatively good national institutional and governance systems also tend to exhibit regional institutional and government systems which are good. Northern and Western European countries tend to exhibit the best-performing governance systems while Southern and Eastern European countries tend to exhibit poorer quality governance systems. However, within individual countries there are also differences in the quality of governance between regions (ibid.), and some of these differences can be very marked. Most importantly for our purposes, and as will be discussed later, there is now also increasing evidence which suggests that these differences are important in terms of the effectiveness of regional policy interventions (Garcilazo and Rodriguez-Pose 2013; Percoco 2013).

There are also differences in the perceived ability of local urban governments regarding the provision of those urban services aimed at enhancing citizens' quality of life (European Commission 2004, 2007, 2010; European Union 2013c). In terms of health and wellbeing issues, EU cities tend to exhibit lower life expectancy levels than Europe's non-urban areas (European Commission 2007). At the same time, the evidence regarding whether the quality of life in European cities is higher than in non-urban areas is mixed. There is evidence to suggest that in rich EU countries there are no real quality of life differences between rural and urban areas whereas urban areas favour relatively better than rural areas in many Eastern and Southern European countries (Shucksmith et al. 2009), while other research finds lower levels of quality of life satisfaction in European urban areas than in rural areas (Sorensen 2014). There is no real evidence that the quality of life is higher in cities in rich European countries. However, for those cities which do display high quality of life rankings, it is generally the small and medium-sized cities in the North and West of Europe which dominate the top echelons of these European rankings (European Commission 2004, 2007, 2010;

European Union 2013c). Similarly, when we consider the top echelons of the 'smart cities' ranking of Europe's medium-sized cities,[7] again these rankings are also dominated by small and medium-sized cities in Northern and Western Europe.

In contrast, most cities with lower perceived quality of life levels are firstly in Eastern Europe and secondly in Southern Europe, and often these cities are also in those regions with the lowest quality of governance rankings. In general, the urban quality of life perceptions on the part of urban citizens tend to follow closely the regional quality of government scorings for the regions in which the cities are located.

The quality of life European rankings are very different to those which are often highlighted in the USA. In the North American case migration is primarily towards southern and western states, with migration flows being associated with amenity and quality of life issues. In particular, the single most important indicator of in-migration flows is the average temperature in January (Partridge 2010), and this suggests that natural climate-related amenities dominate quality of life mobility decisions, although broader amenity-related issues are also likely to play an important role (Storper 2013). Yet, while there is some small evidence of similar north-south flows within rather than between EU countries (Cheshire and Magrini 2006), within Europe it appears that quality of life issues are more closely related to the quality of governance and institutional issues than to natural climate-related issues.

2.3   CONCLUSIONS

The regional and urban characteristics of the European Union are complex and reflect the 'patchwork' nature of the EU economy. The European regional and urban economic system is a result of varying national economies reflecting different institutional and historical economic processes, which have been subsequently overlaid with the processes of European integration. As we see from an examination of these six major perspectives on the EU regional and urban system, there is no single clear-cut description of the EU spatial economy, nor any overall dominant stereotype towards which EU regions and cities are converging. The economic geography experiences are very different in different parts of Europe and as such this deeply rooted heterogeneity precludes both simple aggregate characterisations as well as the drawing of lessons based on overly-simple comparisons with other parts of the world. Any discussions regarding the potential role to be played by regional and urban development policy in the heterogeneous EU context must explicitly take these specific features and differences into consideration. For our purposes a sound understanding of the European regional and urban characteristics is essential in order to ensure that discussions regarding the reforms to EU Cohesion Policy are placed on a sound footing.

NOTES

1. http://bookshop.europa.eu/en/redi-the-regional-entrepreneurship-and-development-index-pbK N0214462/?CatalogCategoryID=cKYKABsttvUAAAEjrpAY4e5L
2. The former phenomenon is known as 'β-convergence' while the latter is known as 'σ-convergence' (Barro and Sala-i-Martin 1992, 1995).
3. The definition of 'urban' employed by the European Commission and Eurostat is consistent with the new OECD definition of 'urban'. In this definition, urban areas can be split into 'cities' and 'towns and suburbs'. Cities can be further differentiated by the size of their urban centre. Metropolitan areas are cities and their commuting zones with a total over 250,000 inhabitants, and Metropolitan regions are NUTS-3 regional proxies of the metropolitan areas.
4. Using the OECD 'urban' definition (OECD 2012a) the OECD data suggests that this gap is much smaller than the MGI or UN data suggests and that almost all of the difference is associated with smaller cities between 500,000 and 1.5 million inhabitants (OECD 2013a).
5. http://bookshop.europa.eu/en/redi-the-regional-entrepreneurship-and-development-index-pbK N0214462/?CatalogCategoryID=cKYKABsttvUAAAEjrpAY4e5L
6. A reformed and more flexible EU-wide approach to climate change mitigation issues was proposed by the European Commission in January 2014. See: http://ec.europa.eu/clima/ policies/2030/index_en.htm
7. http://www.smart-cities.eu/download/smart_cities_final_report.pdf

3. The logic and workings of EU Cohesion Policy

3.1 INTRODUCTION

In this chapter we provide a brief overview and outline of the origins and evolution of EU Cohesion Policy, as well as its current workings and economic impacts. As we see, the policy has evolved over recent decades as Europe itself has evolved and additional features of the policy have been incorporated into the overall policy architecture and logic as a response to particular issues which have arisen as Europe has changed. Fundamentally, however, the policy architecture and logic which existed as of 2013 was still basically the same as that which was originally constructed in 1988, and this chapter explains the basic architecture, logic, and selected impacts of the policy over a 25-year period.

3.2 EUROPEAN REGIONAL DEVELOPMENT POLICIES 1975–2013

The EU regional and urban policy agenda, or more precisely EU Cohesion Policy, on some measures can be considered as being possibly the largest single integrated development programme in the Western and OECD world. The limited evidence available suggests that regional development policies within the USA are probably larger than those operating within Europe (Drabenstott 2005). However, this is open to question[1] because there are no comprehensive and consistent data available on nationally-financed development activities for all EU member states (European Commission 2010b) while at the same time the US policies are somewhat scattered across thousands of different state and sectoral programmes (Drabenstott 2005). In contrast, EU Cohesion Policy works as a regional and urban development policy within a single common overall legal framework applied across EU and, as we will see shortly, the scale of this policy is well-documented.

EU regional and urban development policies date originally back to the 1960s and the early 1970s.[2] These policies originated partly as a result of the area-targeting experience inherent in the 1951 European Coal and Steel Community Treaty (Barca 2009). At the same time, the origin of the ERDF also followed the issues raised by the 1973 accession of the UK and Ireland to the EEC. In particular it reflected the need for some sort of mechanism to give budget contributions back to the UK while at the same time addressing the challenges associated with the advent of new challenges facing old industrial areas in the common market arena. These various issues and experiences led to the European Regional Development Fund (ERDF) being established in 1975.[3] The ERDF is the main budgetary stream in EU Cohesion Policy and funds actions and interventions operating in the areas of infrastructure investments, the promotion of research and development, enhancing innovation, the provision of support for SMEs, and in environmental and energy-related matters. The legal basis of Cohesion Policy is set out in articles 174–178 of the Treaty of the Functioning of the European Union (TFEU) and Article 176 of the TFEU states that the role of the ERDF is 'to help redress the main regional imbalances in the Union through participating in the development and structural adjustment of regions whose development is lagging behind and in the conversion of declining industrial regions'.[4] To further support the structural adjustment effect of Cohesion Policy the Cohesion Fund (CF) was also established in 1993 and operates under Article 177 of the TFEU. The origins of the Cohesion Fund originally lie in the Delors (1989) report on economic and monetary union, which ultimately paved the way for the introduction of the Euro. The Cohesion Fund was originally introduced as part of a deal on EMU giving extra funds for the Southern European countries while also helping to prepare these countries for monetary union. Also, it was at this stage that the first macro-economic conditionality was introduced, although as we will see in the next chapter this was not used until very recently. The Cohesion Fund is designed to help support large-scale environmental and trans-European network projects, and particularly where such actions would pose serious fiscal challenges for the countries concerned. Only member states which have a gross national income (GNI) per head of below 90 per cent of the EU average are eligible for this particular assistance and funding is provided at the national rather than the regional level. The third major funding stream related to Cohesion Policy alongside the ERDF and the CF is the European Social Fund (ESF) which was established in 1957 and its aims as set out in articles 162–164 of the TFEU centre on improving responses to industrial change and the raising of living standards by improving worker employability, increasing employment opportunities and enhancing employment and occupational mobility. Originally the ESF targeted only those who were unemployed but over time it has also shifted towards vocational training and retraining also for those in work. The fourth stream of funding activities relating to Cohesion Policy are the Trans-European Networks (TENs) in energy, transport and telecommunications network systems,[5] and these funding activities support infrastructure investment in these various arenas on the basis of articles 170–172 of the TFEU. There are also specific funding streams relating to rural and maritime regions which as we will see in the following chapter are increasingly working in parallel with the main Structural Funds.[6]

As already mentioned, the suite of development funds and funding actions emerged from the earlier area-targeting experience of the European Iron and Coal Treaty (Barca 2009). However, as well as the area-targeting experience, in part the need for the policy also arose due to the desire by some of the net donor states within what was then the European Economic Community (EEC) to receive some form of compensation payments, and in its early days the policy focus was on regional development (Bachtler et al. 2013). Yet, over time the policy architecture and goals were successively added to in a rather ad hoc manner, thereby expanding the regional development agenda in different ways. By the 1980s the desire by some of the net donor states for greater compensatory receipts had further increased in the light of the restructuring of the European Economic Community (EEC) into the European Community (EC) following the accession of Greece, Portugal and Spain in 1986. In 1988 a wholesale reform of the whole of policy architecture and goals was undertaken by European Commission under the leadership of Jacques Delors. The reforms were implemented in the context of the new multi-annual planning of the EU budget and as such the policy reforms, which also involves a doubling of the policy's resources, were undertaken as a companion to the advent of the European Single Market (Delors 1989; LSE Enterprise 2011; Padoa-Schioppa et al. 1987), the preparations for which at the time were already at a late stage. The Maastricht Treaty and the EU Single Market came into being broadly in its current form at the transition from 1991 to 1992 (Artis and Nixson 2001; Baldwin and Wyplosz 2004; El-Agraa 2001; Hansen 2001; Senior Nello 2005), and meanwhile the new post-1988 regional development policy architecture was now renamed as EU 'Cohesion Policy'.

The 1988 Delors reforms updated the logic and workings of the policy in order to ensure that its role and functioning was appropriate for the new regional development challenges associated with the EU Single Market. Prior to the 1988 reforms, the annual budget procedure and national quotas which were agreed in the referring regulations for the ERDF and the ESF had led to a system of re-funding projects which where selected and introduced by the member states. To overcome this *'juste retour'* logic, the Commission began to develop and finance regional projects on a more autonomous and experimental basis which became the blueprint of Cohesion Policy's method of implementation.[7] Alongside shifts in thinking in regional planning these experiments helped to lead to a greater awareness of the importance of more integrated and 'bottom-up' approaches to regional planning which also involved 'softer' forms of investments alongside 'harder' forms of investments in infrastructure and enterprises.[8] These lessons were incorporated into the design of the 1988 reforms which resulted in a significant movement away from a system of side payments to a more allocative basis for regional policy (Leonardi 2005). In addition, further shifts in thinking regarding the nature, role and design of the policy subsequently emerged as environmental, energy and sustainability issues became increasingly incorporated into the Cohesion Policy remit following the 2001 Gothenburg Strategy.[9] Even allowing for these more recent developments, however, the overall post-1988 system has remained largely intact and the current EU Cohesion Policy architecture up to 2013 is a direct result of these reforms. Indeed, allowing for various changes regarding the definitions of regions, some eligibility criteria, and the bundling of funding streams, taken together the four previous EU Cohesion Policy 'programming periods' of 1988–1993, 1994–1999, 2000–2006 and 2007–2013 as a whole reflect continuity in the policy logic, goals and architecture, even while the European Union itself has changed dramatically during this period.

The change in the policy terminology to EU 'Cohesion Policy' was important in that it underscored that fact that cohesion is an important element of European Treaties. Article 3, third indent, of the Treaty on European Union (TEU) states that: 'the union shall promote economic, social and territorial cohesion, and solidarity among Member States', while Article 2(c) of the Treaty of the Functioning of the European Union (TFEU) provides that: 'Shared competence between the Union and the Member States applies in (...) economic, social and territorial cohesion.' The concept of cohesion highlights the fact that an integrated market can only be successful in the long run if all market participants are able to engage with the market effectively in a manner such that the distribution of the market benefits is spread across the market and does not accrue consistently just to a narrow group of market participants, in this case member states, at the expense of others. The reason is that a Single Market between countries in which all of the benefits accrue to a narrow group of member states is unlikely to be sustainable in the long run politically, institutionally, or economically, and finding ways to avoid such outcomes was seen as being an important dimension underpinning the success of the EU Single Market. In the late 1980s and early 1990s there were very significant productivity and per capita income differences between the European nations, and even a well-working Single Market in which all member states can gain, still exhibits particular situations or contexts in which adjustment challenges can be very real, and cannot be easily overcome simply by the natural workings of the market mechanism. Moreover, as well as significant international differences in wealth and income, there were also significant interregional income and productivity inequalities even within some of the richer countries, and some of these intranational interregional inequalities were even greater than the international inequalities. Therefore, the support for the policy reforms were broadly based, in that economically weaker member states were in favour of the policy because they were obviously the major beneficiaries, while stronger net donor states with significant internal differences such as the UK would also benefit in terms of additional compensation payments. It was therefore both in terms of these international and intranational dimensions that EU Cohesion Policy was seen as a partner to the Single Market, helping to deepen and embed the Single Market by helping certain places facing particularly difficult adjustment problems to better adapt to the new competitive conditions. The argument that EU Cohesion Policy complements the Single Market is still seen as being very relevant today (Monti 2010).

The language of the TEU and the TFEU underscores the fact that cohesion is an important element of the EU, while the reference to 'shared competence' in matters relating to economic, social and territorial cohesion is also important because it concerns the principles governing the relationship between the EU institutions, and in particular the European Commission, and the individual member states. These relationships are based on what are known as 'competences', of which there are three different types. There are areas of 'exclusive competence' where the EU can act while individual member states are not allowed to act independently. Examples here relate to common commercial policy and the customs union. At the other end of the spectrum there are areas of 'supporting competence' whereby the EU can act while individual member states can also act independently. Examples here include tourism, culture and education. In the middle of the spectrum are areas of 'shared competence' in which either the EU or the individual member states may act, but once the EU has acted individual member states may not then act independently. In each case the boundary between independent and EU actions therefore depends on EU legislation. Most of the issues relating to the EU Single Market fall into this category, as does all of Cohesion Policy. Importantly, under the principle of subsidiarity, in areas of shared competences and supporting competences, the EU can only act if it is better placed to do so because of the scale of the actions or the effects of the actions, and around 80 per cent of the EU budget is managed in this way.[10]

3.2.1 Operating Principles

EU Cohesion Policy operates under the principles of 'shared management', whereby individual member states act in conjunction with the EU institutions. EU legislation reflects the fact that it is generally regarded that many aspects of regional and urban development policy are better coordinated at the EU level than by the individual member states. The Single Market arguments outlined above provide a strong defence of this position. In addition, when we also acknowledge the fact that many aspects of urban and regional development exhibit spatial spillover effects, spatial network effects, and economies of scale and agglomeration effects, most of which are largely blind to administrative or national borders, the arguments favouring shared competences in regional development become very persuasive, and underpin the current programming logic.

Many aspects of regional and urban development policy at the national or regional level are undertaken within the context of the overall EU policy logic and rules.[11] However, the specific design of the programmes within each member state depends on the particular development challenges to be responded to in each member state and these must take place in accordance with the EU rules on competition and state aid. The overall design of the broad policy frameworks in each member state are known as 'Operational Programmes' and individual projects, actions and interventions are embedded within the overall umbrella of a specific Operational Programme. Operational Programmes may be constructed at the level of the national member state or at the sub-national regional level, depending on the institutional and governance structure of the member state. During the 2000–2006 programming period there were 230 Operational Programmes running with thousands of individual projects, actions and interventions embedded in them.[12] The development priorities to be responded to by programmes and projects being implemented in each country and region have been set out in National Reform Programmes and in the 2007–2013 period were also detailed in the National Strategic Reference Frameworks (European Communities 2007) of each member state.[13] These documents are produced as a result of discussions and negotiations between the individual member state and the European

Commission and as a result of assessments regarding the key economic, environmental and social challenges facing the member state and also the competences and capabilities of the member state to respond to these challenges.[14]

In terms of day-to-day policy implementation, the actual way in which the policy operates is that each country, or more precisely in EU terminology each member state, receives an individual Cohesion Policy funding allocation, and the value of this is arrived at as a result of EU budget negotiations between all member states which take place every seven years, and which set what is known as the multi-annual financial framework MFF.[15] These negotiations relate to all aspects of the EU budget of which Cohesion Policy is just one, albeit a very significant, component. However, the member state does not negotiate for a budget for their entire country, but rather negotiates a budget which will allocate funding to each category of region within the member state. Funding cannot be shifted between a less developed and more developed region. The negotiations also do not occur on the actual amounts but on the method and the ingredients, and these lead to funding allocations for each category of region within each member state, the sum of which represents the total Cohesion Policy budget allocation for each country.

Once the overall EU Cohesion Policy budget for each country has been agreed, a credit line is then set up for each country via the European Commission with a guaranteed maximum expenditure limit for the EU Cohesion Policy fund. However, this does not mean that member states are simply able to ask for money from Brussels, as is sometimes assumed in the popular press. Rather, at this stage member states and regions within individual member states begin to design their own regional and urban development programmes and projects under the auspices of the overall Cohesion Policy guidelines and rubric. Within individual member states there are multiple programmes and projects embedded within the programmes dealing with a wide range of different issues and also operating at different spatial scales[16] within the member state ranging from very local to nationwide and even cross-border spatial scales. The choice of implemented projects differs between countries, as member states have their own discretion on how to choose the actual projects to be implemented. It is the prerogative of the individual member state to choose the projects to be funded, as is consistent with the subsidiarity principle inherent in much of the logic of the European Union, whereby policy decisions are taken at the lowest levels appropriate, given the policy issue being tackled. Whereas issues relating to, for example, the Euro, must necessarily be taken at the pan-European level of the European Central Bank, in the case of Cohesion Policy the most appropriate level for such decisions to be taken is typically at the national or the regional level. In some cases individual projects are chosen amongst various competing alternatives, and in other cases the competitive aspects are rather more geared towards the relative level of funding for different projects. The specifics depend on the member state concerned and according to the logic of their internal governance structures. The member states initially provide much of the funding for the projects from the public purse, and the member states then apply to the European Commission for reimbursements of many of the costs. The European Commission also makes partial financial advances to the member states at early stages in the programming period (Bubbico and de Michelis 2011; European Commission 2009). As the programmes and projects develop, at various stages during the life of the programmes the individual member states then apply to the European Commission for partial reimbursements of costs of their programmes specifically for those categories of expenditure which are eligible for reimbursements according to the policy regulations. This partnership approach to policy delivery allied with the application of the subsidiarity principle in terms of policy design reflects a multi-level governance approach to institutional relationships which is consistent with the Treaty of the Functioning of the European Union which governs the relationships between member states, regions and the European Commission. Although the EU approach pre-dated the OECD agenda, the logic of this approach is also very consistent with the multi-level governance policy logic which for a long time has been strongly advocated by the OECD for the implementation of development programmes in many different parts of the world (2001a, b, 2004, 2005, 2007, 2009, 2013a, b).

Although the individual Cohesion Policy budget allocations for each member state are technically contained within the seven-year multi-annual financial framework (MFF), and which in the parlance of the policy architecture are referred to as a seven-year 'programming' period, many projects experience time overruns, and there are two main reasons for this. Firstly, many projects, and particularly those involving major infrastructure investments or those dealing with complex environmental challenges, take a long time period to complete. Secondly, the programme and project designers in many member states take several years for their projects to be designed, given that project tenders, project designs, project competitions and project assessments can all take time. These project implementation and completion time-lag challenges are commonplace in all areas of programme and project design well beyond the remit or arena of Cohesion Policy. The effects of these time-lags and overruns is that the actual distribution of Cohesion Policy expenditures and reimbursement claims tends not to be smoothly distributed through-out the programming period, but rather often tends to be heavily weighted towards the latter part of the programming period.[17] The structure of Cohesion Policy funding explicitly assumes that projects will be back-loaded towards the latter parts of the programming period. Cohesion Policy allocations are divided into annual amounts which must normally be spent within two years of the money being allocated. If funding is committed to a project and the funding is not drawn down within two years of the commitment it is lost and the funds are automatically deducted from their financial allocations and go back into the EU budget. This is known as the 'N+2 decommitment rule'. This rule is designed to reduce cost overruns both during the programming period and up to two years after it has expired.[18]

The governments of the member states are responsible for implement-ing the policy and for ensuring that the Cohesion Policy monies are spent correctly while the European Commission is accountable for the EU budget. The European Court of Auditors therefore criticises the European Commission in cases where the member state has made errors. Therefore, eligibility of payments and the time lags inherent in the programmes and projects are also examined as part of an overall and detailed accountabil-ity assessment of all aspects of the policy[19] including any errors in the policy[20] which have to be corrected for by the European Commission. Any errors made by member states have to be corrected by both the member state and the European Commission, and the Commission can insist on corrections and otherwise recover the money or suspend the policy payments. The uncovering of errors in implementation of the policy at the national or local level as well as the correction of these errors are all fundamental aspects of the accountability of the policy.[21] Again the responsibility for good policy implementation is shared between the individual member states and the European Commission as part of an overall EU-wide partnership approach to public accountability.

The co-financing principle implies that the governments, private sector and civil society sectors of each member state are also partially respons-ible for the project funding. This is intended to ensure that member states have an explicit interest in good internal policy design both at their own internal local or regional level, while at the same time also operating via a common set of partnership principles according to a European-wide policy agenda consistent with the various European treaties. Good partnership processes are intended to ensure that programme design and project selection maximise the local leverage possibilities associated with EU funding, thereby also maximising the EU-wide impacts of Cohesion

Policy. However, in each specific case, the actual scale of the Cohesion Policy partial reimbursements from the European Commission depends on the member state's level of development, the level of development of the individual region, and also on the specific nature of the programme implemented and the individual projects operating under these pro-grammes. These are known as the co-financing rates and refer to the relative contributions of EU-funding in comparison to the funding from the domestic government authorities, and these co-financing rates differ between countries according to their levels of development. Moreover, recently, and specifically in response to the impacts of the 2008 global financial crisis and its aftermath, the co-financing arrangements for those member states with the most severe difficulties were temporarily adjusted on an individual basis, in order to help these countries adjust to the unforeseen and extremely adverse circumstances they were facing (European Union 2013).

The partnership principle described above was one of the six key principles on which the 1988 policy reform logic was built, and the 1988 logic and architecture of EU Cohesion Policy is still broadly intact as of the end of the 2007–2013 programming period. However, as well as the partnership principle the policy architecture and logic is also based on five other principles (Bachtler and Turok 1997), namely the principles of 'additionality', 'planning', 'coordination', 'compatibility' and 'concentration', and these principles reflect the intentions of the policy.

In economic policy debates, the principle of 'additionality' generally refers to the intended policy outcomes which are achieved and which should not and could not have been achieved without the policy intervention. In other words, if either the workings of market alone or alternatively the domestic market–public sector interactions would have already achieved such an outcome, then no additionality is evident. This closely relates to the theoretical case for innovation policy examined in Chapter 5. However, technically the use of the term 'additionality' in Cohesion Policy circles refers to the generation of additional growth-enhancing public investments (Barca 2009) on economic development that would otherwise not have been forthcoming, while additional private sector investment stimulated is discussed in terms of a 'leverage' effect. Although the evidence on the additionality effect is positive (Chambon and Rubio 2011) this is only a necessary but not a sufficient condition for ensuring leverage effects or any wider positive output or outcome effects on the regions in question (Wostner and Slander 2009). Moreover, crowding out arguments imply that most economists would only regard the notion of 'additionality' as being meaningful if it is interpreted as a combination of what are here referred to separately as 'additionality' and 'leverage' effects, and indeed this is the way in which the term is interpreted in this book.

In order to maximise the likelihood that the policy does indeed generate the desired additionality effects, all policy actions and interventions need to be carefully designed and properly 'planned' and programmed so as to ensure efficiency and effectiveness. The intention of such careful planning is that this will also help to ensure that the policy programmes, actions and interventions being implemented in each member state are properly coordinated with the wider EU agenda in a manner whereby the national and EU funding objectives are compatible. These principles of planning, coordination and compatibility are all intended to ensure that the partnership principle is adhered to. At the same time, however, the logic and structure of EU Cohesion Policy is also intended to go beyond the relationship between national and European institutions, and as far as possible to also include the local and regional authorities involved in the policy actions in the partnership principle. The coordination of planned actions between national, European and regional authorities which are compatible with wider European goals is intended to ensure that there is a concentration of resources on the development priorities to be responded to, so as to achieve the desired additionality.

A major advantage of the whole logic and architecture of EU Cohesion Policy over domestic regional and urban development activities is the continuity provided by the seven-year programming periods of the policy, which allow for activities to be undertaken independently of short-term domestic political cycles. Moreover, the fact that local and regional authorities are involved as well as central governments, and all actors operate under the wider EU auspices, means that development activities with a wider remit can be undertaken in a manner consistent with the democratic governance and accountability principles of the EU. In particular, any activities which have cross-border implications, as is the case with many transport, energy or environmental activities, can be undertaken with a long-term perspective which is often not possible with domestic actions.

3.2.2   Instruments and Eligibility

The policy has three major funding instruments, namely the European Regional Development Fund (ERDF), the European Social Fund (ESF) and the Cohesion Fund (CF), and the different types of development interventions and actions operate under one common provisions and different fund-specific regulations.[22] The ERDF is the major EU Cohesion Policy funding instrument, and the monies from the ERDF tend to be invested in traditional regional development activities, including the provision or upgrading of transportation infrastructure, the provision or enhancement of R&D infrastructure, human capital and skills enhancement, the provision of credit streams for SMEs, environment-related and energy-related activities, and also land-use and housing-related issues. The ESF funding instrument focuses on combating social issues related to social deprivation, social exclusion, poverty, health and wellbeing, and the actions undertaken via the ESF heavily emphasise the provision or upgrading of employment skills, social integration skills, and the provision of social care facilities and systems for groups, families or individuals. Finally, the CF deals with those specific development challenges whose responses to which would put significant pressure on national budgets and fiscal positions. These tend to relate to very large scale transportation, energy and environmental challenges, and whereas the ERDF and ESF largely operate at a regional level, the CF allocations operate at a national level.

In order for the policy to explicitly address the key regional challenges rather than inadvertently becoming dominated by national sectoral issues, in the 1988 reforms each region of the European Union was classified into different levels of funding eligibility and assistance depending on their relative levels of development. The least developed regions were those defined as having GDP per capita levels of below 75 per cent of the 1988 European Community (EC) average. These regions, which were the weakest in the EU, are those listed as being eligible for the greatest levels of assistance. Other regions eligible for less, but still significant assistance include various other categories of regions which are facing specific problems and societal challenges related to deindustrialisation, industrial restructuring, or severe and persistent problems of local unemployment. Following the establishment of the Single Market at the beginning of 1992 after the enshrining of the European Union in the Maastricht Treaty, the 1988 Cohesion Policy logic and architecture remained largely unchanged in response to the accession of Austria, Sweden and Finland to the EU in 1995, except for the fact that the definition of the EU average changed slightly as these three accession countries were all relatively wealthy.

The grouping of EU regions and the scaling of their development indices according to which regions are classified for Cohesion Policy funding eligibility is determined according to a standardised system known as the NUTS system and which is developed by Eurostat.[23] The NUTS acronym refers to the Nomenclature of Territorial Units for Statistics and this is a statistical system which allows for the comparability of regions across different EU countries, and all EU regions are defined at different levels of spatial aggregation. The highest level of aggregation is NUTS0 and this refers to the national scales of countries. Below this level are the NUTS1 level regional definitions of which, for example, the UK has 12 such regions and The Netherlands has four, each of which typically has around 3–6 million inhabitants. Below this are the NUTS2 level regions of which, for example, France has 27, Italy 22 and Spain 17, each of which typically has 1–3 million inhabitants. Below this level are the NUTS3 regions, which exist at local scale and are typically of the order of less than 1 million inhabitants.[24] For statistical purposes there are even lower city-region and local neighbourhood levels of spatial aggregation embedded inside the NUTS3 classifications.[25] However, NUTS definitions are not only based on population, but also to some extent on geographical areas and also on institutional issues. This is because the efficacy of the NUTS statistical system also depends on the reason for which the statistics are used. For policy implementation purposes, and specifically in the case of EU Cohesion Policy, sub-national governance structures are also very important in that policies are delivered by different tiers of governance in different countries. Therefore, for comparability purposes across different governance and institutional regimes there are also some cases whereby regions are classified both as NUTS1 and NUTS2 regions simultaneously, as is the case, for example, with the nation of Luxembourg which is both a NUTS1 and a NUTS2 region. The different tiers within the NUTS system also coincide largely with the various OECD regional and urban classifications (Dijkstra and Poelman 2011, 2012; OECD 2012, 2013c).[26] Overall, the NUTS system provides a powerful framework for benchmarking the performance and characteristics of regions across many different criteria and objectives, as well as providing an empirical framework within which the whole EU Cohesion Policy framework and negotiations can operate. However, a map of the NUTS regions is not a map of the policy. While NUTS boundaries are important for determining eligibility and financial allocations the member states are not bound to use them for implementation purposes. Moreover, the result of the multi-country and multi-annual EU budget negotiations means that the Cohesion Policy funding allocations are not entirely dependent on the NUTS regions' level of development, but also on other institutional and political economy influences (Bouvet and Dall'erba 2010).

The European Union has evolved significantly over the last two-and-a-half decades. Following on from the Western European countries known collectively as the 'EU-15' member states, the EU itself has both grown and changed in terms of its regional composition. The accession of the 11 new member states from Central and Eastern Europe took place in two waves, namely in 2004 and 2007, while Malta and Cyprus also joined in 2004. Until 2013 these countries were collectively known as the 'EU-12' member states. However, Croatia also joined the EU in mid 2013, so the term used nowadays is the 'EU13' member states. The accession of these countries heavily altered the economic geography of the European Union by increasing the share of the EU population resident in poorer regions and also by reducing the average GDP per capita of the EU as a whole. During 2000–2006 it was the poorer regions of the EU-15, namely the richer EU countries all of which were EU members by 1995 prior to the entry of the EU-12 post-transition economies of Central and Eastern Europe, which were the major recipients of the funding (McCann and Ortega-Argilés 2013a). However, in the previous 2007–2013 programming period, the weakest regions which as we will see below are known as Convergence or Objective 1 regions accounted for some 80 per cent of Cohesion Policy funding (Chambon and Rubio 2011), and amongst this cohort it was the EU-12, the newer member states of the EU, which while accounting for 21 per cent of the EU population now also accounted for 52 per cent of the Cohesion Policy funding (European Commission 2007a, 2009).

As well as these geographic changes, at the same time our understanding of development processes and challenges has itself evolved over recent decades. Therefore, in response to these various changes, new additional categories of Cohesion Policy assistance have been added to the overall Cohesion Policy portfolio. These deal with specific issues[27] such as the challenges faced by rural regions, marine and coastal regions, very peripheral regions, those regions with sparse populations,[28] as well as the major structural challenges associated with land reclamation and environmental degradation, particularly in the Central and Eastern European member states.

The underlying logic and architecture of EU Cohesion Policy has remained largely unchanged during this period. Although the policy had undergone some reforms in both 2000 and 2007 as a result of the reshaping of Europe (European Commission 2007a, 2009) as well as efforts to improve the workings of the policy (Bachtler and Mendez 2013), the fundamental policy logic has remained more or less intact as it was when it was originally constructed in 1988. Although many of the origins of the current shift in the policy logic lie in the 2005 policy reforms aimed at the programming period 2007–2013, the enormous changes both in terms of the geography of the EU as well as the evolving development priorities resulted in shifts in the overall Cohesion Policy funding distribution towards the weaker parts of Europe (European Union 2014). At the same time, this also resulted in rising concerns amongst many of the weaker regions amongst the EU-15 countries regarding the potential losses of Cohesion Policy funding that they were likely to face as a result of these shifts. Many Western European regions whose GDP per capita levels would previously have been under the threshold 75 per cent of the EU average were now finding themselves above this threshold, and therefore ineligible for the same rates of funding as previously.

As well as the changes of the economic geography of the European Union, and also the changes regarding some of the major development challenges being faced, there were also shifts in terms of the terminology employed in the Cohesion Policy arena, and these shifts reflected evolving discourses regarding the wider EU-related agendas. Between 1988 and 1999 the regions eligible for the most funding assistance were so-called Objective 1 regions, measured at the NUTS2 level, and these were the regions with GDP per capita levels of less than 75 per cent of the EU average. They were defined as regions which were 'structurally backward' regions (Bachtler and Turok 1997; European Union 2014). The second group of areas receiving the next most significant levels of assistance were the 'Objective 2' regions. These were areas facing severe localised problems of unemployment and Objective 2 actions were linked to areas smaller than the NUTS-3 regions. From 2000 to 2006 the priority in the Objective 1 regions was to 'counter lagging development' while in Objective 2 areas it was to 'promote competitiveness and employment'. An additional category of region was added at this time, the 'Objective 3' areas, which were focused on the implementation of training systems and employment, along with various additional experimental categories of regions regarding urban, rural, maritime and cross-border issues (European Commission 2007a). From 2007 onwards there were three categories of regions, with the former Objective 1 regions now renamed as those regions within the 'convergence' objective, the former Objective 2 regions were now termed as those regions within the 'competitiveness and employment objective', and the various additional categories of urban, rural, maritime and cross-border issues dealt with in the rather disparate third regional grouping each had a slightly different legal basis within the policy framework, often linking to other EU policies (European Commission 2007a).

The current policy architecture incorporates many different and specific types of actions and elements to the programmes including the cross-border actions known as INTERREG and the important role of the European Investment Bank in providing key supporting finance for particular activities. Moreover, these various elements and actions also evolved throughout the two and half decades as did various kinds of objectives and area eligibility definitions of the programmes since the original 1988 reforms. An overview of these can be gained by referring to a series of publications (European Commission 1996a, 1998, 2000, 2007a).

As we have seen, the policy was initially focused on promoting regional development in difficult contexts, but over time various other remits had been added to Cohesion Policy (Begg 2010), including most recently being tied to the 'convergence' discourse of the Lisbon strategy. Gradually the addition of various new goals to the policy alongside the shifts in terminology and discourses had blurred the relationship between the growth and distributional aspects of the policy (Barca 2009; Begg 2010). The result was that policies aimed at enhancing both convergence and social inclusion were frequently being advocated (Sapir et al. 2004) while ignoring the different complementarities and trade-offs which were likely to be evident in different places (OECD 2011). Tracking these changes in terminology and shifting discourses, what is clearly observable is the heavy influence on Cohesion Policy thinking in the Brussels arena of two quite different and specific lines of argument from economics and other social sciences. These two highly influential strands of thought are the convergence discourse following on primarily from the work of Barro and Sala-i-Martin (1992, 1995) and also the competiveness discourse following on primarily from the work of Porter (1990). During the 1990s both of these lines of argumentation and enquiry had significant impacts on economic thought in general and by the end of the decade they had both also heavily influenced Brussels thinking regarding the role and objectives of Cohesion Policy. Whereas from the 1960s to the early 1990s the dominant discourses and terminology in European regional development policy had all been about assisting regions with severe weaknesses, these discourses had, by the late 1990s, shifted towards rather more optimistic terminology regarding convergence and competitiveness.[29] The emphasis of the terminology had shifted away from the rather more downbeat nomenclature regarding the problems and difficulties holding regions back which need to be challenged to a rather more positive nomenclature regarding the regions' potential for new growth. Such shifts in discourses and terminology are neither entirely superficial nor are they entirely neutral, in that they frame subsequent discussions regarding the nature and efficacy of the policy. Cohesion Policy had become aligned with the Lisbon Strategy goals of competitiveness, growth and jobs, and in the programming period of 2007–2013 some 60 per cent of resources in convergence regions and 75 per cent in the rest of the regions were earmarked for these purposes (Chambon and Rubio 2011).

As we will see in the following chapter, these changes in terminology, language and nomenclature have led to important changes regarding what people consider are the goals of the policy and also therefore on how people discuss the effectiveness of the policy. Some of these changes have provided greater clarity on these matters while others have contributed to a certain degree of unwanted confusion (Begg 2010). The essential elements and nuances of these issues are discussed in detail in the next chapter. However, at this stage it is useful to raise two important issues, namely the scale of the policy and the evidence regarding the economic impacts of the policy.

3.3   THE SCALE AND ECONOMIC IMPACTS OF EU COHESION POLICY

The best reference sources for understanding the historical development of the policy – in terms of scale of the policy, the contexts in which it operates and different goals it is tasked with achieving – are the various 'Cohesion Reports' (European Commission 1996b, 2001, 2004, 2007b, 2010a) and associated documents (European Commission 1994a,b; 1999).

In terms of the scale of the policy for recent, current and forthcoming activities, in the 2007–2013 programming period the total EU Cohesion Policy budget was €347billion, or €49.57bn per annum, and accounted for some 35 per cent of the EU budget (European Commission 2007b, 2009). Along with the CAP Common Agricultural Policy, EU Cohesion Policy is therefore one of the two largest EU policies (McCann and Ortega-Argilés 2013a), The agreed Cohesion Policy budget from the EU budget negotiations of 2013 for the programming period 2014–2020 was €325bn or €47bn per annum in 2011 prices or €366bn in current prices, while for CAP it was €312bn in current prices and €277bn in 2011 prices.[30] In the seven-year 2014–2020 programming period Cohesion Policy accounts for 34 per cent of the total EU budget of €960bn and now is the largest policy of the EU. Every year the policy support tens of thousands of individual projects, actions and interventions across the EU (European Union 2014).

Although the policy is probably the largest single integrated development policy in the Western world, at the same time the scale of the policy in comparison to EU-wide and member state economies should not be overstated. While these figures are very large in absolute terms, the total annual expenditure on Cohesion Policy is less than 0.35 per cent of the European Union's GDP, and significantly smaller than similar expenditures undertaken domestically in many individual EU member states. For example, the annual expenditure figures for Cohesion Policy are equivalent to only 15 per cent of what the UK spends annually on the provision of social welfare and personal social services, some 40 per cent of what the UK spends annually on education, 28 per cent of annual UK health expenditure, and 75 per cent of annual UK government debt interest payments (HM Treasury 2013). In other words, total EU Cohesion Policy expenditure is only a small fraction of similar types of expenditures even within one single large EU member state, which itself accounts for approximately only one-seventh of EU total GDP.

Putting these figures into perspective is very important, given the expectations raised by some of the convergence and competitiveness discourses regarding Cohesion Policy which have evolved over the last decade and as outlined above, have also given rise to some of the critiques which have been raised against EU Cohesion Policy and which will be discussed in detail in the following chapter.

In terms of the evidence regarding the impacts of EU Cohesion Policy, there are numerous evaluation studies of the impacts of specific programmes across all of the different themes, member states and programming periods, as well as evaluations of overall policies during each programming period.[31] As is typical in these types of evaluations, these studies generally use a combination of quantitative, qualitative, cost–benefit and case study techniques (Bachtler and Wren 2006). The various evaluation studies (EPRC and LSE 2013; European Commission 2010b, c, d; Ward et al. 2012) provide detailed assessments of individual programmes.

The broad lesson which emerges from these various studies is that Cohesion Policy is making progress in terms of its intended objectives and that it contributes significantly to achieving local development goals of the recipient regions, particularly when these are measured in terms of outputs such as length of roads (Ward et al. 2013), number of businesses supported or environmental improvements (European Commission 2010b, c). The evidence also points to improvements in connectivity and quality of life (ERPC and LSE 2013; European Commission 2010c, d) as well as in terms of governance features such as compliance with EU directives (Ward et al. 2013), improvements in programming (EPRC and LSE 2013), coordination and cooperation (European Commission 2010d). At the same time, however, these evaluation and assessment exercises also demonstrate that there is a high degree of heterogeneity of outcomes across regions and policies, because projects are affected by delays, by a lack of sufficient definition of goals and targets, by insufficient planning and coordination, by often unrealistic expectations, and by insufficient monitoring. These detailed studies also demonstrate the difficulties in isolating the effects of the policy from other external effects, and these difficulties are often compounded both by the time-lags inherent in the policy effects and also because of the multiplicity of often-vaguely defined objectives which the policy is supposed to address (European Commission 2010b). Moreover, the evaluation of the policy effects on social and territorial cohesion is made all the more difficult due to a lack of appropriate indicators, whereas economic impacts are rather more straightforward to define (ibid.).

However, in terms of the explicit economic outcomes of the policy at a pan-EU level, there are more than 50 research papers which analyse the economic impacts of EU Cohesion Policy using formal economic modelling or econometric modelling techniques. These papers date back from the mid-1990s up to the present day and they employ empirical evidence ranging from the late 1980s through to the end of the 2000–2006 programming period, and in a smaller number of cases also analyses aspects of the 2007–2013 programming period. In these papers various different economic and econometric modelling techniques have been employed ranging from simultaneous equation systems, panel data techniques, technology frontier analysis, data envelopment analysis, spatial econometrics, dynamic input–output models, stochastic computable general equilibrium models, propensity score matching techniques, heterogeneous treatments effect techniques and regression discontinuity models. Most of the papers analyse data derived from the Cohesion Policy experience of the EU15 member states in earlier programming periods, although recently a new set of papers have been able to include some or all of the EU12 member states in their analysis.

The result is that in the same way that the policy has exhibited a high degree of financial accountability in comparison to many intranational policies within many countries, the impacts of the policy have also received a high degree of scrutiny in comparison to almost any other development programme from any part of the world. By undertaking a wide-ranging overview of these papers it is possible to provide a broad brush overview of the economic growth impacts of the policy. The simplest way to do this is to group the papers together according to their overall findings. Although these various papers cover different time periods, use different datasets and employ different econometric techniques, the grouping of the papers provides a reasonably representative summary of the current state of our knowledge.

Firstly, there are more than two-dozen studies which have found broadly positive results for the economic growth effects of EU Cohesion Policy (Arcalean et al. 2012; Bähr 2008; Bayar 2007; Becker et al. 2010,

2012a; Beugelsdijk and Eijffinger 2005; Bouayad-Agha et al. 2014; Bradley et al. 1995, 2007; Cappelen et al. 2003; Dall'erba 2005; de la Fuente and Vives 1995; Ferrara et al. 2010; Gáková et al. 2009; Garcilazo and Rodriguez-Pose 2013; Honohan 1997; In't Veld 2007; LSE Enterprise 2011; Martin and Tyler 2006; Pellegrini et al. 2013; Puigcerver-Peñalver 2007; Ramajo et al. 2008; Sosvilla-Rivero et al. 2006; Varga and In't Veld 2010, 2011). Secondly, there are also more than a dozen or so papers which have found some positive results for Cohesion Policy interventions but these positive results are also found alongside some mixed results (Aiello and Pupo 2012; Becker et al. 2012b; Ederveen et al. 2006; Espositi and Bussoletti 2008; Filippetti and Peyrache 2014; Hagen and Mohl 2008, 2009; LeGallo et al. 2011; Midelfart-Knarvik and Overman 2002; Mohl and Hagen 2011; Percoco 2005, 2013; Soukiazis and Antunes 2006) for the policy which may be weak or not even positive.

Thirdly, there are a dozen or more papers which have not found any positive results for the policy. This group comprises a group of research papers which have found either negligible or insignificant results for the policy with no positive effects (Boldrin and Canova 2001; Corrado et al. 2005; Dall'erba and Hewings 2003; Dall'erba and LeGallo 2008; de Freitas et al. 2003; Fagerberg and Verspagen 1996; Falk and Sinabell 2008; Garcia-Milà and McGuire 2001; Rodriguez-Pose and Fratesi 2004; Sala-i-Martin 1996), along with also a handful of papers which have found negative results or effects (Checherita et al. 2009; Dall'erba and LeGallo 2007; Dall'erba et al. 2009) associated with EU Cohesion Policy.

From this overview it is clear that more than three-quarters of the papers dealing with the growth and development effects of EU Cohesion Policy find either positive effects for the policy or alternatively they find positive but weak or mixed effects of the policy, with just under a quarter of the available studies finding either negligible or negative effects of the policy. What is also very clear from this overview, however, is that the evidence regarding the impacts of the policy are very heterogeneous across regions, with many different factors influencing whether the policy is successful in a particular context, ranging from the governance issues (Garcilazo and Rodriguez-Pose 2013), to national issues (Percoco 2013), to distributional issues (Becker et al. 2010, 2012a, b), and to issues relating to the performance of neighbouring regions (LeGallo et al. 2011).

The results from papers employing spatial econometric techniques (Dall'erba and LeGallo 2007, 2008; Dall'erba et al. 2009) tend to be less favourable than those employing other econometric techniques. However, for policy evaluation purposes doubts have been raised regarding the ability of spatial econometric to address issues of causality and especially so in issues relating to economic geography (Gibbons and Overman 2012). For these types of policy evaluation purposes other econometric approaches aimed at tackling causality issues are argued to be more appropriate (Overman 2013). In this vein and also explicitly aimed at overcoming many of the complications associated with the heterogeneity of Europe's regions, some of the most recent econometric papers aiming to evaluate the impacts of EU Cohesion Policy have employed such techniques (Becker et al. 2010, 2012a, b; Pellegrini et al. 2013). In particular, these papers have used the eligibility criteria of the policy structure itself, which displays a discontinuity above or below the 75 per cent Objective 1 threshold, in order to assess the impacts on like-for-like regions in terms of their levels of development. On the basis of these techniques, these papers have been able to identify positive and significant EU Cohesion Policy growth effects both for the Objective 1 regions and also on the EU as a whole (Becker et al. 2012a). The most recent results (Pellegrini et al. 2013) point to additional growth impacts of EU Cohesion Policy on Objective 1 regions prior to 2007 which are of the order of 0.6–0.9 per cent per annum. Becker at al. (2012a) find even higher estimated additional annual growth impacts of some 1.6 percentage points, but for those regions closest to the Objective 1 cut-off threshold they report a range of 0.8–1.1 per cent, a range which is very consistent with the estimates of Pellegrini et al. (2013). These figures represent somewhere between one-quarter and one-third of the annualised capita growth in these regions prior to 2007, and result in overall GDP increases in these regions of between 7–11 per cent between 1994 and 2006 (Pellegrini et al. 2013). Given that the average annual EU Cohesion Policy investments in the Objective 1 regions including co-financing were of the order of 2.3 per cent during this period in the Pellegrini et al. (2013) dataset, this implies that the long-run multiplier impacts of Cohesion Policy in the EU-15 Objective 1 regions were of the order of 3.0–4.5 over the period 1994–2006, and with a 'payback' period of some 3.5–5.5 years depending on the discount rate applied (European Commission 2008). Moreover, the regional growth impacts suggested by these more recent econometric results (Becker et al. 2010, 2012a; Pellegrini et al. 2013) for EU-15 countries are also broadly consistent (McCann and Ortega-Argilés 2013b) with those also derived from various computable general equilibrium (CGE) simulations (Ferrara et al. 2010; Gáková et al. 2009; LSE Enterprise 2011) for the EU-12 countries. HERMIN estimates point to multipliers in EU12 countries of between 2.3 and 3.9 for EU-12 countries (Gáková et al. 2009), and an average increase in GDP per capita of 2.1 per cent per annum between 2007 and 2016 (Monfort 2012). The estimates derived from prototypes of the full RHOMOLO model suggest that in EU-12 countries the effect of EU Cohesion Policy accounts for some 58 per cent of the Single Market effect (LSE Enterprise 2011; McCann and Ortega-Argilés 2013b). In terms of the overall main beneficiary countries, namely the EU12 plus Greece, Spain, Portugal, the Italian Mezzogiorno and the East German Länders, the HERMIN estates are that per capita GDP was increased by 1.2 per cent per annum between 2007 and 2016 (European Union 2013a). RHOMOLO simulations (Brandsma et al. 2013) for the overall EU-wide multiplier effects of Cohesion Policy provide multiplier values of 1.49 for the programming period 2014–2020 and up to 3.75 for the period 2014–2030 (European Union 2014). These long-run RHOMOLO simulations, which are based on the most advanced computable general equilibrium (CGE) model available at the regional level, and which are also calibrated to coincide with the QUEST CGE national model simulations, are larger than the rather more 'back of the envelope' benefit–cost ratio-type calculations described by Becker et al. (2012b). These simple calculations which are based on the econometric estimates of EU Cohesion Policy on Objective 1 or 'convergence' regions, suggests that the policy generates an EU-wide gain of something of the order 1.2 times the size of the policy (Becker et al. 2012b). In other words, the overall multiplier impacts of the policy across the EU leads to a net gain of 0.2 times the size of the whole policy (ibid.).

While on the one hand the majority of the studies regarding the growth impacts of EU Cohesion Policy have tended to point towards broadly positive results, they have also raised the problem of a lack of consistency of the impacts. The experience of Cohesion Policy suggests that in terms of economic impacts there is a high degree of heterogeneity across European regions (European Union 2010a). Some estimates suggest that when considering crowding out effects, a reallocation of funds towards the weaker regions in more developed countries would generate greater returns (Becker et al. 2012a). The estimates of Becker et al. (2012a) point to an average optimal[32] transfer level to recipient regions of 0.4 per cent of regional GDP and a maximum level of 1.3 per cent of regional GDP across all recipient regions, while the maximum figures for the Cohesion Fund are 0.61 per cent and 1.8 per cent for the Objective 1 transfers. If we compare these estimates of the maximum levels of efficient transfers with the actual allocation figures for these respective funding streams we see that they are 8 per cent and 19 per cent above these estimated maximum values (Becker et al. 2012a), which is not too far out of line. However, again there appears to be a high degree of heterogeneity in the policy effects across individual regions, as has been found in many of the available studies. Becker et al. (2012a) find that 36 per cent of regions exhibit funding streams which are larger than the calculated optimum of 0.4 per cent of GDP and in 18 per cent of regions have inflows larger than the maximum of 1.3 per cent. Similar types of insights are also provided by Garcilazo and Rodriguez-Pose (2013) who find that quality of government improvements are more powerful for promoting growth in regions with lower levels of development. Moreover, beyond annual Cohesion Policy expenditure levels of €120 per person in the recipient region, and there are many regions where per capita expenditure is above this level (European Union 2014), there are no additional regional growth effects unless there are also significant gains in the quality of government.

Becker et al. (2012a) contend that in terms of EU growth the empirical evidence argues for a certain reallocation of funds from the very poorest regions to poorer regions in the wealthier countries. Indeed, the results of the 2013 Multiannual Financial Framework MFF negotiations conducted in the EU Council for the 2014–2020 programming period have led to something of a slight shift in favour of the poorer regions in the wealthier countries (EPRC 2013). However, the poorer EU member states do still account for the majority of Cohesion Policy funding allocations. Moreover, the picture is also further complicated by the fact that different member states choose to internally implement their EU-related regional and urban policies in very different centralised or decentralised ways due to varying governance and institutional systems, and many of the distributional impacts of Cohesion Policy are largely a result of these national governance and institutional choices, rather than issues of funding optimality.

3.4 THE GOVERNANCE AND INSTITUTIONAL CHALLENGES OF THE POLICY

These various pieces of empirical evidence suggest that there may be something of a disconnection between the actual distributional aspects of the policy and the optimal distributional aspects of the policy (Bouvet and Dall'erba 2010). However, this can also be understood as a result of the fact that decisions regarding EU Cohesion Policy budget allocations do not take place in a vacuum. Such decisions do not depend solely on the level of economic development of the region but also on other factors involved in the broader multi-country negotiations regarding the multi-annual financial framework which sets the EU budget. But even allowing for the complexity of the process producing funding allocations, there is still the need to ensure that where funds are spent they are spent wisely and this involves addressing a range of institutional, governance and behavioural issues (Ederveen et al. 2002). Absorption is still very much an overriding concern of member states although in recent years there has been a notable shift in emphasis of discussions within the Cohesion Policy arena away from issues of absorption and towards issues of efficiency and effectiveness. However, the recent evidence suggests that there are still important governance and distributional challenges facing the policy which need to be overcome in order to reduce the heterogeneity of the policy impacts at the local level and many of these also relate to multi-level governance challenges. Absorptive capacity is still very important, but so is governance capacity. Until recently the latter has received much less emphasis than the former, but the European experience of the aftermath of the 2008 Global Financial Crisis has accelerated the urgency to address these governance issues across all EU policy domains including Cohesion Policy. There are now significant movements in the direction of documenting these matters (Charron et al. 2012, 2013, 2014)[33] as a means of highlighting the importance of improving governance for economic development and policy implementation. Yet, one of the policy challenges which needs to be addressed is the fact that the regions with better governance performance and a strong administrative capacity also tend to be those regions in the richer countries (Ederveen et al. 2006). Development funds tend to be most effective in countries or regions with the right policy environment and good institutions (Becker et al. 2012b; Burnside and Dollar 2000; Ederveen et al. 2006; Garcilazo and Rodriguez-Pose 2013) because these good governance environments tend to limit waste and absorption problems (Hervé and Holtzmann 1998). As such, regions with a stronger governance capacity and capability are better able to benefit the most from the policy interventions while at the same time these are also the regions with the least need for public administrative reform and modernisation and the introduction of sound and efficient administration systems (Begg 2009). In contrast, the poorer regions with the weakest administrative capacity are those regions least able to benefit from the policy interventions, yet these are the regions with the greatest need for the public administration reforms to be required of them. Moreover, the available evidence (Becker et al. 2012a; Garcilazo and Rodriguez-Pose 2013) suggests that providing additional funds in the weaker regions alone is unlikely to solve these problems. Yet, it is important to note at this point that this is not an EU-specific problem. As we will see in the following chapter, it is a problem faced in all arenas of development policy, and a successful EU

Cohesion Policy would need to find some ways for better addressing these problems.

3.5 REVIEW AND CONCLUSIONS

EU Cohesion Policy has developed over many decades as a response to the difficult and localised structural and development challenges faced by various localities during the five decades of European integration. The policy has evolved as Europe's circumstances have changed, and over the last three decades the policy has increasingly become structured within a single EU-wide institutional framework. Although there have been some reforms, the logic and architecture of the policy as of 2013 was still largely the same as it was in the late 1980s, and the continuity provided by the policy allows for activities to be undertaken independently of short-term domestic political cycles. The majority of the research studies currently available suggest that the economic effects of the policy are broadly positive. However, it is also clear that there is no totally conclusive proof of the policy impacts of EU Cohesion Policy. This is partly due to the research limitations associated with working with only partially harmonised and not fully comprehensive data, the different methodological approaches employed, and also the heterogeneous implementation and impacts of the policy across member states and regions (Chambon and Rubio 2011). More fundamentally, however, these difficulties also relate to the complex causal relationships at play and also to the relatively tiny scale of the policy, which may limit its ability to significantly alter wide-ranging and longstanding economic relationships (Chambon and Rubio 2011). Taken together Molle (2007) argues that the evidence regarding the effectiveness of EU Cohesion Policy therefore needs to be considered 'in terms of plausibility instead of proof' (p. 231). This principle does not reflect a weak standard of proof, but rather an acceptance of the complex and diverse political economy challenges faced by all development policies and their evaluations, either inside or outside (Rodrik 2007) of the EU. In the case of a policy with a single broad framework and logic such as EU Cohesion Policy, in order to be successful in achieving its intended goals, responding to the economic, geographic, institutional and governance diversity of the regions is clearly a major challenge. In addition, making the development goals of the policy clear is also essential in order to avoid confusion and ambiguity.

NOTES

1. Although Moretti (2011) suggests that they are slightly lower.
2. There is no particular legal provision regarding regional issues, nor any specific overall regional policy framework in the 1957 Treaty of Rome which created the European Economic Community. However, the preamble to the Treaty specifies that one of the objectives of the EEC is: 'to strengthen the unity of [...] economies and to ensure [...] harmonious development by reducing the differences existing between the various regions and the backwardness of the less favoured regions'. In 1958 the European Social Fund (ESF) was established and in 1962 the European Agricultural Guidance and Guarantee Fund (EAGGF) were created, and these policy initiatives reflected the priorities of the founding states (agriculture for France, industrial renewal for Germany). See http://www.europarl.europa.eu/document/activities/cont/200907/20090728ATT59194/20090728ATT59194EN.pdf.
3. An overview of the development of the policy since the 1960s is provided by the European Union (2014) and a very useful summary of the development of the legal basis of the policy over the decades is provided by the European Parliament (2009). See http://www.europarl.europa.eu/document/activities/cont/200907/20090728ATT59194/20090728ATT59194EN.pdf.
4. EU Cohesion Policy operates within context framed by the various EU treaties. The Treaty of Rome (1957) established the European Economic Community, and this has subsequently been updated and amended by the Single European Act (01.07.1987), the Maastricht Treaty (01.11.1993) on the European Union, and the Treaties of Amsterdam (01.05.1999), Nice (01.02.2003) and Lisbon (01.12. 2009), all of which dealt with specific institutional changes to the EU. The Lisbon Treaty which was signed on 13 December 2007, and which came into force on 01.12.2009, amended the original Treaty on the European Union and the Treaty Establishing the European Community, and this latter treaty was renamed as the Treaty on the Functioning of the European Union. There are now two core treaties which together set out the competences of the European Union, namely the Treaty on European Union (TEU), and the Treaty on the Functioning of the European Union (TFEU). See http://www.lisbon-treaty.org; http://www.eur-lex.europa.eu.
5. The legal basis of TENs is soon to be superseded by the Connecting Europe facility proposed by the European Commission in 2011 in order to provide a more streamlined common infrastructure funding framework.
6. These funding instruments were originally part of structural funds but were subsequently removed resulting in a lack of coherence which has been rectified by the reforms discussed in the next chapter. Previously the EU budget for the Common Agricultural Policy (CAP) was administered via the European Agricultural Guidance and Guarantee Fund (EAGGF) but on 01.01.2007 this was replaced by the European Agricultural Guarantee Fund (EAGF) and the European Agricultural Fund for Rural Development (EAFRD). This latter fund is the fund which increasingly will work in partnership with the other Structural Funds in the new 2014–2020 programming period alongside the European Maritime and Fisheries Fund (EMFF) in order to address the specific development challenges raised by rural and maritime regions.
7. These exceptions included the coordination of expenditure by the ERDF, ESF and EAGG and started in 1979 with small pilot projects in Naples and Belfast and a few years later in the Lozer department in southern France. At the beginning of the 1980s, more extensive experimental projects focusing on an integrated approach to regional planning were undertaken in other parts of the Community through the Integrated Development Operations (IDOs). Larger experimental programmes financed at the European level were the Integrated Mediterranean Programmes (IMPs) allocated in 1986 to Greece, Italy and France.
8. See: European Commission (2008) EU Cohesion Policy 1988–2008: Investing in Europe's Future, Inforegio Magazine No. 26, Brussels http://ec.europa.eu/regional_policy/sources/docgener/panorama/pdf/mag26/mag26_en.pdf

9. http://ec.europa.eu/environment/eussd/.
10. http://www.bbc.co.uk/news/world-europe-24823795.
11. In Southern, Central and Eastern European member states Cohesion Policy accounts for a large share of national public investment in this arena, whereas in Western and Northern European member states these shares are small, and also generally smaller than the CAP funds for agriculture in these countries. See Table 4.A1 in Appendix 4.3.
12. http://ec.europa.eu/regional_policy/sources/docgener/evaluation/expost_reaction_en.htm
13. http://ec.europa.eu/regional_policy/atlas2007/fiche/nsrf.pdf.
14. http://ec.europa.eu/regional_policy/country/prordn/index_en.cfm.
15. http://www.bbc.co.uk/news/world-europe-20442880.
    http://www.bbc.co.uk/news/uk-politics-11645975.
16. http://ec.europa.eu/regional_policy/country/prordn/index_en.cfm.
17. http://eur-lex.europa.eu/LexUriServ/LexUriServ.do?uri=COM:2013:0104:FIN:EN:HTML.
18. In a small number of cases during the 2007–2013 programming period this was extended to three years alongside an increase of co-financing designed to help countries facing severe problems in the aftermath of the global financial crisis, and is known as the N+3 rule. See: http://www.europa.eu/rapid/press-release_IP-13-446_en.htm.
19. C:\Documents and Settings\Administrator\My Documents\EU Cohesion Policy Book\EUR-Lex – 52012DC0633 – EN.mht.
20. http://ec.europa.eu/regional_policy/sources/docgener/presenta/errors2011/analysis_errors 2011_en.pdf.
21. The European Court of Auditors (2013) reports that error rates in Cohesion Policy were of the order of 6 per cent in 2011 and affected 59 per cent of transactions and 6.8 per cent in 2012 affecting 49 per cent of transactions. Of these 6–6.8 per cent error rates, some 52 per cent of the error rate (just over 3 per cent of the total policy payments) was associated with failures to comply with public procurement rules while 28 per cent of the error rate (just over 1.5 per cent of the policy payments) was associated with ineligible payments. Similar orders of magnitude for payment errors were reported by an investigation entitled 'Europe's Hidden Billions' published by *The Financial Times* 30.11.2010-03.12.2010. See: http://aboutus.ft.com/2010/11/30/europes-hidden-billions-%E2%80%93-tracking-the-eu%E 2%80%99s-structural-funds/#axzz2lrS3focd.
22. http://eur-lex.europa.eu/JOHtml.do?uri=OJ:L:2013:347:SOM:EN:HTML.
23. *Regions in the European Union: Nomenclature of Territorial Units for Statistics, NUTS2006/EU-27*, Eurostat, European Commission, Luxembourg.
24. Minor adjustments to the classification and definitional schemes are made at various junctures, but the general intention is to keep the classifications and definitions stable in order to allow policy stability as well as analytical comparability over time. The NUTS classification which is currently operating from January 2012 until 31 December 2014 contains 97 NUTS1 regions, 270 NUTS2 regions, 1294 NUTS3 regions. The accession of Croatia (HV) to the EU on 1 July 2013 means that the NUTS classification was extended by 1 NUTS-1, 2 NUTS-2 and 21 NUTS-3 regions. See: http://epp.eurostat.ec.europa.eu/ portal/page/portal/nuts_nomenclature/introduction.
25. NUTS 4 and NUTS 5 areas have been replaced by LAU-1 and LAU-2 (local administrative unit level 1 and level 2). A municipality is typically a LAU-2. A county or district is LAU-1, although not all member states have a LAU-1 level. Luxembourg is simultaneously a NUTS 0, 1 and 2 area.
26. The OECD Territorial Level system is not identical to the NUTS levels. In Belgium, Greece and the Netherlands TL2=NUTS1 and TL3=NUTS2, while in Germany, the OECD uses a spatial planning division that is not linked to the NUTS classification.
27. http://ec.europa.eu/regional_policy/sources/docgener/evaluation/pdf/eval2007/geographical _final1.pdf
28. The accession of Sweden and Finland to the European Union in 1995 brought with it the important criteria relating to sparsely populated regions in Protocol 6 of their accession treaties and led to the establishment of Objective 6 which focuses on the economic development of such regions.

29. By 2012 the *Inforegio* website, the official website of the European Commission regarding regional and urban issues states that: 'EU regional policy is an investment policy. It supports job creation, competitiveness, economic growth, improved quality of life and sustainable development. These investments support the delivery of the Europe 2020 strategy.' See http://ec.europa.eu/regional_policy/what/index_en.cfm.
30. http://europa.eu/rapid/press-release_IP-13-1096_en.htm.
31. http://ec.europa.eu/regional_policy/information/evaluations/guidance_en.cfm.
32. 'Optimal' in this sense used by Becker et al. (2012b) maximises the difference between the local growth and any crowding out effects faced by the net donor regions while a maximum transfer is the level beyond which no additional local growth effects of the policy are evident.
33. This more recent, updated and comprehensive work builds on the first project documenting regional governance in the EU published by the University of Gothenburg entitled 'Measuring the Quality of Government and Subnational Variation', Report for the European Commission Directorate-General for Regional Policy, Directorate Policy Development. See http://ec.europa.eu/regional_policy/sources/docgener/studies/pdf/2010_government_1.pdf.

4.   A reformed EU Cohesion Policy

4.1 INTRODUCTION

As we saw in the previous chapter, even though the policy has undergone various alterations at different stages, the underlying architecture, logic, and workings of EU Cohesion Policy have remained largely intact during the 25 years between 1988 and 2013. As such, while the European Union and its regions have changed dramatically during this period, the basic logic and architecture of EU regional and urban policy has for the most part remained constant. This potential disconnection has given rise to fundamental questions regarding the case for such a policy, and this questioning itself has resulted in a great deal of reflection and reconsideration regarding the case for, the role of and the logic of EU Cohesion Policy in the coming years.

The case for a reformed EU Cohesion Policy has three broad aspects to it. The first aspect of the case for a reformed EU Cohesion Policy relates to the workings of the policy and the extent to which the policy works – or in other words is successful in achieving what it is intended to achieve. The second aspect of the case for EU Cohesion Policy relates to the distributional features of the policy and the question of whether EU development policy should be focused only on the very poorest parts of the EU, or whether weaker regions in wealthier countries should also be eligible for assistance. The third aspect of the case for a reformed Cohesion Policy raises the question of whether the policy should engage with localities and regions and sub-national levels of governance as well as with central governments.

Regarding the first aspect of the case for a reformed Cohesion Policy, namely the extent to which the policy works in the sense that it achieves its intended goals, the evidence regarding the specifically economic growth effects of the policy have been outlined in the previous chapter. As we have seen the majority of empirical evidence appears to be broadly supportive of the policy, although this is still not entirely conclusive, and the heterogeneity of impacts is a key challenge. However, apart from the complexities already outlined in the previous chapter, as we will see in this chapter one of the issues which needs to be clarified concerns the intended objectives and goals of the policy, because these issues have become somewhat blurred over recent decades, leading also to ambiguities in terms of the performance assessment of the policy.

Regarding the second aspect of the case for a reformed Cohesion Policy, namely the distributional aspects of the policy, this is a broader political economy question regarding the ability of different countries to engage with, and benefit from, EU policies. This also raises the question of the extent to which the policy is in reality perceived to be, or intended to be, simply a fiscal transfer policy or rather a real development policy.

The third aspect of the case for a reformed Cohesion Policy relates to the role of economic geography, and whether a development policy should be 'place-based' or 'space-blind'. Taken together, the debates over recent years regarding the reforms to EU Cohesion Policy have resulted in a reformed policy 2014–2020 which is characterised by specific methods for clarifying exactly what the intended effects of the policy are, a policy which is clearly intended to be real development policy and not simply a fiscal transfer policy, and finally a policy which is explicitly a 'place-based' policy and not a 'space-blind' policy.

This chapter aims to explain the nature and rationale for the reformed EU Cohesion Policy which is being implemented 2014–2020, by focusing on the intended objectives of the policy, its distributional aspects and its underlying place-based logic. In order to do this we will explain the process of the rethinking of the policy, and in particular the impacts on EU debates of the place-based recommendations of the Barca (2009) report, alongside various other influential reports emerging from both within and outside the EU, all of which have heavily shaped the European discussions and decisions regarding the reforms to EU Cohesion Policy. The new policy proposals being implemented during the programming period 2014–2020 reflect the wide-ranging lessons regarding modern development policies which have resulted from this rethinking and also from the experiences of many different parts of the world. As we will see here, the reformed Cohesion Policy is one in which the intended goals of the policy are to be made absolutely explicit at all stages. Moreover, the distributional aspects of the policy reflect the fact that it is always intended as being a development policy and not simply a fiscal transfer policy. Furthermore, both of these aspects of the case for a reformed Cohesion Policy are also inherently intertwined with the place-based logic underlying the policy. Therefore, it is the various aspects of the place-based logic of the policy which is the central focus of this chapter, and the discussions of this aspect of the policy will be used to frame these other aspects. Finally, after explaining the basic case for a reformed Cohesion Policy the chapter will conclude with a discussion of the actual key features of the new policy logic and architecture which has been proposed and will be being implemented in the 2014–2020 programming period.

4.2   THE RETHINKING OF THE POLICY

As we have already seen, during the two decades since the existing Cohesion Policy architecture and logic was constructed in 1988, Europe, and for that matter the whole global economy, has undergone enormous changes. At the same time our understanding of the nature of development processes, including as we will see in subsequent chapters also those relating to innovation, have changed fundamentally. Various changes to the policy workings had been implemented at different stages, including in the most recent programming period post 2006 (Bachtler and Mendez 2013; Bachtler et al. 2013), and these provided some of the groundwork for any future reconsideration of the policy's role and objectives. However, the scale of the changes witnessed in the global economy alongside the major changes in our understanding of development processes all gave rise to a need for a fundamental rethinking of the whole case for and against Cohesion Policy, as well as considering the arguments regarding different types of possible policy systems, architectures and logics.

In 2008 such a rethinking was called for by the then EU Commissioner for Regional Policy, Danuta Hübner. Following on from this call a series of hearings and consultations took place in Brussels with more than 50 scholars from all over the world working in many different arenas of academia, government and international organisations. The deliberations and discussions taking place at these hearings provided the inputs to the final independent report (Barca 2009) written by the rapporteur of the hearings Fabrizio Barca, then a Director-General of the Italian Treasury, under the title of *An Agenda for A Reformed Cohesion Policy: A Place-Based Approach to Meeting European Union Challenges and Expectations*, with additional support from John Bachtler of the European Policies Research Centre EPRC at the University of Strathclyde, Scotland. This document is generally referred to as the Barca Report, and for reasons of brevity this is also the terminology we will adopt here.

The analytical case emerging from the Barca report was that EU Cohesion Policy is a development policy, and as such has an important and constructive role to play in the EU agenda as long as the policy returns in many ways to its original roots while also incorporating new insights and experiences from the wide experience of development worldwide. The Barca report argued that the appropriate logic underpinning the policy in order to allow it to be successful in its role is a place-based logic. A place-based logic, the details of which are discussed both below and also in the appendices, is argued to best respond to the local development challenges faced by EU regions while at the same time also being very consistent with the governance and institutional issues inherent in the EU logic. The Barca report in some sense was also a direct response to the challenges to EU Cohesion Policy posed by an earlier report (Hall 2005; Sapir et al. 2004) and also to the some of space-blind arguments emerging at the same time (World Bank 2009). These issues are discussed in detail in Appendix 4A.2 and also elsewhere (Barca et al. 2012; Menzes 2013).

In terms of the development policy logic and policy systems, the Barca report advocated an explicit place-based approach to EU Cohesion Policy, whereby the place-based approach aims at encouraging local policy design and delivery so as to maximise the local engagement of different actors and institutions. The objective here is to foster the local engagement of as wide a range of actors and institutions as possible in order to act for the common good (Ostrom 1990, 1998, 2005, 2007). However, this local engagement is not assumed to be based on altruism or coercion or a communitarian vision of spatial equality (Barca 2011), but rather on quasi-market-based systems of incentives and objectives. The role of public policy is to provide the appropriately-tailored public goods necessary to galvanise such activities but such activities also have to be primarily 'bottom-up' and cannot be designed or imposed from a top-down perspective. In order to facilitate such a bottom-up and place-based policy logic, a remodelled multi-level governance commitment must be adopted across the EU. This remodelled multi-level governance commitment emphasises the primacy of local and regional actors in terms of policy design and delivery while the national and EU-wide authorities have the primacy in terms of setting out in advance the overall 'rules of the game' as a result of transparent and wide-ranging public debate. Barca (2009) argued that as well as being consistent with the policy logic which for a long time has been advocated by the OECD (2004, 2005a, 2007, 2008, 2009a), this multi-level governance approach to institutional relationships is also consistent with the various EU Treaties relating to the relationships between member states, regions, and the European Commission. These issues are each discussed in detail below.

4.2.1   The Critique of the Policy

The Barca report heavily criticised many aspects of the policy as it currently existed and recommended fundamental changes to the policy. Moreover, the report also contained numerous observations, arguments and specific recommendations for improvements to the policy. After a four-year period of reflection, rethinking and redesigning, it is clear that not all of the specific Barca recommendations have been incorporated into the reforms of EU Cohesion Policy. However, overall, the major thrust of the report has been heavily utilised to underpin the EU Cohesion Policy reforms, and many of the key recommendations of Barca are indeed being implemented in various ways. Most notably, the basic conceptual case emerging from the Barca report regarding the nature of the policy and also the essential principles for implementation, have in the main been adopted. For our purposes we can summarise here the key arguments of the Barca report as they relate to the actual policy reforms being implemented.

In terms of the criticisms of the existing EU Cohesion Policy the Barca report argued that there was currently:

- A lack of focus of the policy and explicitly a failure to distinguish between the policy goals related to promoting efficiency and those goals related to promoting social cohesion and reducing social exclusion.
- A lack of information or data provision.
- A failure to use the data available to analyse the impacts of the policy at the local level.
- A deficit in strategic planning and a lack of any real territorial perspective.
- A lack of consideration of the broader issues relating to wellbeing.
- An absence of the needed contractual relationships required for ensuring institutional changes appropriate to the locality.

There are obviously various responses to these searing criticisms, one of which is to abandon the policy altogether. However, Barca (2009) argued that even in spite of these criticisms there is indeed a strong case in favour of the policy, as long as the policy is heavily re-adjusted and, in effect, returns to its original roots and to its original objectives, as correctly specified for today's challenges.

Regarding the first aspect of the case for Cohesion Policy, namely the nature and role of the policy, the Barca report explicitly argued that ever since the 1960s and 1970s, Cohesion Policy was always intended to be, and should always now be, understood primarily as a development policy focused on assisting particular areas facing severe transition challenges, and not as a policy of fiscal redistribution. Moreover, all of the reforms to Cohesion Policy at different times over various decades also point exactly to this conclusion. In contrast, an efficient redistributive policy would work simply on the basis of fiscal transfers between member states and all of the architecture and logic of Cohesion Policy that had been developed over many decades would be largely irrelevant and unnecessary. EU Cohesion Policy should not be perceived as, or used as, a 'back door' fiscal transfer system from richer states to poorer states.

Regarding the second aspect of the case for a reformed EU Cohesion Policy, namely the extent to which the policy 'works' – in the sense that it achieves what it is intended to achieve – Barca (2009) argued that the objectives of the policy over time had become blurred as additional issues and discourses had been incorporated into the policy in a somewhat ad hoc manner (Begg 2010). This had made it difficult to assess the performance of the policy because its role had become confused by the addition of multiple objectives. In addition, this also questions evaluations of the effectiveness of the policy which are based simply on economic convergence criteria (De Michelis and Monfort 2008). As such, clarifying the fact that the policy was a development policy aimed at helping regions facing structural adjustment and transformation problems, and as such is applicable to regions in all countries facing transition problems, is an important step forward. However, building on this basic premise, the specific policy goals require urgent clarification, and here the Barca report made very clear recommendations, as we will see below. On this development policy logic, as we have already seen, although the findings are not conclusive, most of the evidence regarding the local economic growth effects of the policy tends to be favourable.

On the third aspect of the case for a reformed EU Cohesion Policy, namely the question of which regions should be eligible for assistance, Barca (2009) was absolutely clear. On the argument that EU Cohesion Policy is a development policy aimed at assisting regions facing major structural and adjustment challenges, the development policy logic of the policy clearly does include regions in richer countries facing significant adjustment challenges,[1] albeit most likely with different levels of assistance.

Having argued for both the nature and geographical coverage of the policy on the basis of the local development policy logic, the question then turns to the workings of the policy itself. In order to address the current failures and deficits the Barca report called for the existing working of the policy to be heavily adjusted so as to incorporate the wide-ranging lessons learned from the experience of successful international development practices. These lessons relate primarily to methods for countering, and as far as possible overcoming, the types of local governance and institutional failures which are likely to contribute to many of the local development traps. In particular, Barca (2009) focused on the key policy-implementation challenges to be addressed within the political economy of Cohesion Policy and the critical need to overcome the behaviour, actions and system failures which often subvert the workings of the policy within the EU arena. The Barca report focused on the imperative for implementing those principles, instruments, techniques and systems which are designed to deal with problems of incentives, information asymmetries, moral hazard, principal–agent problems, conflicting goals, and the monopoly and monopsony positions of local elites. These five key principles, instruments, techniques and systems relate to:

- An explicit place-based logic to the policy to allow for differentiation, heterogeneity and the mobilisation of local knowledge.
- The need for explicit multi-level governance partnerships between local, regional, national and EU-wide institutions.
- The need for policies to be explicitly results-oriented or outcome-oriented in nature, with in-built and ongoing (internal and external) monitoring and evaluation systems in order to deal with the learning and incentives issues.
- The establishment of clear development priorities and goals distinguishing between efficiency and social inclusion priorities.
- The use of 'conditionalities' in order to deal with the contractual issues.

Many elements of the reform agenda were already in place in one form or another, but the Barca proposals argued for a rediscovery of many of the essential underlying objectives which were central to the 1988 policy reform and evident in the mid-1990s policy environment (Bachtler and Turok 1997). However, as well as a call to return to its original core intentions, the Barca report also included many novelties derived from the modern experience of international development programmes which allowed the whole policy logic to be reframed in a modern format. The Barca report argued that if taken together as a whole and properly incorporated into EU Cohesion Policy these five sets of features will as a group help to ensure that the policy plays the role it is designed for in the service of the European Union. As such, Barca (2009) argued that in order for a renewed and re-invigorated EU Cohesion Policy to be best-equipped to achieve its intended objectives, it is imperative that each of these five sets of principles and features are indeed implemented.

4.2.2 The Place-Based Imperative

In the case of Europe the major challenges faced by EU Cohesion Policy relate to implementing development policy in an environment of greatly varying institutional capacity and greatly varying levels of economic development. The Barca report explicitly recommended a place-based response to these challenges to allow for differentiation, heterogeneity and the mobilisation of local knowledge.

The modern place-based arguments operate at the interface between institutional analysis and economic geography (Storper 2013). The starting point of the modern place-based approach is that institutions and their interactions *really* matter for development, and that understanding institutions and their roles at the local level is critical in order to promote development. The reason is that the market mechanisms highlighted by economic geography and urban economics operate in specific and heterogeneous institutional contexts, and these institutional and governance contexts in turn heavily shape and mould these economic geography market processes (OECD 2012a). Geography is regarded not simply as a blank page or a form of wallpaper providing little more than backdrop to market mechanisms. Rather, the geographical market mechanisms both shape and are shaped by the institutional and governance issues, and vice versa. Modern place-based approaches do not in any way ignore economic geography. On the contrary, the modern place-based approach explicitly acknowledges and incorporates the lessons and insights from economic geography, regional science and urban economics (Barca 2011; Barca and McCann 2010), but aims to set them squarely also in the real world political economy of governance and institutional systems. As such, a modern place-based logic or policies derived from this logic do not imply ignoring economic geography, limiting agglomeration or promoting an anti-urban agenda (Barca 2011; Barca et al. 2012; McCann and Rodriguez-Pose 2011) as some people have suggested (Gill 2010). Rather, place-based approaches emphasise that institutional issues regarding many aspects of governance are central to questions of development and how such issues can best be responded to. In particular, the place-based approach emphasises the need to tap into the development possibilities on offer by mobilising local actors, assets and institutions (Barca 2009; Barca et al. 2012).

In terms of development policy this has profound implications. In particular, the modern place-based arguments assume that many local development traps are to some extent due to failures in governance and institutional systems, and that overcoming these systems failures is essential in order to overcome as far as possible these local development traps. The modern place-based approach therefore argues for the prioritis-ation of different types of actions or interventions in different contexts (Rodrik 2007). Here the emphasis is on recognition of territorial diversity in terms of needs and opportunities, the importance of harmonising and coordinating actors and institutions, and the need to assess the impacts of all actions both on the place in question and also on other places.[2]

In terms of questions of development policy, the starting point of modern place-based argument explicitly starts from the position that central governments do *not* have sufficient knowledge in order to correct market failures, in order to be effective, or in order to guide economic development for the common good. In many cases and regarding many aspects the central state is regarded as being profoundly ignorant (Barca and McCann 2010) and this is particularly the case for development issues. Nor, however, are local governments assumed to exhibit such competences. Indeed, the modern place-based approach assumes that all levels and tiers of governance including central government only have limited competences in this regard. But the place-based approach is also specific in its interpretation of these limitations, assuming that central government has very limited competences regarding specifically local development issues and that local actors, including local government, typically have much more knowledge than is often assumed. On the other hand, local actors tend to be poorly placed to provide a broad framework for development beyond their own horizons and interests. Importantly, however, both exhibit different competences, and according to the place-based logic it is these differences which need to be exploited. These assumptions are rather different to many frequently-held precon-ceptions. Many observers have traditionally assumed that central govern-ment actors have greater knowledge than local actors because local actors tend to display myopic interests whereas central government actors have a more panoramic perspective, and similarly local government appoint-ments generally display lower competition for professional appointments than central governments. However, social capital and principal–agent arguments tend to overturn this logic, emphasising that central govern-ment actors are more distant from the development realities, and as such, often have much less knowledge about these realities and also a much more limited ability to effect any constructive changes at the local level than is typically assumed (Barca et al. 2012). At the same time, this does not necessarily imply that localism should have primacy, as this often tends to foster precisely the types of locally myopic monopoly-type behaviours which need to be avoided. As such, neither centralised top-down policies nor bottom-up localised policies are fully able to respond to the challenges of maximising local development potential (Barca et al. 2012).

Regarding who has the knowledge to take the lead in these development roles, the place-based approach takes its lead from the insights of authors including Sen (1988, 1989, 1993), Ostrom (1990, 1998, 2005, 2007), Acemoglu and Robinson (2000), Acemoglu and Johnson (2006a, b), Rodrik (2004, 2007) and Storper (2013). These approaches argue that much of the local knowledge which is required to unlock development potential at the local level does not pre-exist exogenously either locally or centrally. Rather, such knowledge can only be extracted by means of a deliberative process (Sen 1988, 1989, 1993) of debate and engagement between local, regional and central parties, actors and institutions with different interests, preferences and competences (Stiglitz et al. 2009). Neo-classical models assume that knowledge is largely disembodied, exogenous and distributed, while endogenous growth models assume it is embodied in factors and is transmitted via spillovers. However, the arguments of Sen (1988, 1989, 1993) and Ostrom (1990, 1998, 2005, 2007) are that for many aspects of development such exogeneity simply does not exist, and has to be extracted and built upon by engagement. This is particularly so for matters related to interest groups, and these insights also tie in very closely to many of the social capital and trust-building arguments (Storper 2013). Processes of engagement and cooperation both extract knowledge and build knowledge via the experience of interacting and also facilitate the better alignment of incentives. In many cases such processes also require a degree of experimentation in order that communities can 'discover' aspects of their own development potential (Hausmann and Rodrik 2003). It is the very fact that many aspects of development knowledge are not simply exogenous which underpins the idea that actors and institutions have to be mobilised in order to generate and build on such knowledge (Storper 2013).

4.2.3 The Multi-Level Governance Imperative

Therefore, in terms of designing the most appropriate development policy for responding to local development traps, the key to overcoming the knowledge and information limitations as far as possible is therefore to foster certain types of vertical and horizontal multi-level governance arrangements tailored to the context (OECD 2004, 2005a, 2007a, 2008). In these tailored arrangements it is essential that the incentive systems are designed so as to ensure that different tiers and arenas of governance employ those competences for which they are best-suited while working in tandem and parallel with each other. These institutional arguments are central to the modern place-based logic (OECD 2012a) and reflect the insights of economic geography (Storper 2013) and also the advice and experience of many international organisations (OECD 2001a, b, 2004, 2005a, 2007b, 2009a, 2011a,b, 2012a, 2013a; World Bank 2006, 2010; Zoellick 2012). Moreover, they also push the principles of shared management and subsidiarity under which Cohesion Policy currently operates to their logical conclusions. The important elements of such multi-level governance approaches are the ability to tailor actions and interventions to the local context in order to correct for local market or systems failures and the multi-level governance agenda is essential in order to enable different competences at different levels and arenas of governance to be employed. Moreover, governance in this context is not restricted to public government, but explicitly aims to include private sector and civil society actors. Broadly, central government takes advantage of its overall panoramic perspective in order to play the more strategic role of setting the broad 'rules of the game' and then local and regional actors working in partnership are allowed to build on their more specific and detailed knowledge by being given the freedom by central government to be able to differentiate their actions and interventions according to local specificities. The importance of being able to differentiate local actions is consistent with the recommendations of Prager and Thisse (2012). Policy differentiation which is appropriate to the context often requires the explicit coordination of interventions across different themes so as to avoid the types of policy duplication which is typically found with parallel and largely unconnected sectoral interventions. However, such multi-level governance arrangements require real and genuine partnerships between different levels, tiers and jurisdictions of governance, and building the requisite trust to employ such systems is also a critical capacity-building aspect of multi-level governance and place-based arrangements. In many cases they also require the breaking down of institutional 'silos' in order to allow for policy programming aimed at integrated and multi-dimensional objectives.[3] Indeed, the overcoming of government and institutional inertia so as to forge such partnerships is often a major part of place-based policy initiatives.

The multi-level governance approach to the local differentiation of policies very much reflects a key component of the modern place based approach to regional development policy which has been advocated for a long time by the OECD (2003, 2005b, 2009b, c, 2011c, 2012a). As we see in Table 4.1, the key elements of the new place-based approach to regional development policy are very different from the approaches of traditional regional development policies, which tended to be dominated

Table 4.1   Traditional and modern approaches to regional policy

	Traditional Regional Policy	Modern Regional Policy
Objectives	Compensating temporarily for location disadvantages of lagging regions	Tapping into underutilised potential in all regions to enhance development in all regions
Unit of Intervention	Administrative units	Functional economic areas
Strategies	Sectoral approach	Integrated development projects
Tools	Subsidies and state aids	Mix of hard capital (infrastructure) and 'soft' capital (business support, credit availability, networking systems)
Actors	Central government	Multi-level governance involving different tiers or level of local, regional and national government working in partnership and alongside the private and civil society sectors

Source: OECD (2009c).

by decisions taken nationally by central government along primarily sectoral lines. The only geographical aspect to these traditional sectoral policies concerned the spatial definition of the administrative areas which would receive these primarily sectorally-targeted subsidies. In contrast, modern place-based approaches to development policy aim to tap into the under-utilised potential of localities by not only engaging different levels of government simultaneously but also by mobilising private sector and civil society actors in parallel. The tools used for this include a range of 'soft' interventions associated with business support and networking systems along with revolving loan finance for SMEs targeted at training, research and development. Importantly, the mobilisation of local actors working in partnership with regional and national actors requires a careful consideration of the incentives and sanctions associated with institutional engagement. Following the lessons from decades of development policies, the place-based approach therefore explicitly aims at fostering institutional structures and governance systems which are capable of supporting a healthy, sustainable market-based system while being explicitly aware that these are highly specific to local conditions (Rodrik 1999). Finding ways to mobilise local, regional and national actors such that they are able to work together for the common good is central to the place-based approach, and the appropriate multi-level governance arrangements must be constructed in ways which overcome the misalignment of incentives. This is achieved by adoption of an outcome-oriented or results-oriented policy logic.

4.2.4 The Results-Oriented Imperative

One of the key implications of the fact that so many aspects of economic development are inherently local and place-based in nature (Hughes 2012; Moretti 2012) is that there is no single top-down 'one-size-fits-all' policy which can be imposed or designed for all regions (Prager and Thisse 2012). Following Rodrik's (2007 pp. 4–5 and p. 57) insights Prager and Thisse (2012 p. 70) emphasise that context matters so strongly that 'the straightforward borrowing of policies without a full understanding of the context that enabled them to be successful is a recipe for disaster'. This in turn means that 'there are of course general, abstract principles that are desirable everywhere. But turning these general principles into operational policies requires considerable knowledge of local specificities.' In the particular case of regional development, 'although economic geography and urban economics should serve as guidelines, they must be applied with pragmatism and based on rigorous and detailed assessments of the specific case in question' (Prager and Thisse 2012, p. 70). Policy design at the local level has to be very carefully considered. Analysis should always precede prescription, based on the best data and evidence available (Rodrik 2007) and this is a critical element of the tailoring of policies to the local context. Once evidence and data has been gathered policymakers have to decide the most appropriate way forward for the local development policy to proceed. However, all policy choices are difficult because not all interested parties will receive benefits and the political economy of these issues can seriously complicate and even derail good policymaking. These pressures are even greater in times of severe budget cuts, as experienced by most regions in the aftermath of the 2008 global financial crisis. However, in the end it is policymakers who have to decide and this is correct, as long as the basis on which they decide is clear and transparent so as to maximise the levels of accountability and agreement (Stiglitz et al. 2009). Once a policy has been decided on the basis of the best data and evidence available, then the policy must be monitored and evaluated throughout the life of the policy. This is in order to assess whether the policy is working or needs to be adjusted, and information feedbacks and reflection are all part of the modern policy-learning process (Rodrik 2007). Such approaches require the use of explicit 'outcome indicators' in Anglo-Saxon terminology or 'results indicators' in the EU terminology. Outcome/results indicators are required not because the results or outcomes of the policy are known in advance, but precisely because they are *not* known (Rodrik 2004). They are required in order to learn about the effectiveness of the policy and to help policy-makers and the public understand the extent to which the policy is making progress towards the explicit objectives it was designed to address. This allows for the progress towards reaching the policy objectives to be considered in the light of the counterfactual case of no policy (Mouqué 2012). In the case of regional policy this has been a longstanding principle (Martin and Tyler 2006; Moore and Rhodes 1973), and applies equally to each of the economic, environmental and social dimensions of development reflected in the Europe 2020 Agenda (European Union 2010a). The task of facilitating this learning process comes down to the monitoring and evaluation exercises, and ongoing monitoring and evaluation should be natural elements of a modern policy design and delivery cycle.

4.2.5 The Policy Goals Imperative

In order for place-based, multi-level governance and results-oriented policies to be effective, the intended thematic priorities as well as the specific goals of the policy must be specified clearly in advance. Otherwise, the monitoring and evaluation activities are simply not realistic or meaningful. The Barca report recommended six possible pillars for the overall thematic priorities of the policy with different broadly-defined objectives. The first pair of priorities are, respectively, innovation and climate change, with efficiency being the primary objective in these cases; the second two are migration and children, with social inclusion being the primary objective in these cases; and the third two are skills and ageing, with the efficiency and social inclusion objectives being equally prioritised in these cases. The key issue these possible thematic suggestions raises is that the objectives of EU Cohesion Policy do differ substantially because they are responding to the various different dimensions of development referred to in Europe 2020. In each case, these different objectives should be made explicit so that the criteria against which policy actions or interventions are taken are correctly specified. At the same time, stating explicitly the thematic priorities is also essential because priorities have to be chosen even before specific individual actions are decided upon. Otherwise, it will be impossible to ensure a concentration of resources. In development policy arenas such as this, the experience from numerous international examples suggests that all political actors desire to receive some payments in order to satisfy or mollify their own constituencies. The problem with this political logic, however, is that this automatically undermines the ability to concentrate resources on the most pressing challenges. As such, a political logic regarding resource allocation tends to subvert the development needs and policy efficacy. Making the policy objectives transparent right from the beginning and then designing programmes and projects which are explicitly results-oriented all helps to break this political logic.

If the intended local development objectives of the policy are made explicit in advance then all interested parties understand in advance what the specific policy interventions and actions are intended to achieve and allows for them all to be continually monitored and assessed against these stated objectives (OECD 2009c). In good policy environments, potentially all policy programmes and projects ought to be data-generating exercises in their own right. As we have already seen in Chapter 1, the Europe 2020 Agenda of 'smart, sustainable and inclusive' growth (European Commission 2010a) which represents the umbrella agenda under which all EU programmes and policies will operate, also chimes with the work and views of various international commissions and international bodies as well as with the all of the major international development organisations. These approaches highlight the fact that development is a multi-dimensional phenomenon incorporating eco-nomic, environmental and social dimensions simultaneously, and in the long run real development progress requires making significant progress on all three aspects.[4] Development policy necessarily works across all of these dimensions, with different priorities at different stages and in different contexts. In line with both the Europe 2020 Agenda and also with these other high-level international reports and agreements (OECD 2009b, c, 2012a; World Bank 2003), the Barca (2009) approach interprets development and growth in a broad multi-dimensional framework which also emphasises the environment, wellbeing (OECD 2009c, 2011c; World Bank 2003), social inclusion (Atkinson et al. 2002; Berg and Ostry 2011; Frazer et al. 2010; Marlier et al. 2008; OECD 2011d; *The Economist* 2013) and quality of life issues (OECD 2011d; Stiglitz et al. 2009). All of these different issues are central to regional development processes and many of the most important and also the most difficult challenges of development are actually related to the interrelationships between these different economic, environmental and social dimensions, rather than related to specific dimensions in isolation. The likely trade-offs and complementarities between these different dimensions will differ between regions and localities (Braga de Macedo and Oliveira-Martins 2008, 2010; Braga de Macedo et al. 2013; Farole et al. 2011; OECD 2011c). Therefore, where policy is being considered at the local or regional level it is essential in each case for policymakers to clarify these likely trade-offs and complementarities so that the positioning and role of the policy is properly specified. EU Cohesion Policy is uniquely positioned within the EU policy portfolio to make progress on a range of fronts simultaneously. The multi-dimensional and integrated development possibilities afforded by EU Cohesion Policy mean that these issues need to be stated as clearly as possible in order to ensure transparency and effectiveness. Whatever priorities are chosen and whichever specific local challenges are being addressed, it is always absolutely essential from the beginning to make the chosen priorities clear and understandable, to explain publicly the basis on which these priorities are chosen, and to describe transparently the arrangements for ongoing monitoring and evaluation. As we have already seen the objectives of the policies must be made as measurable and as verifiable as possible, so that the impacts of policies can be evaluated according to their specified objectives. This is essential in order to build public accountability and trust, and to develop a policy-learning culture.

4.2.6 The Conditionalities Imperative

In terms of governance matters, the place-based approach advocates greater policy flexibility and autonomy on the part of the local funding recipients in order to foster local engagement in the policy process and to allow for enhanced local policy design and delivery. This of course raises the classic principal–agent problem of how to ensure good behaviour on the part of the funding recipients. The Barca report agreed with the Sapir et al. (2004) assessment that the 'Open Method of Coordination', in which the European Commission issues guidelines, agrees benchmarks and compares performance in the past has been useful for promoting dialogue but in reality in certain situations is wholly insufficient for ensuring that the policy goals are achieved. In the case of Cohesion Policy the Barca report argued that entirely different systems of incentives and sanctions – 'carrots and sticks' – are required in order to ensure good policy design, delivery, evaluation and learning. The system proposed by Barca (2009) was that EU Cohesion Policy should make explicit and clear use of 'conditionalities' in almost all aspects of the policy, in return for these greater levels of local flexibility and autonomy. The imperative to use conditionalities in all aspects of development policy arises from the experience of many international organisations including the World Bank (2005), the International Monetary Fund (Dreher 2009) and the OECD (2007). Conditionalities are the binding legal agreements regarding the rules, the roles and the responsibilities on the part of all funding beneficiaries. Conditionalities are not intended to refer to the micro-management or design or delivery of specific programmes of projects, which are left as far as possible to the discretion of the funding recipients. Instead, conditionalities refer to the broad 'rules of the game' which cannot and must not be altered. In the case of the EU Cohesion Policy the conditionalities need to refer to the issues raised by Barca (2009) regarding the specification of the policy thematic priorities and intended results, the results-orientation processes of monitoring and evaluation, and the essential need for multi-level governance partnerships, all of which should provide for EU-wide transparency and accountability. Conditionalities are essential alongside these other aspects in order to ensure that the incentives of all potential funding recipients are correctly aligned with the overall philosophy of EU Cohesion Policy. As such, while the 'carrot' which is offered to local and regional authorities is much greater local flexibility and autonomy in terms of policy design and delivery, the 'stick' is represented by the conditionalities. The experience of numerous international development cases is that this type of 'carrot and stick' approach is essential in order to ensure the correct incentives for both the policy design and appropriate institutional reforms. In particular, conditionalities require that all of the commitments undertaken by policy funding beneficiaries are verifiable by third parties. As such, a renewed role for the European Commission is to facilitate the role of the EU-wide verification of good policy design and delivery and evaluation, in order to ensure that development funds are well spent, in addition to the questions of absorption and accountability which are already well-established.

4.3 THE IMPACTS OF THE POLICY REFORM DEBATE

When the Barca report was published at first it was met with a rather mixed reception. In some academic and policymaking quarters it was received with enthusiasm whereas in other policymaking arenas, including many EU-related circles, it was initially met with scepticism as being politically unpalatable. In some cases the reasons for this scepticism ostensibly appeared to be analytical differences (Gill 2010), particularly in the light of the widespread academic profile received by the 'space-blind' approach advocated by 2009 World Development Report Reshaping Economic Geography (World Bank 2009). However, the responses to this scepticism (Barca and McCann 2010) alongside the appearance more or less contemporaneously of a suite of other reports arriving at similar conclusions (CAF 2010; OECD 2009a, b), subsequently provoked a widespread international debate spanning many parts of the world regarding the place-based case for regional development policies (Barca et al. 2012; Farole et al. 2011; Garretsen et al. 2013; OECD 2011c). In the case of Europe, moreover, the Barca report had not only explicitly focused attention on the critical economic development role played by governance and institutional reform, but more importantly it had proposed specific mechanisms for promoting good governance and institutional reform. As such, the Barca report had gone a long way beyond previous reports (Sapir et al. 2004).

During 2010 as the Greek crisis unfolded followed by the wider Euro-crisis, EU policymakers not only within Brussels but also across all parts of the EU started to search for new policy options and potential solutions to the new realities. As the discourses shifted and concern mounted regarding the economic situation across many parts of Europe it became clear that in many governance quarters ranging across many countries there was an increasing consensus that nothing was 'off-the-table' and that all potential policies should be considered on their own merit. The sense of crisis and the need to consider all options contributed to allaying much of the earlier scepticism and encouraged wide-ranging debates across many of the different Directorates within the European Commission, as well as between different arenas of governance and research across Europe. Increasingly, a groundswell of opinion emerged in many arenas that the Cohesion Policy reform proposals outlined by Barca (2009) were important, realistic, and provided a workable long-term response to some of the most serious development challenges faced by EU regions in the aftermath of the 2008 global financial crisis. However, this emerging groundswell of opinion only marked the beginning of the EU-wide process of debate and deliberation which continued in earnest through to 2013. This process of debate included the deliberations of various high-level expert groups working on all of the major aspects of the potential policy reforms backed up by various discussion papers produced under the auspices of Commissioner Hübner during 2008–2009 and by the interim Commissioner Pavel Samecki in 2009–2010. The actual outcomes of these deliberations do not exactly reflect the Barca (2009) recommendations as many other issues subsequently entered into these discussions. However, as we will see in the following sections, the conditionalities inherent in the new generation of EU Cohesion Policies do underpin: the imperative to build genuine multi-level governance partnerships, the imperatives regarding evidence-gathering and ex ante analysis, the imperative for policies being results-orientated and open to detailed monitoring and evaluation, and the critical need to tailor policies to the local context rather than copying or employing one-size-fits-all policies. These are all now enshrined in the new EU Cohesion Policy regulations.

4.4   THE PROPOSALS FOR A REFORMED EU COHESION POLICY

On 6 October 2011 a detailed new architecture and logic for EU Cohesion Policy for the 2014–2020 'programming period' was proposed by the European Commission (European Commission 2011a). These reflect the prototype regulations which from the perspective of the EU represent the 'rules of the game' which will have to be adhered to in order to qualify for funding. The final regulations are agreed via multinational and multilateral negotiations between member states, within the Council of Ministers and with the European Parliament, and the negotiation process lasted from the autumn of 2011 to late 2013.[5] The final negotiations and agreements which took place on 7–8 February 2013 were ratified by the Council[6] on 12 November 2013 and by the European Parliament on 20 November 2013[7] and the policy regulations were finally published on 20 December 2013.[8] The major elements of the proposed reforms to Cohesion Policy remained largely intact following the negotiations, with some elements even being more robust than was originally suggested. These negotiations and regulations relate to all aspects of the workings of the portfolio of EU Cohesion Policy funding streams which within the EU were known collectively as the 'Structural Funds' prior to 2013 and as the 'Structural and Investment Funds' from 2013 onwards. The Structural and Investment Funds comprise the European Regional Development Fund (ERDF), the European Social Fund (ESF), the Cohesion Fund (CF), the European Agricultural Fund for Rural Development (EAFRD), and the European Maritime and Fisheries Fund (EMFF). Within the overall EU multi-annual financial framework (MAFF) the agreed negotiated budget in 2011 prices for the whole of EU Cohesion Policy for the programming period 2014–2020 was €325bn over the seven-year period or some €47bn per annum.[9] This level of funding is expected to leverage some €100.00bn of additional national and regional resources, leading to a total investment of well over

€400.00bn over the seven-year 2014–2020 programming period.[10] Cohesion Policy currently accounts for 33.85 per cent of the total EU budget of €960bn over the seven-year programming period and Cohesion Policy is therefore now the largest single EU policy investment in the real economy (European Commission 2014).[11] Within this overall budget, the individual national allocations are the outcome of the complex multi-country, multilateral and multi-fund negotiations (Bachtler et al. 2013; EPRC 2013). If we also include the other funds earmarked for the development of rural regions (€85bn) and maritime and fisheries regions (€8.5bn), the total European Structural and Investment Funds amount to €418bn. Although in absolute terms this represented a cut from the previous programming period as the overall EU budget decreased, the share of the total EU budget accounted for by the Structural and Investment Funds actually increased from 42.2 per cent to 43.6 per cent (Petzold 2013).

Within the European Union both policies and also reforms to policies, are developed by a specific process and political economy logic (Petzold 2013). The European Commission, which is the civil service of the European Union, is the sole institution which is able to formally propose and design EU legislation. The 28 EU Commissioners are the European ministers responsible for each particular European-wide policy portfolio and they are appointed by the 28 EU member states. The political influence comes via the EU Commissioners, although their work is specifically related to a particular policy portfolio, and as such reflects an EU-wide mandate rather than a specifically national agenda. Decisions are agreed between the member states in the European Council, which comprises the individual national ministers responsible for the particular portfolio, and all policy proposals go through more or less the same scrutiny and legislative process (European Union 2012a). In the case of EU Cohesion Policy, the Commissioner responsible for Regional Policy between 2010 and 2014 was Johannes Hahn who was in the lead as regards the proposals for common provisions for all funds and more specifically the ERDF and the Cohesion Fund. An Austrian by background, Johannes Hahn came to the post with a wide-ranging academic and business career behind him, as well as both city-regional and national governmental experience. Building on the groundwork laid by the previous commissioners Hübner and Samecki alongside the increasingly influential effects of the report produced by Fabrizio Barca (Barca 2009), in many ways Johannes Hahn was the ideal person to drive the reform agenda forward having already experienced many of these issues personally from different viewpoints. Under his leadership, the new Cohesion Policy proposals emerging from the European Commission for the new programming period 2014–2020 reflected many of the issues first raised in the Barca report. At the same time, in many ways the proposals also sought to be even more radical on specific issues. However, the new proposals were intended to re-establish these in a new overall setting which gave real teeth to the European Commission returning them in some cases to the influence they had in the mid 1990s (Bachtler and Turok 1997). Obviously, such proposals were bound to cause much contention and debate and this proved to be the case. However, after more than one and a half years of multinational and multilateral negotiations an amended policy construction was accepted by all EU member states in the summer of 2013 and these govern the some 320 regional and national operational programmes envisaged in the 2014–2020 programming period (Petzold 2013).[12] Although there were numerous specific amendments to the proposed policy regulations, the vast majority of what was originally proposed in October 2013 has remained intact in the agreed policy architecture (ibid.), and certainly far more of the intended changes to the policy have been accepted than many sceptics initially assumed would be the case. Part of the reason for this was the quality and transparency of the discussions around the Cohesion Policy reforms which involved multiple local, regional and sectoral stakeholders as well as the advice of numerous academic experts and the inputs from multiple directorates of the European Commission working alongside the European Parliament (Tell Cremades 2014) and the Council of Ministers (Petzold 2013).

The proposed architecture and logic of the reformed EU Cohesion Policy contains many features which are very new to EU Cohesion Policy and in some cases fundamentally different from the previous elements. Many of the novel features relate to the Barca (2009) proposals but also various features are quite distinct from those mooted by Barca. There are many specific and detailed issues involved in the policy architecture and logic but the individual pieces do not represent the policy reforms, and nor even does the sum of the individual pieces fully represent the policy reforms. Rather, taken together it is the way in which the various pieces are intended to connect with each other which reflects the novel radical thinking underpinning the policy reforms (McCann and Ortega-Argilés 2013a). These interconnecting elements, which can be interpreted as representing the individual jigsaw pieces which in combination paint a larger picture, are intended to affect policymaking behaviour in ways which are consistent with the latest thinking regarding what constitutes good development policy.

The main elements of the reforms to EU Cohesion Policy are summarised by the European Commission.[13] However, for our purposes we can group the major features of the overall Cohesion Policy reforms into seven major elements. These seven elements are: (i) the role of the policy in the aggregate EU growth agenda, (ii) a greater coordination of actions across different dimensions, (iii) the explicit use of conditionalities, (iv) an explicit results orientation of policy actions, (v) a more robust approach to partnership and shared multi-level governance, (vi) some changes in geographical coverage and a greater emphasis on urban issues, and finally (vii) a central role for regional innovation strategies underpinned by a smart specialisation logic (McCann and Ortega-Argilés 2013b).

(i) Firstly, all future EU policy frameworks are required to operate under the umbrella agenda of the Europe 2020 strategy (European Commission 2010a). This EU growth agenda mirrors closely the growth strategy of both the OECD (2011a) and USA,[14] and the perspectives of OECD (2011c, 2012c) and the US government already referred to earlier in the book make clear that addressing regional and local issues is central to this growth agenda. As such, the Barca (2009) argument that EU Cohesion Policy always has been, and should still be understood as, a development policy and not a redistribution policy, has been generally accepted (European Union 2012c), and the policy is therefore ideally positioned to play a central role in the Europe 2020 strategy. The core principles of the multi-dimensional growth and development agenda set out by the Europe 2020 strategy is to emphasise and to prioritise as far as possible policies which enhance growth and development across all of these dimensions simultaneously. Making progress on various fronts at the same time can be very difficult because of the inherent trade-offs which often arise. However, at the same time, it is also essential to search for the potential complementarities between different dimensions of growth wherever possible and in particular to build links across them. This is exactly the arena where the provision of appropriately-tailored public goods may be able to make a difference (Barca 2009; OECD 2009b, 2011a). Yet, the distribution of the potential trade-offs and complementarities, and consequently the possibilities for local policy alignment, will differ between regions (European Commission 2008; OECD 2011a), and identifying these possibilities is exactly the rationale underpinning the place-based approach (OECD 2009a). The differentiation of local actions and interventions according to the local priorities and possibilities (Prager and Thisse 2012) under the multi-dimensional growth and development agenda underpinning Europe 2020 is very consistent with the approach advocated in Barca (2009).

Following the Barca (2009) recommendations that all programmes and policies should be clearly linked to thematic development pillars which need to be explicitly distinguished according to efficiency or social inclusion criteria and goals, the reformed EU Cohesion Policy is now tied explicitly to the Europe 2020 strategy. All programmes and policies now have to be explicitly tied to at least one of the Europe 2020 thematic priorities of:

(a) strengthening research, technological development and innovation;
(b) enhancing access to and use and quality of information and communication technologies;
(c) enhancing the competitiveness of small and medium-sized enterprises, the agricultural sector (for the EAFRD) and fisheries and aquaculture sector (for the EMFF);
(d) supporting the shift towards a low-carbon economy in all sectors;
(e) promoting climate change adaptation, risk prevention and management;
(f) protecting the environment and promoting resource efficiency;
(g) promoting sustainable transport and removing bottlenecks in key network infrastructures;
(h) promoting employment and supporting labour mobility;
(i) promoting social inclusion and combating poverty;
(j) investing in education, skills and lifelong learning;
(k) enhancing institutional capacity and an efficient public administration.

Each of these 11 thematic priorities also contains sub-priorities related to more specific categories of policy goals and interventions, and again at this more detailed level all policy actions need to be clear about which of the Europe 2020 objectives are being prioritised.[15] This is very important for three reasons: firstly, by explicitly tying all policy actions and interventions to the specific Europe 2020 thematic priorities the intention is to provide clarity regarding the policy objectives of each particular intervention and action and the expected role which the overall policy plays in the wider European growth and development agenda; secondly, this also helps to clarify what are the appropriate performance assessment criteria which need to be established and which do not confuse efficiency with social inclusion objectives (Barca 2009); thirdly, it is also intended to help to establish the appropriate spatial scale over which such actions should be assessed (McCann 2011).

On some issues, however, aspects of the EU Cohesion Policy reforms actually go further or in a somewhat different direction than anything suggested in the Barca (2009) report. In particular Cohesion Policy funding adjustments have been linked to a so-called 'macroeconomic conditionality'. The European Commission is able to request that member states adjust certain policies or programmes in order to support key structural reforms aimed especially at deficit reductions. This macroeconomic conditionality is triggered automatically in a situation where a member state is both in excessive deficit position and also has repeatedly ignored and breached the recommendations on these matters from the European Commission (European Parliament 2012a, b). As regards Cohesion Policy, the linking of the policy to this conditionality means that the ultimate sanction is therefore the suspension of development policy funds.[16] The pressure leading to these macroeconomic conditionalities has arisen primarily in the aftermath of the Greek crisis and the subsequent Euro crisis, in which there has emerged a general consensus that the 'open method of coordination' has been found to be wanting in a severe and adverse economic climate and that certain new structural elements need to be in place in order to ensure better micro–macroeconomic policy alignment (European Commission 2012a, b).

(ii) Secondly, a much greater degree of coordination and alignment between different Cohesion Policy funding streams is allowed for by the establishment and strengthening of what is known as the CSF Common Strategic Framework (European Commission 2012b).[17] The improved coordination of funding streams across different types of development actions, interventions and thematic priorities is essential in order to exploit potential policy complementarities (OECD 2011a) and to foster the types of integrated and locally-tailored policies advocated by the place-based approach.[18] As we have seen, within the EU the portfolio of funding streams related to regional development are collectively known as the 'Structural and Investment Funds'. The Structural Funds which are related to regional development matters comprise the European Regional Development Fund (ERDF), the European Social Fund (ESF), the Cohesion Fund (CF), and also now have re-integrated the European Agricultural Fund for Rural Development (EAFRD), and the European Maritime and Fisheries Fund (EMFF) into the overall portfolio. Skills-training and social inclusion actions come primarily under the ESF European Social Fund,[19] while innovation-related actions and infrastructure investments primarily come under the ERDF European Regional Development Fund. Regional development in rural, maritime or sparsely populated regions comes under the EAFRD and EMFF as well as the ERDF and ESF (European Commission 2011a). As a legal instrument, the Common Strategic Framework allows funding from the different streams to be bundled together in tailored packages, and it also makes it easier to link Cohesion Policy actions with Horizon 2020 initiatives (European Commission 2014).[20] The ability to link different funding streams together into tailored packages is very important in order to exploit the potential policy complementarities (OECD 2011c) necessary to foster the more integrated and multi-dimensional approaches to development advocated by the Europe 2020 agenda. Funding streams focusing on the rural, coastal or sparsely populated regions facing specific development challenges are also now fully integrated into the overall framework in ways which were previously not possible, thereby allowing these integrated and place-based development principles to be applied in all regions. As mentioned above, regions and member states are able to choose their policy priorities from a menu of themes which themselves closely relate to the Europe 2020 strategy, with the choice options available to more advanced regions being narrower than those for less developed regions. Finally, there is also a specific funding allocation of some €63–66billion which is earmarked for the promotion and completion of trans-European transport and energy networks (European Commission 2012a, 2014).[21]

(iii) The third element of the reform is the explicit use of ex ante conditionalities in the policy framework. Conditionalities are the agreed and binding arrangements relating to many aspects of the policy design, delivery and implementation process. These are required in order to ensure that the agreed 'rules of the game' represented by the agreed policy regulations are indeed adhered to at all levels. The important point about conditionalities is that they are specified and agreed ex ante, and therefore set out in advance what is to be expected and undertaken by the policy designers and beneficiaries. In the case of EU Cohesion Policy these conditionalities relate to the design of the development strategies, the role and nature of the partnership in the programming, the need for data provision, the importance of performance transparency, as well as the macro-economic conditionality outlined above. The experience from numerous development actors and agencies from around the world confirms that ex ante conditionalities are essential for ensuring good policy design and delivery and for avoiding rent-seeking and overcoming principal-agent and information asymmetry problems (Dreher 2009; OECD 2007a, b; World Bank 2005). The lack of any clear conditionalities in earlier periods of EU Cohesion Policy was a major criticism in the Barca (2009) report, but conditionalities can only be effective if they are allied with credible and enforceable sanctions. In this regard a 'perform-ance reserve' of 6 per cent of the potential funding available is held in reserve, ready to be released on the receipt of robust evidence that recipients are achieving certain progress targets in terms of their policy delivery. These progress targets relate primarily to procedural matters.[22] There are some complex issues regarding the balance between the incentive and sanctioning effects of these conditionalities (European Parliament 2012a), although the fact that the reserve is already included in the budget allocations rather than being an additional resource leads to doubts as to its potential incentive effects. Overall, however, the general consensus amongst most observers is that these conditionalities are required in order to ensure the alignment of Cohesion Policy actions with the overall EU agenda.

(iv) The fourth key element in the reforms to EU Cohesion Policy is the incorporation of an explicit outcome-oriented agenda, or rather in EU terminology, an explicit 'results-oriented' agenda (Gaffey 2013a, b).[23] The results-oriented or outcome-oriented nature of all policy actions or interventions is a central element in modern development policy design. The idea of results orientation is to establish right from the beginning the intended results and outcomes of the policy as a way of imposing a discipline on the whole policy process based on the objectives of the policy, and not on a primarily political logic. Funding allocations which are determined primarily on political grounds tend to undermine the policy because all potential actors wish to receive some funding in order to mollify their respective stakeholders and constituencies. A primarily political logic to funding generally means that funds are scattered and fragmented in a manner unrelated to the development challenges which need to be addressed. As such, this political logic inherently goes against the need for the concentration of funding on specific priorities and therefore tends to undermine the policy effectiveness in the vast majority of cases where the concentration and prioritisation of funding is warranted. Instead, making the intended results and outcomes of the policy transparent from the beginning helps to break the political funding logic and to develop a policy-funding logic tied to the development challenges. These ideas follow much of the recent thinking on modern forms of industrial and development policy which have arisen in the last decade (Rodrik 2004). These ideas emphasise that in order for policies to be most effective the whole policy cycle encompassing policy design, delivery, monitoring and evaluation should be an interactive and recursive process which allows for both learning and adjustment. All project design and delivery mechanisms should be undertaken with explicitly stated ex ante objectives and goals, and the delivery of the policy must be accompanied by real-time monitoring and evaluation of all of the embedded programmes and projects. To aid both monitoring and evaluation policymakers are required by explicit conditionalities to choose appropriate outcome indicators or, in EU terminology, appropriate results indicators. To reiterate, and as Rodrik (2004) makes explicit, the use of outcome indicators or results indicators is not because policymakers know the results in advance, but rather precisely the opposite. The use of results indicators is essential precisely because policymakers do not know the results in advance, and these indicators are required in order to help track the progress of the policy towards its intended goals. Making results indicators an inherent element of all programme and projects allows policymakers to observe the progress of the policy. At the same time, it also allows policymakers wherever possible or appropriate to make real-time adjustments of the projects on the basis of the new information which emerges during the life of the project. In addition, observation of the programmes and projects allows for the possibility for learning from the projects (Glennerster 2012; Bryson et al. 2012). The more that programmes and projects can become data-generating exercises in their own right, the better will be the overall policy design, delivery and results. However, in order for this outcome-oriented or results-oriented culture to become automatic, it is necessary to develop a system of baseline data resources covering all aspects of the local economy. These allow the starting points for each policy to be established, against which progress should be measured. The evaluation process itself should combine both quantitative and qualitative evaluation and monitoring techniques.

The European Commission[24] has provided detailed guidance regarding all aspects of the evaluation and monitoring process including the construction and choice of results indicators based on the latest thinking regarding policy monitoring and evaluation principles (Barca and McCann 2011). The European Commission also provides examples of different approaches to the use of both quantitative and qualitative evaluation techniques along with the case study examples from around the world of good practice,[25] and additional guidance for the evaluation of innovation-related actions is provided (Technopolis Group and MIOIR 2012). The use of explicit monitoring and evaluation techniques in the policy design and delivery process is essential in order to link the ex ante intended policy objectives to ongoing interim and ex post evaluation (Davies et al. 2000; Farrow and Zerbe 2013; Link and Vonortas 2013; Pawson 2006; Priemus et al. 2008; Sedlacko and Martinuzzi 2012; Stockmann 2011). The terminology underpinning the logic of the monitoring and evaluation processes in the reformed EU Cohesion Policy context has been clarified (European Commission 2012a; Gaffey

2013a, b) such that the inputs represent the financial resources committed to the projects, the outputs represent the immediately measurable actions whose intention is to produce results, and the impact is the contribution of the policy which can be credibly attributed to the change in the result indicator. This contribution is to be assessed and evaluated by observing the changes in the results indicators in the light of all of the various additional factors potentially influencing changes in the results indicators as well as the policy itself. Moreover, these results-indicator approaches are just as relevant for environmental actions in cities and regions (Piacentini and Rosina 2012; EEA 2010, 2012) as they are for innovation and labour-related actions. The European Commission has also required that certain common output indicators will have to be published by all funding recipients in order to ensure that aggregate data is available on various key outputs.

As well as improved monitoring and evaluation the greater results orientation of EU Cohesion Policy also aids much-needed governance capabilities and institutional capacity building in weaker regions. From an institutional capacity perspective all of the baseline assessment, monitoring and evaluation activities are essential components of learning processes on the part of policymakers, and the more such learning becomes a natural part of the policy process, the better will be the governance capacity of the localities undertaking such activities. Moreover, clarity regarding the intended policy objectives, policy learning and policy transparency are not only all parts of good governance and public accountability but they are also essential in order to improve the targeting, design and effectiveness of policies. The required transparency is also bolstered by the subsequent publication of the performance of programmes and projects based on the data derived from the projects, and this publicity acts as a further bulwark against the danger that a political and rent-seeking logic resurfaces in the funding allocation logic. All of these developments respond directly to one of the major criticisms of previous generations of EU Cohesion Policy which had been raised in the Barca report, namely that there had been little use made of the potential programme and project data which could have been derived from the policy itself. The use of such data, and the ensuing learning processes discussed above are all critical in order to identify policy additionality. Although on one hand counterfactual analyses depend on data which is specific to the context, at the same time data derived from many different types of programmes and projects should also better allow for counterfactual impact assessments to be undertaken at a later stage (Mouqué 2012). The generation and use of these types of data is argued for both in the Barca report and also in a range of key papers (Martin and

Tyler 2006; Moore and Rhodes 1973; Swales 1997, 2009) and books
(Ferrara 2010) on regional policy evaluation. The overall results-oriented
approach is necessary in order to correct for both weaknesses in policy
assessment and also to guard against a primarily political logic to funding
allocations (OECD 2008, 2009d).

(v) The fifth key element in the EU Cohesion Policy reforms is the
strengthening of the partnership principle in policy design and delivery
(European Union 2012b). Partnership is an essential feature of many EU
activities. Many European policies operate under principles of partnership and shared responsibility between the member states of the EU and
the European Commission (McCann and Ortega-Argilés 2013b). However, in the case of EU Cohesion Policy since the 1988 design of the
policy the principle of partnership was understood in a very specific
sense in that all EU, national and sub-national governance actors were
expected to work in partnership with each other in a manner which is
consistent with the policy logic (Bachtler and Turok 2007). While in
principle this is correct, the current reforms to EU Cohesion Policy
actually take this agenda much further, and for the first time make
institutional reform and capacity-building key thematic objectives of the
policy (Bachtler et al. 2013). As an essential feature of the place-based
logic of the reforms, all member states will be required to develop and
sign an investment and development Partnership Agreement with the
European Commission (European Commission 2011a; European Commission 2012b) explaining in detail the role and activities of all of the
different regional, local, private-sector and civil society actors and
institutions involved in the design and delivery of the programmes and
projects. As such, there is to be an explicit acknowledgement of exactly
how the principles of partnership[26] are in reality being translated into the
policy process. The importance of the partnership principle, not just in
terms of a concept, but also in terms of actual activities and engagements,
is that it underpins the promotion of the vertical and horizontal multi-
level governance agenda (Committee of the Regions 2012a, b) which is
regarded as being so critical for fostering a successful place-based
development policy logic (OECD 2004, 2005a, 2007). The types of
multi-level governance partnerships which are envisioned in a reformed
EU Cohesion Policy are expected to lead to the mobilisation of as many
private sector and civil society actors as possible as well as engaging all
levels of government in the policy process. In addition, multi-level
governance activities are also central to the successful establishment and
ongoing formation of coordinated cross-border policy actions. Within the
EU cross-border actions are particularly important in matters relating to

environmental issues (European Commission 2010b, 2011c) and these are the types of actions which require careful long-term management on the part of multiple stakeholders. Good multi-level governance is essential in these cases. In this respect, the European Commission proposed in January 2014 a delegated regulation on a 'European code of conduct' which is now legally binding for partnership arrangements and lays down objectives and criteria to support their implementation including the sharing of information, experience, results and good practices among member states. Finally, and linked to the above discussions, in order to further enhance institutional learning and good governance capacity-building, there are also provisions in the policy regulations which allow weaker regions with more limited institutional capacity to work with experts and advisors from stronger regions. This represents an important and a proactive practical approach to the enhancing of institutional capacity-building via the fostering of technological spillovers in terms of governance and institutional issues (McCann and Ortega-Argilés 2013a, b).

(vi) The sixth key element in the reforms is the change in some aspects of the geographical coverage of the policy as well as an increasing attention on urban issues alongside regional issues (European Commission 2011).

The changes in the geographical logic relates to the introduction of a category of 'transition regions', in which regions that previously were eligible for higher levels of funding are still able to receive lower funding levels, rather than losing almost all of their funding once they reach a particular threshold. The new systems allocated EU regions to one of three categories, namely Less Developed regions, Transition regions and More Developed regions. Less Developed regions exhibit GDP per capita of less than 75 per cent of the EU-27 average, Transition regions are regions with GDP per capita levels of between 75 per cent and 90 per cent of the EU-27 average, and More Developed regions are those with per capita levels which are above 90 per cent of the EU-27 average. These different categories of regions will face different investment requirements relating to each of the Europe 2020 dimensions. ERDF investments in innovation and research, SME support and the digital agenda must account for 80 per cent of ERDF expenditure in More Developed regions, 60 per cent in Transition regions and 50 per cent in Less Developed regions (European Commission 2014). For low-carbon energy efficiency and renewables initiatives the ERDF expenditure requirements are 12 per cent for Less Developed regions and 20 per cent for both Transition and More Developed regions. For ESF investments there are similar rules with more than 20 per cent of ESF resources having to be allocated to promoting social inclusion and combating poverty (European Commission 2014). Taken together the More Developed regions will be required to spend more than half of their overall funding on skills-related and social inclusion issues and up to one-third on innovation-related actions focused on SMEs, whereas less advanced regions in Central and Eastern Europe in particular will be able to spend more on infrastructure-related investments. Member states are also required to target ERDF support to the particular challenges identified in their National Reform Programmes and their country-specific recommendations (European Commission 2014).

The aim of these geographical coverage changes is to better target the types of investment distributions so that they are most appropriate to the types of the regions. As we have seen in the previous chapter and as we will also see in the following chapter, regions with different levels of development are found to respond better to different types of actions and interventions, and these investment prioritisation rules closely reflect these findings. At the same time, the intention of these changes is also to ensure the continued development momentum in those regions which are already making good development progress. Regions with per capita GDP levels originally below 75 per cent of the EU average at the start of the previous 2006 programming period which have subsequently been making good development progress will tend to exhibit increasing GDP per capita levels. However, on the basis of the previous regional classification scheme some of these regions will face the prospect of losing much of their funding support at a level of development which is still relatively very low. This itself may act as a disincentive to continue with good development policy, and in order not to stall or stifle such progress on the basis of strict cut-off rules, the new transition regions is designed to maintain the development momentum by providing a more finely-tuned tapering of assistance regimes. This category of region is also widely distributed amongst the richer countries, and in many cases these regions need ongoing assistance, as is now offered by this Transition region category.

Another aspect of the changing geographical logic of the reformed Cohesion Policy relates to the increasing urban agenda. Urban issues, and in particular the roles which cities play in growth and development, are increasing in visibility in many parts of the world (MGI 2011; World Bank 2009). Urban issues are seen as being central to Europe's future growth and development[27] as more and more of Europe's population are expected to be living in cities over the coming decades (European Commission 2014). Cohesion Policy provides a variety of actions and interventions in the urban arena (European Commission 2010d) including land rehabilitation and reclamation, urban regeneration, housing and transport, and the promotion of rural–urban linkages, and the pattern of interventions differs between member states according to their specific needs and priorities.[28]

As we have already seen, while the growth-enhancing role of cities is widely discussed (Storper 2013), there are also major internal differences both within and between member states in terms of the role played by cities in growth. In the EU-15 much of the economic growth since the millennium has been shifting away from many of the larger core urban areas, whereas these core and capital cities continue to dominate economic growth in the EU-12 countries (Dijkstra et al. 2013; OECD 2012a). The increased urban agenda therefore has to be sufficiently flexible to respond to the enormous variation in urban experiences across Europe. However, as well as growth, urban issues are also increasingly playing a key part in policy discussions regarding environmental sustainability, energy conservation and low carbon innovations (European Commission 2012c; OECD 2010, 2012b). While rural regions also play an important role in addressing climate change-related challenges (OECD 2012c), the challenges faced by cities in this arena are rather different. The governance mechanisms which cities have at their disposal to make progress on these fronts are nowadays widely discussed and the importance of governance coordination within cities is underscored by the recent OECD (2014a) findings which demonstrate that institutional fragmentation can mitigate all potential gains from urban scale or density (ibid.). Getting the integrated urban governance arrangements right so as to ensure scale and focus is essential in order to maximise productivity growth. Cities, however, are not always 'good news' stories. Segregation, social exclusion, poverty and low levels of wellbeing and quality of life are also at their highest levels in many of Europe's cities, including some of Europe's richest cities (European Union 2014). Again, the role which good governance (Charron et al. 2012, 2013, 2014; OECD 2013a, 2014b, c) plays in countering these adverse trends has become high on the urban agenda.

A major problem which many cities within Europe face is that as well as institutional fragmentation many cities also exhibit a lack of governance flexibility and autonomy even where better coordination may be achievable, and as such, many cities face a serious deficit in terms of the policy levers required to respond to the locally-specific urban challenges (OECD 2013a, 2014b, c). Moreover, the fact that the shared management principles of Cohesion Policy operate via national governments and also regional authorities means that these local urban deficits may persist.

An increasing urban agenda in the Cohesion Policy reforms is therefore designed to help offset these strategic deficits, and particularly so in the arena of integrated urban development. At present approximately 40 per cent of ERDF monies are invested in cities (European Commission 2014) whereas just under 73 per cent of the EU's population are currently urban residents, so the increasing urban agenda is designed to correct for some of these imbalances. At least 5 per cent of ERDF resources are to be set aside for promoting sustainable urban development responses to social, economic and environmental challenges through the use of 'integrated actions' to be managed by the cities themselves, and these resources are in addition to other spending on urban issues (European Commission 2014). EU Cohesion Policy already has widespread experience operating in urban development arena (European Commission 2012c; European Union 2013a) and the previous programming periods have also trialled various different types of urban community development initiatives, networks and research programmes[29] (European Commission 2007, 2010b). The parts of the Cohesion Policy reforms prioritising urban development issues are intended to build on the knowledge gained from these experiences. In addition, the reforms have also built on the knowledge gained from the local and community-led local initiatives which have been trialled under the LEADER programme for rural development.[30] Bringing together these different experiences, each of which can be regarded as representing the type of experimental self-discovery approach to finding 'what works' (Rodrik 2007), has meant that important parts of the EU Cohesion Policy reforms now allow for the use of what are known as Community Led Local Development (CLLD) initiatives and Integrated Territorial Investments (ITIs) to help drive this higher profile urban agenda. The intention here is to allow for more locally-based and well-tailored integrated solutions to be sought for local urban development initiatives. This is important because the specifics of different urban development challenges will differ markedly in each locality, with different mixes between innovation and skills issues, energy and environmental considerations, and social and heritage matters evident in different cases. Real estate-related interventions in the local land market involving the provision of new infrastructure, the refurbishment of the built environment, or land-use transformations, will demand locally-tailored solutions. Increasingly this will require the integration of Cohesion Policy grants with revolving-loan advanced finance instruments (European Union 2012c). Different institutional structures and 'special purpose vehicles' with different management systems will therefore be required in different situations, and the opportunity to employ the CLLD and ITI approaches is intended to foster exactly these types of locally-tailored responses. The programmes spearheaded by the European Investment Bank already provide significant expertise and experience regarding the use of advanced financial instruments designed for such purposes[31] and the JESSICA[32] initiative in particular is designed to provide the modern financial frameworks for enhancing the urban sustainability agenda. Such initiatives are likely to become increasingly important in the 2014–2020 programming period and beyond as both the use of modern financial instruments for development (European Union 2013a), alongside the increasing urban and environmental agendas, are regarded as being major priorities in the reformed and modernised EU Cohesion Policy.

A final aspect of the evolving geography of EU Cohesion Policy relates to the shift towards greater cross-border cooperation on policy initiatives, including the adoption of what are known as 'macro regional strategies'. There have been various initiatives designed to foster research-led cross-border cooperation in policymaking under the headings of INTERREG programmes (European Union 2010b) and these provide valuable learning and experience of cross-border cooperation (Cultplan 2007),[33] not all of which is positive (European Commission 2010e; OECD 2013b). These programmes are now being extended under the umbrella of the European Territorial Cooperation initiative (European Union 2011) with different funding availability to support cross-border, trans-national, and interregional cooperation (European Union 2012b). At the same time, EU Cohesion Policy already has gained experience in large-scale cross-border cooperation programmes dealing with complex environmental challenges in cases where multi-country actions are required. These are known as 'macro-regional strategies' and the best known of these macro-regional strategies are the Baltic Sea Strategy (European Commission 2010c) and the Danube Region Strategy (European Commission 2011c). These programmes involve no new formal institutional structures or configurations, and no formal and comprehensive evaluations of these relatively recent programmes have as yet been undertaken. However, these types of programmes are being afforded greater priority in the Cohesion Policy reforms and their experience has also encouraged the development of other similar types for the new programming period and beyond, including a strategy for the Adriatic-Ionian Region, and the Alpine Region. The Danube Region Strategy, the Adriatic-Ionian Region Strategy and the Alpine Region Strategy[34] also all involve non-EU nations as well as EU nations (European Union 2013b).

The seventh key element of the reforms to EU Cohesion Policy is that of the regional innovation and 'smart specialisation' agenda, which focuses on the role played by policy actions in fostering innovation and entrepreneurship at the local and regional level. In the 2007–2013 programming period close to 25 per cent of structural funds, or some €86bn, were spent on R&D and innovation-related activities (European Commission 2014). As we have seen for the 2014–2020 programming period these shares are being significantly increased. The growth challenges facing Europe in the aftermath of the global financial crisis are very real, and this has spurred the search for new ideas and initiatives which orient Cohesion Policy towards growth-enhancing actions and measures. As we will see in Chapter 6, smart specialisation is central to this re-orientation but this is also based on shifts in our understanding of the nature and role of regional innovation as a process and a phenomenon underpinning aggregate innovation. The changes in thinking regarding regional innovation are discussed in the next chapter, and the various aspects of the smart specialisation approach are discussed in detail in the subsequent chapter.

A final point is that the 'N+2' decommitment rule – whereby resources have to be claimed within two years of the financial commitments, and which predominated in the 2007–2013 programming period – has now been shifted in the 2014–2020 programming period to an 'N+3' decommitment rule.[35] As such monies have to be claimed within three years of the financial commitments.

4.5 CONCLUSIONS

In the last few years the debates surrounding the role and future of EU Cohesion Policy have been highly transparent and involved multiple stakeholders. This transparency has itself contributed to the success of the reform process and the debates have meant, at least in terms of the newly-adopted legal regulations, that the whole policy has undergone major changes in its intervention logic. These changes are based on the latest thinking regarding modern development policy, innovation policy and economic geography. They are reflected both in the new systems of incentives and sanctions, as well as in the changes in the policy architecture and the new opportunities to initiate more locally-tailored development structures. In terms of institutional-impact assessments, detailed assessments of the likely impacts of the various changes to EU Cohesion Policy have been undertaken by the European Parliament (Committee of the Regions, 2012a, b; European Parliament 2012a, b) and the Council of the European Union in conjunction with the European Court of Auditors (Council of the European Union 2012). While all of the changes have potentially positive effects as was always intended in their design, some of them also face difficulties which in some cases potentially can lead to counterproductive effects (European Parliament 2012a, b). However, having acknowledged and examined these different impacts, the assessments undertaken by these various institutional-impact investigations have all found that the overall reforms to EU Cohesion Policy are both workable and also consistent with EU Treaties (Committee of the Regions, 2012a, b; Council of the European Union 2012; European Parliament 2012a, b). Even so, while from an institutional perspective the balance of the effects of the EU Cohesion Policy reforms is likely to be broadly positive, the most important effects are the actual development impacts on the ground. As we have seen, while the effects of Cohesion Policy in the past have been varied, there is now a growing body of evidence which suggests that the overall economic impacts of the policy have been broadly positive. Yet, it still remains to be seen whether the reforms outlined here also lead to more positive local and regional economic development impacts than those which are currently observed.

A central issue here is the role which EU Cohesion Policy can play in fostering innovation. Innovation is understood to be a key element of growth and development processes, and in the aftermath of the global financial crisis and the subsequent economic difficulties faced by EU member states, the role which Cohesion Policy can play in helping to drive innovation at the local level has become very much centre-stage in European debates. As we will see in the following two chapters, a great deal of thinking regarding innovation policy has shifted over recent decades from the aggregate national level to the local and regional level. While this is a global shift it is particularly evident at the European scale, and this shift has heavily influenced recent EU policy discussions, and in particular those involving Cohesion Policy. EU Cohesion Policy is now understood as being a policy which invests for development and growth at the local and regional level across a wide range of different activities and places. As such, because of its new results orientation as well as its size, the reformed EU Cohesion Policy is now perceived as playing an important role in the overall European post-crisis recovery process, alongside other macroeconomic and institutional reforms. In order to understand why this is the case it is important to understand the contemporary role which innovation policy at the local and regional level is now widely understood to play. The case for regional innovation policy is the topic of Chapter 5. Then building on this regional innovation understanding the EU Cohesion Policy agenda has gone on to prioritise what is known as the 'smart specialisation' approach to policy design and implementation. This smart specialisation approach to policy design is built on deep analytical roots, and is a powerful vehicle for ensuring both good and realistic policy design. This will be the subject of Chapter 6.

NOTES

1. A simple thought exercise serves to clarify this point. Consistent with a one-sector neo-classical adjustment mechanism (Barro and Sala-i-Martin 1995; Borts and Stein 1964), since the Single Market integration process many of the fastest growing regions in Europe have been in the lower income countries (World Bank 2012; MGI 2013). If the policy were simply an EU redistributive policy, then the fact that a redistributive process was already being driven by the spatial factor reallocations associated with market integration means that it is entirely unclear on political economy grounds as to why public funds should be provided for these countries when the market mechanism is already achieving exactly this result. In contrast, if Cohesion Policy is understood as a development policy aimed at overcoming local bottlenecks and missing links and institution-related local development traps, then the local public goods arguments inherent in development policies become perfectly reasonable for these weaker countries and regions when either convergence or divergence is observed. Moreover, on this argument the policy also applies to weaker regions in richer countries (Begg 2009), exactly as the Barca (2009) report made clear. Furthermore, participation in the policy by all member states and regions, albeit to different degrees, also allows for policy learning and the sharing of best practice between all regions. This not only provides for important forms of pan-EU capacity-building and institutional technology transfer between regions, but in the light of the current reforms this also facilitates pan-EU transparency regarding good practice.
2. See, for example, the publication *Place-Based Territorially Sensitive and Integrated Approach* published by the Polish Ministry of Regional Development in 2013 as a result of its chairing of the European Council during 2011.
3. See http://www.whitehouse.gov/sites/default/files/omb/assets/memoranda_2010/m10-21.pdf.
4. See http://www.stiglitz-sen-fitoussi.fr/en/index.htm.
   See also 'Monitoring economic performance, quality of life and sustainability' jointly produced by the French 'Conseil d'analyse économique' and the German Council of Economic Experts, December 2010. Available at: http://www.cae.gouv.fr/IMG/pdf/095_ANG.pdf.
5. These negotiations also depend on the legal assessments undertaken by the European Court of Auditors (Council of the European Union 2012) and also the policy scrutiny committees within the European Parliament (Committee of the Regions, 2012a, b; European Parliament 2012a, b).
6. http://www.consilium.europa.eu/uedocs/cms_data/docs/pressdata/en/ecofin/139448.pdf.
   http://www.bbc.co.uk/news/world-europe-24909708.
7. http://ec.europa.eu/regional_policy/newsroom/detail.cfm?LAN=en&id=1145&lang=en.
8. http://eur-lex.europa.eu/LexUriServ/LexUriServ.do?uri=OJ:L:2013:347:0320:0469:EN:PDF.
9. These figures are derived from the MFF negotiations which are based on 2011 'constant' prices, and these 2011 constant price figures are then adjusted according to an expected 2 per cent costs increase per annum over the programming period in order to arrive at current prices. In terms of current prices these negotiated figures for Cohesion Policy therefore translate into €351.8bn of actual expenditure (European Commission 2014). See Table 4.A1 in Appendix 4A.3 for details of the allocations in current prices.
10. http://ec.europa.eu/regional_policy/newsroom/detail.cfm?LAN=en&id=1057&lang=en
11. The 2007–2013 Cohesion Policy budget was €347bn, or alternatively some €49.57bn per annum, and the agreed 2014–2020 budget represented a 9.4 per cent reduction in the funds allocated to the policy as a result of the overall cuts in the EU budget.
12. http://ec.europa.eu/regional_policy/what/future/proposals_2014_2020_en.cfm#1
13. http://ec.europa.eu/regional_policy/newsroom/detail.cfm?LAN=en&id=1057&lang=en

14. See http://www.whitehouse.gov/blog/2010/06/30/place-based-investments
15. Both the rural EAFRD and maritime EMFF development funds contribute to six or four of the thematic priorities (Petzold 2013).
16. http://ec.europa.eu/regional_policy/newsroom/detail.cfm?LAN=en&id=1057&lang=en
17. The programming period 2007–2013 used Community Strategic Guidelines adopted by the Council of ministers and which set out investment priorities used to shape the National Strategic Reference Frameworks produced by each member state. In poorer regions 60 per cent and in richer regions 75 per cent of resources were to be invested in order to deliver the Lisbon Strategy goals of jobs and growth. The new CSF objectives will be a legal requirement.
18. These principles were already evident in previous eras of the policy, but were largely abandoned in a shift towards a more sectoral approach following the Lisbon Agenda (Bachtler et al. 2013)
19. Around €70billion – or some 23.1 per cent of the Cohesion Policy budget – is accounted for by ESF investments in employment training and life-long learning, fighting poverty and promoting social inclusion. Of this, each member state must invest at least 20 per cent in social inclusion measures. See http://ec.europa.eu/regional_policy/newsroom/detail.cfm?LAN=en&id=1057&lang=en
20. The linking of Horizon 2020 funds with Cohesion Policy funds is referred to in the regulations as 'Stairway to Excellence' and has also been described variously as 'Teaming for Excellence' or 'Twinning for Excellence'.
21. http://ec.europa.eu/regional_policy/newsroom/detail.cfm?LAN=en&id=1057&lang=en.
22. http://ec.europa.eu/regional_policy/newsroom/detail.cfm?LAN=en&id=1057&lang=en.
23. The official EU results-oriented monitoring and evaluation guidance documents can be found at: http://ec.europa.eu/regional_policy/information/evaluations/guidance_en.cfm.
24. http://ec.europa.eu/regional_policy/information/evaluations/guidance_en.cfm.
25. http://ec.europa.eu/regional_policy/information/evaluations/guidance_en.cfm#1.
26. http://ec.europa.eu/regional_policy/what/future/index_en.cfm#2.
27. http://ec.europa.eu/regional_policy/activity/urban/index_en.cfm
28. http://ec.europa.eu/regional_policy/activity/urban/index_en.cfm#1.
    http://ec.europa.eu/regional_policy/activity/statistics/2007_urban.pdf
29. See the Urban Audit research base at www.urbanaudit.org and the URBACT programme of projects at http://urbact.eu
30. When empowering local communities one of the issues raised by evaluations of the LEADER programme is the need to avoid an over-concentration of decision-making power at the local level in a small number of key actors, because this leads to local monopoly and monopsony positions. See European Court of Auditors, 2010, *Implementation of the LEADER Approach for Rural Development, Special Report No 5.* http://eca.europa.eu/portal/pls/portal/docs/1/7912812.PDF.
31. http://www.eib.org/attachments/strategies/environdoc_en.pdf
    http://www.eib.org/projects/priorities/urban/index.htm.
    http://www.eib.org/attachments/thematic/elena_en.pdf.
    http://www.eib.org/infocentre/publications/all/shaping-sustainable-cities.htm.
32. http://www.eib.org/products/jessica/index.htm.
    http://www.eib.europa.eu/products/jessica/index.htm.
    http://ec.europa.eu/regional_policy/thefunds/instruments/jessica_network_en.cfm.
33. So far there have been three generations of such programmes. See European Union (2007, 2010b)
34. In its meeting of 18/19 December 2013 the European Council invited the European Commission to elaborate a macro-regional strategy for the Alpine Region until June 2015 (Bauer 2014).
35. Article 136 on page 347 of the Common Provisions Regulation.

APPENDIX 4A.1:   THE SPACE-BLIND ARGUMENT

Within economics there is an analytical case which eschews development policy altogether, and there is also an analytical case which eschews policies with some element of targeting for weaker regions. The former case is an extreme neo-classical view which would see regional development policy as having either negligible or counterproductive effects, irrespective of which part of the world the policies are engaged in, and irrespective of which aspect (such as environment, transport, or education) they are focused on. Trade deregulation and market and institutional reform alone are of themselves always assumed to be sufficient to maximise growth. It would be fair to say that nowadays such an approach is not widely accepted amongst either the academic community or the wider arena of international organisations, and for our purposes here no further discussion of this approach is particularly required. Instead we focus on the areas of general policy-related discussion and debate relevant to the case for or against regional interventions.

European regional development policies have been criticised on the basis of retarding efficiency-generating processes of migration, agglomeration and concentration (Martin 2005; Puga 2002), and retarding these processes is argued to lead to aggregate losses of productivity and welfare (Charlot et al. 2006). These arguments assume that there is largely an automatic trade-off between spatial concentration and performance. However, the veracity of these arguments depends heavily on the assumptions made regarding social utility functions, production functions and the purported trade-offs related to geography, of which there are a range of different theoretical views (Martin 2008; Storper 2013). In addition, in the European case at least, the empirical basis for the trade-off arguments is not strong (Martin 2008).

Given this, Prager and Thisse (2012 pp. 70–72) argue that there is a spectrum of approaches to economic development, and at the extreme opposite ends of the spectrum are two opposing views. They argue that on the one hand there is the 'space-blind' argument associated with the Word Bank (2009), while on the opposite end of the spectrum according to Prager and Thisse (2012 pp. 70–72) there is an interventionist logic which derives from the classic public economics view of the world whereby the government is best placed to 'fix' (Prager and Thisse 2012 p. 70) or correct for market failures. Prager and Thisse (2012) argue that this latter approach assumes that the government is 'knowledgeable, benevolent and effective' (p.70), and they also contend (p.71) that this reflects the 'official policy stance of the European Union'.[1] However, this claim can be contested. As we see in these chapters, while Cohesion Policy has for a long time been an official and important policy of the EU and the principle of 'territorial cohesion' is indeed officially enshrined in EU treaties, the debates since 2008 make it clear that no such assumptions are made regarding the knowledge, benevolence and effectiveness competences of central governments or the supra-national EU institutions. In actual fact the place-based approach underpinning the EU Cohesion Policy reforms are based on the assumption that this is explicitly not the case. Following the discussions of Barca (2009, 2011) which are heavily influenced by the arguments of Rodrik (2007 p. 2), the place-based approach adopts a 'second-best' approach to local institutional design and transformation in the sense that there is no expectation that ideal 'best practice' institutions are necessarily or automatically likely to emerge, nor that top-down central government policy-design is unilaterally capable of designing appropriate best practice local and regional policies. However, it is still important for our purposes here to examine the origin of these claims because there are now many important arguments which suggest that issues are rather more complex and nuanced than this simple type of description suggests.

The pure 'space-blind' approach to economic development has been recently advocated amongst others by the 2009 World Development Report (World Bank 2009). Prager and Thisse (2012) argue that this pure 'space-blind' approach eschews any interventions aimed at 'correcting' for market failures and instead emphasises the need to liberalise market forces, to foster agglomeration effects, to promote density and to facilitate migration and spatial factor adjustments. Taking its lead, at least ostensibly, from aspects of urban economics and new economic geography, the space-blind approach, as reflected in the 2009 World Development Report (World Bank 2009) argues that development policy should be 'space-blind'. As Prager and Thisse (2012) explain this approach argues that the only real role for space-specific policies is to mitigate the congestion effects arising in large metropolises, to provide a minimum level of local public goods and services, and to promote connectivity. In this pure space-blind approach, no minimum public good quality, accessibility or distributional requirements are specified, and resource re-distributional mechanisms should be neutral with respect to geography. If development policies are indeed to be advocated, they should be focused on 'people-based' interventions – such as education, skills training and institutional reform – rather than on 'place-based' interventions, and the issues related to geography and place will be responded to in an efficient manner by the spatial adjustment processes of factor mobility. Where location-specific interventions such as transportation infrastructure are to be implemented, in order to maximise national growth these should be prioritised for overcoming congestion problems in the core agglomerated regions and for connecting weaker regions to stronger regions. Any place-based interventions favouring non-core regions are assumed to stifle the efficient workings of the market, at the expense of society as a whole.[2] Additional issues related to the fostering of innovation and good institutions are also raised in this line of argument, although the mechanisms by which such issues are to be addressed are left largely unspecified.

As mentioned above, on the opposite end of the spectrum according to Prager and Thisse (2012 pp. 70–72) there is an interventionist logic which derives from the classic public economics view of the world whereby the government is best placed to 'fix' (p. 70) or correct for market failures. According to Prager and Thisse such policies assume that the government is 'knowledgeable, benevolent and effective' (p. 70) and aims to use spatial policies in order to guide the geography of economic development. The aim of these policies guiding the geography of development is to correct for the market failures in a manner which increases aggregate social welfare from the levels which would exist under purely free market conditions. Prager and Thisse (2012 p. 71) contend that the most extreme form of this approach underpinned socialist planning, and in a milder form has also heavily influenced development policy in France and Italy and to a lesser extent the UK.[3] Prager and Thisse (2012) argue that modern economic geography theory does provide some support for the public economics argument and that market failures do in some sense need to be corrected for by development policy.

Some advocates of the space-blind approach (Gill 2010) may wish prima facie to interpret the logic of the Barca (2009) report as reflecting the interventionist type of logic described above by Prager and Thisse (2012). In particular, the space-blind logic criticises place-based approaches arguing that 'people-based' interventions are far more important and effective than 'place-based' interventions. However, the modern place-based approaches are different to early 1960s' 'place-based versus people-based' discussions in which institutional issues were almost entirely absent. As such, the modern place-based approach argues that such discourses reflect an outdated rhetorical dichotomy which the 2009 World Development Report unfortunately draws from (Barca et al. 2012). Simple dichotomies such as 'place-based versus people-based' policy approaches are largely meaningless (Barca et al. 2012; McCann 2013), and 'place-based in order to be people-based' rather than 'place-based versus people-based' represents a more accurate description of a place-based understanding of development processes (Barca et al. 2012).

More realistically, the Barca (2009) report, along with a suite of other high level place-based reports (OECD 2009 b, c; OECD 2011c, 2012a; CAF 2010) emerging from different parts of the world around the same time, take a quite different position to either of these extreme positions described by Prager and Thisse (2012) and do not necessarily sit anywhere in the purported spectrum between them. The reason is that the modern place-based arguments, as distinct from the 1960s types of 'place-based versus people-based' discussions motivating much of the space-blind discourses (Barca et al. 2012; McCann 2013; McCann and Rodriguez-Pose 2011) operate at the interface between institutional arguments and spatial economics and, in particular, assume that governments are not knowledgeable and that many factors and institutions are not even approximately freely mobile. The partial ignorance and partial competence of the government is explicitly a starting point of the place-based approach, as is the assumption of the limited mobility of factors and institutions, and the place-based approach therefore argues that the space-blind approach adopts a naïve approach to institutional questions. Modern place-based approaches situate the interactions between institutional and geographical issues at the centre of the development discussion. In particular, following the arguments of Rodrik (2008, p. 2), the place-based approach adopts a 'second-best' approach to local institutional design and transformation in the sense that there is neither any expectation that ideal 'best practice' institutions are necessarily or automatically likely to emerge, nor that top-down central government policy design is unilaterally capable of designing appropriate local and regional policies. Over recent decades the so-called 'Washington consensus' towards issues of structural change has meant that many of the international organisations including the World Bank, IMF and WTO (*The Economist* 14.12.2013) have advocated a development approach which is heavily oriented towards the implementation of a 'best practice' model (Rodrik 2007). Such an approach largely ignores the market and government failures which are related to the context and also ignores the context-specific complications associated with institutional reform. This ignorance serves only to narrow rather than to widen the policy options (Rodrik 2007 p. 10), because from the perspective of local stakeholders the knowledge on which these top-down and ideally-constructed approaches to institutional matters are based fails to meet the requirements of credibility, legitimacy and salience (Cash and Buizer 2005; Cash et al. 2003) necessary for development policies to be effective.

This starting point regarding the limited knowledge and limited institutional-design and transformation capabilities of top-down government reflects a very different set of starting assumptions to either of those embodied in the two polar positions described in Prager and Thisse (2012). At first, while it may appear that the place-based approach is in reality situated somewhere in the middle of the spectrum suggested by Prager and Thisse (2012), in reality, however, if there is a spectrum in which modern place-based arguments are situated, it is between pure institutionalist arguments and those which reflect pure space-blind factor-mobility-related arguments, rather than on a spectrum between interventionist or space-blind poles. The place-based approach reflects a combination of economic geography with contemporary institutional approaches (Rodrik 2004, 2007), and assumes that both institutional issues and geography issues (Sachs 2003, 2012) play critical roles in local development. The place-based approach argues that the most powerful responses to local development challenges typically involve finding ways to reconfigure and improve the workings of the local institutional context so as to best respond to the challenges associated with economic geography.

The approach views space-blind policy narratives (World Bank 2009) in reality as ignoring many of the most powerful forces shaping economic geography (Barca 2011; McCann and Rodriguez-Pose 2011; Prager and Thisse 2012). By largely ignoring governance issues in policy frameworks, the space-blind analysis also limits the ability of regions to search for differentiated policy solutions appropriate to the local or regional context (Barca et al. 2012), the importance of which has also been highlighted by Prager and Thisse (2012), Moretti (2012), Hughes (2012) and the World Bank (2010), amongst others.

Rather than being somewhere in the spectrum described by Prager and Thisse (2012) it is more realistic to position modern place-based arguments at a triangulation point drawing in part from both poles, but at the same time containing fundamental and very distinct elements which concur with neither the space-blind nor interventionist logic.

In order to understand these points it is necessary to consider some aspects of the philosophical logic as well as the policy-implementation logic of the apparently space-blind argument. On the one hand while space-blind approaches ostensibly eschew any attempts to 'correct' for market failures via spatial targeting of any form, at the same time, as Crafts (2010, 2012) points out, market failure arguments for intervention also include agglomeration. In space-blind discussions, promoting agglomeration spillovers is seen as being critical for growth (World Bank 2009), and therefore attempts are made to promote agglomerations and to correct for any market failures associated with agglomeration processes. As such, the argument proceeds to suggest that development interventions should be prioritised on the stronger regions so as to maximise national growth, or in some cases also linking weaker with strong regions. Yet, while economic theory can provide arguments regarding the conditions under which policy interventions or actions might be justified, these same arguments are largely unable to explain what exactly should be done in specific cases of, for example, innovation-related actions (Hughes 2012) or where infrastructure investments should be targeted (Estache and Fay 2010). As such, when the apparently space-blind logic advocates that such growth-enhancing interventions are to be undertaken then policy actions are indeed aiming to correct for market failures in particular places, and as such, these apparently 'space-blind' approaches are therefore neither space-blind nor are they non-interventionist. Someone has to decide what has to be done and where. Such decisions neither take place in a vacuum nor on a blank page and therefore the actual basis on which decisions are made cannot be space-blind.

Secondly, and following directly on from the first point, the policy prioritisation process in the space-blind discourse is entirely opaque in that the discourse hides how such processes operate behind a space-blind veil. As such it therefore fails to expose the risks associated with development policy being made primarily in response to the pressures associated with excessive lobbying by powerful and overly-narrow corporate interest groups (Barca and McCann 2010). As Prager and Thisse (2012 p. 73) explain: 'most policies have consequences for the location of economic activity, albeit with variable intensity. The key issues for governments ... is deciding where to locate infrastructure exhibiting large scale economies (for example, large hospitals or universities) and what should be the policy priorities for each region (more education and if so what educational level, or more transportation infrastructure)'. They continue by pointing out that governments

> intervene extensively in technology policies, for example by financing large research centers, sometimes via military spending, while economic and innovation strategies are never spatially neutral, whether in advanced or emerging countries. Furthermore, spatial neutrality is counterproductive when geographical constraints combine with a shortage of human and social capital to plunge entire regions into 'underdevelopment traps'. (pp.73–74)

which is exactly as the place-based approach advocated by the Barca report argued. Given that development is a very long-term process and interventions such as infrastructure have very long-term impacts, even in an apparently space-blind environment, in order to best identify which infrastructure should be implemented in which places and in which form and in which scale, there is always the requirement that there must be a minimum level of governance which in some sense is 'knowledgeable, benevolent and effective' (Prager and Thisse 2012 p. 70). Otherwise how can governments choose infrastructure projects to enhance long-term growth via agglomeration and connectivity effects? Clearly, central government cannot be entirely ignorant otherwise governance and planning functions have no foundation beyond pure politics and rent-seeking. The modern place-based argument consequently heavily criticises the space-blind approach (Barca et al. 2012) precisely because in reality the infrastructure choices and policy decisions made by central government in the 'national' interest following the space-blind approach do indeed rest on the assumption of a central government which is either totally 'knowledgeable, benevolent and effective' or likely to be acting heavily under the influence of overly-narrow lobbies and interest groups (Barca and McCann 2010). Much of the space-blind approach is therefore actually not at all space-blind but often simply reduces to a capital city-favouring argument in which policy decisions are driven primarily by capital city elites (Barca and McCann 2010; Barca et al. 2012). The 'space-blind' nomenclature therefore hides much of the reality of the approach and its implications (Barca et al. 2012). The place-based approach aims to describe these economic geography processes in as explicit a manner as possible also incorporating these institutional and governance issues. This ensures that the real economic geography effects of sectoral policies are not hidden under an apparent 'space-blind' rhetorical veil and such analytical transparency should both improve the design of sectoral policies as well as spatial policies while making more publicly-accountable the basis on which decisions are being made.

More realistically, of course, it is perfectly possible to argue that governments are not *totally* 'knowledgeable, benevolent and effective', but in a democratic and mixed economy environment very few people would argue with this point anyway. In a modern state the preconditions regarding government competences being in some sense 'knowledgeable, benevolent and effective' must be common to whatever development approach is advocated, irrespective of whether it is interventionist, space-blind or place-placed. As such, these competence preconditions cannot reflect the assumptions at one end of a spectrum of development approaches, as argued by Prager and Thisse (2012), unless the other end of the spectrum is anarchy.

APPENDIX 4A.2: THE SAPIR ET AL. REPORT

The Sapir et al. (2004) report was an important document because it questioned the rationale and workings of many aspects of the EU and forced a debate regarding polices such as Cohesion Policy. The Sapir report argued that EU aggregate growth was best served by targeting funding only at the national governments of member states with no regional dimension, and with a focus on innovation promotion and the fostering of institutional reforms (Sapir et al. 2004; World Bank 2012). The argument at first appears rather straightforward and well-founded. However, following the initial response from Hall (2005), the approach advocated by the Sapir report was further challenged head-on by the Barca report, which highlight three critical weaknesses of the Sapir et al. (2004) approach. The first critique of the Barca report regarding the Sapir logic was that there was no obvious way via the Sapir proposals to ensure or even motivate many of the much-needed governance and institutional reforms which the report discussed (Barca 2009; Barca et al. 2012). The reason is that the Sapir et al. report employs a largely 'top-down' perspective and as such does not tackle the complex 'bottom-up' challenges associated with the varied interactions between institutions and geography. Secondly, the Barca report argued that the Sapir report was also unclear on the underlying logic, goals and trade-offs of Cohesion Policy, and such a lack of clarity led to confusion and a mixing up of different issues. Thirdly, was the fact that there is also the problem of external expertise associated with the European Commission. The European Commission has neither the ability to design or to micro-manage the industrial or development policies of member states and nor does it have the legitimacy to do so (Barca 2009). In this arena the European Commission only has the role of ensuring that the overall framework conditions for the Single Market are respected and the agreed rules for policy interventions are all adhered to.

APPENDIX 4A.3

Table 4A.1   Cohesion policy allocations in current prices

	Cohesion Fund	Less Developed Regions	Transition Regions	More Developed Regions	Outermost and northern sparsely populated regions	European Territorial Cooperation		Youth Employment Initiative (additional allocation)	Total cohesion policy	Rural Development	CAP Direct Payments	Total
						Cross-Border Co-operation	Trans-national Co-operation					
BE	–	–	1,039.7	938.6	–	219.0	44.2	42.4	**2,283.9**	551.8	3,146.4	**5,982.1**
BG	2,278.3	5,089.3	–	–	–	134.2	31.5	55.2	**7,588.4**	2,338.8	4,540.1	**14,467.3**
CZ	6,258.9	15,282.5	–	88.2	–	296.7	43.0	13.6	**21,982.9**	2,170.3	5,241.9	**29,395.1**
DK	–	–	71.4	255.1	–	204.2	22.7	–	**553.4**	629.4	5,416.8	**6,599.6**
DE	–	–	9,771.5	8,498.0	–	626.7	338.7	–	**19,234.9**	8,217.9	30,575.3	**58,028.1**
EE	1,073.3	2,461.2	–	–	–	49.9	5.5	–	**3,590.0**	725.9	837.9	**5,153.8**
IE	–	–	–	951.6	–	150.5	18.3	68.1	**1,188.6**	2,190.0	7,279.5	**10,658.1**
EL	3,250.2	7,034.2	2,306.1	2,528.2	–	185.3	46.4	171.5	**15,521.9**	4,196.0	12,008.8	**31,726.7**
ES	–	2,040.4	13,399.5	11,074.4	484.1	430.0	187.6	943.5	**28,559.5**	8,290.8	29,168.1	**66,018.4**
FR	–	3,407.8	4,253.3	6,348.5	443.3	824.7	264.6	310.2	**15,852.5**	9,909.7	45,049.5	**70,811.7**
HR	2,559.5	5,837.5	–	–	–	127.8	18.3	66.2	**8,609.4**	2,325.2	1,065.1	**11,999.7**
IT	–	22,324.6	1,102.0	7,692.2	–	890.0	246.7	567.5	**32,823.0**	10,429.7	22,962.1	**66,214.8**
CY	269.5	–	–	421.8	–	29.5	3.3	11.6	**735.6**	132.2	299.8	**1,167.6**
LV	1,349.4	3,039.8	–	–	–	84.3	9.3	29.0	**4,511.8**	969.0	1,414.6	**6,895.4**
LT	2,048.9	4,628.7	–	–	–	99.9	13.9	31.8	**6,823.1**	1,613.1	2,729.8	**11,166.0**
LU	–	–	–	39.6	–	18.2	2.0	–	**59.7**	100.6	201.2	**361.5**
HU	6,025.4	15,005.2	–	463.7	–	320.4	41.4	49.8	**21,905.9**	3,455.3	7,622.3	**32,983.5**

MT	217.7	–	490.2	–	–	15.3	1.7	–	725.0	99.0	29.8	853.8
NL	–	–	–	1,014.6	–	321.8	67.9	–	1,404.3	607.3	4,574.8	6,586.4
AT	–	–	72.3	906.0	–	222.9	34.4	–	1,235.6	3,937.6	4,154.4	9,327.6
PL	23,208.0	51,163.6	–	2,242.4	–	543.2	157.3	252.4	77,567.0	10,941.2	3,469.6	91,977.8
PT	2,861.7	16,671.2	257.6	1,275.5	115.7	78.6	43.8	160.8	21,465.0	4,057.8	3,469.6	28,992.4
RO	6,935.0	15,058.8	–	441.3	–	364.0	88.7	106.0	22,993.8	8,015.7	10,490.7	41,500.2
SI	895.4	1,260.0	–	847.3	–	54.5	8.4	9.2	3,074.8	837.9	819.4	4,732.1
SK	4,168.3	9,483.7	–	44.2	–	201.1	22.3	72.2	13,991.7	1,890.2	2,314.4	18,196.3
FI	–	–	–	999.1	305.3	139.4	21.9	–	1,465.8	2,380.4	3,142.2	6,988.4
SE	–	–	–	1,512.4	206.9	304.2	38.1	44.2	2,105.8	1,745.3	4,186.8	8,037.9
UK	–	2,383.2	2,617.4	5,767.6	–	612.3	253.3	206.1	11,839.9	2,580.2	21,411.0	35,831.1
Interregional cooperation									571.6			571.6
Urban innovative actions									371.9			371.9
Technical assistance									1,217.6	238.9		1,456.5
EU28	63,399.7	182,171.8	35,381.1	54,350.5	1,555.4	7,548.4	2,075.0	3,211.2	351,854.2	95,577.2	237,621.9	685,053.3

Note: * Breakdown by category of allocations subject to transfers between categories at the request of the Member States.

Sources:
Cohesion policy allocations (DG REGIO):
http://ec.europa.eu/regional_policy/what/future/eligibility/index_en.cfm
Cohesion Policy Factsheet for Each Country:
http://ec.europa.eu/regional_policy/information/cohesion-policy-achievement-and-future-investment/index.cfm
Common Agricultural Policy CAP direct/market payments and rural development/EFARD (DG AGRI):
http://ec.europa.eu/agriculture/cap-funding/budget/mff-2014-2020/mff-figures-and-cap_en.pdf

Notes

1. Following the arguments of Barca (2009, 2011) and Rodrik (2007 p. 2), the place-based approach adopts a 'second-best' approach to local institutional design and transformation in the sense that there is no expectation that ideal 'best practice' institutions are necessarily or automatically likely to emerge, nor that top-down central government policy design is unilaterally capable of designing appropriate best practice local and regional policies.

2. Some forms of the space-blind argument go even further and argue that on aggregate welfare grounds 'taxing' the core regions to 'subside' weaker regions via the provision place based interventions in these regions, should be avoided at all costs. Note, however, that if core regions exhibit on average higher wages, then this extreme space-blind argument is actually not an argument against place-based interventions, but instead it is an argument against any form of taxation, including income tax, sales tax, or even flat rate taxes. The only tax which is admissible with this argument is a poll tax, whereby every citizen pays the same absolute level of tax irrespective of income or wealth. Alternatively it implies that all taxes should be only locally raised and also only locally spent, a degree of autonomy and institutional fragmentation which implies that national states become reduced to states defined by metropolitan areas.

3. As Crafts (2010, 2012) notes, UK regional policy in the 1960s and 1970s accounted for as much as 5 per cent of UK GDP. However, since the 1980s it has accounted for a very tiny fraction of one percentage point of UK overall GDP. Similarly, in the case of EU Cohesion Policy in relative terms regional development expenditure is approximately one-fifteenth of the figure noted by Crafts, so both for the UK and also for the case of Europe this argument is not particularly pertinent.

5. Innovation, regions and the case for regional innovation policies

5.1 INTRODUCTION

We have already seen in previous chapters that Europe's regions are highly heterogeneous in terms of their characteristics and also they are very heterogeneous in terms of the complex and varied development challenges they face. In terms of the policy logic and policy architecture, this also implies that the challenges facing the design and redesign of EU Cohesion Policy needs to be both sufficiently flexible to respond to these different local challenges, while at the same time, maintaining a coherent overall logic and discipline to the design and the delivery of the policy in all of the regions of Europe.

One of the central themes in today's debates regarding development policy, and one which has emerged both from a wide variety of different academic fields as well as the wide-ranging experience of national and international development agencies, is the issue of innovation. It is nowadays widely accepted that economic growth and development depend critically on promoting and enhancing innovation and entrepreneurship at all levels and stages of development and across all areas of the economy and society. The literature on innovation systems (Iammarino and McCann 2013) argues that the processes driving innovation will be different in different contexts (Iammarino and McCann 2006), and that there is no single blueprint or template for promoting innovation and entrepreneurship. Innovation-promoting policies must therefore be adaptable to different contexts, and in particular must dovetail with, and aim to enhance, the capabilities and capacity of the local people, actors and institutions. This is particularly so in the case of regions, which are not only highly heterogeneous in terms of all of these features but are also critical formation grounds, test-beds and nurseries, out of which many aspects of innovation and entrepreneurship emerge (Hughes 2012; McCann and Ortega-Argilés 2013; Moretti 2012).

The relationship between innovation generation and regional, urban and local issues is critical for the reforms to EU Cohesion Policy for two reasons. Firstly, innovation promotion is seen as being central to the growth and development agenda of the EU, and in particular via the smart specialisation approach discussed in the following chapter, and secondly, Cohesion Policy is the single largest source of innovation-related policy interventions in the EU (Bachtler et al. 2013). A good understanding of the links between innovation and regions will therefore help with improved policy design and will also facilitate tailoring of EU Cohesion Policy to local possibilities and conditions. However, the insights into these issues arise from global discussions and are based on evidence from all over the world. These wider issues and lessons are first discussed in detail in this chapter and the evidence and arguments presented here regarding these wider global debates follow closely the arguments contained in McCann and Ortega-Argilés (2013). Then in the following chapter these insights are taken on board and adapted to the specific context of the European Union, and in particular the development of the EU smart specialisation agenda.

These contemporary lines of thinking reflect fundamental shifts in our understanding over the last four decades. Modern policy approaches to innovation promotion, and specifically those policies which operate in part or wholly at the regional level, have emerged increasingly into the mainstream of public policy thinking after more than four decades of analysis, empirics and policy experiences. Collectively, the policy experience and the academic analysis running in parallel have reframed our understanding of the role played by innovation in economic growth and wider aspects of economic development. In particular, one of the key issues which has emerged over the last couple of decades is an increasing awareness of the role played by geography in influencing and shaping processes of innovation and entrepreneurship. Therefore, a tradition which started out from a relatively narrow sectoral, science-based and R&D-led mode of thinking about innovation processes and the appropriate policy responses, has now subsequently evolved into a much broader multi-dimensional policy approach. This more modern approach to innovation policy is becoming increasingly prevalent nowadays in many different arenas. It is an approach which moves away from a narrowly defined science-based agenda and instead also allows for other issues to heavily influence innovation processes, including issues relating to institutions, geography and broader linkage development challenges. The journey from the early science-led policy approaches to innovation to the current broader innovation policy framework is therefore the culmination of various shifts in both analytical and empirical thinking, as well as policy experiences across the world.

In the case of Europe, the particular ways in which innovation-promoting and entrepreneurship-promoting activities have today been incorporated into the EU Cohesion Policy reforms closely reflects the lesson learned from this journey. As we have already seen, the regions of Europe differ significantly in terms of their economic structure, their economic history, their skills and technological profiles, their institutional and governance architectures, and their capacity, capabilities and performance across each of these dimensions. Therefore, European development policies aimed at fostering regional innovation and entre-preneurship must not only be able to respond to these differences, but wherever possible must also identify ways to build on these differences as potential sources of competitive advantage. As Prager and Thisse (2012) have emphasised, finding ways to exploit locally distinctive capabilities in order to enhance differentiation is essential for fostering regional development. A modern view of growth therefore suggests that the exploitation of local distinctiveness and enhancing the advantages associated with local differentiation should very much be a central tenet not only of regional policies, but in particular those focused on enhancing innovation and entrepreneurship.

The reforms to EU Cohesion Policy have explicitly embodied and addressed these challenges in their redesign. The overall approach to fostering innovation and entrepreneurship via this logic is known as *smart specialisation*. The smart specialisation approach provides a policy prioritisation logic which is explicitly tailored to the local context and is based on a region's economic potential. The policy approach is built on a powerful intellectual tradition combining both conceptual analyses with hard-headed empirical evidence, and emerged explicitly from enquiries into the nature of the innovation and entrepreneurial processes within the EU. However, as well as responding to specifically European challenges, the smart specialisation approach also reflects the wider emerging academic consensus regarding the role played by regions in innovation and the likely priorities for regional innovation policies. Moreover, even though it originally emerged from a quite different background context, the smart specialisation approach to policy design is also very consistent with both the place-based logic of the Barca (2009) report as well as the spirit of the new Coherent Policy regulations including the results-oriented logic. The outcome of all of these intellectual synergies is that smart specialisation has now emerged as a key component of the EU Cohesion Policy reforms.

These next two chapters explain the background and the reasons why smart specialisation has emerged as a key component of the EU Cohesion Policy reforms. In order to do this, it is first necessary in this chapter to discuss the wider issues regarding innovation and innovation policies per se, without any reference to regions as such. The focus here is largely on the early science-related and R&D-led understanding of innovation, and the emergence of systems views of innovation. The discussion in this chapter then moves on to explain how the consensus regarding innovation policies has itself shifted over recent decades, as our understanding of innovation and entrepreneurship processes has itself shifted. In particular, a rapidly improving understanding of the role played by geography in influencing innovation and entrepreneurial processes has been one of the key elements underpinning this shift. This shift itself has partly underpinned the modern case per se for selective industrial policy, of which innovation policy is one such example. Yet, the case for regional innovation policy goes further than the case for industrial policy per se, precisely because of our awareness of the role of geography in shaping innovation. As we will see in this chapter, the role played by local issues in facilitating or inhibiting innovation processes is now widely accepted and modern innovation policy is increasingly aimed at addressing many of these local issues. This provides the backdrop to the discussion in the following chapter regarding smart specialisation in European regions.

Following on from the development of the case for regional innovation policies, we are then in a position in the next chapter to examine the specific EU Cohesion Policy response to these matters, known as smart specialisation. This concept emerged out of discussions concerning the emergence of the so-called 'transatlantic productivity gap' and rising concerns regarding the competitiveness of the EU economy and was not originally or explicitly related to regional issues. However, the concept has nowadays become explicitly related to the case of EU regions, linking the earlier innovation and entrepreneurship insights from science-policy analyses to more recent economic geography insights. Prima facie, the smart specialisation logic may appear to some observers to be inconsistent with the objectives of EU Cohesion Policy. However, the next chapter will explain why it is indeed very much consistent not only with the EU Cohesion Policy objectives, but also more generally with modern regional policy approaches. Importantly, however, smart specialisation offers a perfectly workable logic to policy design and delivery based on a policy prioritisation approach which encourages capacity-building and institutional-learning. Finally, the smart specialisation approach also reflects the Stiglitz et al. (2009) position that in the end policymakers need to make decisions for the common good based on the best available information, including data, evidence but also the knowledge embedded in the community's actors and institutions. The next chapter will finally go on to explain the practical interventions put in place by the European Commission in order to help EU regions develop their smart specialisation approaches.

5.2 INNOVATION AND ECONOMIC GROWTH: ANALYTICAL ISSUES

Innovation is nowadays understood as the process of converting new ideas into marketable outcomes (Gordon and McCann 2005), but more specifically, outcomes which are not only new, but represent novel improvements on previous blueprints, and are designed as far as possible to overcome uncertainty. Innovation can be understood either as a phenomenon or as a process, in which knowledge and learning clearly are both essential components. However, identifying appropriate policy frameworks for promoting innovation and entrepreneurship require a deep understanding of the innovation process. The role which innovation plays in driving economic growth has evolved significantly over the last two decades, and the evolution in our understanding of innovation reflects shifts in both analytical thinking and also in our empirical experiences. In terms of this chapter, the aim of which is to situate smart specialisation and its role in the EU Cohesion Policy reforms within the wider academic and policy debates, it is useful at first to consider these analytical shifts and the shifts in our empirical experience over the last few decades separately. This will then help to set the scene for us to examine how the smart specialisation concept arose and the implications of this approach for innovation policy design at the regional level.

In terms of analytical issues, the roles which knowledge and learning play in national economic development can be considered to be both stock and flow variables. In other words, the stock of knowledge assets is likely to be critical. The more such assets an economy has, the greater ought to be the potential for the economy's further development, particularly given the fact that the importance of knowledge in the contemporary 'weightless economy' (Quah 2001) is nowadays generally understood to be increasing (Jorgensen et al. 2008; OECD 2004). At the same time, however, the academic literature suggests that the stock of knowledge assets is only one part of the story, and that the knowledge flows emerging from the knowledge assets, and the resulting processes of learning which arise from these knowledge flows, are at least as important as the assets themselves. In other words, by way of an example of knowledge assets, having a large number of universities is likely to be very important for growth and development. However, this is not sufficient to foster growth. At least as important are the impacts of the knowledge flows emerging from the universities, in terms of graduate human capital (Faggian and McCann 2006, 2009a, b), university–industry collaborations and wider knowledge spillovers, all of which critically matter for knowledge and learning processes. The hoped-for outcomes of the knowledge flows emerging from the knowledge assets include entrepreneurial actions and innovation. Yet whether such outcomes are observed depends on processes and systems; phenomena which go well beyond simply questions of economic structure.

Over the last three decades academic research in economics, technology sciences and management sciences, along with an increasing wealth of case study experience from diverse industrial and commercial examples, has emphasised the role played by innovation in driving economic growth. Innovation driven by large companies and multinational firms in particular, has been a central focus of research for many years (Iammarino and McCann 2013). Over the last two decades, however, the link between entrepreneurial activities and innovation has also become a central focus of policy debates. All discussions regarding innovation, however, have shifted over recent decades as our understanding of innovation as a phenomenon and as a process has itself evolved.

Before the 1980s, discussions of innovation and entrepreneurship were largely peripheral to mainstream economic thought. Economic growth was primarily understood in terms of a neo-classical growth accounting framework, in which the technological nature of total factor productivity residuals was largely barely ever discussed. While the small number of scholars who were working on the topics of innovation and entrepreneurship often referred to Schumpeterian ideas, none of these lines of enquiry were at the time regarded as being central to economic thought, because the implicit or explicit assumption was that efficient factor allocations will automatically lead to the maximisation of the technology levels and diffusion rates. However, this approach treats technology as being largely disembodied from, or exogenous to, production factors, whereas increasingly we have come to understand that technology is embodied not only in production factors, but also very much in the feedbacks and interrelationships between these factors both within firms and also between firms. Simply discussing factor stocks and factor prices is not sufficient for understanding technological evolutions.

The idea that economic growth operates via feedbacks between factors within the firm had first been formally established in neo-classical frameworks by Arrow (1962). Although some rather more heterodox approaches (Kaldor 1975) had attempted to make progress on these issues, this idea had lain largely dormant for almost two and half decades until the work of Romer (1986). Building somewhat on the original insights of Arrow (1962), the work of Romer (1986, 1990) argued that many aspects of growth reflect endogenous processes driven by spillovers and feedbacks. A parallel line of argument was initiated by Lucas (1988) who emphasised the importance of the knowledge and know-how embedded in human capital. What had previously been seen in the earlier growth-accounting models as stocks of disembodied technological residuals was increasingly understood as reflecting flows of knowledge between factors as well as stocks of knowledge embodied within those same factors. These 'new growth' models were aimed at linking stocks of factor inputs, including expenditures on education, science, research and development (R&D), to economic growth.

At this stage the nature and role of innovation as being central to growth processes was still discussed largely outside of mainstream economics, and mainly in the technology policy (Pavitt 1984), management (Porter 1985) and management science literatures. Meanwhile, there had been some early theoretical work on the nature of entrepreneurship and the role of the entrepreneur in searching out new intra-marginal profit opportunities (Casson 1982). While this work was also structured within a neo-classical framework, it was well over two decades before it received its rightful recognition (Casson et al. 2006), and somewhat too late to influence many of the mainstream aggregate theoretical approaches.

In terms of formal analytical frameworks, it was in the work of Aghion and Howitt (1992) that innovation was finally situated as a central element in growth models. These types of approaches aimed to incorporate Schumpeterian ideas into growth models, whereby innovation was viewed as a latent element in the growth process. Traditionally, in growth models innovation was typically associated with either R&D or total factor productivity. However, the Aghion and Howitt (1992) theoretical framework and the Crépon et al (1998) conceptual framework extended this approach to allow for a structure in which innovation is both an intermediate input and an intermediate output, controlling for selectivity and simultaneity. The role played by innovation was that of linking technological and factor inputs to growth outcomes. As such, growth is understood as being a multi-stage process in which factors inputs and competition effects create profit-making opportunities which are exploited by firms engaging in innovative activities, which are themselves designed to maximise the chances of achieving these profitable outcomes. Subsequent work by various authors (Carlaw and Lipsey 2006; Crépon et al. 1998; Lipsey et al. 2006) has continued to develop these ideas both in terms of measuring the importance of these different elements, and also refining our understanding of the nature of these processes. Although structural models of a Crépon et al. (1998) type are sensitive to the specific model structure and estimation techniques employed, the important point is that they characterise innovation as part of a sequential structure or system. More recent research has also sought to identify and measure the different roles played by innovation and technology. Of central importance here is the need to distinguish between the role played by general purpose technologies and their diffusion impacts across all parts of the economy, from the impacts of more specific purpose technologies, which tend to affect particular sectors or particular types of activities.

General purpose technologies, such as electricity grids, plastics, nano-technologies or information technologies, are seen to impact on the whole economy, but they tend to emerge only sporadically, with long periods between the next new waves of general purpose technologies. In contrast, specific purpose technologies arise frequently, but often in something of an uncoordinated and haphazard manner, and differently affect different types of arenas in the economy. General purpose tech-nologies are transformative in nature, in that almost all aspects of the economy and society are affected by their introduction, and sometimes the emergence of such technologies also requires a rethinking of the methods for assessing different aspects of economic growth. In particular an earlier generation of growth-accounting conventions was largely unable to capture the nature of modern information and communications technologies (ICTs), as reflected in the so-called 'Solow paradox' (Solow 1987). A re-assessment of the nature of the economic benefits of ICTs has itself given rise to a re-assessment of the methods for measuring economic growth. In particular, the price of the capital assets involved in ICTs, such as computers or smart phones, has been falling dramatically over recent decades as enormous increases in micro-processing power associated with minaturisation have continued apace. These develop-ments, which are often reflected in what is commonly known as 'Moore's law',[1] imply that the prices of such assets per unit of processing power fall as processing power increases. However, traditional measurements based on capital stock values misrepresented the economic benefits associated with these price falls. In reality, it is the value of the flows of services associated with these capital goods which are the dominant feature of ICTs, rather than the value of the capital assets themselves. The adjustments in the methods for valuing economic growth from stock values to values of the flows of services provided by the assets,[2] itself reflects a shift of the compositions and workings of the economy as a whole. The modern 'weightless economy' (Quah 2001) which emerged in the latter part of the twentieth century is increasingly driven by know-ledge flows and knowledge exchanges, and much less so by physical capital assets. Flows of knowledge, which are generated by the inter-actions between human capital and physical capital, are increasingly seen as being the backbone of the modern economy. As well as leading to changes in growth measurement techniques, a gradual awareness of these real shifts in the nature of much of the modern economy, has also increasingly brought to the fore the importance of both innovation and entrepreneurship in the modern economy. The conversion of knowledge and new ideas into marketable and profitable products and services, and the establishment and growth of the types of firms designed to facilitate and exploit these conversion activities, is nowadays widely accepted as being critical for economic growth.

Over recent years, it has become increasingly accepted that innovation is both a phenomenon and a process, but in the 1980s and 1990s these ideas were largely confined to what became known as the 'innovations systems' literature. This literature had emerged from a combination of rather heterodox approaches to economics along with management, engineering, sociology, and science policy. While these lines of research adopted largely a Schumpeterian approach (Schumpeter 1934) to entrepreneurship (Casson 1982) and innovation (Kline and Rosenberg 1986), they did so from a systemic perspective which focused on the examination of the links between behavioural influences on innovation and the structural characteristics of the economy. Moreover, because the field had originally developed very much at the interface between different disciplines, this led to something of a hybrid blend of different methodologies and influences.

Over time innovation came to be understood as the result of a system (Freeman 1995), but the systems approach to innovation has itself also exhibited changes. The earlier generations of these innovations-systems approaches largely avoided the formality of the abstract modelling frameworks typical in most branches of economics. Instead, where modelling was employed, they tended to focus more on models based on engineering production functions (Morroni 1992). As we will see in a moment, at the time there were very good reasons for the emphasis on engineering approaches, but an unintended outcome of this was that during the 1980s these heterodox approaches to innovation remained largely outside of theoretical developments in orthodox economics. Central to the emergence of the early systems approach to innovation were the evolutionary ideas of Nelson and Winter (1982) who argued that while micro-level feedbacks and interactions within the firms are important, meso-level interactions between firms and other actors and institutions are also critical for innovation.

Apart from different analytical traditions, the development of the rather heterodox approaches to innovation and the rise of the innovations-systems approaches was in part also catalysed by the rise of the Japanese and Asian multinational firms during the 1980s, and in particular in sectors such as automobiles and electronics. These firms increasingly made inroads into western domestic consumer markets and captured market share not only on the basis of new or improved products but also on the basis of new production processes (Best 1990; Piore and Sabel 1984; Schonberger 1981). The critical importance of systems and processes in fostering innovation emerged primarily in the production engineering literature which uncovered the innovation-related advantages afforded by new management and operations practices such as just-in-time production systems, quality circles and total quality management (TQM). These developments highlighted the links between systems and outputs, and these experiences and observations were also bolstered by a burgeoning management literature based on numerous case studies of firms (Porter 1985).

The impact of these new competitive developments from Asian multi-national firms gave rise to a profound reconsideration of the role of innovation in all aspects of growth. In particular, the management literature and also the engineering-related literature both emphasised the importance of different types of innovation for fostering firm competitiveness and the supply chain mechanisms via which these innovations are embodied. Innovations are seen to emerge from different sources either within or outside of the sector in which they are observed (Pavitt 1984), depending on the ways in which the knowledge is embedded in intermediate inputs, capital goods or human capital. Earlier understandings of innovation largely focused on manufacturing and engineering sectors but over recent years our understanding of the nature and role of innovation has shifted so that it is nowadays widely understood that innovation is not only both a latent phenomenon and process linking firm decisions to aggregate growth, but also that the knowledge investments driving innovation very much include both the implementation of non-technological developments in marketing, network formation, research collaboration (Arita and McCann 2000; Teece 2011), or organisational issues, as well as the adoption of more traditional technological issues related to new equipment, new machinery and new capital goods.

A third and final shift in our understanding of innovation relates to the motivation for innovation and the conditions under which innovation is cultivated. Innovation is nowadays widely understood as being a latent phenomenon which itself is an outcome of knowledge investments. However, the outcomes of these investments are themselves uncertain, because these investments take place in an environment of risk. Innovation actions are therefore intended and designed to translate knowledge investments and new ideas into growth outcomes. This is because while invention relates to new ideas, innovation also implies that these ideas can be successfully converted into commercially viable and profitable outcomes. In other words, in the end it is the market which distinguishes an innovation from an invention. As such, the three common features of all innovations are: firstly, that they display newness or novelty; secondly, that they represent an improvement over previous blueprints or templates; and thirdly, that they are undertaken in the short or medium term as an attempt to reduce long-term risk (Gordon and McCann 2005). These tripartite generic features are common to all possible types of innovations. Yet, the important point here is that while early production function approaches tended to suggest that knowledge investments lead to growth, modern approaches to innovation imply that such investments are not of themselves sufficient to promote growth. This is because economic growth also depends on the success in translating those investments to commercially successful outcomes (Kline and Rosenberg 1986). As we have already seen, modern systemic approaches to the analysis of innovation view innovation itself both as a latent feature as well as an outcome of a process.

5.3   INNOVATION AND ECONOMIC GROWTH: EMPIRICAL AND MEASUREMENT ISSUES

Much of our recent understanding of innovation as a meta-phenomenon and a meta-process linking factor inputs to growth outcomes has been spurred by empirical developments. Empirical improvements have been observed in terms of better innovation classification systems, in terms of improved measurement systems and also in terms of more advanced empirical methods, and these have sought to throw light on difficult challenges associated with interpreting many aggregate empirical observations. In particular, economic growth is not solely related to industrial structure and other issues are clearly important, of which innovation is widely regarded as being one such key issue.

Aggregate data shows us that different countries exhibit different economic and industrial structures and very different factor shares for human capital, physical capital, total factor productivity (TFP) and employment. What are known as growth-accounting techniques measure these differences, and also the different contributions to growth made by different factor inputs. As an example, if we use the US as a benchmark of 100 per cent on each of these indicators, observations from OECD countries suggest that TFP ranges from 52 per cent in Japan, to 64.1 per cent in Australia–New Zealand, to 67.8 per cent across the EU+EFTA countries and to 72 per cent in Canada. Meanwhile, the rest of the world including the BRICs countries are all below one-third of the US's TFP score (OECD 2010). Moreover, this is not simply a matter of assets. In terms of physical capital Japan has approximately one-third more capital assets per capita than the US although its overall productivity is still much lower. Similarly, the EU+EFTA countries, along with Canada, Australia and New Zealand, also all have more physical capital inputs than the US. Again productivity is lower in all of these countries than in the US. On the other hand, what is noticeable about the US is that the share of business R&D in US firms is on average higher than in almost any other country. We know that across all OECD countries and across all areas of manufacturing industry, ranging from high technology to medium technology and to low technology, the shares of R&D do differ significantly. However, the US economy appears to be more systematic-ally geared towards the higher end of the technology value-chains than other countries (OECD 2010). Moreover, the US economy also appears to have higher human capital inputs than other countries, even adjusting for differences in the number of labour input hours (ibid.). Yet, while a superficial reading of the data may imply that stocks of physical capital – known as 'tangibles' investments – or education-related human capital investments, must together determine economic growth, what we see today is that in many advanced economies including the Nordic coun-tries, the UK and the US, the share of investments in 'intangibles' is actually now greater than investments in physical capital 'tangibles'. What we mean here by the term 'intangibles' are those investments in activities such as new marketing initiatives, new intellectual property, new organisational systems and new managerial capability, and invest-ments in these types of activities all appear nowadays to be at least as important as the types of factor stocks which were traditionally under-stood to be critical for growth (ibid.). This is not to say that the more traditional tangible types of factor inputs are not important. It is just that intangibles are becoming increasingly important in many countries, and indeed in some countries they are now the most important factors determining growth and development. The relationship between factor stocks and economic growth therefore depends not only on the stocks of assets, but also on the flows of services and complementary activities which are associated with those assets. While this is true for factors in general, this is nowadays increasingly true for knowledge assets them-selves. Innovation and entrepreneurship are the intermediate outcomes of the knowledge flows emerging from an economy's knowledge assets, and in particular, these are the intermediate outcomes widely regarded as linking knowledge to economic growth.

The rapid growth of ICTs in the mid 1990s focused attention on the complementary investments required in order to exploit the opportunities associated with these investments (Hulten 2013). However, neither the production function model of the firm typical in microeconomics nor the prevailing growth accounting conventions (ibid.) were well-suited to these developments. Even now, aggregate growth accounting techniques are still largely unable to capture empirically the meta-phenomena associated with innovation, and other empirical techniques have therefore been devised to do this. Early empirical work on classifying innovation focused largely on the technological innovations relating to new products and processes, and as with the theoretical developments also evident in the 1980s, the empirical analyses tended to focus on manufacturing industries. This type of analysis was aimed at identifying the technological inputs embodied in new products and processes, and underpins the construction of the Pavitt (1984) taxonomy. The Pavitt approach identified the sources of innovation in the context of backward and forward linkages, and specifically in terms of whether the new technologies embodied in industry innovations were originally internal or external to the sector. One of the important insights of the Pavitt taxonomy is that many sectors grow by absorbing and embodying the innovations initially developed in other sectors or in other parts of the supply chains, and such sectors may be as successful as those which develop numerous new technologies and innovations internally. An important implication of the Pavitt approach is therefore that indicators of R&D activities often misrepresent the knowledge content of the sector concerned, and such indicators need to be bolstered with other measures of knowledge content and knowledge embodiment. For more than two decades the Pavitt taxonomy was regarded as the standard classification approach to innovation in sectors producing tangibles.

Following on from the Pavitt (1984) approach, one of the major steps forward in the empirical analysis of innovation was the use of patent data, the use of which dominated most early econometric work on innovation (Jaffe 1986; Levin et al. 1987; Mansfield et al. 1981; Scherer 1965; Teece 1986), and patents are still the most widely used indicators of innovation in many parts of the world. Over time, however, other indicators increasingly became adopted as indicators of innovation including the value of sales devoted to new products (Acs and Audretsch 1988, 1990). The use of these other indicators since the 1990s led to a concerted and coordinated effort across countries and research agendas to

develop better innovation data sources and indicators above patent data
(Hong et al. 2012; OECD 2010). These are two reasons why the
development and use of a wider set of indices of innovation are
important. Firstly, it is well-known that patents fail to capture the
majority of innovation emerging in service industries. This gap in our
knowledge associated with patents is particularly important given that
services account for almost 70 per cent of value-added in advanced
economies. Secondly, patents also poorly reflect the variety of innovations, including non-technological innovations, which also emerge even
in many tangibles-producing sectors. As such, an over-reliance on patent
data misses many of the innovation processes and outcomes evident in
the economy.

During the 1990s and 2000s the increasing awareness both of the role
played by innovation in service sectors and also the fact that many
innovations in both the service and manufacturing industries are of a
non-technological nature gave rise to efforts to develop a revised Pavitt-
type taxonomy (Pavitt 2000; Tidd et al. 1997). In particular, the aim was
to develop an innovation taxonomy which better reflected the contemporary understanding of innovation as being much broader than the earlier
science-based and R&D-focused views of innovation. This was also
essential because various firm-level innovation surveys were emerging
from different countries, but comparability between these was very
limited as there was no agreed methodology for the design of such
surveys (Hong et al. 2012). The *Frascati Manual* (OECD 2002) and the
Oslo Manual (OECD 2005) provided the templates on which modern
surveys on R&D and on innovation, respectively, are now built in most
countries (Hong et al. 2012). These two OECD manuals provide the
internationally agreed and standardised system for data collection, vali-
dation, or comparison when constructing innovation surveys, and these
are the frameworks on which the EU *Community Innovation Survey* is
nowadays built.

Many important empirical findings have emerged both from the use of
these new innovation classification schemes and also from the improved
survey-based innovation data and indices. In particular, innovation is
based on a much wider set of linkages and issues than earlier technology-
led approaches had suggested and typically spans simply sector-specific
or firm-specific distinctions. Important insights include: the levels of
innovation in service sectors are generally seen to be lower and also more
variable than in the case of manufacturing firms, except for knowledge-
intensive business services (KIBS), which are found to innovate at
equivalent or even higher rates as high-technology manufacturing firms
(OECD 2010; Ortega-Argilés et al. 2011); many firms typically employ

mixed modes of innovation, undertaking both technological and non-technological forms of innovation simultaneously (Ortega-Argilés and Moreno 2007; OECD 2010); and the wider growth benefits associated with the technological innovations generated by the tangibles sectors are also increasingly seen to depend on innovations in service sectors (Ortega-Argilés 2012). As such, the growth impacts of innovation are understood to depend heavily on the linkages or transmission effects between firms and between sectors, rather than just activities within firms or sectors.

The major features of the broadly accepted consensus regarding both the sources of innovation and also the outcomes of innovation related investments are summarised in McCann and Ortega-Argilés (2013) on the basis of the detailed analysis of the OECD (2010) and a range of other sources. With regard to the various sources of innovation, the evidence suggests that firms operating in international markets are some 40–70 per cent more likely to innovate than domestically-oriented firms (Crépon et al. 1998; Ortega-Argilés et al. 2005). In particular, the links between internationalisation and innovation appear to be particularly strong for inward or outward foreign direct investment (FDI) which can be a major source of innovation (OECD 2010). Moreover, not only are these links strong, but there is also much evidence to suggest that this importance is increasing (Iammarino and McCann 2013).

In terms of the links between collaboration and innovation, firms involved in collaboration are typically some 20–50 per cent more likely to innovate than other non-collaborating firms, and large firms tend to engage more in collaboration (OECD 2010) than small firms. Yet, this also raises the issue of firm size, and the wide-ranging consensus for all of the available evidence is that there is a non-linear relationship between firm size and innovation, with both small firms and large firms appearing to be the most innovative types of firms, while medium-sized firms exhibit lower levels of innovation (Tether et al. 1997). However, the likelihood of innovation is not simply a matter of scale, with innovation being highly skewed to a relatively small number of firms. The reason is that while a majority of firms in advanced economies do innovate in some way, the majority of innovation expenditures and outputs are accounted for by only a very small number of firms (Iammarino and McCann 2013; OECD 2010; Ortega-Argilés et al. 2005) and only a very small number of firms account for the vast majority of the new employment growth associated with SMEs (Haltiwanger et al. 2010; NESTA 2009).

In terms of funding issues, there is a wide range of evidence to suggest that venture capital-backed firms outperform non-venture-capital-backed firms in terms of employment and revenue. In addition, firms receiving public funding invest 40–70 per cent more than non-supported firms (OECD 2010). Moreover, in the arena of venture capital and angel investments, the evidence suggests that many parts of the EU and Asia are not only catching the US up, but in some cases they are actually moving ahead of the US, and this appears to be the case both for seed-funding and start-up finance, as well as for early development and expansion funds (McCann and Ortega-Argilés 2013; OECD 2010).

In terms of the outcomes of innovation, it is clear that innovation is highly beneficial. Firms with higher innovation sales intensities achieve higher productivity and higher survival prospects than firms with low innovation sales intensities (OECD 2010; Ortega-Argilés 2012; Ortega-Argilés and Moreno 2009). Moreover, these effects are strengthened the broader is the innovation base, such that firms undertaking product and process innovations are found to achieve some 30 per cent more innovation sales per employee than those introducing only product innovations (ibid.). In contrast, firms which are well below the technology frontier invest less and achieve lower returns to innovation, although the innovation probability of a firm is independent of its level of productivity. On the other hand, the evidence is that such firms also respond well to public policy in that the public support for firms well below the technology frontier has a greater induced effect on innovation-expenditure relative to similar non-supported firms (Kumbhakar et al. 2012; OECD 2010).

Although these typical aggregate results are not always realised in every case, it is these types of insights which motivate many innovation policy actions. In particular, the wide-ranging observations regarding the different aspects of innovation also underlie the shift away from the narrower 'hard science' and capital-expenditure view of innovation typical in the early days and increasingly towards an emphasis on the role of 'soft' factors and systems-issues in promoting innovation as is more widely accepted nowadays.

Taken together, the mix of case-study evidence from the 1980s and 1990s onwards, allied with increasing econometric evidence emerging since the 1990s and 2000s and summarised here, has shifted our understanding of the nature of innovation as an essential ingredient in growth such that it has moved beyond invention and technology to incorporate all of the elements involved in the commercialisation of new ideas (Hulten 2013). This broader understanding of innovation includes activities related to marketing, customer support, skills-training and organisational issues, and there is now a greater awareness of the importance of knowledge-based capital or intangible capital investments for economic growth (ibid.). Indeed, the evidence shows that investments related to this wider range of activities are much more important for growth than R&D investments alone (ibid.). However, as we have already seen, there are also differences between countries, with tangible capital investments being relatively more important in manufacturing-led countries such as Germany, China and Japan than in the US, UK or France, where investments in intangibles play a greater role (ibid.).

Innovation is no longer seen as a latent element in a largely linear growth process, but rather as both a latent element in, and also an outcome of, a system of mechanisms, feedbacks and processes operating within and between firms and institutions (Hughes 2012; OECD 2010). The configuration of the system as well as the elements of the system are all seen as being crucial (Hughes 2012). Moreover, beyond productivity growth, innovation is now also widely seen as being central to the success of our responses to all global and societal challenges including all environmental, health and wellbeing challenges (OECD 2010). The various empirical and conceptual developments described above have been reflected in the fact that our understanding of innovation has shifted over time as more evidence has emerged (Hughes 2012). Over the last two decades, the systems approach, which interprets innovation performance in the context of the specific relationships between firms and institutions, has been extended to questions of geography, and these approaches are nowadays becoming increasingly influential in policy-circles.

5.4 INNOVATION AND ECONOMIC GEOGRAPHY

The role which geography plays in innovation is an issue which reflects fundamental shifts in our understanding of the nature of innovation as a phenomenon and a process. These shifts have emerged from various different literatures including management (Porter 1990, 1998a,b), economics (Acs and Audretsch 1990) as well as science policy and international business (Iammarino and McCann 2006, 2013). However, as well as providing new analytical insights, it can also be argued that the shifts in our understanding of innovation are also a result of the emerging empirical evidence which strongly points to the fact that the nature of innovation itself has also changed over recent years. Such changes are seen to be due most notably to the technological and structural developments (Timmer et al. 2013) associated with the advent of modern information and communications technologies (ICTs) and also the increasing importance of global value-chains (Baldwin and Evenett 2012;

OECD 2013a). These technological and structural changes imply that the links between the application of knowledge and its embodiment in innovations throughout the production process are altered throughout the value-chain (Iammarino and McCann 2013). Indeed, the emerging empirical evidence does suggest that fundamental changes within global value chains are evident in terms of the international patterns of value-added and the profit distributions (OECD 2013a; Timmer et al. 2013) as a result of changing geographical patterns in knowledge content (Baldwin and Evenett 2012; Hughes 2012; Iammarino and McCann 2013). The recently-emerging general purpose technologies of information and communications technologies (ICTs) have proved to be primarily complements for those knowledge-intensive activities requiring highly frequent face-to-face interactions (Gaspar and Glaeser 1998; McCann 2007), while at the same acting as substitutes for routinised activities (McCann 2008). A result of the dramatically changing transactions costs is that ICTs have themselves helped to engender a more uneven interregional and international spatial distribution of activities according to the degrees of knowledge intensity embodied in activities (McCann 2008; McCann and Acs 2011). Combined with these changes in transactions costs associated with the economic geography of globalisation (McCann 2008), the technological shifts and the reconfiguration of global value chains also implies that the incentives and opportunities associated with location decisions will have also been altered over recent years. In particular those location decisions related to the access, exploitation, or application of knowledge would appear to be those which are likely to have been the most affected (Iammarino and McCann 2013; McCann 2011) and indeed, there is widespread evidence that today's geographical patterns of knowledge activities and knowledge distributions differ fundamentally from those patterns which pertained even as recently as the late 1980s (McCann 2008). This consequently has led to reconsideration of the development role played by the interactions between geography and innovation at both a local and a global scale (World Bank 2010) and has resulted in new insights into the nature of development processes (OECD 2013b). At the same time, one of the major impacts of the emergence of internationally agreed innovation survey-design templates is that the role played by geography in fostering innovation has become increasingly apparent in ways which were largely absent in the early generation of innovation taxonomies and surveys (Hong et al. 2012). As well as analytical and intellectual shifts, this burgeoning empirical evidence has also contributed nowadays to placing regional and geography issues very much centre stage in discussions of innovation.

Early systems approaches emphasised country-specific influences on the national innovation systems (Lundvall 1992; Nelson 1993). These approaches were subsequently adapted to include industry and technology features, leading to approaches focused on sectoral systems of innovation (Dosi et al. 1995, 1997; Nelson and Winter 1982), technological systems of innovation (Foray and Freeman 1993; Malerba and Orsenigo 1997; Malerba et al. 1999). Observing changes in the nature and role of innovation systems in different time periods and contexts, Freeman (1995) agreed with Porter (1990) that the role of the home country appeared to be becoming even more important in the global context, even though globalisation processes were advancing. While such observations could be made consistent with various new trade theory and new economic geography arguments, for Porter (1990), however, the reason was that sub-national local and regional factors were critical in fostering innovation. He went further than previous innovation theorists in terms of highlighting the important role played by the local and regional context in innovation systems, arguing that the role of the region is central in shaping the innovation-related responses to global competition (Porter 1990, 1998a, b). Over time, other innovation-systems theorists subsequently concurred with this line of argument as more and more data emerged on these issues. Following the early empirical work of Jaffe et al. (1993), Feldman (1994), Audretsch and Feldman (1996) and Anselin et al. (1997), a wide-ranging literature has now emerged which empirically examines the relationships between geography and innovation (Breschi and Malerba 2005). There is now overwhelming evidence from numerous studies all over the world that as well as countries (European Commission 2014a), certain regions are also systematically more disposed towards innovation than others (Crescenzi and Rodriguez-Pose 2011; ESPON 2012; European Commission 2014b; OECD 2011). The reasons for the differences in the extent to which regions are oriented towards innovation are argued to relate variously to issues of urban agglomeration externalities (Acs 2002; Van Oort 2004) associated with city population or employment density (Carlino et al. 2007; Ciccone and Hall 1996), the regional industrial structure (Iammarino and McCann 2006), the presence of knowledge-related institutions (Morgan 1997), the environment for entrepreneurship (Sternberg 2011), and research (Cozza et al. 2012; Ortega-Argilés and Moreno 2009), the institutional context (Polenske 2007), changes in knowledge transactions costs (McCann 2007, 2008), and the role of global companies (Iammarino and McCann 2013).

The arguments regarding the role played by cities in fostering innovation are closely tied to the standard urban agglomeration arguments, in which proximity and density are assumed to foster knowledge spillovers between people and between firms. The evidence regarding the relationships between productivity and city size, density and diversity suggests that in many cases there are indeed statistically significant relationships, although as we have seen in Chapter 2, the associated elasticities are rather small and subject to a great deal of heterogeneity. Following on from these lines of argument, some observers have also found evidence that innovation (Carlino et al. 2007; Nathan and Lee 2013) and entrepreneurship (Acs 2002) are related to employment or population density, while others have found evidence that innovation-related activities such as knowledge-intensive business services (Shearmur and Doloreux 2008) are also higher in cities than in non-urban areas. In contrast, there is also evidence which suggest that cities (Shearmur 2011, 2012; Shearmur and Doloreux 2013) and more densely populated urban areas do not necessarily enjoy systematic advantages related to innovation (Macpherson 2008) or to entrepreneurship (Sternberg 2011). The reasons for this appear to be that innovation also depends on other aspects or dimensions of proximity, including technological, cultural or institutional proximity, as well as on the ability of firms to develop non-local knowledge-related linkages (Boschma 2005). From this perspective, population or employment density is therefore seen to be something of a 'catch-all' phenomenon incorporating many different types of linkages and interactions, with density itself being associated with the centrifugal forces resulting from relatively higher land and labour costs (Brakman and van Marrewijk 2013). As such, once a firm's linkages with other firms, institutions and different labour markets are properly accounted for, then innovation appears to be less likely to be related to density due to these associated centrifugal costs and more likely to be related to the extent of the links with both local and non-local knowledge sources (Simonen and McCann 2008, 2010). These various findings highlight the importance of understanding the relationship between the local context and the type and frequency (McCann 2007) of knowledge linkages, knowledge exchanges, and knowledge transmission-effects which are essential for innovation. In particular, the degree of connectivity (McCann and Acs 2011) between an individual region and other external sources of knowledge appears to be essential for innovation. Such connectivity can be related to other firms and other institutions and these other firms or institutions can be either locally or externally located. Obviously not all knowledge flows are local, and it is likely that the frequency (McCann 2007) and intensity (Shearmur and Doloreux 2013) of the knowledge interactions between firms and other knowledge sources will differ according to both the geographical context and also the nature of the knowledge being generated or acquired. Nor is it necessarily the case that the most innovative activities are the most geographically clustered (Macpherson 2008).

Many urban economic arguments (Glaeser 2011: Glaeser et al. 2010) largely treat the links between geography, entrepreneurship and innovation as being analogous to the arguments relating cities to local knowledge spillovers, yet the available evidence (OECD 2011, 2013b) suggests that in reality these relationships are far more complex, varied and nuanced than this simple analogy suggests. Innovation emerges from many different types of spatial and institutional systems and the links between innovation, entrepreneurship and cities remain rather less clearcut than is often assumed. The different arguments and approaches can be reduced to the basic question of how important local or non-local interactions are for innovation, and consequently how important for innovation it is to be in or out of a particular place (Boschma and Frenken 2011; Gertler 2003; Lagendijk and Oinas 2005; McCann 2007; Torre and Rallet 2005). Following the Pavitt (1984) approach to classifying the sources of innovation according to the nature and characteristics of knowledge (Pavitt 2000; Iammarino and Mccann 2006, 2013), there are many arguments which suggest that the knowledge-transactions mechanisms driving innovation may differ markedly between places (Iammarino and McCann 2006, 2013). These differences depend on the nature of the local firm and industrial structures, the types of knowledge investments made, and the knowledge-related objectives of the firms. Firms whose knowledge-exchange requirements are less frequent than others are more likely to locate in more peripheral and cheaper locations, while firms with more frequent knowledge-exchange requirements will tend to favour greater proximity and more expensive urban areas (McCann 2007). At the same time, however, these location choices also depend on the extent to which the knowledge is freely available in a disembodied form or rather embodied in particular human capital (Iammarino and McCann 2006). Many advanced technology knowledge breakthroughs and innovations are accomplished in a closed environment, with employees working largely under conditions of secrecy and silence (Grindley and Teece 1997) irrespective of the employment or population density of the local urban area (McCann and Arita 2006), and many highly innovative activities take place in non-clustered locations. What these observations imply is that whereas urban economists typically assume that the more localised knowledge spillovers are likely to be associated with higher knowledge-content exchanges, this may not necessarily be the case at all, and the opposite may often be true. The need for secrecy to protect proprietary information and to avoid unintended outward knowledge spillovers means that where knowledge exchanges do take place across large geographical distances, these cases often reflect low frequency but high knowledge-intensity and high knowledge-content interactions (McCann 2007), whereas many local and urban knowledge interactions often reflect high frequency but low intensity or low knowledge content exchanges (Iammarino and McCann 2006, 2013).

These knowledge-spillover risk arguments suggest that urban locations will offer an environment favourable to the dissemination and diffusion of non-fundamental technological changes, whereas other types of environments may be more conducive to more fundamental technological progress. Indeed, evidence from the UK's small and medium-sized enterprises (Lee and Rodriguez-Pose 2013) shows that while the levels of innovation are higher in urban areas than in non-urban areas, these advantages are not large (Nathan and Lee 2013) and the major advantages for innovation within urban areas tend to be in the form of product and process innovations which are new to the firm but not to the industry (Lee and Rodriguez-Pose 2013). In other words, while urban clustering somewhat favours innovation, it tends to favour incremental innovations comprised largely of imitating, mimicking or copying, rather than fundamental technological innovations. Urban scale and density only capture part of the innovation story, and many aspects of the role played by geography in fostering innovation and entrepreneurship appear to be related to other issues.

Recently, a new widespread and growing body of evidence has emerged demonstrating that the relationship between geography and innovation is also shaped by technological proximity, or more precisely, what is known as 'technological relatedness' (Frenken et al. 2007). Empirical evidence on the relationships between the economic geography of innovation and growth is closely connected to the relatedness of the emerging technologies and skills (Neffke et al. 2011), and particularly at the regional level (Boschma and Iammarino 2009; Boschma et al. 2012). What this approach implies is that the likelihood of new technological developments to emerge, to survive, and to develop in a particular location, is higher if the technological developments are in a similar technological class to the activities in which the location already has strength and experience. Moreover, the empirical evidence suggests that this principle applies not only to new technological innovations, but also to new sales, new exports (Hausmann et al. 2013) and to new skills (Neffke et al. 2011). Regions are more likely to grow steadily over time if they develop according to the principle of 'related variety', whereby a region diversifies slowly on the basis of the technologies and skills in which it already has longstanding experience and skills. The conceptual underpinnings of these empirical findings follow on naturally from many of the insights of the economics of knowledge (Foray 2004, 2009), which posits that many aspects of growth are associated with new knowledge developments which proceed along evolutionary principles (Boschma and Martin 2010). However, these evolutionary principles do not imply that growth is random or cumulative, but rather that innovation-led growth is heavily shaped by the prevailing levels of cognitive proximity between firms and other institutions, which in turn depends on the existing linkages and connections between them. Innovation can only take place of the requisite skills and technologies are already in place, and therefore, if skills and technological profiles differ across regions, the patterns of growth will be closely related to these existing patterns, and will only diverge slowly from the existing long run trajectories. As such, the role of innovation in driving economic growth is argued to be shaped by, and embedded in, the existing technological frameworks, routines, institutional systems and communities of practice. These routines, systems and communities of practice are also argued to be heavily influenced by cultural and institutional issues, which are likely to have emerged over many years. As such, economic and technological history is consequently argued to matter critically in terms of linking innovation to economic geography, over and above simply questions of scale. Taken together, these various arguments therefore imply that there is no automatic advantage for innovation associated with either geographical proximity (Boschma 2005) or with being in an urban location, because in addition it appears to depend on other dimensions of proximity, including cognitive, cultural, institutional and technological proximity (Boschma and Frenken 2011). This therefore represents quite a different understanding of the relationship between innovation, entrepreneurship and economic geography than the scale-based and density-based approach advocated by many urban economists.

While firms in all regions are able to generate innovations, the broad range of available evidence suggests that the dominant modes of innovation in each region will tend to differ according to a region's industrial structure, its economic history, technological profile, institutional arrangements and its degree of geographical peripherality (ESPON 2012; OECD 2011, 2013b). Similarly, the importance of innovation generation or innovation absorption in a region's growth profile also differs markedly between regions (OECD 2011, 2013b). Some regions are well-known for leading in the development of new technologies, and innovations in these regions therefore tend to be concentrated at the technological frontiers. This is typically the case, for example, with regions dominated by many high-technology activities, and these regions are described as innovation-producing regions (ibid.). On the other hand, the growth profile of many other regions is often characterised more by adoption of innovations developed in other sectors or regions, which are then adapted for use in different settings from which they initially emerged. These regions are known as innovation-absorbing regions (ibid.) and may, for example, include regions with little or no R&D capacity, as is often the case in peripheral or sparsely populated areas (ESPON 2012). As we have seen, innovation is increasingly understood as being multi-faceted, and while formal R&D-based innovation is one mode of innovation, non-formal R&D-based forms of innovation such as practice-based innovation are also very important in many contexts, as also are various types of social and business innovations (Paunov 2013). Many of the innovations which occur in developing regions are of these non-formal-R&D types of innovation (ibid.). At the same time, some advanced and wealthy regions, including many of the world's leading financial centres, often reflect these types of innovation-using regions, whereby innovations from the information and communications technologies are adopted, adapted and embodied in the products, services and systems of the financial markets (OECD 2011, 2013b).

These alternative regional pathways linking innovations and economic growth, as reflected by the relative importance of innovation-using activities or innovation-producing activities (European Commission 2012), or alternatively between R&D-based innovation and non-R&D-based innovation, all follow naturally from the seminal Pavitt (1984) logic. Again, these different pathways to innovation highlight the importance of having a broad systemic view of innovation; such a view is underpinned by an awareness of the different elements and modes of innovation which are likely to differ significantly between different contexts and places. Indeed, the available survey data suggests that while firms in all regions do innovate, the composite indicators of regional innovation performance (European Commission 2012) demonstrate that regional differences in innovation performance still tend to be very marked and persistent. In some cases these differences can give rise to what are sometimes known as 'islands of excellence', which can co-exist with many low productivity activities. These types of situations result in large productivity gaps between firms (Paunov 2013), and also between places, and this phenomenon has been particularly marked in some parts of central Europe (Baláž 2007; Paunov 2013). This raises the challenge of identifying the best ways both foster excellence while at the same time encouraging and facilitating the diffusion of knowledge, so as to help the overall growth and development process by reducing inequalities and widening opportunities (Paunov 2013).

The complex systemic nature of innovation, the different potential pathways to innovation, and the enormous heterogeneity of regions in terms of their innovation capacity, all provide the backdrop against which innovation policies operate. Having examined the key features of innovation, the shifts in our understanding of the nature of innovation both as a process and as a phenomenon, and finally the ways in which we now capture the features of innovation empirically, it is now time to consider the case for innovation policy per se, and in particular at the level of the region, and specifically the form that such policies should take. These are the issues to which we now turn.

5.5 THE CASE FOR INNOVATION POLICY AT THE REGIONAL LEVEL: MARKET FAILURES AND SYSTEMS FAILURES

Nowadays it is widely accepted that knowledge-related investment activities generally benefit from good horizontal and economy-wide framework policies relating to issues such as the ease of tax compliance, business foundation, market deregulation and the upgrading of human capital, as well as macroeconomic stability. However, there is also a growing consensus internationally that when it comes to questions of innovation carefully designed policy interventions can play an important and constructive role in fostering knowledge-related activities. In particular, in terms of promoting growth and development, a key aim of modern innovation policy is to counter the types of market failures which restrict knowledge-related investments (OECD 2010). In order to achieve this, policy interventions are designed to stimulate private R&D and innovation-related investments in those specific situations where the social rates of return of knowledge investments are likely to be much greater than the private rates of return on these investments (Ortega-Argilés 2012; Scotchmer 2004). Policy actions such as patent protection measures and R&D subsidies have often been advocated as important elements in the policy toolkit (Ortega-Argilés 2012), and in some cases these interventions are applied generally as horizontal policy actions underpinning economy-wide framework conditions, while in other cases they have been applied in a rather more selective manner (OECD 2010, 2011, 2013b). More recently, there has also been an increased emphasis on the role that the scale advantages and reduced uncertainty associated with public procurement schemes may play in driving demand-led innovation, and these may be particularly important in helping to overcome certain nationwide aspects of technological inertia (OECD

2012). However, the discussions regarding the conditions under which innovation-related interventions and actions should be applied generally or selectively are very important for our purposes because regions differ markedly. Therefore, as with the case for regional development policy as a whole, it is essential to consider the justification for innovation policy having some selective elements to it which are related to regional issues. At this stage we are not considering the nature of these potentially selective elements, but rather what the underlying case is for an innovation policy having some regionally-specific selective features. After dealing with these issues we then move on to the arguments regarding what such features might look like, as derived from the smart specialisation logic.

The theoretical arguments which underpin innovation policy fall into two broad groups, namely market-failure arguments and systems-failure arguments (McCann and Ortega-Argilés 2013). To begin with, we will first examine both sets of arguments, before setting these rather generic arguments into context of geography. As we will see shortly, translating the basic non-spatial innovation policy arguments into an explicitly geographical and regional setting somewhat alters various aspects of these arguments, and as we will see this translation process itself underpins and justifies the application of smart specialisation principles at the level of the region.

In neo-classical models, apart from broad-based horizontal policies, there are also various theoretical arguments which underpin the case for industrial policy, of which innovation policy might be one such policy option. Regarding the broad conceptual case for industrial policy per se, and more specifically here we focus on innovation policy, the case for *selective* policies rests on three broad lines of market failure arguments, namely infant industry arguments, agglomeration and spillovers, and rent-switching arguments (Crafts 2010, 2012). As regards regional issues and innovation issues, it is just the first two market failure arguments which are relevant for our purposes here.

The first market failure argument favouring selective industrial policy is based on an infant industry argument and this argument rests on the assumption that new firms in new industries require a certain degree of support or protection from market forces until they are sufficiently resilient to withstand competition effects. This argument is often deemed to be particularly pertinent in the case of new and emerging technologies which offer significant opportunities for broad-based development but which also involve high levels of risk in the early life-cycle stages of the technologies. The high levels of risk may overly deter investments in these key technologies at a critical juncture in their development, thereby limiting the possibilities for embedding these new technologies in the wider economic system.

The second market failure argument justifying selective industrial policy relates to the question of the potential spillovers associated with agglomeration and industrial clustering. Many commentators argue in favour of dismantling many of the land-use regulations associated with restrictive planning regimes in order to foster growth and development. The argument here is that restrictive planning regimes impose unnecessary costs on business and households which reduce both utility and profits, and the removal of many of these artificial barriers across a country will consequently encourage growth in the appropriate locations. Yet, many of these nationwide land-use deregulation arguments can be considered to be largely akin to more general horizontal framework policies such as market deregulation actions, improved business foundation and compliance procedures, and as such, are not directly related to the case for selective industrial policy. It is only if such deregulation policies were implemented in a specific subset of locations that such arguments would come under the heading of industrial policies

For example, decisions to build specific pieces of key infrastructure in particular locations, or decisions to support particular developments in particular locations via subsidies or specific legal actions, do indeed fall under the broad heading of selective industrial policy. The reason is that such actions are designed to influence the behaviour and outcomes of a particular set of firms or commercial actors, defined in this case primarily in locational terms rather than in sectoral terms, although these two dimensions often overlap. While such policies are often presented by their advocates as being 'national' issues, such interventions are selective by nature. Similarly, as we have already seen, almost all ostensibly 'space-blind' sectoral policies have a locational dimension to them, irrespective of whether this was explicitly stated or intended (Barca et al. 2012). As such, any regional or urban policies, infrastructure policies, or specific land-use policies, which have a particular locational focus, can indeed be considered in some sense to be forms of selective industrial policy, albeit ones which may or may not have a particular sectoral dimension to them. Some cluster policies, for example, have both an explicit sectoral dimension as well as a locational dimension, although this is not always the case (Ketels 2013).

In terms of specific innovation policy issues rather than industrial policy issues per se, the economic geography argument is rather more complex, and actually has rather conflicting sides to it. Firstly, following the logic of economic geography, if agglomerations are associated with higher levels of knowledge spillovers, any obstacles that restrict the growth of agglomerations should be removed, and incentives for promoting agglomeration, via infrastructure investments, housing subsidies or land-release schemes, should be promoted (Crafts 2010, 2012). In some ways these actions can be seen as the spatial parallels of the arguments favouring R&D subsidies, R&D tax relief, or policies providing support for patenting activities, in that they are designed to foster knowledge engagements. On the other hand, however, the field of knowledge economics also offers a different twist on these arguments. While the spatial clustering of activities increases the chances of firms benefiting from unintended inward knowledge spillovers, such clustering also increases the likelihood that firms will experience unintended outward knowledge spillovers (Grindley and Teece 1997). The potential beneficiaries of these spillovers will exhibit free-rider behaviour and are likely to be those with lower knowledge investments. In contrast, those firms with greater knowledge investments also have the most to lose from such unintended outward knowledge spillovers. For high knowledge-intensive activities, and in particular those innovation activities involving significant levels of R&D investments, it is likely that the balance of the net benefits and risks associated with unintended knowledge inflows and unintended knowledge outflows shifts in favour of firms aiming to avoid any unintended outward knowledge spillovers. In such cases, either knowledge-intensive firms will relocate elsewhere away from the cluster or alternatively the remaining clustered firms will not invest in sufficient quantities because of the risks of failing to protect their proprietary knowledge (Iammarino and McCann 2006, 2013; McCann and Mudambi 2004, 2005). In these cases innovation policies based on R&D subsidies may be justified in promoting innovation on the grounds that they are needed to counter the negative externalities associated with the inherent risks associated with clustering. The aim of such a policy would be to promote investment in exactly those types of activities which will then provide positive externalities at a later stage.

In terms of innovation, the difficulty here with the market failure treatment of the agglomeration argument is that the two externality mechanisms linking innovation and geography actually work in the opposite direction (McCann and Arita 2006). Many commentators will tend to assume that for innovation purposes the beneficial aspects of clustering or agglomeration are likely to be dominant, but the basic point here is that there is no simple innovation-clustering relationship, as we have already seen.

These two broad lines of market failure argumentation both share a common thread, in that it is assumed that the inherent market failures mean that the types of investments required for innovation are likely to be insufficiently realised and therefore that partial public support for these types of investments may be required. Whether this argument holds in practice depends not only on the public good nature of knowledge but also the types of knowledge and the levels of knowledge being generated. Here, the particular features of knowledge which determine its level of production are described as 'appropriability' and 'cumulativeness', and these terms are widely used in the literature on the economics of knowledge and technological change (Fagerberg et al. 2005; Foray 2004; Swann 2009). The term 'appropriability' describes the firm's ability to protect and internalise its own knowledge so that the firm's investors can reap the benefits from the firm's use of this knowledge. The term 'cumulativeness' reflects the ability of the firm to build on its previous knowledge and also the extent to which the firm's current production and use of new knowledge is dependent on its previous knowledge. Although all forms of knowledge exhibit public good characteristics, different types of knowledge exhibit different levels of appropriability and cumulativeness.

Firms use different methods to maximise the 'appropriability' of their knowledge such as acquiring patents, undertaking R&D in highly secretive and restrictive laboratory facilities, or designing specific employment contracts with explicit secrecy requirements, depending on the characteristics of the knowledge. However, even allowing for these measures, there are still many situations where it remains very difficult for firms to appropriate all of the potential benefits of their own internal knowledge investments, due to the costs associated with patenting and enforcing specific employment contracts. Moreover, these difficulties are likely to be magnified in the case of start-ups and small firms, because the costs to these firms of undertaking patenting activities and enforcing restrictive and secretive employment contracts may be too great. Such market failures are therefore likely to reduce the level of knowledge-related investments undertaken by small firms to a greater degree than large firms, and therefore given the perceived importance of start-ups and SMEs to the innovation performance of the whole economy (NESTA 2009; Tether et al. 1997), these market failure arguments often emphasise the policy priority for helping SMEs overcome such knowledge-related investment difficulties.

Empirically, many studies analysing the returns to R&D do regard appropriability as a real problem (Ortega-Argilés 2012). Therefore, in order to maximise knowledge-related investments there is a need to ensure that knowledge investors receive their due entrepreneurial rewards while avoiding as many of the free-rider problems and public good problems associated with knowledge as possible. Importantly for our purposes, such problems may be particularly acute in the case of clustered or agglomerated firms such that clustering or agglomeration does not automatically imply increased knowledge accumulation. Ironically, the increased local knowledge spillovers associated with industrial clustering are also likely to *reduce* the levels of knowledge-related investments (Iammarino and McCann 2006, 2013), such that the overall net knowledge-related investment effect of clustering is actually rather ambiguous. The reason is that the actual net knowledge-related outcomes of geographical behaviour also depend heavily on the institutional mechanisms governing the knowledge-related transactions operating in the industry and these in turn comprise specific types of contractual and legal mechanism designed both to facilitate knowledge-related exchanges while at the same time restricting unintended knowledge spillovers. The results of these arguments are that the effects of clustering on knowledge-related investments will also tend to depend heavily on the types of industries locally present and the types of knowledge-related investments they typically undertake (Iammarino and McCann 2006, 2013).

While in general most observers tend to assume that the relationship between the levels of knowledge-related investments and the size of a region and its cities is positive, the important point here is that fostering clusters or agglomerations alone is itself unlikely to display strong positive impacts on knowledge-related investments. As already discussed, this is because when it comes to the issues linking knowledge investments, innovation and economic growth, there are many other influences and factors at work beyond simply geographical scale issues (McCann and Acs 2011; Iammarino and McCann 2013), the net effects of which can be rather ambiguous. As such, when land use policies designed to increase city sizes are predicated primarily on arguments about fostering innovation they become rather weak, because there are many other geographical influences on innovation, many of which are likely to be conditioned by technological and institutional phenomena, and almost all of which differ by locality (Moretti 2012).

Given the heterogeneous role which local factors play in fostering innovation, the broad consensus is that policies aimed at identifying ways to foster entrepreneurship, creativity and the exploitation of new ideas must pay explicit attention to the specifics of the local context (Hughes 2012; OECD 2011, 2013b; World Bank 2010, 2011). This is because:

> like politics, all innovation is local: each community has its own comparative advantages. Local government must build on their existing capabilities by leveraging local strengths and expertise. The use of public funds to create jobs must be reserved for cases where there are important market failures and the

community has a credible chance of building a self-sustaining cluster. Ultimately policy-makers should realize that when it comes to local development, there is no free lunch. (Moretti 2012 p. 214)

At the same time, the complex links between geography and innovation mean that the case for innovation policy with a regional dimension is clearly broader than just supply-side market failure arguments, and explicitly involves the types of innovation-systems arguments which nowadays dominate contemporary thinking about innovation. As Hughes (2012) explains, market failure arguments 'provide important rationales for public sector intervention, but rarely provide sufficient guidance for the degree of intervention in particular instances; nor do they address the many other potential institutional and connection failures which may arise in an innovation system' (Hughes 2012, p. 38). Innovation policy design goes much further than the standard market failure arguments, with actions and interventions aimed at identifying and fostering the technological transitions which are best suited to the specific context (Hughes 2012).

In the case of the role played by geography in innovation these policy considerations are paramount because, as we have already seen, the complex relationships between the beneficial effects of unintended inward knowledge outflows geography itself may themselves contribute to local institutional and systems failures. Moreover, following on from the innovation-systems and evolutionary economic geography arguments, such problems may be further magnified by system failures associated with transition and lock-in problems (David 1985), which limit or inhibit the ability of a particular local system to adjust towards new technological structures (Boschma and Martin 2010). As well as information problems, such difficulties can also be due to the inertia or sunk costs associated with existing public- or private-sector investments, and previous policy decisions. As Hughes (2012) points out, depending on the local systems configuration, these institutional features may either stifle or enhance the knowledge flows necessary for innovation. The innovation-systems approach therefore argues that a key role of innovation policy should be to overcome local systems-configuration failures by helping to improve the alignment of institutional incentives, the pathways for knowledge diffusion and the mechanisms for fostering collaboration. This systems type of thinking therefore implies that while the market failure justifications for innovation policy are very important, they are not necessarily the complete rationale, and there is no reason to assume that the implementation of such corrective interventions will automatically lead to some form of 'innovation equilibrium'.

Taken together, all of the above arguments imply that in addition to addressing market failure issues, the aims of modern innovation policies therefore also include addressing both national and local systems-failures issues (McCann and Ortega-Argilés 2013). Importantly, the role which the heterogeneity of localities plays in influencing different innovation pathways implies that as well as ensuring that the broader and national horizontal framework conditions are in place, good innovation policy also requires a specifically local dimension. In this sense good innovation policy is also likely to be in part a selective industrial policy.

The local dimension of innovation policies is to be derived from the involvement of, and engagement with, local institutions and local knowledge assets in the policy development, policy design and policy delivery processes. This is necessary in order that all aspects of the policy can most beneficially leverage as far as possible off the insights, experiences and influences of these local actors. Indeed, systemic approaches to innovation applied at the regional level (Cooke and Morgan 1998; Morgan 1997), which emphasise these local and specific relationships between firms and institutions, have become increasingly popular and influential in many academic and policy arenas (Cooke et al. 2006; McCann and Ortega-Argilés 2013; Moulaert and Sekia 2003).

In terms of policy efficacy, all of the above arguments imply that policies which build on and foster local engagement will best respond to the geographic heterogeneity associated with innovation processes and the ensuing locally-tailored solutions will help to maximise the viability of policy interventions, as long as all incentives are correctly aligned. Obviously this local or regional dimension to innovation policy is also entirely consistent with the broader place-based approach to economic development, which as we have already seen, advocates engaging with and enabling local institutions and actors to be key elements of the policy design and delivery processes.

In terms of fostering innovation in different types of countries and regions the World Bank (2010 p. 19) advocates the setting of 'strategic focal points' according to the technological and institutional capabilities of the country, an approach which is similar to the arguments of Iammarino and McCann (2006, 2013). The priority in countries with high knowledge and technological potential and a strong institutional framework would be the promotion of innovation-related clusters and the enhancing of the value-added in supply chains.[3] There are many debates regarding the veracity of such approaches including sceptics (Martin and Sunley 2003) and supporters (Ketels 2013) of cluster-type arguments. However, if cluster building is perceived as being largely akin to small-scale new industrial town development, as is argued by Duranton

(2011), then this represents a very different view of clusters as is typically understood nowadays or implemented in the EU case. On this point, US comparisons are not particularly instructive for many European discussions. During the last two decades there have been many local policies ostensibly operating under a 'cluster' label in the US,[4] but where such policies occur they tend to be primarily sectoral rather than place-based in nature (Landabaso and Rosenfeld 2009), emerging from a plethora of different combinations of state, industry and federal policies (Drabenstott 2005). Indeed, outside of East Asia (Sonobe and Keijiro 2006) most of the available evidence (Van der Linde 2003) suggests that in the advanced economies the type of cluster policies described by Duranton (2011) are actually not very common. While there are indeed examples of these types of approaches in Europe, some of which appear to have had some success (Viladecans-Marsal and Arauzo-Carod 2012) and some of which appear to have not (Martin et al. 2011), the vast majority of actions in Europe implemented via EU Cohesion Policy under a 'cluster' heading tend to follow the intra-industry linkage-development logic (Landabaso and Rosenfeld 2009) of the sectoral approach to innovation systems (Hughes 2012) and global value-chain literatures (OECD 2013a), rather than the small-scale new industrial town development model described by Duranton (2011). In Europe the latter type of initiative represents only a tiny fraction of overall EU Cohesion Policy expenditure,[5] which in terms of innovation-related issues heavily emphasises SME funding, R&D investments, skills-training and infra-structure investment. Where initiatives under the heading of 'cluster' policies do exist in Europe (Borrás and Tsagdis 2008; Landabaso and Rosenfeld 2009) they are far more likely to emerge primarily from the actions of sectoral ministries than from primarily regional actions, or from largely sectoral-led combinations of both.

In middle-income countries or regions, including those in some parts of Central, Eastern and Southern Europe, for those with a weaker but improving institutional context the World Bank (2010) argues that the innovation-policy priority should be on improving the value-added of the wealth from natural resources wealth, increased value-adding in supply chains, and also the increased commercialisation of technology, and in particular around the enhancement of niche and non-traditional exports. These regions can also benefit from inward FDI flows and wider education policies. In contrast, in very weak institutional contexts the innovation-policy priority should be on the building up and enhancing of those small 'pockets of dynamism' which are observed to exist and also on basic institutional capacity-building (World Bank 2010).

At this point it is important to raise and respond to two criticisms of these types of approaches which reappear intermittently. A first possible concern which has been raised against such a policy logic is that the information requirements necessary to implement these types of policies may be overly onerous. Indeed, as we have seen in Chapter 4, if the intention was for central government policy planners to design optimal and differentiated policies from a top-down perspective this would indeed be a valid criticism. In contrast, however, the place-based approach to such policies advocated in the Cohesion Policy reforms follows very much a bottom-up logic as well as a top-down logic, whereby local institutions and actors are intended to be key providers of the bottom-up local knowledge inputs to the policy design process. If such bottom-up activities are indeed evident then the information requirements are no longer overly onerous. Indeed, the information requirements mean that it is often at the lower regional or technological levels that innovation policies are most appropriately designed and targeted in order to increase the likelihood of success (Hughes 2012). This is why the involvement and engagement of local institutions is so critical for effective innovation policy design and delivery, as is consistent with wider arguments regarding the importance of multi-level governance.

A second criticism of these types of policies which appears frequently is that inevitably such policies will end up as policies of 'picking winners'. As Hughes (2012) argues, however, the critique that modern innovation policy is a matter of 'picking winners' is incorrect and is based on an outdated perspective of the role of such policies. The 'picking winners' critique emerged from the shortcomings of the out-moded industrial relations and trade-protection environment of earlier decades in which governments were often using policies to bolster and protect national champions in a range of sectors, at the expense of the public welfare gains associated with deregulation and liberalisation. However, today, the importance of open and contestable markets and deregulated industries is almost universally accepted, and therefore the picking winners critique is also outdated. Instead, the types of innovation policy interventions advocated here reflect rather more a matter of what Hughes (2012) describes as being analogous to 'choosing races and placing bets'.

This analogy of Hughes (2012) reflects a country such as the UK where gambling is a leisure pursuit for many members of the general public who are continuously betting on horse-races or dog-races. Such people carefully study the recent performance of the horses and dogs, the weather conditions of the venue and the track surface, the recent performances of the other competitors, as well as the constraints (handicaps) faced by each competitor in terms of the weights they are required to carry. Then in response to the outcomes and results of the races these gamblers then adjust their subsequent betting strategies. Such gamblers are continuously studying the evidence and adjusting their strategies in the light of the results and outcomes.

This analogy of Hughes (2012) also succinctly captures the idea the policymakers should always base the logic and design of policy interventions as far as possible on baseline evidence and in response to a detailed analysis of the alternative possibilities, opportunities and constraints. This represents the strategic element of policy design in which the intended results and outcomes of the policy are clarified and the policy delivery process begins. Then, once policy actions are underway the policy process also requires ongoing monitoring and evaluation in order to identify the extent to which the various elements of the strategy are successful or not. This represents the implementation phase of the policy delivery process. Finally, in response to the qualitative and quantitative data which emerges as a result of both of the earlier phases of the policy cycle, these data are then compiled and reflected upon and subsequent policy interventions are adjusted in the light of the intended.

This type of evidence-based policy cycle is explicitly results-oriented, and allows for learning by doing (Arrow 1962), because the three phases of the cycle overlap and involve feedbacks and recursive links. For example, some policy actions may be adjusted at earlier points than others in response to the emerging evidence. In fact, this type of innovation policy logic had already been advocated in the UK as early as 2007 (Hughes 2012). In their advice to central government, the UK Council for Science and Technology (CST 2007), the most senior science policy advisory body in the UK, proposed that in order to foster innovation and technological progress, innovation policy should follow a step-by-step approach based: firstly, on the compilation of all of the available evidence concerning how the nature and distinctiveness of technological competence is related to each specific context; secondly, an analysis of the potential market size for any successful innovations in the relevant technology space; and thirdly, the identification of potential private sector collaboration based on a global value-chain analysis. This stepwise approach should then also be viewed in the context of wider societal benefits of successful innovation, the risks and effects of policy failures, and finally the governance and institutional capacity design and delivery of the policy (Hughes 2012).

The type of policy approach described by Hughes (2012) shares many of the well-designed industrial policy features advocated by Rodrik (2007) which allow for trial and error actions, policy experimentation and policy learning, policy monitoring and the adjustment of policy interventions in the light of new evidence derived from processes of monitoring and evaluation. This type of policy logic which is analogous to 'choosing races and placing bets' (Hughes 2012) is clearly a very long way away from an environment of 'picking winners'.

While at this stage we can allay the two major concerns raised against modern policy approaches, and particularly those applied at the local level, at this stage it is still necessary for us to consider exactly what form of policy approach or policy framework reflects all of these desired properties and is also applicable at the regional level. As we have already seen, in particular situations the general market failure arguments described above are not especially informative as to what specific form policy interventions or actions should take (Hughes 2012). Similarly, the types of spillover discussions common in urban and regional economics are not particularly useful in terms of informing innovation policy design, because they tend to be rather cursory and very superficial, and ignore most of the specific and complex features of knowledge spillovers and their interactions with institutional issues. Much more detailed discussions of these issues are evident in other fields including the economics of knowledge and technological change (Foray 2004; Swann 2009), and linking these discussions to economic geography is therefore also essential for informing policy design (Iammarino and McCann 2006, 2013). As we will see in the following chapter, within the European regional and urban policy, many of the important elements of modern regional innovation policy design have in fact emerged from those fields which explicitly examine the economics of knowledge and technological change.

5.6 CONCLUSIONS

This chapter has outlined the broad case for the types of innovation policies which have explicitly regional or local components as fundamental elements of their policy logic and framework. Not all innovation-related or knowledge-related growth policies will have local or regional elements to them, and early science policy and innovation policy discussions rarely involved questions of geography. However, over time as our understanding of innovation has evolved, the role played by geography in innovation has also become increasingly central to such discussions. Nowadays there is a widespread understanding of the role which local or regional factors can play both in shaping innovation processes and innovation outcomes, and these shifts in our understanding have heavily influenced recent policy debates. Over the last decade in particular, an increasing awareness of the role played by local factors in fostering or inhibiting innovation processes has resulted in various shifts in innovation policy thinking. In particular, there have been increased emphases towards both broader notions of innovation and also the importance of addressing the local market failures and systems failures inhibiting innovation. These notions move well beyond simply arguments about urban expansion and increasingly put institutional and governance challenges centre stage.

NOTES

1. http://en.wikipedia.org/wiki/Moore's_law
2. https://www1.oecd.org/eco/growth/2496902.pdf
   http://www.oecd.org/sti/ieconomy/measuringtheinformationeconomy.htm
3. See:http://www.whitehouse.gov/sites/default/files/omb/assets/memoranda_2010/m10-21.pdf
   http://www.whitehouse.gov/blog/2010/06/30/place-based-investments
   http://yosemite.epa.gov/opa/admpress.nsf/0/75E1F57EB6D0FCEC8525788CA0063A5CB
4. http://www.isc.hbs.edu/cluster-mapping-project.htm
5. There are of course activities of this type in Europe such as the European Cluster Observatory (http://www.clusterobservatory.eu/index.html) but the basic point that such actions only represent a very tiny fraction of EU Cohesion Policy interventions (Landabaso and Rosenfeld 2009) remains valid.

6. Smart specialisation and European regions

6.1 INTRODUCTION

In the case of the EU Cohesion Policy programming period 2014–2020, the major regional innovation agenda is known as *smart specialisation.* As already discussed in the previous chapter, many of the insights into regional innovation policy actually emerged initially from outside of the arenas of regional economics, urban economics or economic geography, and this is also the case with the European regional innovation agenda. Smart specialisation as a concept originally emerged from the fields examining the economics of knowledge and technological change (Foray 2004; Swann 2009). However, this original non-spatial and largely theoretical concept has been slowly translated into an explicitly geographical and primarily pragmatic schema which is proving to be a powerful and workable policy tool. Interestingly, this process of translating a non-spatial and theoretical concept to an explicitly regional and pragmatic tool has involved the adoption of new knowledge and its adaptation to a specific context, exactly along the lines advocated by the concept itself. As such, in terms of innovation issues, the policy development process inherent in the reforms to EU Cohesion Policy itself largely mirrors the logic of the smart specialisation concept.

The smart specialisation concept is now an important element in both the new 'Innovation Union' flagship programme of the European Commission and also the EU Cohesion Policy reforms.[1] The aim of this chapter is to explain how the concept has been adopted and adapted in the context of EU Cohesion Policy and also how the policy logic inherent in smart specialisation has been implemented in practical terms. There is now widespread interest in the policy implications of the approach and it is important to clarify the important role which smart specialisation can play in the Cohesion Policy arena, as well as to correct a few misunderstandings and to dispel a few myths which have emerged regarding the concept and its application in EU policies. In order to do this, the chapter will first explain the background to the emergence of the concept. The smart specialisation idea evolved out of discussions regarding rather puzzling and serious empirical observations concerning the performance of the European economies. In particular, these observations relate to what is known as the 'Transatlantic Productivity Gap'. Understanding the backdrop to the theoretical development of the early smart specialisation concept is important as it situates the original conceptual discussions in a very real empirical context addressing very real empirical challenges. Having examined the backdrop to the emergence of the smart specialisation concept we are able to discuss the various features of the original non-spatial and theoretical concept and also to explain how the concept has been subsequently adapted and applied in a geographical setting suitable for responding to regional issues.

At this point it is also important for us to address two major concerns which could be raised by some commentators regarding the efficacy and workability of the concept in European regions. Firstly, to some observers these different agendas of Innovation Union and EU Cohesion Policy may appear to display conflicting goals. In particular, while on the one hand the aims of the EU Innovation Union programme are to generate and disseminate EU-wide economies of scale in knowledge-intensive sectors, on the other hand EU Cohesion Policy seeks to promote the development of many of the EU's weaker regions. Consequently, a cursory reading of much of the literature from economic geography and from urban and regional economics suggests, at least prima facie, that these different aims may be mutually incompatible. Secondly, some observers may conclude that smart specialisation only favours stronger regions and that there is little to be gained by adopting this approach by weaker regions. However, as will be argued in this chapter, neither of these criticisms are valid and the following sections are intended to specifically address and counter these concerns. In order to do this we will build on much of the material already discussed in the previous chapter regarding the case for selective industrial policy, the specific case for innovation policy, and ultimately the case for modern approaches to innovation policy at the level of the region. In particular, it will become apparent smart specialisation emerges as being especially useful for many non-core regions as a way of prioritising policy initiatives and ensuring resource concentration, and doing so in a manner which provides weaker regions with the greatest potential benefits from EU Cohesion Policy. As we will see, one of the key benefits for regions of smart specialisation is the potential for learning, capacity-building and 'self discovery' (Hausmann and Rodrik 2003) on the part of local and regional institutions which is associated with the processes of analysis, engagement and knowledge exchange essential in the smart specialisation logic.

Finally, having addressed all of the various conceptual issues concerning both the theoretical validity of the concept and also its practical workability in EU regions, the chapter will move on to explain the various initiatives which have been implemented by the European Commission in order to aid regions in their smart specialisation policy design, development and delivery processes. What will become apparent in these following sections, which draw heavily from McCann and Ortega-Argilés (2014a) and Ortega-Argilés (2012) as well as from McCann and Ortega-Argilés (2013a, b), is that the particular way that the smart specialisation concept is being applied in European regions potentially allows for the objectives of both the Innovation Union and also EU Cohesion Policy to be simultaneously addressed. The reason is that from a regional policy perspective the smart specialisation approach offers a range of advantages for the design of appropriate innovation policymaking, while allowing for the varied evolutionary nature of regional economies (OECD 2012a).

6.2 THE ORIGINS OF THE SMART SPECIALISATION CONCEPT: THE TRANSATLANTIC PRODUCTIVITY GAP

The smart specialisation agenda has been developed in response to the particular innovation policy challenges faced by the EU, but more over recent years the concept has become of broader interest for policymakers in a wide range of other OECD countries (OECD 2012a). The concept is not meant to be a wholly self-contained and independent analytical device, but rather one which provides a practical framework for dealing with the difficult prioritisation challenges faced by policymakers dealing with innovation-related matters. As the OECD (2012a) points out, the smart specialisation concept contains many elements which were already evident in the innovation-systems literature, the entrepreneurship and growth literatures, and in the various transactions costs literatures, as well as the innovation policy advice given to the UK government in 2007 (CST 2007). However, as the OECD (2012a) also makes very clear, a distinctive and important feature of smart specialisation is that it provides a clear policy-prioritisation logic which is well-suited and adaptable to fostering innovation in different types of regional settings including in weaker regions as well as in stronger regions. This feature is particularly important in the highly heterogeneous context of the European regional system.

Yet the original smart specialisation concept had no explicitly geo-graphical aspects to it and was not especially intended to respond to regional matters. Rather, the concept was originally developed out of growing concerns over the last two decades regarding the productivity performance of Europe and the need to envision a European response to the growth challenges of the twenty-first century. The concerns had arisen because in the mid 1990s it became increasingly apparent that the European economies were falling behind the North American economies; a phenomenon known as the 'transatlantic productivity gap' (Ortega-Argilés 2012). This observation was particularly puzzling because the productivity gap emerged at a time which was concurrent with the establishment of the EU Single Market and in the wake of many decades during which Europe had been rapidly catching up with North America. As such, most commentators would have expected exactly the opposite to occur at this time. The observed emergence of this transatlantic produc-tivity gap consequently led to rising concerns as to its causes both in policy circles and in academic circles and spawned a completely new literature aiming to identify its causal factors (Ortega-Argilés et al. 2010, 2014). Many explanations for the evolving productivity gap were offered including arguments relating to differences in labour markets, in manage-ment performance, in organisation issues and in market deregulation. However, the mounting empirical evidence increasingly pointed to the critical role played by new information and communications technologies (ICTs), and in particular the differing experiences of these new tech-nologies between the North American and the European contexts (Ortega-Argilés 2012, 2013). There are two major aspects to these differing experiences.

Firstly, during the 1990s it was the North American ICT-producing sectors which were driving the productivity gap. The US software, hardware, semiconductor and electronics firms were in the vanguard of these new high technological developments in the late 1980s and early to mid 1990s, and generally they out-performed their European counter-parts. Although the ICT-intensive industries in Europe performed better than Europe's non-ICT industries during this period, during the first part of the 1990s the performance of the European ICT-producing firms as a whole was still well below that of their US competitors. The North American high technology firms proved to be intrinsically more competi-tive than their European counterparts and this intrinsic effect is some-times referred to as the 'Silicon Valley' effect (Ortega-Argilés 2012, 2013).

Secondly, by the beginning of the 2000s, the intrinsic effect appeared to have largely disappeared, although the productivity gap persisted well into the next decade beyond the millennium. The reason was that the causes of the persistent productivity gap between the North American and European economies had shifted away from the earlier intrinsic effect to an ensuing 'structural effect'. This structural effect relates to the differences in the composition of competing economies and differences in the various ways in which sectors are interlinked (Ortega-Argilés 2012, 2013). From the mid 1990s onwards the evidence showed that rather than the ICT producers, it was the ICT-using sectors, such as market services and retailing, which were the industries that most accounted for the productivity growth differences between the US and EU (Timmer et al. 2011). It became increasingly apparent from the empirical evidence that cross-sectoral knowledge spillovers and technological linkages related to ICTs were simply much stronger in the North American case than in Europe, and that after the initial positive shock effect of the advent of these new technologies it was the ICT-using sectors rather than ICT-producing sectors which continued to drive the observed productivity gaps. This particular manifestation of the so-called 'new economy' or 'weightless economy' (Quah 2001) has often been referred to in the literature as the 'Walmart Effect', and the evidence pointed to much more significant knowledge-related transmission effects between North American industries than between the equivalent European sectors. The North American sectors which were not producing new ICTs appeared to be far more adept at adopting these new technologies and rapidly adapting them to their specific needs than were the European firms. In contrast, the European economies appeared to be much less able to absorb and transmit new knowledge (Storper 2013) across sectors (Ortega-Argilés 2012) and across regions (Cozza et al. 2012; Ortega-Argilés 2013).

The particularly puzzling aspects of these observed productivity trends was that they were seen to emerge at exactly the very moment that much contemporary economic logic suggested that precisely the opposite would be more likely to occur. ICTs represented the latest genre of general purpose technologies whose impacts would be expected to spread across all sectors, industries and activities, thereby enhancing productivity across a wide range of arenas. Furthermore, at the beginning of the 1990s Europe had just fully embarked on the Single Market project with its massively reduced institutional barriers, and these would be expected to be exploited by opportunities created by the newly-established world wide web which had also just been invented (McCann 2008). To many observers, therefore, this mix of concurrent developments ought to have been exactly the moment when European industry would begin to display greatly increased pan-European economies of scale and increased global competitiveness. Moreover, the assumed increases in global competitiveness would be particularly expected in those activities either developing or harnessing these new ICT-related general purpose technologies.

In marked contrast, however, the observed productivity differences associated with the transatlantic productivity gap, and in particular the causes of the productivity differences, demonstrated just how far EU-wide market deregulation, market integration and structural reforms, still had to go in order to achieve European-wide technology-related and knowledge-related economies of scale (Ortega-Argilés, 2012). The need to overcome market fragmentation and to generate European-wide economies of scale was, of course, a major driving force underpinning the creation of the EU Single Market. However, the experience of the transatlantic productivity gap and the relatively limited ability of Europe's industries to facilitate the transmission and dissemination of newly-emerging knowledge and technologies between sectors, called for a major reconsideration of Europe's economic strengths and weaknesses and possible policy responses.

The policy responses to these growing concerns were in part reflected in the construction of the European Research Area (ERA) agenda. The schemes operating under the ERA agenda provided for European-wide and international consortia to undertake collaborative research projects, and a key intention of such schemes was to foster pan-European knowledge generation and diffusion. However, the emergence and scale of the transatlantic productivity gap, which traversed almost all sectors of the economy including apparently many non-knowledge-intensive sectors, suggested that the European knowledge-related growth challenges extended far beyond simply the research community or just high technology sectors. Consequently, a more fundamental rethinking of the productivity challenges facing Europe was urgently called for, and a rethinking which would move well beyond the confines of the ERA agenda. In order to address these challenges a 'Knowledge for Growth'[2] expert group (K4G) was set up in order to advise the then European Commissioner for Research, Janez Potočnik. The group undertook detailed analytical reflections combined with observations of real-world case studies, and their discussions were conveyed in a series of nine briefing papers published between 2006 and 2009. The deliberations amongst this highly distinguished group of scholars led to the development of a new conceptual framework for thinking about a policy-prioritisation logic which could usefully underpin a range of EU policies aimed at promoting growth. This framework they labelled smart specialisation.

6.3   THE NON-SPATIAL SMART SPECIALISATION CONCEPT

The original non-spatial smart specialisation concept is in some ways a rather abstract construct. However, what initially appears to be a rather abstract and conceptual schema has profound real-world applications, and in particular in the context of regions. In order to understand the importance and applicability of the concept in a regional and spatial setting, it is first essential to discuss the original theoretical concept and to identify its major themes, and then to translate these arguments into a framework which is consistent with economic geography thinking. Finally, we are then able to sketch out the policy implications of the smart specialisation logic for the regional context, and also to address the various concerns which have been raised against the idea.

In order to best grasp the smart specialisation concept it is important to understand the background context from which it emerged. The original non-spatial smart specialisation concept was developed on the basis of a line of reasoning which is related to the observed experience of the weaknesses of the European economy in the wake of the emerging transatlantic productivity gap. As we have already discussed, the central issue here was Europe's systemic weaknesses in terms of the diffusion of new knowledge and new technologies across sectors. At the same time, the concept is also based on a set of theoretical arguments derived from the field of the economics of knowledge and technological change and intended to construct a logical framework which would help in policy prioritisation efforts aimed at countering these weaknesses.

The original non-spatial smart specialisation concept (David et al. 2009; Foray et al. 2009, 2011) assumes that the context in which technological change takes place really matters for the potential technological evolution of innovation systems, and the contextual nature of knowledge and technological change is termed the *knowledge ecology*. In other words, the context in which technological progress operates is not purely exogenous to technological developments but also inherently endogenous. As such, the potential pathways for innovation are argued to depend on the evolutionary experience of the system, and this in turn is assumed to also depend on the inherited structures, institutions and actors present in the system as well as their interrelationships. Moreover, the critical role of a system's knowledge ecology is assumed to hold irrespective of whether the observed technological change is incremental or transformational. One of the key implications of this argument is that knowledge and technology are not perfectly malleable, commutable, flexible or transferrable between sectors and fields, and that technological change and knowledge growth are heavily embedded in and also constrained by the context. Naturally, therefore, different countries and regions will tend to specialise in different fields of knowledge and technology according to their capabilities and their past technological trajectories. These assumptions were already implicit in much of the logic underpinning the ERA, but smart specialisation made these assumptions explicit, and then aimed to develop a policy-prioritisation logic from this perspective. This tendency towards knowledge specialisation based on previous technological trajectories is the first element of the original non-spatial smart specialisation concept.

The next two elements of the original smart specialisation concept are secondly, that of an entrepreneurial search process, and thirdly, that of a domain (David et al. 2009; Foray et al. 2009, 2011). These two elements capture the idea that technological change is driven by entrepreneurs who search out the opportunities for innovation within their particular knowledge domain, by adopting and adapting new technologies and knowledge to different situations, sectors and challenges. The domain in this sense is the technological space within which certain sets of knowledge operate, and this technological space can span science, firms, institutions and other actors, depending on the particular situation. One of the key imperatives of economic policy should be to find ways to enhance these entrepreneurial search processes, because technological progress in general depends on the variety, scale efficiency and effectiveness of these entrepreneurial search processes.

Not all domains are the same, however, and according to the smart specialisation logic, the fourth critical element of the domain is its relevant size. What is understood here by the idea of relevant size is the range of commercial activities or sectors in which the new technological adaptations can most realistically and most likely be applied to a beneficial effect. In particular, as well as the generation of innovations, of particular importance here is the potential beneficial role of spillovers to entrepreneurs within the relevant domain. Given the knowledge economy logic, spillovers were primarily understood as operating intra-sectorally, although inter-sectoral spillovers are also acknowledged (David et al. 2009).

The fifth and final element of the original non-spatial smart specialisation concept is that of the connectedness of the domain. This captures the fact that domains which are highly interconnected with other domains are likely to offer greater learning possibilities than domains which are less connected. The potential for system-learning effects is regarded as being essential for technological progress as well as learning on the part of individual actors, and being connected with other knowledge domains facilitates this.

Of the smart specialisation elements, the knowledge ecology and technological trajectory elements are both evident in the innovation-systems and evolutionary economics literatures. The entrepreneurial search element is evident in the entrepreneurship literature, while the relevant size and the connectedness elements are both evident in the literature on network systems.

The original non-spatial concept of smart specialisation focuses on the elements required to maximise the likely economic potential of entrepreneurial actions, given the technological context. Following McCann and Ortega-Argilés (2014a) it is possible to summarise the various processes and mechanisms by which such potential is most likely to be realised in the following way. Within a particular domain the entrepreneurial search process leads to the identification of the distribution of potential opportunities for technological improvements to be embodied in a range of sectors, activities and occupations; the relevant size issue relates to the potential magnitude of the innovation outcomes associated with these opportunities; and the connectedness issue relates to the potential for learning about both these opportunities and magnitudes (McCann and Ortega-Argilés 2014a).

The original smart specialisation concept highlighted the importance of R&D, and in particular R&D in high-technology and multinational sectors, and this is understandable given the scientific background of the K4G experts as well as the early evidence regarding the transatlantic productivity gap which provided the backdrop to the initial deliberations of the expert advisory group. However, it is also very noticeable that as one moves through the nine policy briefs produced by the expert group between 2006 and 2009 and then on to the subsequent papers (David et al. 2009; Foray et al. 2011), there is a marked shift away from the early emphasis on pure R&D and towards the wider institutional and governance issues fostering, inhibiting or shaping the adoption and adaptation of new knowledge and technologies. In many cases EU member states and regions were comparable in terms of pure technology with many North American regions, while most of the factors inhibiting the EU regional performance were associated with institutional, social, geographical and governance issues (Fagerberg et al. 2014). As such what emerges as being the most critical issue is the importance of enhancing the technological and institutional linkages between all forms of knowledge-generation processes, including formal R&D, at all stages of the value-chain from the lower-order activities through to the high-technology components, and from upstream suppliers through to downstream final producers. Building knowledge-linkages at all stages of the value chain and across a wide range of activities and sectors is critically important. This is because strong linkages of this type are critical in order to promote the dissemination of the new and emerging knowledge and technologies essential for fostering entrepreneurship and innovation (McCann and Ortega-Argilés 2013).

As already explained, the original smart specialisation concept emerged from non-spatial and largely sectoral lines of thinking. However, the debates underlying the emergence of the concept increasingly shifted their focus to consider the role which regions and the regional context might play in providing a concrete application of the concept, and also potentially shaping its application. Regions and their performance are fundamental building blocks of European and national growth issues, and adopting the knowledge-linkage perspective, David et al. (2009) argue that one of the features of many European regions are weak linkages between a region's R&D capabilities, its skills-training specialisations and its industrial structure. Indeed, the weak linkages and frequent disconnections between R&D, skills-training and employment demands in Europe has again been highlighted recently (MGI 2014). Consequently, an obvious regional policy recommendation to emerge from the knowledge-linkage approach of the smart specialisation would be to eschew top-down and centrally-designed 'one-size-fits-all' policies and instead to prioritise the local development of systems which increase the alignments, knowledge linkages and synergies between these different aspects of the local economy. The aim of such a policy would be, for example, to promote a local skills base which can facilitate widespread local incremental improvements across a range of the region's economic activities, as well as developing more specialised application technologies in the region.

David et al. (2009) provide two possible examples of possible policy initiatives. Firstly, they suggest reorienting the skills-training dimensions of a region to better align with the region's existing industrial structure and its existing R&D capabilities. This does not imply necessarily prioritising high-technology skills, and nor does it imply aiming for the generic upgrading of skills per se. Rather it implies designing skills-training programmes which prioritise human capital formation for the new and specific 'knowledge needs' of the region's traditional industries which are starting to adapt and apply newly emerging technologies. As such, the aim is to galvanise precisely those existing sectors and activities of the region's economy which best offer opportunities for achieving scale effects if they are able to better adopt and adapt to the new technological opportunities emerging from elsewhere. Secondly, and in order to help with the absorption of new technological ideas, David et al. (2009) suggest that the establishment of a network development programme which subsidises a 'follower region's' access to the knowledge expertise contained within a leader region could be fruitful. Such programmes may involve, for example, exchanges between researchers in different regions.

Various other previous concepts have also made similar types of policy recommendations along these broad lines (Boschma 2014; Cooke et al. 2006). However, an additional twist to the recommendations offered by smart specialisation, but also one which is absolutely fundamental to the whole smart specialisation logic, is that rather than tending to prioritise high-technology sectors over others, as had been both typical and widespread in the 1990s and 2000s across many parts of Europe and the OECD, the aim here is to better link the new and emerging technologies, sectors and activities with the region's existing activities displaying longstanding scale and depth in the region. Yet, while these recommendations were quite different from much of what was currently fashionable in policy circles at the time, the emphasis on enhancing the knowledge capabilities and linkages of a region's traditional and existing activities and sectors actually emerges quite naturally out of the original non-spatial concept, because of the aspects of relevant scale and connectedness. For example, in many cases, attempts to attract or to encourage the local development of new high-technology activities within a region, which are either entirely new or largely new to the region, will have very limited chances of success. The reason is that the lack of any longstanding local experience or established depth in these new sectors or activities means that there will be little or no technological or skills congruence between the region's existing activities and the new activities. As such, there are unlikely to be any relevant scale effects associated with these new sectors as well as little or no connections between the existing activities and sectors.[3]

The novelty of the smart specialisation concept was that although it emerged from the literature on the economics of knowledge and technology, it provided a policy-prioritisation logic and a policy agenda which was rather different to most of the currently popular technology policy recommendations, although it was based on ostensibly the same underlying rationale, namely that of enhancing innovation, technology and growth. The earlier generation of policy recommendations tended to favour high-technology sectors, and there were numerous papers in both professional and academic journals advocating these types of approaches, all of which were based on our earlier understandings of the nature of innovation, as well as our earlier experience of the 'structural effects' of the transatlantic productivity gap. In contrast, the smart specialisation concept reflects our more recent understanding of the role of innovation systems, and our more recent experience of the important role played by the 'intrinsic effects' associated with the transatlantic productivity gap. As such, the smart specialisation logic emphasised building better linkages between a region's activities and sectors so as to enhance the region's knowledge-dissemination processes and its knowledge-diffusion effects. In particular, linking a region's knowledge-intensive sectors and activities with its broader, more traditional and established activities and sectors, is seen as being essential. Often these more traditional sectors and fields and activities are less well able to adapt to changing technologies than new high-technology SMEs and activities, and finding ways to enhance these mechanisms is essential. Similarly, these more traditional, established and longstanding sectors and activities are often also much less adept at acquiring policy assistance for innovation-related activities than, for example, high-technology SMEs. Yet, according to the smart specialisation logic, finding ways to shift the balance of policy support in favour of fostering local innovation-related knowledge-transmission effects between high-technology, medium-technology and even low-technology activities, is deemed to be absolutely critical for overall regional development.

Most importantly for our purposes, although smart specialisation built on a range of earlier non-spatial literatures in order to provide a major twist in terms of contemporary economic policy thinking, much of this logic has turned out to be especially relevant for the case of regional policy. The approach encourages regions not to be introspective in terms of their policy logic and to develop a strategy which is built explicitly on an understanding of the position and growth potential of the region in the wider global competitive context. This is why smart specialisation has emerged as one of the fundamental building-blocks of the EU Cohesion Policy reforms. However, as with all policy interventions, the types of policies implied by smart specialisation logic also need to be carefully designed in order to work, because one of the key issues which arises from the knowledge economics literature (David 1985) is the problem of economic systems becoming 'locked-in' to undesirable technological trajectories. This problem is also particularly relevant for matters relating to policy design, and it is essential to avoid the types of moral hazard, adverse selection and opportunism problems which might lead to such undesirable lock-in outcomes.

While the need to avoid unintended and adverse policy lock-in effects is essential, it is also important to ensure that the approach is applicable to different contexts. One of the implications of the original non-spatial smart specialisation concept is a shift away from an over-emphasis of high technology sectors and activities so as to encompass the wider picture in which knowledge-linkages operate. If we transfer this logic to an explicitly spatial and regional context this implies that policy should not over-emphasise successful regions, and should consider ways of fostering knowledge-related development in other types of regions. As we have already seen, David et al. (2009) suggest that network-development programmes linking researchers from different regions may be a fruitful way forward. However, what we know from economic geography is that translating this type of non-spatial logic to the explicitly spatial and geographical context of regions is rather more complicated than this. One obvious reason for this is that improved network-connectedness between a leading core region and a weaker follower non-core region does not automatically engender development in the follower region, because of the danger of what is known as the 'shadow' effect (Fujita et al. 1999). Improved interregional linkages can expose weaker non-core regions to more intense competition emerging from stronger core regions enjoying agglomeration advantages. Alternatively, the up-skilling of local labour to improve labour demand–supply synergies may actually induce their out-migration by increasing their attractiveness to high wage-paying employers in other regions (Faggian and McCann 2006, 2009a, b). As such, unless the policies aimed at enhancing connected or synergies are carefully designed, policy actions aimed at promoting interregional connectedness so as to foster and enhance local knowledge linkages may actually favour the core regions by undermining the attempts by the local activities and sectors to shift onto new technological trajectories. Clearly, therefore, while the need to avoid unintended 'lock-in' effects is critical (David et al. 2009), the need to avoid unintended 'lock-out' effects is also just as important. These examples immediately call into question the translation of the non-spatial smart specialisation concept to the explicitly spatial and regional level.

In the previous chapter we have seen that core regions and larger urban areas often tend to display various advantages over non-core regions regarding the knowledge-related processes driving innovation and entrepreneurship. Although this is not always the case, and particularly so in Europe (Dijkstra et al. 2013; Sternberg 2011), these interregional differences might be interpreted as implying that policy actions aimed at fostering knowledge growth, knowledge diffusion and knowledge transmission will tend to realise greater leverage effects in more advanced and core regions. This line of argument is also bolstered by the fact that the impacts of the adoption and adaptation of information and communications technologies (ICTs) which underpin most of today's general purpose technologies (GPTs) have also tended to favour core regions and to exacerbate interregional differences (McCann 2008; McCann and Acs 2011). As such, following our earlier terminology, much of the economic geography literature might suggest that core regions offer greater potential rewards to the entrepreneurial search process in terms of the distribution, the magnitude and the capacity for learning. Prima facie, to some observers the smart specialisation logic would therefore appear to systematically favour core 'knowledge regions' at the expense of non-core follower regions, and as such, while it is largely consistent with the knowledge-enhancement logic of the EU Innovation Union agenda, it would appear to be at odds with the logic of EU Cohesion Policy.

In reality, however, this is not at all the case because smart specialisation does not inherently imply favouring high technology or leading regions, and nor is this the rationale for the smart specialisation idea.[4] Rather, a focus on technological (European Commission 2011a, b), skills, network and governance innovations which can help to cut across sectors, firms and institutional barriers so as to diffuse new knowledge and innovations as much as possible across the regional economy is to be prioritised (Coffano and Foray 2014). There are always difficulties with aligning innovation incentives where entrepreneurs will wish to appropriate as many of the rents associated with their innovations as possible while at the same time there is the imperative to diffuse this knowledge throughout the regional system as soon and as widely as possible (Coffano and Foray 2014; Rodrik 2004). However, these alignment issues are always present in research and innovation policies, and in each case they require a careful design of the policy in partnership with potential entrepreneurs and funding recipients. Involving a wide variety of entrepreneurs in the programme and policy settings is absolutely essential, whereby 'entrepreneurs' are here broadly understood to include all institutions with entrepreneurial capabilities – such as universities, research institutes, large companies as well as SME small companies, business associations, individual inventors and self-employed individuals. It is the local culture of entrepreneurship which is to be enhanced (Acs et al. 2014) and this can be facilitated by addressing the structural, institutional and governance bottlenecks evident in the region (Boschma 2014).

Taken together, the intention of smart specialisation is to better guide policy prioritisation logic (Coffano and Foray 2014) in different contexts based on a systems way of thinking which assumes that for reasons of history and hysteresis regions vary not only in terms of their technological and industrial competences, but also in terms of their potential evolutionary trajectories. In this policy-prioritisation role, smart specialisation can indeed provide a powerful and perfectly workable policy tool which is both flexible and amenable to a wide range of different types of regions, and one which is especially pertinent in the case of non-core regions. As such, the smart specialisation logic is very consistent with the aims of EU Cohesion Policy. Yet, in order to see why this is the case, it is essential to translate the non-spatial smart specialisation concept into an explicitly spatial construct which is appropriate for regional policy thinking, although this is not entirely straightforward. The original non-spatial smart specialisation concept can indeed be adapted to an explicitly spatial and geographical setting and then adopted in the regional policy context, but there are some major economic geography issues which need to be first considered in order for this to be the case.

6.4   TRANSLATING THE SMART SPECIALISATION CONCEPT TO A SPATIAL CONSTRUCT

In order to properly apply the smart specialisation logic in the regional context we must translate three of the key elements of the non-spatial smart specialisation concept – namely the domain, the relevant size, and the level of connectedness – into their explicitly spatial equivalents. In economic geography terminology the explicitly spatial equivalent concepts of these three non-spatial smart specialisation elements are relatedness, embeddedness and connectivity.

In explicitly spatial and geographical terms, the domain and the relevant size of a region have two distinct aspects to them. Firstly, the technological relatedness of activities describes their degree of technological proximity. Various types of different activities share technological commonalities or skills commonalities, and the degree of relatedness captures the extent of these commonalities. The more closely related are activities, the easier it is to switch between them via adjustments in production systems, skills-training programmes, or organisational changes. Conversely, the less closely related are different activities, the greater are the challenges and costs associated with making such adjustments.

Secondly, technologies, activities or sectors must display what economic geographers describe as embeddedness. 'Embeddedness' refers to the extent to which particular activities display depth and linkages with a broad range of other local activities, local skills or local institutions. Some activities may display high levels of embeddedness in the form of a few narrow and specific but also deep and strong inter-connections with other local activities, while other activities may display high levels of embeddedness via a wide range of shallow linkages across a broad range of different sectors. The embeddedness captures both the scale and congruence between activities, technologies or sectors, and in a sense reflects the goodness of fit between activities, as well as the size of the activities. However, embeddedness is not just understood at a local level. The degree of embeddedness of local activities needs to be considered against the backdrop of evolving global value-chains which are fragmenting, modifying and reconfiguring interregional linkages.

Thirdly, connectivity reflects how all of the simultaneous dimensions by which individuals, firms, institutions or other such actors in a region are linked to knowledge sources, including via transport links, interpersonal links and financial links. Most importantly, connectivity refers to decision-making linkages, and the ability and autonomy of actors to absorb knowledge from a wide range of connections and to act on that knowledge accordingly. A region is not simply the spatial analogy of a domain, because regions are themselves inherently very open constructs with linkages throughout to multiple global value chains, and the connectivity of a region captures this dimension of openness.

Using these concepts of technological relatedness, embeddedness and connectivity, the smart specialisation logic argues that in order to foster innovation and growth regions should aim to prioritise those activities fostering and enhancing entrepreneurial search initiatives in activities which are aimed at technologically diversifying those activities which are both highly embedded within a region and also highly connected to other regions. At the same time, however, in order for these policy priorities to realise longstanding benefits for the whole region, the policy actions should also aim explicitly to increase both the levels of local embeddedness and local connectivity, as well as global connectivity.

The technological relatedness argument arises from evolutionary economics (Boschma and Frenken 2011; Frenken and Boschma 2007). As such, the most promising pathways for a region's growth are those pathways which build on its existing dominant technological and skills profile and capabilities, but then diversify around this core base. This growth logic both minimises the adjustment costs and also maximises the chances of success. There is nowadays strong and growing empirical evidence (Boschma and Iammarino 2009; Boschma et al. 2012; Neffke et al. 2011) that regions grow more successfully and are more resilient if their growth patterns are more related to their historical trajectories. For example, the inflow and successful survival rates of new firms and the founding of new local firms are both systematically higher in diversified technological fields which are closely related to the existing dominant fields of the region (Neffke et al. 2011). Similar findings also exist for the growth of exports and also of employment. Indeed, the evidence suggests that the impact of this technological relatedness argument is even more pronounced at the regional scale that at the national scale (Boschma et al. 2012).

The smart specialisation logic does not imply that regions should become more specialised (Coffano and Foray 2014), because we know from urban economics that this can make regions increasingly vulnerable to shocks. At the same time, the relatedness argument also implies that it is not diversification per se which is important for growth, as is often argued in much of the urban economics literature, but the patterns of specialised diversification across related technologies which are important for growth (McCann and Ortega-Argilés 2014a). Smart specialisation requires regions to develop a strategy which best allows them to diversify, but around those activities in which it is already specialised, and in which it also displays both scale and connectivity.

In terms of identifying and measuring these various features, the levels of embeddedness of different activities can be identified by various means, including regional input–output models, the analysis of regional employment distributions, an analysis of the region's trade linkages and the competitive arenas for a region's exports or imports (Thissen et al. 2013), or via case study information regarding the organisational and institutional behaviour of various actors or sectors, including local university–industry links, and other similar sources of evidence regarding local knowledge spillovers, knowledge exchanges, or social and institutional participation activities (McCann 2007). Relatedness can be measured in terms of skills distributions, technological profiling and network analyses. Taken together, the technological relatedness and embeddedness concepts well understood in economic geography translate the non-spatial smart specialisation idea of a relevant size domain into a workable and practicable setting.

In economic geography the idea of connectedness is discussed in terms of connectivity. This is a sociological concept widely employed in the global cities literature (McCann and Acs 2011; Sassen 2002; Taylor 2004) and is used to capture all of the knowledge and decision-making linkages and capabilities which are situated at a particular location. Following the relatedness and embeddedness arguments, a region's likely growth patterns will be enhanced where the local knowledge and decision-making linkages are also closely aligned with the region's existing technological fields (Boschma and Iammarino 2009). Knowledge flows from external sources are essential in order to help regions keep as close to the technological frontier as possible, exactly as argued by the original non-spatial smart specialisation concept (David et al. 2009; Foray et al. 2009). However, it is often observed that particular types of knowledge, according to the technology, the sector or the activity, can flow more easily between regions than within regions, depending on the institutional and corporate structures (McCann and Acs 2011). Therefore, in order to ensure that local entrepreneurial initiatives have longstanding local impacts it is essential that policy actions also lead to the further development of strong local knowledge linkages within the region. For sustainable and resilient long-term development, displaying strong internal connectivity across all actors and institutions within the region is just as important as displaying strong external connectivity to other regions. These two notions of connectivity both relate specifically to the 'softer' institutional, governance and coordination issues which determine the contextual aspects of innovation systems (Hughes 2012). These issues emphasise the importance of ensuring the correct alignment of incentives across public and private actors, and unsurprisingly are also underpinned by the analogous 'bonding' and 'bridging' dimensions of social capital (Putnam 1996), both of which are crucial for building good institutional systems.

Combining all of the elements we arrive at a simple smart specialisation policy prescription formula:

The smart specialisation logic argues that policymakers should prioritise those actions which foster entrepreneurship and innovation in activities which are novel and which are also closely related technologically to those activities in the region already displaying potential scale, embeddedness and connectivity, and which do so in ways which also increase local regional knowledge linkages.

6.5 OPERATIONALISING SMART SPECIALISATION IN EU COHESION POLICY

The smart specialisation model provides a logical framework by which policymakers can frame their long-term innovation-related development agendas. What the specialisation concept offers is a powerful organising framework which helps regions to develop their strategies in a manner which is consistent with modern thinking regarding the nature of innovation and its crucial role in local growth, and one which has emerged from much reflection on the specifics of the EU geographical, institutional and policy context (Landabaso 1997: Landabaso and Mouton 2005; Landabaso and Reid 1999; Landabaso et al. 2001). The logic of smart specialisation also implies that the actual priorities chosen should be different in different types of regions, or at least in ostensibly similar regions the balance of different priorities should differ markedly between regions. The distributions of programme and project funding ought to reflect differences in industrial structures, trajectories and innovation pathways. The first point we must therefore address in understanding how the concept is likely to be operationalised is to consider the likely impact of the concept on different types of regions. Secondly, implementing the concept as a policy-prioritisation tool when designing a region's innovation-related actions requires various forms of knowledge acquisition and mobilisation. On the one hand, much of the evidence needed to develop such strategies is more or less all available in every EU region, due to the wide-ranging empirical research which is nowadays publicly available (Annoni and Dijkstra 2013; ERAWATCH 2011; ESPON 2012). However, in reality of course, no policy schema or agenda should be either totally prescriptive or exclusive and must adapt to the local context. Policymakers will be working within budget constraints and facing multiple and competing claims on their funds, and although policy prioritisation is essential, it cannot always be an exact science. In certain cases, there may be innovation-related funding actions and policy interventions in different regions which do not fall naturally or fit easily into the broad relatedness, embeddedness and connectivity categories advocated by the explicitly smart specialisation logic. However, in principle, the majority of innovation-related actions and interventions should indeed be based on this logic, and in individual situations where this is not the case, the logic of smart specialisation ought to be reflected upon in order to test the logic of the alternative innovation-related intervention. At the same time, operationalising the concept requires putting in place systems and measures to monitor and evaluate the policies so that the types of learning mechanisms described by Hughes (2012) as 'choosing races and placing bets' can become a natural part of the smart specialisation agenda. How the policy prioritisation process actually works in different contexts is itself something that now needs to be considered.

6.5.1   Smart Specialisation and Different Types of Regions

As we have already seen, the smart specialisation policy-prioritisation logic suggests that at the regional context the policy recommendations may well be very different in different places, depending on the region's geography, institutional structure, industrial structure and technological profile. Regions differ enormously in terms of their characteristics and it is important to consider how the applicability of the smart specialisation approach differs across different types of regions. In order to help us do this we need to classify regions according to various features and in earlier chapters we have already come across various regional classification schemes. In terms of discussing the different types of regions from an orthodox economic geography logic we can refer here to the OECD (2013a) typology of regions which categorises regions according to predominantly urban regions, predominantly intermediate regions and predominantly rural regions. There are also other more specific geographical classification schemes, including the detailed urban classification scheme developed by the OECD (2012c) and used by the European Union and Eurostat (Dijkstra and Poelman 2012; European Union 2013a), plus those developed on the basis of different characteristics and themes (ESPON 2012). However, for our purposes here the general OECD (2013a) classification scheme is perfectly sufficient to explain the geographically-specific implementation issues associated with smart specialisation.

In large, densely populated and very diversified urban centres or leading research-intensive regions (OECD 2011a), it may appear that the smart specialisation argument is somewhat less relevant than in other regions in that almost all sectors and technological fields will be evident in the local economy. A sufficiently large and concentrated population base may be expected to generate agglomeration-related spillover effects, and high quality human capital inflows from outside will generally be expected to respond to local labour demands and to overcome any perceived local skills mismatches. Moreover, if these types of core regions are also economically buoyant as is generally assumed, then such regions are also less likely to be the target for significant amounts of regional policy funding. Therefore, to some observers, smart specialisation arguments may appear to be of limited relevance to these types of cases. However, the smart specialisation logic is still important in these regions and there are three main reasons for this.

Firstly, high demand core locations are indeed increasingly observed to face constraints in particular skills sets or skills profiles and these tend to be in many of the middle-skills, technical or applied types of activities (Gordon and Kaplanis 2014). One of the impacts of modern globalisation is that much of the outsourcing and offshoring that has taken place over the last two decades has been in activities which are relatively routinised and standardised and which form middle-range activities within value chains (OECD 2013b). These types of activities tend typically to be in the middle skills and middle income categories, and the dramatic fall in many of these types of roles in even prosperous and buoyant regions means that these groups of workers increasingly have to compete with the lowest skills groups, thereby depressing the wages of both the middle and lower skills groups (Autor et al. 1998; Goos et al. 2009). Nowadays, many buoyant cities and regions are becoming increasingly unequal in terms of income, with an emerging bimodal income distribution dominated by high skills and high wage groups at one end of the spectrum and large numbers of low wage groups at the other end of the spectrum, with a shrinking number of middle skills and middle incomes in the middle of the distribution (Gordon and Kaplanis 2014). The land market effects of these bimodal income distributions are increasing spatial segregation. In terms of local and regional innovation the effects of these changes in skills profiles and employment opportunities mean that many parts of the global value chain become more vulnerable to technological changes and an innovation-systems approach argues that one or two such 'bottlenecks' or 'missing links' may lead to widespread systemic failures. Clearly, even buoyant regions are vulnerable to technological shocks.

Secondly, public policy budgets face severe constraints in almost all EU countries in the aftermath of the 2008 global financial crisis and also in core regions and prosperous areas. Moreover, smart specialisation advocates and implements a policy discipline and policy-learning process which in terms of good governance and governance innovation is of equal importance in all types of regions. Furthermore, as we have already seen in the previous chapter, agglomeration benefits do not necessarily imply innovation gains in all fields, so strategic thinking is still important.

Thirdly, as we have already seen in earlier chapters, many cities in Europe, including major cities, are facing severe problems of unemployment, social exclusion and deprivation (Dijkstra et al. 2013). Indeed, cities appear to exacerbate the effects of the global financial crisis such that countries which have emerged reasonably well from the crisis are being led out of it by their cities, while countries which are struggling in the post-crisis era are being held back and weighed down by their cities (European Union 2013a). Being urban and being large is therefore not all a good news story about learning, sharing and matching (Duranton and Puga 2004), and today in Europe it is just as much a story about the need to respond to difficult challenges and to search for good policy solutions focused on growth.

For intermediate regions containing both urban and rural areas, as well as for many smaller sized regions with urban centres, the smart specialisation argument would seem to be very well suited. The spatial patterns of these types of regions often exhibit polycentric features, and while as a group these regions display diverse features their heterogeneity means that they also individually tend to be somewhat more narrowly defined in terms of their economic structures. Intermediate regions do not exhibit the highly diversified systems of large cities and core regions, but on the other hand they also tend not to exhibit many of the high land price and congestion problems faced by core regions. Therefore, if properly organised and well-coordinated across locations, intermediate types of regions ought to be well able to develop stronger local and interregional network-type effects which can act as a different or an alternative route for innovation-related knowledge flows. At both the local level and also the interregional scale, their heterogeneity and the resulting need to search for complementarities in terms of technologies, skills and policy options, means that these regions would appear to be particularly suited to a mix of R&D, training and networking programmes. In the case of Europe these issues would appear to be particularly pertinent. Europe has numerous such regions with multiple interfaces and interactions between the urban and the rural dimensions. At present, intermediate and smaller regions account for well over half, and also an increasing share, of economic growth in OECD countries (OECD 2012b), and they are not only particularly important in Western Europe, but their importance to the overall European economy is actually growing faster than any other type of region (Dijkstra et al. 2013). As such, both in terms of their aggregate economic growth potential and also the knowledge-network possibilities offered by their polycentric types of spatial structures, these intermediate regions would appear to be ideal targets for the policy-prioritisation logic inherent in smart specialisation.

For rural regions, the smart specialisation logic can be applied as well. Rural regions are surprisingly heterogeneous in terms of their features and behaviour and also surprisingly buoyant and resilient to many observers (OECD 2013c). Over recent years, rural regions across the OECD (ibid.), and in particular in Western Europe (Dijkstra et al. 2013), have generally performed well. However, there is also significant heterogeneity amongst rural regions. Rural regions near urban regions have performed particularly well experiencing relatively weaker adverse effects on productivity and employment than many other types of regions (OECD 2013c). Remote rural regions have tended to suffer more from the demographic effects associated with population outflows than from adverse productivity trends, but the picture is very varied with highly heterogeneous responses by region. Non-farm-related entrepreneurship and innovation in non-agricultural activities such as tourism, lifestyle and leisure activities, as well as high value design and consultancy services linking to urban consumers, are becoming increasingly important in many rural economies (ibid.). The smart specialisation approach ought to be particularly helpful in fostering such processes, and again because population-based scale effects are not possible the smart specialisation focus will tend to be on specific local and interregional network-building effects, and in particular the possibilities offered by wireless IT-based systems point towards technology-based network-building solutions in many rural regions.

Regions differ markedly in terms of their explicitly geographical and land use features and are categorised in these terms as being urban, intermediate and rural regions. At the same time, even within these individual geographical categories discussed here, regions also differ markedly in terms of both their innovation characteristics and their innovation processes. As such, we also need to consider these innovation-related features.

As we have already seen, there are many different types of regions according to their observable innovation features (OECD 2011b; Tödtling and Trippl 2005) or their innovation systems (ESPON 2012) and different classification systems are useful for different types of analysis. For our purposes here we can again refer to the OECD (2011b) typology of different types of regions, which is a typology reflecting the major innovation features of the region, and one which also closely mirrors the earlier Tödtling and Trippl (2005) regional innovation classification scheme. The OECD regional innovation typology groups regions into three broad types, namely knowledge regions, industrial production zones and non-science and technology (S&T)-driven regions, and this latter category typically represents the weakest regions. This classification approach is useful in demonstrating the dominant features of a region's innovation system, and all OECD regions are classified into one of these three categories. In addition, each category has a series of sub-categories and again all OECD regions are grouped into one of the sub-categories. This exercise, and other such similar types of exercises (Camagni et al. 2014; ESPON 2012; Tödtling and Trippl 2005), are very useful for helping policymakers identify the key innovation features and mechanisms of their localities, and the major innovation-related challenges that they face.

Regions which exhibit the features of knowledge regions tend to display many of the R&D-led growth or R&D-inspired innovation mechanisms advocated in the literature. In these cases, many local entrepreneurial processes are often already related directly to local R&D activities. These knowledge regions can be variously large core urban areas, university-city regions, or even agricultural regions housing applied science and industrial research centres. As we have already seen in the previous chapter, being urban and being knowledge-driven are not synonymous, and Europe's most prosperous knowledge regions contains regions displaying each of these features. Yet, as we have already seen in the previous chapter, when it comes to knowledge-related activities and knowledge-related investments, there will still be particular market failures and systems failures evident even in these types of regions. The smart specialisation logic argues that even in these types of regions such challenges are to be discovered and responded to in collaboration with private-sector actors explicitly on the basis of data, evidence and on an explicit statement of the problem being addressed, and not primarily on the basis of any particular sectoral or rent-seeking logic. In these types of regions, regional innovation policies will therefore typically tend to focus on maintaining or enhancing their existing knowledge-related strengths rather than on promoting innovation per se, because such regions are already regarded as being conducive to innovation (McCann and Ortega-Argilés 2014a), and this is consistent with the smart specialisation logic. In these cases, the specific policy actions will tend to emphasise the fostering and enhancing of public–private collaborations, the promotion of further and deeper knowledge exchanges, the engagement of local SMEs in networks, and the strengthening of business links with local universities and research centres. In each case, however, the interventions need to be backed up by systems of monitoring and evaluation which allow for policy adjustments as new information emerges.

Industrial production zones, by their very nature, tend to be primarily urban regions or primarily intermediate regions. In terms of technological profiles and skills specialisations industrial production zones are a very heterogeneous group, and for this reason the fortunes of these types of regions are seen to vary significantly. Some of these regions are currently performing very well indeed, building competitive and innovation systems based on particular technological profiles in those specific segments of global value chains where demand is expanding and in which investment is growing. The local and regional multiplier effects (Moretti 2010) of these positive demand trends are likely to be strengthened the greater are the local degrees of embeddedness and relatedness displayed by these key activities and technologies within the overall regional system. In these buoyant regions, many of the smart specialisation actions will mirror those already evident in knowledge regions. In particular, in order to avoid bottlenecks in the value chains there is likely to be an emphasis on ensuring appropriate specialised skills training for the demands of the local activities, as originally recommended by David et al. (2009).

In contrast, many other industrial production zones are currently operating within technological regimes situated in declining segments of global value chains. Many of these regions now exhibit severe and adverse lock-in problems, manifested by falling local employment and falling wages and declining investment levels. Furthermore, the greater are the levels of local embeddedness of these declining technologies, the greater will be negative local multiplier effects, thereby magnifying the adjustment problems facing these regions. Severe adjustment problems in these cases are also often exacerbated by a shrinking capacity to act on the part of public sector, due both to declining budgets and also institutional ossification. Moreover, it is important for our purposes to note that within Europe a major effect of the 2008 global financial crisis has been to transform many industrial production zone regions from those experiencing positive demand trends into those experiencing severe adverse shocks as their national economies have experienced rapid repositioning within global value chains (European Union 2013a; MGI 2013; OECD 2013c; Timmer et al. 2013; World Bank 2012). These effects, whereby regions have suddenly shifted in terms of their development trajectories, unsurprisingly, have been especially evident in regions across Southern Europe. Moreover, the scale of these shocks as well as the scale of the regions makes these particularly important cases as well as particularly difficult cases for any form of economic policy to address.

The development priority in these regions will be to try to help local commercial activities adjust to these changing circumstances in ways centred on the fostering of entrepreneurship and innovation, even in these difficult circumstances. The smart specialisation logic in many of these types of regions will be to focus on helping the region's core activities to diversify away from many of their current activities, but to do so by diversifying around their existing technological strengths and skills profiles, exactly as the related variety argument suggests. The aims will be to increase the number of firms engaging in innovative activities, and again by establishing or building up the region's collaborative networks so as to foster the emerging local and interregional knowledge exchanges. There have already been examples of regions which have successfully facilitated such transitions (Foray et al. 2012).

In terms of non-S&T-driven regions, these regions again represent diverse cases. There are some non-S&T-driven regions facing relatively few difficult challenges, in that they exhibit low unemployment rates and a reasonable growth performance. These regions tend to be dominated by tourism, leisure and amenity-related activities, and in particular, those segments of the leisure and tourism market dominated by middle and higher income consumers. Moreover, these regions also often benefit from inflows of new and higher income residents, thereby expanding the local income and population base. While these appear to be broadly positive shocks, a significant portion of these inflows may be in the form of weekend or holiday-home investment inflows from external regions, which can lead to local social disruption and skills shortages in key segments of the economy if land prices become exorbitant. Many of the smart specialisation recommendations in these regions typically tend to mirror those evident in the prosperous rural regions, focusing on enhancing connectivity with the core urban areas. Where exorbitant land prices lead to local skills shortages, particularly amongst young people, smart specialisation logic will tend to emphasise specialist skills training in the leisure and tourism activities, alongside activities relating to the local environmental and amenity conditions.

Some non-S&T-driven regions are primarily agricultural regions, and all agricultural regions are vulnerable to global price fluctuations and shifting global demands, even allowing for the stabilising role of the Common Agricultural Policy (CAP) operations within the EU. In these types of rural regions, as we have already seen, the focus will often tend to be on fostering local entrepreneurship in non-agricultural activities in order to help diversify the rural economy away from purely agricultural activities to a wider range of non-farm activities.

In non-rural regions, some of the most challenging cases relate to those non-S&T-driven regions which are dominated by production systems based on imitation and adaptation of external ideas, rather than on local fundamental R&D. Following the original Pavitt (1984) logic this is not an uncommon type of region which also includes some prosperous service-oriented urban regions (Iammarino and McCann 2006; Lee and Rodriguez-Pose 2013). In fact there are many such regions across all parts of Europe (Camagni et al. 2014; ESPON 2012). Apart from prosperous service-oriented urban regions, these types of non-S&T-driven regions include some which benefit primarily from inflows of foreign direct investment in response to low local factor prices, some which rely primarily on traditional family and craft-based industries (Best 1990) and some which were former industrial production zones. In these diverse cases, alongside specialist skills training, the logic of smart specialisation is also likely to emphasise enhancing both local and interregional connectivity in the region's most embedded activities in order to ensure that knowledge inflows continue to operate in order to fuel local innovative activities. At the same time as well, policy interventions to help with, for example, patenting activities, will be important to help these regions in their formal R&D activities, so as to increase their long-run resilience.

Finally, amongst the non-S&T-driven regions there is a specific group which faces particularly severe challenges in the current global environment, and these are the very poorest regions, most of which are facing population decline, outflows of young people and environmental problems. Many of the convergence regions in the EU exhibit per capita GDP levels which are typical of middle income countries, while some of the very weakest regions within the EU display productivity levels more reminiscent of those exhibited by the richer group of nations amongst the developing country group. In these very challenging circumstances advice on how to foster innovation in these types of non-S&T-driven regions is provided by the World Bank (2010) which, reflecting the general shift in our understanding of innovation over recent years, argues that innovation should be understood as the dissemination of something new in a given context, not in absolute terms nor purely in science or technology terms.

> Innovation is distinct from research and development and in fact need not result from it … Innovation … is fundamentally a social process … Distinguishing between high technology from low technology is not very useful, particularly in low and medium income countries. High technology may not generate jobs and wealth, while low technology developments and the exploitation of indigenous knowledge can lead to significant economic growth and welfare. The use of high technology in all sorts of products, processes and services can be more important than producing it. (World Bank 2010 p. 3)

Clearly, the experience of the World Bank working in numerous regions in developing countries (World Bank 2010) and in the lower income regions of the EU (World Bank 2011) is very much in line with the arguments of smart specialisation, which at its core was about the dissemination, adoption and adaptation of new technologies and ideas across as wide a range of industries as possible. In weaker regions, finding ways to embody ICTs and new technologies within a wide range of products and services is critical (Paunov 2013). Moreover, the evidence suggests that ICTs have not particularly disadvantaged many weaker regions (ibid.), and if anything in Europe the reverse appears to be the case (Dijkstra et al. 2013; European Commission 2010), such that broadband-type initiatives would appear to offer real traction in these cases. However, the heterogeneity of regions combined with the systemic nature of innovation (Hughes 2012) means that finding ways to different innovation pathways in different contexts is critical (von Tunzelmann 2009). This holistic perspective advocated by the World Bank (2010) and OECD (Paunov 2013) understands innovation as something that should be approached from an organic and evolutionary perspective (McCann and Ortega-Argilés 2013) rather than simply a science-led perspective, and this is very consistent with the embeddedness and related variety underpinnings of smart specialisation. In terms of enabling innovation, only this type of broad-based development perspective which allows for local variation and specificities can be fully capable of fostering growth which is also sustainable and inclusive (UNCTAD 2012). Indeed, from the arena of international development there is already widespread case-study evidence and experience offering viable approaches to fostering innovation even in these particularly challenging environments. However, the development of 'inclusive innovations', whereby innovations are developed in conjunction with technology-using rather than technology-producing activities such as agriculture, banking, marine industries, health and education, can also prove to be highly beneficial, as long as ways to achieve sufficient scale or network effects can be identified (Paunov 2013).

In order to avoid inadvertently favouring buoyant regions, it may seem slightly ironic, therefore, that in order for the staged approach to regional smart specialisation strategies to be successful, the innovation-related funding for SMEs from the EU Cohesion Policy budget might in its early stages actually need to be as space-neutral as is possible. What is meant here by space-neutral is not what the 2009 World Development Report (World Bank 2009) discusses as space-blind policies, but rather that SME innovation-related funding should not be earmarked primarily in the dominant knowledge centres even within different tiers and types of regions, but instead initially spread as randomly as possible across all places in response to funding applications. Only in the light of a successful peer-review performance evaluation taking place after a predefined period of time should any such seed-funding be continued. Indeed, there are already programmes such as those implemented in the US by the National Research Council (NRC 2009) which explicitly adopt this particular type of space-blind logic specifically so as not to systematically favour strong regions or strong sectors and to provide opportunities for a wide range of entrepreneurs.

The smart specialisation logic, as the original proponents of the concept themselves acknowledge (David et al. 2009), does imply a policy-prioritisation logic which is based somewhat on a fledgling-industry type of argument. However, the smart specialisation concept also introduces a few twists on the standard fledgling-industry argument, which always suffers from the problem that the medium- to long-term outcomes of such a fledgling-industry policy are by definition unknown, and as such are very risky. In contrast, however, if we apply the smart specialisation logic in a regional context, in which the dimensions of embeddedness, relatedness and connectivity are emphasised, then the empirical evidence from the related variety literature (Boschma and Iammarino 2009; Boschma and Frenken 2011; Boschma et al. 2012; Frenken et al. 2007; Hausmann et al. 2013) suggests that the policy prioritisation logic is built on a much sounder footing than the standard fledgling industry arguments. Importantly, this also implies that within individual regions, within particular types of regions, or within specific tiers of regions, any policy-prioritisation of SME funding streams should be based primarily on the smart specialisation features of embeddedness, relatedness and connectivity, and not automatically on either a geographical logic favouring stronger parts within each type of region or on particular new technologies, unless their features happen to chime with the smart specialisation logic. These important nuances and subtleties to the policy-prioritisation logic pose implementation challenges which must be explicitly considered and addressed.

A growing body of evidence (OECD 2012b) suggests that different types of interventions are appropriate for different types of regions with differing levels of development, and this is particularly so in the case of Europe (Crescenzi and Rodriguez-Pose 2012). Evidence from across the range of OECD countries suggests that 'hard' investments such as transport infrastructure tend to have a bigger impact at lower levels of economic development, but only as long as they are also allied with human capital investments (OECD 2012b), with the effects of these 'hard' infrastructure investments largely disappearing at the higher levels of development (ibid.). In contrast, 'soft' knowledge-related and innovation-related investments have the largest impacts in the more advanced regions (Crescenzi and Rodriguez-Pose 2012). However, moving beyond board categories such as 'hard' of 'soft' infrastructure and choosing exactly which actions or interventions to employ in which specific cases is still a major challenge, and the response to this challenge is exactly where smart specialisation is designed to help (McCann and Ortega-Argilés 2014b).

6.5.2 Smart Specialisation Tools, Techniques and Implementation Challenges

Nowadays, a wide range of different techniques, tools, actions and interventions are employed in policies aimed at fostering entrepreneurship and innovation (McCann and Ortega-Argilés 2013c). Examples include the use of matching grants, mini-grants, venture capital schemes, open innovation programmes, university–business linkage schemes (Abreu et al. 2009; Hughes and Kitson 2013; OECD 2007), innovation parks, incubators, angel investor programmes (McCann and Ortega-Argilés 2013c; World Bank 2010), network programmes linking SMEs with multinational firms (OECD 2007), schemes fostering university–business links (European Commission 2011a; OECD 2007), alongside the more traditional funding schemes aimed at promoting R&D. Moreover the smart specialisation approach is also as well suited to responding to the innovation challenges associated with environmental issues, although the analytical and policy approaches differ somewhat from other types of research and innovation issues (European Union 2013b,c). The World Bank (2012 p. 15) provides a detailed checklist of the advantages and disadvantages of the different types of schemes aimed at increasing R&D investments (McCann and Ortega-Argilés 2013c) and as with all innovation policy actions and interventions, not all such schemes display positive results in all cases (OECD 2013d). In particular, our knowledge of service innovations is still very limited in comparison to manufacturing and science-based activities (OECD 2011a) so policy actions or interventions in this arena are likely to require particular care in terms of follow-up monitoring and evaluation.

In terms of which individual policy tools to use in which specific cases, the smart specialisation approach is largely agnostic. Instead, following the smart specialisation logic the answers to these types of questions depend on the regional setting, the region's major challenges and the region's likely potential, and the onus is on the local and regional actors working in partnership with government to identify appropriate actions and interventions using the best evidence available and using the logic provided by the smart specialisation approach.

Following on from the original transatlantic productivity gap backdrop to the original emergence of the concept, as we have seen one of the key issues which emerged at an early stage was the importance of the adoption, adaptation and diffusion of general purpose technologies, and in particular modern information and communications technologies (ICTs). Policy actions aimed at providing the skills and systems required for enhancing adoption and adaptation may be critical in many situations, including specialised human capital programmes, university–industry links, network-development programmes and other such interventions. However, the local adoption of ICTs may not always be a local priority given that EU interregional disparities are neither exclusively, nor in many cases even primarily, due to ICT-related issues. Although ICT-related issues are indeed likely to play a major role in many policy actions in a wide range of regions, as with the earlier fashion for prioritising high-technology sectors, an exclusive focus on the ICT-related sectors may inadvertently lead to sectoral rent-seeking, an outcome which is precisely the type of adverse 'lock-in' problem to be avoided (David et al. 2009). Rather, the important role which ICT-related actions are likely to play in many regions in order to foster knowledge dissemination needs to be understood in the context of the broader entrepreneurial and innovation-related challenges faced by the region. ICT-based solutions are an important subset of a broader range of possible interventions.

Another issue to be addressed here regarding the operationalisation of the smart specialisation concept relates to the region's entrepreneurial search processes, which it is hoped will identify the medium-term innovation-related opportunities locally available. The emphasis on using this particular policy-prioritisation logic in EU Cohesion Policy in order to help promote entrepreneurial search processes is perfectly consistent with the remit of EU Cohesion Policy, which is currently the largest source of credit for small and medium-sized enterprises (SMEs) within the whole EU policy portfolio (European Union 2013d). Yet, the fact that it is the entrepreneurs and not the policymakers who are understood as being best placed for identifying the innovation-related opportunities therefore implies that there will need to be some place-specific criteria for the SME credit provision; criteria which are consistent with the smart specialisation policy-prioritisation logic (European Union 2013b; McCann and Ortega-Argilés 2014a,b). In particular, in many cases SME credit availability will need to be prioritised for those firms whose entrepreneurial goals are specifically aligned with the technological diversification of the region's most embedded activities and industries (McCann and Ortega-Argilés 2014a,b). At the same time, however, in order to avoid the charge of 'picking winners' it is always necessary to follow the 'staged approach' advocated by Council for Science and Technology (CST 2007) reminiscent of the 'choosing races and placing bets' logic of Hughes (2012), and there are several governance aspects here which need to be highlighted, namely governance experimentalism, governance innovation, governance coordination and governance impartiality.

First, in order for the smart specialisation approach to work it is essential to develop systems of indicators for monitoring, evaluation and learning. These are essential elements not only of programme implementation but also of institutional capacity-building on the part of public sector as well as private sector and civil society actors. There is already a large literature on project and policy evaluation (Davies et al. 2000; Pawson 2006), and there are established guidelines as to how evaluation should be undertaken for innovation actions (Technopolis Group and MIOIR 2012). However, in specific settings policy learning is still challenging, and requires experimentation in each particular context in order to observe what works and what does not. The importance of experimentation has been underscored primarily by the work of Hausmann and Rodrik (2003) and Rodrik (2007) and is based on the experience of numerous development initiatives from around the world (Rodrik 2007). In good governance systems trial and error and governance experimentalism should be key features of the modern policy process. Good policy design, policy delivery and policy learning processes are linked via the identification of what works in each particular setting. This requires the use of policy outcome indicators or policy results indicators, and the use of such indicators is not because we know the outcomes or results of the policy in advance, but precisely because we do not know the outcomes (Rodrik 2004). On the other hand, in good governance systems what we do know in advance are the intended results and intended outcomes of the policy. Therefore, it is essential to explicitly link the ex ante intended outcomes and intended results of the policy to the implementation experience via systems of monitoring and evaluation (Gault 2013). This outcome-oriented or results-oriented approach offers policymakers and stakeholders the greatest possibilities for identifying which aspects of the policy design and delivery – ranging from the original intended outcome and intended results through to the implementation and management systems – work and which do not work, and for understanding why some aspects work while others do not. Moreover, in the case of innovation-related issues in some ways this experimentation imperative is even more important than in other cases. The reason is that innovation processes by their very nature require failures to occur, and it is only by observing what works and what does not that we can identify innovations.

Second, for innovation policies, the need for public sector actors (European Union 2013d; Osborne and Brown 2013; Technopolis 2012) to become more innovative so as to complement the innovative actions of private sector and civil society actors is greater than ever and governance innovation is nowadays widely understood as being central to governance capacity-building processes. These innovation-related governance imperatives pose challenges to the culture of many civil service organizations which in the past have often worked almost entirely within vertical logic. In contrast, the smart specialisation approach emphasises policy frameworks for facilitating processes of entrepreneurial discovery, and one key means of achieving this is by searching for complementarities between different policy domains (Foray et al. 2012; Foray and Goenaga 2013; Foray and Rainaldi 2013; OECD 2011a, 2013d). Many policy arenas directly linked to innovation often operate within institutional 'silos' constrained within vertically-organised ministerial structures, and the search for complementarities between policy domains and actions is not always natural to experienced policymakers or policy managers working within a primarily vertical organisational logic.

However, in many cases, such vertical demarcation lines between jurisdictions must be overcome if an integrated approach to innovation-related and entrepreneurship-related issues is going to be provided (OECD 2011a, 2013d). Ironically, many horizontal policy framework conditions are easily delivered by vertical sectorally-organised governance systems whereas a more vertical policy logic only makes sense with more horizontal governance frameworks (Coffano and Foray 2014). Otherwise a largely sectoral approach to 'picking winners' is the most likely outcome. This is why in order to leverage the policy complementarities (Braga de Macedo and Oliveira-Martins 2010) required for smart specialisation there is such an imperative to overcome a purely vertical governance logic and to develop a more transversal and horizontal logic which also facilitates innovations and learning on the part of public governance actors (Hughes et al. 2011).

Third, in terms of deploying the smart specialisation approach in the service of EU Cohesion Policy, as we have already discussed in previous chapters, EU Cohesion Policy as a whole, and now also the smart specialisation dimensions of Cohesion Policy, both have an explicitly place-based logic underpinning their implementation. Place-based governance coordination is an essential feature of smart specialisation and such coordination has various dimensions to it, the most important of which is that of partnership. The shifts in thinking regarding the importance of partnership in facilitating governance coordination also involve a reconsideration of the possible roles of different levels of governance (OECD 2009a, b; 2011a, b). This is important because when applied in a regional setting the smart specialisation logic puts the onus onto the local and regional policy designers and potential funding recipients to clearly identify the perceived market failures or systems failures (Hughes 2012) which are being corrected. As Hughes (2012) argues, textbook market failure arguments are of no particular use regarding the design of policy interventions or actions in specific cases, and it is therefore essential to extract and build on the knowledge of the local actors and stakeholders, exactly as the modern place-based argument contends. However, as we will see in a moment, a trend towards 'localism' must also be avoided and higher levels of governance must necessarily also be part of the policy process to ensure that the system remains open and follows the overall intended logic of a good policy process. These principles are all very consistent with the approach of Rodrik (2004) and Barca (2009) in which multi-level and multi-jurisdictional partnerships between the public, private and civil society actors are required in order to elicit the local knowledge regarding the most severe obstacles to growth, the major bottlenecks or missing links, and the most likely remedies.

Fourth, as has already been discussed in the earlier chapters and also here in terms of smart specialisation, in the case of public policy interventions it is important that the interventions themselves do not lead to adverse 'lock-in' outcomes, and this can only be ensured by governance impartiality. Such adverse lock-in outcomes could involve activities becoming tied to declining or outmoded technologies, or alternatively they could involve the rent-capturing behaviour of particular elites leading to clientelist-type relations between donors and recipients. In the regional context, it is therefore essential to ensure that powerful sectors in individual regions are not able to enhance their acquisition of public funds by systematically exploiting the advocacy advantages they exhibit on the basis of their local monopoly and monopsony positions. At the same time, as we have also seen, from a technological perspective it is also essential that policy actions do not lead to adverse 'lock-out' effects whereby a too-rapid exposure to external markets and global value chains undermines the local activities' attempts at shifting onto new technological trajectories. On face value, one might assume that smart specialisation policy actions and interventions are continuously 'walking a tightrope', aiming at achieving constructive outcomes within only a narrow band of possibilities, flanked by lock-in and lock-out scenarios. However, this is not at all the case, because smart specialisation involves opening up and democratising knowledge-related and innovation-related policy discussions, it involves reciprocal responsibilities. In terms of democratisation of the knowledge-related and innovation-related aspects of policy, smart specialisation policy actions should be aimed at building new local intra-regional knowledge linkages and diversifying and enhancing existing knowledge linkages, as well as fostering interregional knowledge exchanges and cooperative actions. This systematic and evidence-based approach should be inherently both a democratic and inclusive type of policy process, based on the gathering of evidence and data, the building of public–private partnerships, and the monitoring of all policy actions and interventions. The transparency, openness and inclusiveness of the policy process should itself help to avoid the fragmented and localised sectoral rent-seeking likely to undermine the drive for resource prioritisation and concentration.

Part of the transparency and democratisation dimensions of smart specialisation also arise from the fact that smart specialisation policy prioritisation logic does not necessarily imply favouring particular actors, particular sectors or particular places over others, unless there are clear smart specialisation reasons as to why this should be the case, and all policy beneficiaries also have reciprocal responsibilities to the wider community in terms of transparency and engagement. In the language of development policy, as we have already seen in earlier chapters, these reciprocal responsibilities are known as 'conditionalities'. However, the logic of smart specialisation, which also requires engagement with local stakeholders and institutions in order to extract and build on their local knowledge so as to develop locally-tailored agendas, means that policy-makers may sometimes come into conflict with local elites who choose either not to be part of the smart specialisation policy agenda, or alternatively seek to fashion the agenda in their own interests. Local knowledge-related issues, and policy-design issues in particular, often face issues of externalities, problems of information asymmetries and principal–agent problems (McCann and Ortega-Argilés 2014a), and in some cases the smart specialisation logic may pose a threat to some locally-entrenched monopoly positions. The specialised diversification aspect of the smart specialisation policy logic implies the local promotion of newness, variation and differentiation, as Prager and Thisse (2012) have called for, and all of which are features of innovation. However, these novel characteristics themselves may threaten the monopoly positions of local elites, who may then aim to limit openness and restrict the pursuit of the novelties and variations to domains over which they still maintain control. Therefore, in order to counter these potential threats, the experience of the World Bank, the OECD and the European Commission (Barca 2009) suggests that the way to overcome these problems, as we have already discussed in detail in earlier chapters, is by the use of both conditionalities and also outcome indicators. In the 2014–2020 programming period conditionalities are to be attached to EU regional innovation funding regarding issues of transparency, along with the use of results/outcome indicators and monitoring, and the role of peer review and mutual learning. The reason is that these elements all help to foster the inclusiveness and public accountability of the policy process.

What is very clear is that the smart specialisation approach does not advocate particular interventions or policy models in specific contexts, but rather provides guidance regarding 12 different broad types of approaches, each containing multiple different types of possible actions, which might be adopted in different circumstances,[5] and combinations of these approaches are encouraged as much as possible. Importantly, the smart specialisation approach is explicitly agnostic regarding the desirability or efficacy of any particular approach, and instead is focussed on the workings of the policy process regarding how to prioritise the use of public funding in different regional contexts in the most appropriate manner. Moreover, the smart specialisation approach is also designed to be applicable to all three of the smart, sustainable (European Union 2013b, c) and inclusive (European Union 2013d) dimensions of Europe 2002, as is consistent with the overall reforms to EU Cohesion Policy.

In order to help with the deliberation, transparency and accountability features which are essential elements in the smart specialisation policy process, a peer-review and mutual learning arena has been set up by the European Commission in the form of a support facility, known as the RIS3 (Research and Innovation Strategies for Smart Specialisation) Platform,[6] in the European Commission Joint Research Centre, the Institute for Prospective Technological Studies (IPTS) in Seville, Spain. This facility provides an arena in which delegates and decision-makers from different EU regions can interact and discuss their policy priorities and are also able to be peer-reviewed by each other, so as to foster mutual learning. Advice, support systems and guidance publications[7] on all aspects of the regional innovation policy context are available regarding different policy initiatives, evidence-building, data-gathering and governance challenges,[8] and at the time of writing there were 151 EU regions and 14 countries participating in the activities of the RIS3 Platform, together accounting for some 90 per cent of Europe's NUTS2 regions. In addition, other EU member states were setting up their own 'in-house' facilities modelled on the Seville facility. These activities are exactly the types of institutional mobilisation processes envisaged by the Barca (2009) report, and the European Parliament has also provided strong support for the smart specialisation agenda within the EU Cohesion Policy reforms.[9] Designing good strategies is not simple and requires careful consideration of difficult questions in each case (Iacobucci 2014). However, designing good strategies is essential in order for the public sector to help foster entrepreneurship and innovation so that the effectiveness of Cohesion Policy interventions can be maximised for the long-run good of the European economy (Landabaso 2014).

Finally, there have been two high-level independent assessments of the smart specialisation approach. The first report undertaken by the Science and Technology Directorate of the OECD (2012a, 2013e) examines both the overall logic of the approach and its feasibility more generally both in the EU and further afield internationally. The second report by the Fraunhofer ISI (2013) institute examines the implementation of the approach at the level of EU regions within the EU Cohesion Policy reforms. Both reports are remarkably positive, constructive and realistic in their assessments. The OECD (2012a, 2013e) report finds that many of the elements of smart specialisation were already evident in different existing lines of the literature. However, the novelty of the approach is the way in which these various elements are combined in order to provide a policy-prioritisation logic which is appropriate for the context. The approach can be feasibly adapted to different countries across the OECD and is not purely related to the EU context, although it serves an important role in EU Cohesion Policy, given the specifics of the EU context.

The Fraunhofer ISI report analysed the responses by regions and member states to the new approach, investigating also the perceptions, responses and roles played by local and regional stakeholders in their various institutional engagement activities in the policy process. The report argues that smart specialisation will not change the world of regional innovation and nor will it rapidly transform the inherent innovation-related problems facing many EU regions. However, the Fraunhofer ISI (2013) report also argues that this is exactly the strength of the smart specialisation approach which is focused on the 'conscious review, fine-tuning and improving effectiveness which is a good approach to tackle the heterogeneous world of European regions'. As such, the approach represents a 'good fertilizer rather than the tree itself'. Moreover, Fraunhofer ISI (2013) argue that the experience of the smart specialisation preparatory efforts of regions and EU member states in the run-up to the new programming period 2014–2020, which has been characterised by a surprising degree of initial openness, highlights the fact that 'regional intelligence/experience counts'. A major potential effect of smart specialisation is to shift the focus of policymakers on to what is feasible, attainable and realistic, and to emphasise the importance of safeguarding, securing, fine-tuning and improving what has already been achieved, rather than aiming to reach too far too quickly for unrealistic objectives. The report argues that there is a general sense amongst EU regions that smart specialisation 'helps to improve rather than create anew', by making the regions do the work themselves and therefore emphasising the importance of the regions remaining in focus. Again, this reflects exactly the place-based logic advocated by the Barca (2009) report, whereby the systems and incentives should be designed so as to mobilise and maximise the engagement of local actors. At the same time, the transparency afforded by this evidence-based approach explicitly acknowledges the socio-economic and institutional issues limiting the approach in each case. In particular, Fraunhofer ISI (2013) highlight issues such as leveraging private-sector co-financing will always remain challenges, and must therefore remain priorities in all cases. However, monitoring must be employed in order to help improve the policies and Fraunhofer ISI (2013) conclude that overall the approach has been remarkably positively received across Europe, even with regard to the EU Cohesion Policy conditionality requirements for monitoring and evaluation.

6.6 REVIEW AND CONCLUSIONS

The smart specialisation concept is essentially a way of thinking about local knowledge-enhancement and learning-enhancement systems. It is a powerful lens through which policymakers can design and articulate local development policies, and these various discussions make it clear that there is no 'one-size-fits-all' policy prescription associated with smart specialisation. Nor is there any top-down central government sectoral planning logic associated with smart specialisation either. Rather, smart specialisation has always been understood very much as a partnership-type approach between various stakeholders aimed at fostering entrepreneurship and innovation in ways which are most beneficial to the wider economy (Foray et al. 2012). An advantage of the approach is that it forces policy priorities to be established in a pragmatic way and on a solid basis which is explicitly related to the region's features, challenges and likely potential. A greater degree of differentiation and tailoring of innovation polices is needed across EU member states (European Union 2013e) and smart specialisation provides a way to help achieve this. This framework allows any proposed projects to be ranked against other competing alternatives on the basis of the best available evidence and on a self-reflection of the region's likely potential. The approach is neither sectoral in nature, nor is it focused necessarily on the prioritisation of high technologies, but rather reflects the broader understanding of innovation which has emerged over recent years (OECD 2011a, c, 2013d; World Bank 2010, 2011). Instead, it is focused on entrepreneurs and innovators engaging in activities with the likely potential to provide wider knowledge-diffusion benefits across the regional economy.

To some observers, smart specialisation and similar such policy approaches (*The Economist* 2013) may appear to raise concerns regarding 'picking winners' (David et al. 2009). Yet, smart specialisation was never conceived of as a top-down government planning system for championing particular sectors or imposing sectoral specialisation (McCann and Ortega-Argilés 2013b). As the advocates of smart specialisation themselves always emphasised, it is critically important for entrepreneurship and innovation to have good horizontal framework conditions in place, including low regulatory barriers, clear and simple tax systems, good education systems, the enforcement of contracts, and good infrastructure provision (OECD 2011c; World Bank 2011). However, as Hughes (2012) explains, such 'picking winners' concerns largely ignore the differentiated and nuanced logic of these modern policies and thereby miss the central point of what these policy approaches are trying to achieve. Rather, these types of policy approaches have always been understood as reflecting a partnership-based policy process of discovery and learning on the part of both policymakers and entrepreneurs. As such, these types of policies are situated explicitly in the recent thinking regarding role and logic of industrial policy (Rodrik 2004), research policies (Trajtenberg 2009; Soete 2009a, b) and regional innovation policies (McCann and Ortega-Argilés 2013a; Tödtling and Trippl 2005). Such holistic approaches are advocated by the World Bank (2010) and OECD (2011a, c). Moreover, they are also very much in line with the principles of Stiglitz et al. (2009), whereby as an essential feature of public accountability, the priorities underpinning programme or project selection are made as transparent as possible.

These various new lines of thinking suggest that public policy may be able to play a more strategic role in fostering entrepreneurship and innovation. In particular, the recent experience of the 'valley of death' (House of Commons 2013) problem[10] in which many parts of Europe in particular (European Commission 2011b) have faced serious difficulties in translating academic ideas into marketable products has led many observers to advocate policies aimed at better enabling the development of cross-over technologies and the targeting of wider new applications for sector-specific technologies (European Commission 2011b). Smart specialisation falls into this line of thinking. As we have seen, the original idea emerged from a non-spatial setting, but it quickly became apparent that the regional setting was very much the context in which the idea was best-suited. As well as being appropriate for a wide range of regions, the smart specialisation approach also warns against recommending off-the-shelf or 'one-size-fits-all' policy solutions imposed from above, and instead emphasises the need for locally-tailored policy recommendations, based on the region's existing knowledge-related assets. The emphasis on using the smart specialisation concept within the service of EU Cohesion Policy arises both because it provides a policy-prioritisation organising framework which is based on modern thinking about innovation policy and regions (McCann and Ortega-Argilés 2013c), which can respond to all of the elements of Europe2020,[11] and which also fits perfectly with the overall place-based logic of EU Cohesion Policy.

NOTES

1. See http://s3platform.jrc.ec.europa.eu/s3pguide
   http://ec.europa.eu/regional_policy/newsroom/detail.cfm?id=361&LAN=EN.
2. http://ec.europa.eu/invest-in-research/monitoring/knowledge_en.htm

3. Much of the 'clusters' discourses in Europe emerged after 2001 in the light of the primarily sectoral Lisbon Agenda (Borrás and Tsagdis 2008) which tended to emphasise a largely top-down policy perspectives (Bachtler et al. 2013) focused on high-technology sectors. Following this type of logic some observers (Cooke 2012) have criticised smart specialisation for encouraging greater sectoral specialisation based on a cluster type of approach. However, and consistent with the arguments of Cooke (2012) and Cooke et al. (2006), smart specialisiation adopts a regional innovation systems approach which emphasises the building of transverse cross-sectoral linkages via platform technologies and knowledge networks, as is made clear by the official publications on these matters (Foray et al. 2012). See also: http//: www.s3platform.jrc.ec.europa.eu/guides

4. 'Smart specialisation is a good yardstick for identifying growth priorities. Smart special-isation can help innovation and competitiveness in all regions in Europe, even the least developed. Innovation is certainly not just about high-tech.' Máire Geoghegan-Quinn, European Commissioner for Research and Innovation. *Smart Specialisation and Europe's Growth Agenda*, European Commission, 2014, Publications Office, Brussels, April.

5. A 'clusters' type approach is just one of these twelve generic approaches suggested for consideration. See: http://ec.europa.eu/research/evaluations/pdf/archive/other_reports_ studies_and_documents/clusters_smart_spec2013.pdf. However, no particular policy model is advocated or recommended by smart specialisation. Rather all of the official EU guidance material encourages policymakers to consider a wide range of options. However, on the basis of some US and UK observations some commentators have claimed that smart specialisation is simply a new wave of cluster policies (Nathan and Overman 2013) whereby clusters in this are understood largely as in the proto-model described by Duranton (2011). Yet smart specialisation is not a model but a policy prioritisation framework providing guidance as to how to best undertake the policy-process, something which cluster approaches have always largely lacked (Ketels 2013). A cluster approach may provide one of the 12 generic approaches which can be utilised in smart specialisation but clusters and smart specialisation are not at all equivalent. Further evidence regarding this point comes from the fact that proponents of clusters (Ketels 2013) themselves do not see smart specialisation as being equivalent to a clusters approach. Likewise, apart from the reference referred to above, within the other 1050 pages and 642,000 words of material contained in 15 of the official guidance documents published by the European Commission which are aimed at assisting with the development of smart specialisation strategies, the words 'cluster', 'clusters', 'clustering' 'clustered' and so on appear only 51 times. Finally, in order to avoid any misconceptions that clusters, smart specialisation and regional policy are the same thing, in the 225 pages of text governing the regulations to the reformed EU Cohesion Policy 2014–2020 the word 'clusters' appears only once out of more than 185,000 words. All four of these observations suggest that the rather sceptical claims (Nathan and Overman 2013) that regional policy and smart specialisation are in fact simply a revamped cluster policy are in reality likely to be seriously misplaced.

6. http://s3platform.jrc.ec.europa.eu/home

7. http://s3platform.jrc.ec.europa.eu/resources

8. http://s3platform.jrc.ec.europa.eu/documents/10157/15789/Governance%20Guide%20RIS 3_15_11_2013_def.pdf

9. http://www.europarl.europa.eu/meetdocs/2009_2014/organes/regi/regi_20131014_1500. htm

10. http://www.whitehouse.gov/blog/2011/10/28/lab-market-initiatives-transforming-new-ideas-new-jobs
    http://www.aau.edu/WorkArea/DownloadAsset.aspx?id=14535

11. http://ec.europa.eu/regional_policy/sources/docgener/guides/synergy/synergies_en.pdf

7. Conclusions on the reforms to the regional and urban policy in the European Union

7.1 A REVIEW OF THE MAJOR THEMES OF THE EU COHESION POLICY REFORMS

The aim of this book is to explain the nature and rationale for the reforms to EU Cohesion Policy, the European Union's regional and urban development policy. In essence EU Cohesion Policy aims to promote the growth and development of Europe's economically weaker regions so that they are able to play a more enhanced role in Europe's Single Market. This is to be realised by means of policy interventions and actions intended to foster many of the positive aspects of local growth and to mitigate some of the most severe and adverse aspects of local decline. The policy has already received a great deal of scrutiny over many years, as is warranted for major policies such as this. However, all aspects of the policy have received a fundamental reconsideration over recent years as a result of many different intellectual, practical and political economy influences deriving from many different quarters. These influences have ranged from openly hostile critiques to many different recommendations for reform based on different insights and experiences. These various critiques and recommendations have been incorporated into a wide-ranging reconsideration and redesign of the policy which has been implemented from 2014 onwards.

In the light of these intellectual, practical and political economy influences, this book sets out to explain the broad development case for the policy and also the conceptual basis underpinning its current reforms. In order to achieve this the explanation built by the book is developed by: articulating the intended objectives of the policy as a consequence of its evolution over several decades; by examining its underlying and modern place-based logic; by highlighting the centrality of the promotion of entrepreneurship and innovation in the new approach; and by sketching out the broad picture of the actual details of the reforms being implemented in the light of these various issues. As is consistent with the place-based approach, the book emphasises the importance of the inter-actions between the local economic and institutional context and all of the discussions regarding the reformed policy are explicitly positioned in the context of the institutional and geographical features of the EU. We discuss in detail the regional and urban economic features of the European Union alongside the heterogeneous governance characteristics of the EU geography. These are seen to be key determining factors regarding both the role and also the efficacy of the policy. At the same time, we also examine these discussions against the backdrop of the recent and current European political economy debates emerging both prior to, and in the aftermath of, the 2008 global financial crisis.

The basic underlying thread running through all aspects of the reforms outlined in the book is that EU Cohesion Policy does play a real and constructive role in both the EU's overall agenda and in Europe's regions and cities. However, in order for this role to be enhanced and improved for the twenty-first century challenges it must be tailored to the local context and this tailoring requires institutional and governance improve-ments in all aspects of the policy design and delivery. These institutional and governance improvements need to start from the initial policy prioritisation process and the overall policy strategic design, through to implementation and delivery, on to monitoring, evaluation and assess-ment, and finally to learning and policy adjustment. Each of these aspects of the policy cycle needs to be underpinned by greater levels of awareness and consideration of the available data, the data and evidence which can be generated by the programmes and projects, a great involvement of different partners, and a greater role for building on the bottom-up knowledge and capabilities of local actors. These requirements are critically relevant both in weaker regions and stronger regions, as well as in urban, rural or intermediate regions. Moreover, these require-ments are not specifically European issues, but are based on lessons derived from worldwide insights and experience. These lessons have then been applied and tailored to the specific economic, geographical and institutional characteristics of the European economy.

Chapter 1 examined the impact of two major influences on the current EU Cohesion Policy debates, namely the Europe 2020 strategy and also the 2008 global financial crisis. The Europe 2020 strategy has reshaped and reframed many aspects of the discussions regarding Europe's pre-ferred growth and development trajectory within the context of the Single Market, but as we see this reshaping also reflects the reframing of such debates at the wider international and global scales. A broader and more comprehensive understanding of growth and development processes has been emerging over the last two decades as a result of the different development experiences of different parts of the world, and in particular in the light of modern globalisation. Chapter 1 articulates this broader understanding and also highlights the specific features which are particularly pertinent to the European context in which Cohesion Policy operates. In particular, Chapter 1 also sets these discussions in the context of the regional and urban impacts of the 2008 global financial crisis which are seen to be highly heterogeneous. There is no simple story associated with these impacts, other than a recent reversal of many of the longstanding pan-EU convergence processes, and the role played by cities and regions in the trend changes vary significantly between countries. An awareness of the nuances of these shifts is very important in order to best situate the discussions regarding the role of the policy and its likely outcomes.

Chapter 2 sets out explicitly the geographical and institutional characteristics of Europe's cities and regions in a manner which also allows for comparisons with other parts of the world. This is important in order to provide appropriate benchmarks and comparators against which the regional economies of Europe can be understood. What we see is that while Europe's regions and cities display many of the characteristics of cities and regions in other parts of the world, there are also many specific and unique features of the European regional and urban system which differ markedly from other parts of the global economy. These discussions are developed in Chapter 2 in an explicitly geographical setting and across a range of different themes including: productivity and innovation; city sizes and city size-distributions; connectivity and accessibility; labour markets, mobility and inequality; demographic change; environmental matters; and governance and institutional issues. The book makes no normative claims regarding the nature of these geographical issues, but simply documents what we actually know about them. This is important because possible lessons for Europe deriving from observations in other parts of the world including North America and Asia are often casually applied to the European context, with little or no real understanding of the specifics of the European context.

Chapters 1 and 2 together provide a detailed backdrop against which we are able to begin our discussions in earnest in Chapter 3 regarding the nature of EU Cohesion Policy, the European Union's regional and urban policy. As we see in Chapter 3 the current policy logic and architecture is a product of a range of earlier developments and previous decisions based on different criteria at different stages in the life of the Common Market, the European Community and the European Union, respectively. While the policy has undergone various adjustments at specific points, until now the overall logic and architecture of the policy retains most of the key elements devised in the late 1980s, and some specific aspects of these various elements remain largely unchanged from that period while others have changed significantly. However, both the European Union and also the whole of the global economy have changed dramatically since the late 1980s, and this raises the question as to whether a policy devised in an earlier era is still appropriate for the current period. These questions touch on many aspects of economics, economic geography, political science, environmental science and sociology amongst others, and no single discipline has a monopoly of knowledge or insights into these matters. As we see in Chapter 3 there has been a great deal of scrutiny as to the economic performance of the policy and this provides insights and lessons regarding the possible ways in which the policy needs to be adapted or improved. However, when discussing the policy's reform, in order to build up a comprehensive and coherent overall picture of the policy across its various different dimensions and roles, a broad conceptual approach is required based on insights and lessons from a range of fields.

The approach employed in this book is also the approach which underpins the policy reform, namely the place-based approach. In Chapter 4 this approach positions the relationship between economic geography and institutional matters at the centre of the debate regarding the case for regional and urban policy, and emphasises the importance of a multi-level governance agenda which combines both bottom-up local and regional activities with top-down activities. The central argument here is that traditional regional policy based on a centrally determined and top-down sectoral approach applied at a regional level is not realistic for fostering regional development as it is inconsistent with the requisite institutional and governance structures appropriate for mobilising local actors and for building on local knowledge. To some observers, the idea that regional and urban policy can be anything other than place-based may appear to be rather surprising. However, some of the issues raised by the place-based discussion of regional and urban policy arise in part as a result of the space-blind critique of regional policy advocated by various commentators and institutions, and most notably by the 2009 World Development Report published by the World Bank. Again, to some observers these may appear to be rather esoteric theoretical arguments but in actual fact these discussions relate to concrete matters of real substance, quite literally, and addressing these theoretical challenges head-on is important to ensure that the conceptual approach underpinning Europe's regional and urban policy has strong foundations. These issues are dealt with in the appendix to Chapter 4, while the main text in the chapter discusses the major place-based critique of existing EU Cohesion

Policy outlined by the Barca (2009) report, and spells out the major requirements identified for a successful policy reform. These include the need for a results-orientation of the policy and also the use of condition-alities, all of which have arisen not just from European debates, but also from the experience of diverse actors within the global development arena. The chapter then proceeds to outline the major features of the actual reforms to EU Cohesion Policy being implemented in the period 2014–2020

One of the key features of the reform, as discussed in detail in Chapters 5 and 6, is the emphasis put on the need for fostering local and regional innovation. The broad case for policies aimed at enhancing regional innovation which is derived from the experience of many different countries and institutions is discussed in Chapter 5. This then forms the backdrop to the discussions in Chapter 6 which examine the particular approach to innovation policy prioritisation which is advocated in the EU Cohesion Policy reforms, and which is known as 'smart specialisation'. The smart specialisation agenda provides a framework for prioritising the allocation of innovation-related policy resources in a manner which is appropriate for the regional context. The movement towards an innovation-oriented policy as the core of the development agenda in weaker regions is a major shift of emphasis for EU Cohesion Policy. This shift is consistent with the view that 'EU regional policy is an investment policy. It supports job creation, competitiveness, economic growth, improved quality of life and sustainable development. These investments support the delivery of the Europe 2020 strategy' while at the same time being consistent with the principle that 'Regional policy is also the expression of the EU's solidarity with less developed countries and regions, concentrating funds on the areas and sectors where they can make the most difference. Regional policy aims to reduce the significant economic, social and territorial disparities that still exist between Europe's regions.'[1] As is appropriate for all innovation-related actions in the private sector and in the civil society sector as well as in the public sector, such approaches must also be explicitly results-oriented and based on processes of trialling and experimentation (Rodrik 2007). The promotion of innovation and entrepreneurship are never without risks, and yet they are inherently aimed at the overcoming of risks and uncertainty (Gordon and McCann 2005). The fragility and lack of resilience of many of Europe's regions in the aftermath of the 2008 global financial crisis has highlighted the need for a reorientation of the approaches to local development adopted in European regions. As we see in Chapter 6, while the insights and thinking which underpin the approach advocated in the policy reforms are derived from multiple sources, the specifics of the approach are based on the particularities of the EU context. The need for a tailored approach aimed at fostering local entrepreneurship and innovation in a manner which is appropriate for the local context is central to all of this thinking.

Behind all of these initiatives is the need for fostering the right types of local institutional and governance arrangements for achieving the desired local development goals. This includes not only ensuring good quality institutions and governance systems but also ones which are appropriate for the challenges being addressed. The importance of getting the institutional and governance settings right cannot be over-emphasised. Indeed the keys to addressing many of the technical, technological and skills-related challenges evident in our regions and cities actually lie in the arena of governance and institutional systems (Storper 2013). In particular, multi-level governance settings with a strong local or regional component are essential in order to bind together different sectoral policies. While trade-offs arise spontaneously, the search for tailored policy complementarities requires building, trialling and testing, and such activities are generally much easier and more effective at a local or regional scale than at a national level.

As we see in Chapters 2 and 3, however, there are major variations in the quality of regional governance within Europe, and these variations significantly impact on the efficacy of EU Cohesion Policy actions and interventions. A poor institutional context heavily limits development potential, and such governance systems require reforms in order to improve development potential. At the same time, having good institutions but ones which are inappropriate for the challenges ahead is just as problematic, because good institutions are very hard to reform even when such reforms would be desirable. This is because such institutions tend to have strong legal foundations, strong brand identities, strong constituencies and motivated memberships, all of which will tend to militate against reforms. Reforming either poor institutions or good-but-inappropriate institutions are both challenging issues, with the former being more prevalent in economically weaker economies while the latter are more prevalent in economically stronger economies. In all such cases, implementing the proportionality principles inherent in good multi-level governance arrangements, whereby roles, responsibilities' resources and incentives are correctly aligned, are essential features of ensuring good governance. This also implies that in cases where the macro-economic conditionality is applied there needs to be a mechanism whereby cities or regions implementing good policies are not penalised as a result of poor governance performance on the part of national authorities or other regions. Otherwise such fears in member states facing difficult budgetary conditions will lead to the widespread design and implementation of conservative policies focusing on relatively easy goals rather than on innovative policies designed to re-orient regional trajectories. The different quality of government variations in the EU and the heterogeneity of Europe's regional institutional settings, alongside the diversity of Europe's regional per-capita income levels, means that the importance of getting these various governance issues right is at least as critical in the case of Europe's regions as it in other parts of the world.

The EU Cohesion Policy approach in the 2014–2020 programming period and beyond essentially requires policy efforts to be aimed at tailoring rather than copying, based on actions designed to foster differentiation rather than mimicking, and driven by strategies focused on prioritisation and concentration rather than on the politically driven fragmentation and dispersion of funds. The desired good governance policy settings are based on an explicit result-orientation culture combined with a strong partnership theme and a policy-prioritisation logic appropriate for the local context. Good governance is to be ensured by accountability and transparency regarding all aspects of the policy process throughout all stages of the policy cycle, and not just in terms of expenditure and accounting. In many regions these changes will necessarily imply significant changes in the culture of policymaking and policy-implementation processes. At the same time, often this approach will also require us to consider the opportunities and potential associated with a wider range of actors with a broader portfolio of ideas than are currently represented in local policy discourses.

As we have seen in this book, the EU Cohesion Policy reforms have been informed on the basis of a wide-ranging reflection and reconsideration of the policy experience and on the insights of numerous academic and policy experts. Yet, as with many policy innovations, and especially in the case of development policy innovations, whether the reforms will engender sufficient levels of the desired behavioural and institutional changes so as to be successful cannot be realistically assessed for many years. As we saw in Chapter 3 our present understanding of the performance of the policy is based on data from previous programming periods and similarly our understanding of the impacts of the current policy reforms will only emerge in future time periods. However, the experience from development activities worldwide suggests that evidence in the short and medium terms of ongoing and credible behavioural and institutional changes is likely to underpin the long-term success of the policy reforms. This underscores the importance of ensuring that the policy reform process is accepted and adopted as soon as possible and as widely as possible and that all activities relating to good policy design, monitoring and evaluation begin in earnest as soon as possible.

7.2 POTENTIAL WEAKNESSES, THREATS AND RESISTANCE TO THE EU COHESION POLICY REFORMS

The widespread acceptance and adoption of the EU Cohesion Policy reforms is not without challenges or threats. There are potential weaknesses in the manner in which the reform logic has been translated into actual provisions and regulations as well as real behavioural and institutional threats to their implementation. All of these need to be explicitly acknowledged, as they each have the potential to derail many of the forward-looking innovations inherent in the new policy design logic.

7.2.1 Weaknesses in the Policy Provisions and Regulations

One potential weakness of the policy regulations is the rather vague nature of some of the investment priorities. In order to ensure that programmes and projects are well targeted a much sharper focus is often required than some of the broadly and rather vaguely-defined headings permit. Following the smart specialisation approach, it is essential that policy programming is as explicitly and sharply defined as possible in order to facilitate the whole results-orientation agenda. Otherwise, the emphasis on resource prioritisation and concentration may be somewhat watered down.

A second potential weakness of the policy provisions concerns the tension between the whole results-orientation agenda, which may incline managing authorities and policymakers towards a more sectoral approach, and that of the territorial agenda – including the integrated and the urban strategies – which do not have an explicit results-orientation requirement. In the former case, the logic of the smart specialisation agenda means that these strategies need to be explicitly place-based in their approach, tailored to the territorial context, and aimed at diversifying regional technological profiles via the facilitation of entrepreneurial search processes. However, as we will see below there will be many incentives for major sectoral actors to push this agenda towards a largely 'insider–outsider' (Lindbeck and Snower 1988) sectoral logic in order to help capture policy rents. In the latter case of the territorial agenda, rather than needing to be explicitly results-orientated, these programmes only have a requirement for their outputs to be tracked back to the sectoral priorities from which they draw their funding. While these approaches will generally prioritise integrated territorial-based thinking, it is essential that actions and interventions under these headings still adopt as much of a results-orientation logic as is possible. Otherwise again, it will be very difficult to engender learning, to identify performance, and ultimately to determine whether the interventions have been effective or not.

A third potential weakness of the implemented policy reforms, and one which was an outcome of the complex negotiations between member states and the European Commission, is that the N+2 decommitment rule which predominated in the 2007–2013 programming period has changed to an N+3 decommitment rule. These extended reimbursement time periods potentially reduce the incentives for early and proactive action regarding programme design and implementation. As a result the distribution of policy actions, interventions and projects is likely to be increasingly back-loaded towards the latter part of the programming period. Unfortunately, this also militates against the promotion of early insights and learning being derived from the required project monitoring and evaluation activities. Moreover, the potential paucity of data and evidence during the middle years of the current programming period will complicate the subsequent preparations for negotiations regarding the next programming period.

A fourth potential weakness of the policy reforms as implemented, and again one which was an outcome of the complex negotiations, is that the performance framework has emerged as something of a double sanction, rather than as a 'carrot and stick' combination of incentives and sanctions, as is argued for in modern development policy literature. The reason is that in the final agreed policy regulations, the resources are programmed from the beginning, so in order to be able to draw down the performance reserve it is necessary to implement the programmes as originally planned. From a development policy perspective, in terms of incentive structures, a much better arrangement would have been for the performance reserve to be exactly that, a reward for good performance, and this would also include policy adjustments in the light of real-time learning derived from the monitoring and evaluation activities. A crucial dimension of the results-orientation philosophy, including the whole monitoring and evaluation agenda, is to ensure that policies are also explicitly 'delivery-oriented' in nature. Being delivery-oriented is not simply a matter of programming and then implementing as programmed, but also of adjusting as required on the basis of the emerging evidence. Following the key features of the original of the 1998 reforms (Bachtler and Turok 1997) programming is an essential feature of good policy design. But the contemporary thinking on good results-oriented and good delivery-oriented policies include many additional and essential features and the appropriate performance criteria should reflect these. Furthermore, in the contemporary EU context good place-based policy also requires that multi-level governance partnership principles are properly adhered to, although the evidence suggests that across Europe's cities and regions the adoption of these principles is ad hoc (CoR 2014) and there is still some way to go to achieve these goals.[2] This brings up the question of the likely sources of institutional resistance to the policy changes.

7.2.2 Institutional Resistance to the Policy Reform Logic

At the same time as potential design-weaknesses within the policy regulations themselves, another set of obstacles to the success of the policy relates to institutional resistance. Taken together the wide-ranging changes to EU Cohesion Policy are likely to be rather threatening to certain established individuals, institutions, organisations and consistencies, and the experience of development policies from around the world suggests that there are typical patterns to these threats. As such the policy reforms are likely to face significant resistance from a range of different sources including local, central and sectoral actors. Indeed, any parties who fear that their existing monopoly positions are likely to be challenged are likely to be a source of resistance and the majority of these parties will display incentive structures oriented towards limiting, diverting or even subverting the reforms. Moreover, the resistance to these reforms may arise via various different mechanisms, some of which may at first appear to be rather innocuous but which in reality are potent. On this point, two of the most common and threatening resistance mechanisms aimed at limiting, diverting or subverting policy reforms are via the use of 'tick-the-box' exercises and also via the design of strategies which are too general in nature to be meaningful. Both of these approaches reflect a form of tokenism designed to reduce transparency and real accountability.

In terms of 'tick-the-box' type approaches to policy design and policy compliance, the key problem is that what actually takes place 'on the ground' is very different to what appears on paper. If the agreements between the various multi-level governance actors are based on what is written on paper without any other strong and independent forms of verification or oversight being possible, then such agreements will be based on weak foundations. There are many common examples of this type of behaviour. For example, Partnership Agreements may contain lists of actors and institutions who ostensibly are partners in the policy-design process but in reality have little or no influence on what takes place. 'Tick-the-box' types of approaches tend to work when there is a hierarchical policy-governance structure in which lower-level and smaller actors have little or no voice, and where all of the communication regarding the policy emerges from the high-level decision-makers. It is therefore essential that the policy negotiations between the European Commission and the member states regarding the design of the pro-grammes also involve discussions regarding the credible involvement of different multi-level governance parties and the verification of the various partnership roles throughout the life of the programmes.

An alternative tactic to limiting, diverting or subverting policy reforms is via the design or policy programmes based on strategies which are too general in terms of their intended objectives. Such a tactic typically involves designing a policy whose stated objectives are too broad to be captured by the use of a small number of realistic, measurable and practical results indicators. This also relates to the vagueness of some of the investment priorities, as alluded to above. Instead these types of policies typically set out vague and over-general aspirations which cannot be clearly or narrowly defined. This tactic militates against the usefulness of any policy monitoring and evaluation activities as the goals of the policy are insufficiently narrow to clearly be articulated. It thereby also undermines the whole results-orientation approach of the policy reforms. In addition, this tactic is also particularly attractive to certain parties because it makes it easier for policymakers to alter their policies in an ad hoc fashion according to other politically-motivated criteria.

Both of the two tactics, namely employing 'tick-the-box' exercises and alternatively setting out overly-general objectives, can be used as 'back-door' routes towards policies which are largely space-blind in nature. Such approaches are often used to undermine the territorial logic of the policy reforms because a place-based and territorial approach tends not to prioritise the preferences or interests of national or capital city elites. Rather, as we have seen, a place-based multi-level governance approach seeks to balance the interests and agendas of local and regional actors alongside national actors in order to maximise the wellbeing of local people in the regions being targeted. Some national or capital city actors will be threatened by such approaches in situations where these imply a certain devolution of responsibilities. In terms of central government institutions, many policymakers and high-level government actors oper-ating in hierarchically-driven and top-down governance systems are likely to be very reluctant to cede responsibility for important aspects of policy design and delivery to lower levels actors and institutions. The reason is that such a loss of responsibility and control also often involves a loss of employment status, job satisfaction, and personal sense of self-worth. Moreover, traditional hierarchical governance roles are doubly threatened by such shifts where they are allowed to take place, because if indeed it subsequently turns out that lower-level local actors can be successful in such policymaking activities, this would undermine any claims by central government actors that they have superior and specific capabilities which are unavailable to local actors. As we have seen, the place-based approach explicitly allows for such claims to be tested and challenged. Yet, as long as central government maintains all such policy levers, then many of these claims can never be challenged. As such, the fear not only of losing control but also of losing credibility means that significant resistance to more locally-driven innovation-policy approaches may emerge from central government policymakers used to top-down policymaking and who are thereby reluctant to cede much of their previous power. Central government policymakers may seek to limit the transfer of powers and responsibility from central to local actors using other issues as pretexts, including legal issues, data and information restrictions, and public finance controls. Taken together, these various types of activities represent the major top-down challenge to the types of multi-level governance approaches required for a healthy place-based policy.

In terms of local institutional challenges to the policy reforms, resistance to more locally-driven policy innovations may emerge from those local vested interests and elites who currently command local monopoly and monopsony positions and who thereby feel threatened by such changes in policy approaches. These types of fears will be magnified if there is a sense that central government actors will also be playing an increasingly important oversight role consistent with the place-based approach and which demands greater transparency and accountability both at the national as well as at the local level. In particular, local elites and vested interests are likely to feel threatened by smart specialisation policies aimed at promoting the diversification of the existing regional technological and institutional trajectories. The reason is that the promotion of such diversification and novelty may imply a degree of policy prioritisation towards actors and institutions who are rather different from those represented by the existing elites and therefore such actors may fear that these policy initiatives may partially undermine their monopoly positions. As a response, such local vested interests and elites may try to block or at least limit many of the potentially innovative policy approaches. Alternatively, they may seek to 'capture' the policy processes and to restrict the role of other newer or less influential actors by positioning themselves as the dominant players in the local policy discourses so as to capture the lion's share of any policy-related rents.

This type of 'insider–outsider' behaviour is common in many fields of political economy including labour negotiations (Lindbeck and Snower 1988), and the rental-capture aspects of these relations are particularly relevant where policy resources are made available. These types of tactics associated with either limiting or capturing the policy process and policy changes represent the major local and bottom-up challenges to the types of multi-level governance approaches required for healthy place-based policy.

A third potential institutional source of resistance to the more locally-driven innovative policy approaches arises from sectoral interests. Many large companies or large and well-organised business and institutional groupings are especially adept at capturing policy-related rents via lobbying and industry self-promotion activities. Some business sectors display particularly well-oiled lobbying activities and the complex relationships between government and these key sectors is often highly influential in shaping government policies, and most notably those involving industrial policy. Yet, such adept and influential lobbying activities are not in any way confined to the private sector. Highly influential sectoral lobbying is also evident in various arenas of both the public sector and civil society sectors. Many of the major actors undertaking these sectoral lobbying roles within the private sector, the civil society sector and also the public sector may feel significantly threatened by policy-related shifts advocating more of place-based rather than a sector-based approach. The structure and composition of these sectors and their lobbying interests will determine the nature of the different attempts at blocking, limiting or capturing policy innovations and a variety of such actions are likely to ensue in many arenas. One of the most obvious tactics in the current context is for sectoral interests to try to translate the smart specialisation concept into a sectoral specialisation policy in which particular sectors lobby in order to divert the policy resources towards supporting their own sectoral rather than regional and place-based interests. The actual pattern of these tactics may be quite diverse and will depend on the policies being advocated and the specific issues facing these lobbying bodies. Moreover, such tactics may impact differently on local or central actors and institutions, according to their nature and pattern. Yet, these types of activities whereby sectoral interests will lobby in order to dilute the place-based dimensions of the policy represent the major sectoral challenges to the place-based innovation-related policies.

A fourth set of institutional challenges to the policy reforms relate to the relationships between the central government of the EU member states and the role of the European Commission. One of the key elements in the reforms to EU Cohesion Policy is that fact that the explicit use of conditionalities relating to all aspects of ex ante policy design, ongoing policy delivery and monitoring and ex post policy evaluation means that the role of the European Commission as guardian of good governance of the policy on behalf of all EU citizens is enhanced. In some sense this can be seen as returning to and reaffirming the original intentions of the 1988 Delors reform. Yet, the fact that these conditionalities are being implemented at exactly the same time that localities have greater flexibility than ever to pool resources from different streams using the Common Strategic Framework and to cooperate on the basis of different types of the partnerships, means that the multi-level governance principles are being enhanced at an EU-wide level. The 'carrot and stick' approach is central to the fostering of healthy multi-level governance partnerships aimed at combining the good aspects of both central and local governance. For Cohesion Policy this is exactly as it should be if the policy is to serve in the best interests of EU citizens. Yet, these movements towards better multi-level governance may be impacted upon by various domestic issues within individual member states. Much of the opposition to the role played by supra-national institutions which is currently evident in the domestic political discourses of various European countries may be used in some cases as a pretext to limit the application of EU-wide good multi-level governance principles and to weaken the enhanced supervisory role of the European Commission. Given the patterns of these domestic debates, these objections are probably more likely to emerge from some of the richer member states.

In other cases, claims that different levels of national and local government do not have the capacity or capabilities to implement modern regional development approaches are more likely to emerge from economically weaker countries. Yet, the reforms have been explicitly designed to encourage policy-tailoring which is appropriate to the context, and this also takes into consideration different institutional capabilities. The obvious riposte to these claims is that such approaches themselves encourage processes of policy learning and institutional capacity-building and galvanising these processes is an essential element of the reforms. Moreover, the regulations provide for the funding of technical support and assistance via the development of capacity-building linkages with other regions and expertise. The development of these types of cooperation arrangements are a form of technology transfer in their own right.

A final institutional threat to the policy reforms comes from the workings of the European Commission itself, in that a lack of vigilance or capacity on the part of the European Commission regarding specific aspects of the policy reform may inadvertently end up limiting the effectiveness of the overall reforms. For example, compliance on almost all conditionalities but an unwillingness to ensure that the use of results indicators is properly adhered to in all cases will undermine the whole monitoring, evaluation and results-orientation aspects of the reforms. Similarly, an unwillingness on the part of the European Commission to challenge the assumptions underlying the proposed smart specialisation strategies is likely to lead to already-privileged institutions and actors capturing most of the policy rents. Again, a lack of serious questioning regarding the true nature of the partnership roles discussed in the partnership agreements is likely to undermine the whole multi-level governance and territorial aspects of the place-based approach. Therefore, in order to ensure the credibility of the whole policy and its reforms it is essential that the European Commission acts on behalf of all member states and all EU citizens to ensure that the conditionalities are properly enforced. These conditionalities relate to each of the key aspects of the policy reform outlined in Chapter 4, and it is also essential that the European Commission invests in the much-needed expertise to monitor the application, and ensure the enforcement, of the all of the conditionalities. The different elements of the policy reform only work as a whole as long as all of the reform elements are adhered to by policymakers in the recipient regions.

The lessons from international development activities show that the co-dependency relations often evident between different types of policy donors and recipients generally act as a bar to policy innovations. The incentive structures inherent in such institutional relations mean that actors will automatically seek to limit the impacts of any policy changes and this opposition thereby contributes to the ongoing sclerosis of existing institutional settings. Moreover, these various forms and mechanisms of institutional resistance may also arise from more than one source at a time, and this obviously complicates the picture. However, the various alternative mechanisms which are used in order to limit the effectiveness of policy innovations by different types of actors and institutions in different local, central, sectoral or national monopoly positions are well known within the economics and political science literatures, and are traditionally analysed using frameworks such as game theory, principal-agent theory and bilateral monopoly models. As a direct response to these threats, therefore, modern development theory stresses the need to trial and to experiment with policy actions and interventions in order to identify what works and thereby to overcome such sclerotic tendencies (Rodrik 2007). It is therefore essential that the reformed EU Cohesion Policy regulations are implemented in a manner in which policy innovation is encouraged, and any performance reserve sanctions are only applied for a failure to implement policies according to the spirit of these modern development policy principles, rather than on the basis of whether a specific policy action or intervention was deemed to be successful or not in the short run.

More generally, however, the most robust defence against each of these various different forms of institutional resistance to change and the strongest tonic for promoting good policies based on good governance principles is to reiterate, reinforce and publicise the whole results-orientation logic of the policy. All aspects of the programmes, projects, actions and interventions ranging from the original scoping and ex ante baseline analysis activities through to the policy prioritisation process and then on to the monitoring and evaluation activities, should be publicised as much as possible in all regions and all countries and in all stages of the programmes, not just after the programmes have finished. The transparency of: the policy intentions, aims and objectives; the role and engagement activities of the partners and stakeholders; the policy delivery mechanisms; and the ongoing performance monitoring and evaluation activities, are all essential features of accountability, in addition to robust accounting for expenditure. Such transparency fosters good policymaking and helps to build trust. At the same time, and in order not to undermine these good governance and accountability principles, any sanctions should only be applied for non-compliance with these principles, and never on the basis of whether performance results are as good as expected. Otherwise stakeholders will never try to innovate for fear of failure and will automatically revert to conservative policy positions, thereby undermining the whole innovation culture.

Obviously, the new legal provisions and the revised performance framework are intended to make implementation more consistent and effective (Petzold 2013). However, on the basis of these various potential weaknesses and different potential sources of institutional resistance, it still remains to be seen whether the new Cohesion Policies narratives – results-orientation, place-based and territorial, prioritisation and concentration, smart specialisation, integrated actions, partnership and multilevel governance – in reality do take hold to the degree intended in very different EU regional and national contexts. While on the one hand commentators emphasise the importance of 'Europeanising' national–regional policies and capacity-building (Bachtler et al. 2014), the economic, geographic, and governance heterogeneity of EU regional settings suggests that these processes may still remain somewhat fragile, varied and rather context-dependent (Petzold 2013).

7.3 FINAL THOUGHTS

Given the scale of the policy and also the types of issues addressed by the policy the future performance of EU Cohesion Policy is of major significance for the performance of the European Union as a whole. Good results-oriented policymaking also requires good data and reconnaissance and the whole results-oriented approach has also been heavily supported by major advances in EU regional data availability. A large number of different sources of different types of EU regional and urban data are now available and many of these sources and publications have been referred to in this book. The most comprehensive overall assessments are provided by the three-yearly Cohesion Reports (European Commission 2010; European Union 2014), but just as important in many ways are the intervening Progress Reports (European Union 2011, 2013) which document key current trends in regional and urban transformations and particularly recent changes in these trends. The enormous trend changes in EU regions in the aftermath of the 2008 global financial crisis underline the importance for policymakers of receiving such timely and frequently updated overviews of the type provided for by these progress reports

At the same time, many of the issues discussed here are not unique to Europe. While there are many particular aspects which are specific to Europe many of the issues arising here also have major lessons for other parts of the world which are considering shifting their policy settings along similar lines. The reforms described here are based on worldwide consultations, and as a result are underpinned by the latest thinking on a range of different issues, and most importantly on the need to foster policy innovation in order to spur innovation more generally. Consistent with these international arguments, the policy reforms contain large elements of trialing and experimentation and the willingness of policymakers to adopt, adapt and implement new ideas is central to the whole smart specialisation logic. As such, the modern development policy principles have also been learned and applied by EU policymakers themselves in terms of the design of the overall Cohesion Policy reforms.

The fact that such policy innovations should have emerged from the EU may be something of a surprise to some observers who are accustomed to descriptions in their respective popular and domestically-oriented national presses which often depict EU institutions and activities as being dominated by institutional sclerosis. Yet it is the non-party-political nature of the EU's institutions and also the lack of domination of the EU's institutions by individual member states which has allowed such policy innovations to be considered on the basis of the best external advice and expertise. Hopefully, the contents of this book will go some way to changing some of the misplaced views about the EU's institutions and policy settings, and will also underscore the role that new ideas can play in fostering policy innovations (Rodrik 2014; Foray 2015).

NOTES

1. http://ec.europa.eu/regional_policy/what/index_en.cfm
2. See also https://portal.cor.europa.eu/europe2020/Documents/Executive%20summary_CoR%20Europe%202020%20mid-term%20assessment%20report.pdf
   http://cor.europa.eu/en/activities/governance/Documents/vdb-opinion-mlg/cdr273-2011_fin_ac_en.pdf

Bibliography

CHAPTER 1

Addison. J.T., and Siebert, W.S., 1997, (eds.), *Labour Markets in Europe: Issues of Harmonization and Regulation*, Dryden Press, London

Aghion, P., Besley, T., Browne, J., Caselli, F., Lambert, R., Lomax, R., Pissarides, C., Stern, N., and Van Reenen, J., 2013, *Investing for Prosperity: Skills, Infrastructure and Innovation*, Report of the LSE Growth Commission in Partnership with the Institute for Government, Centre for Economic Performance, London

Alesina, A., and Giavazzi, F., 2006, *The Future of Europe: Reform or Decline*, MIT Press, Cambridge MA

Arestis, P., and Sawyer, M., 2012, (eds.), *The Euro Crisis*, Palgrave Macmillan, Basingstoke.

Armstrong, H.W., and Vickerman, R.W., 1995, *Convergence and Divergence Among European Regions*, Pion, London

Artobolevsky, S.S., 1997, *Regional Policy in Europe*, Jessica Kingsley, London

Bachtler, J., and Turok, I., 1997, (eds.), *The Coherence of Regional Policy: Contrasting Perspectives on the Structural Funds*, Jessica Kingsley, London

Bachtler, J., Mendez, C., and Wishlade, F., 2013, *EU Cohesion Policy and European Integration: The Dynamics of EU Budget and Regional Policy Reform*, Ashgate, Aldershot

Baldwin, R., Cohen, D., Sapir, A., and Venables, A. (eds), 1999, *Market Integration, Regionalism and the Global Economy*, Cambridge University Press, Cambridge

Barca, F., 2009, *An Agenda for A Reformed Cohesion Policy: A Place-Based Approach to Meeting European Union Challenges and Expectations*, Independent Report Prepared at the Request of the European Commissioner for Regional Policy, Danuta Hübner, European Commission, Brussels

Bellini, N., and Hilpert, U., 2013, *Europe's Changing Geography: The Impact of Inter-Regional Networks*, Routledge, London

Berg, A.G., and Ostry, J.D., 2011, "Inequality and Unsustainable Growth: Two Sides of the Same Coin", IMF Staff Discussion Note, SDN/11/08, International Monetary Fund, Washington DC

Berglund, S., Duvold, K., Ekman, J., and Schymik, C., 2009, *Where Does Europe End?: Borders, Limits and the Directions of the EU*, Edward Elgar, Cheltenham

BIS, 2011, *The Economic Consequences for the UK and the EU of Completing the Single Market*, BIS Economics Paper No.11, Department for Business Innovation and Skills, February

BIS/DFID, 2011, *The UK and the Single Market*, Trade and Investment Analytical Papers Topic 4 of 18, Department for Business, Innovation and Skills Department for International Development Joint BIS/DFID Trade Policy Unit

Bliss, C., and Braga de Macedo, J., 1990, (eds.), *Unity with Diversity in the European Economy: The Community's Southern Frontier*, Cambridge University Press, Cambridge

Blokker, P., and Dallago, B., 2009, (eds.), *Regional Diversity and Local Development in the New Member States*, Palgrave Macmillan, Basingstoke

Boltho, A., and Eichengreen, B., 2008, *Economic Impact of European Integration*, Centre for Economic Policy Research CEPR, London

Button, K., and Pentecost, E., 1999, *Regional Economic Performance within the European Union*, Edward Elgar, Cheltenham, UK and Northampton, MA, USA

Cappelin, R., and Batey, P.W.J., 1993, (eds.), *Regional Networks, Border Regions and European Integration*, Pion, London

CBI, 2013, *Our Global Future: The Business Vision for a Reformed EU*, Confederation of British Industry, London

Cecchini, P., Catinat, M., and Jacquemin, A., 1988, *The European Challenge 1992: The Benefits of a Single Market*, Report for The Commission of the European Communities, Brussels

Cheshire, P.C., and Gordon, I.R., 1995, (eds.), *Territorial Competition in an Integrating Europe*, Avebury, Aldershot

Cole, J., and Cole, F., 1993, *The Geography of the European Community*, Routledge, London

Commission of the European Communities, 1990, *European Economy: One Market One Money – An Evaluation of the Potential Benefits and Costs of Forming and Economic and Monetary Union*, No 44, October, Directorate-General for Economic and Financial Affairs, Brussels. See: http://ec.europa.eu/economy_finance/publications/publication_summary 7520_en.htm

CoR, 2014, *A Mid-Term Assessment of Europe 2020 from the Standpoint of EU Regions and Cities*, Committee of the Regions, Brussels

Crafts, N., and Toniolo, G., 1996, (eds.), *Economic Growth in Europe Since 1945*, Cambridge University Press, Cambridge

David, P.A., 1969, 'Transport Innovations and Economic Growth: Professor Fogel On and Off the Rails', *Economic History Review*, 22.3, 506–524, reprinted in David, P.A., 1975, *Technical Choice, Innovation and Economic Growth: Essays on American and British Experience in the Nineteenth Century*, Cambridge University Press, Cambridge

Delamaide, D., 1994, *The New Superregions of Europe*, Dutton, New York

DG Regio, 2008, *Regions 2020: Demographic Challenges for European Regions*, EU Directorate General for Regional Policy, Brussels

DG Regio, 2009a, *Regions 2020: Globalisation Challenges for European Regions*, EU Directorate General for Regional Policy, Brussels

DG Regio, 2009b, *Regions 2020: The Climate Change Challenge for European Regions*, EU Directorate General for Regional Policy, Brussels

DG Regio, 2013, *Information Tools*, EU Directorate General for Regional and Urban Policy, Brussels

Dijkstra, L., 2010, "The Regional Lisbon Index", *Regional Focus 03/2010*, Directorate-General for Regional Policy, Brussels

Donaldson, D., and Hornbeck, R., 2013, "Railroads and American Economic Growth: A Market Access Approach", NBER Working Paper 19213, National Bureau of Economic Research, Cambridge MA. See http://www.nber.org/papers/w19213.pdf?new_window=1

Dotti, N.F., and Bubbico, R., 2014, "New Challenges for Structural Funds: The New Territorial Capital Approach in the Perspective of the Evolution of the EU Regional Policy", *European Structural and Investment Funds Journal*, forthcoming

Eichengreen, B., 2007, *The European Economy Since 1945: Coordinated Capitalism and Beyond*, Princeton University Press, Princeton NJ

Emerson, M., Aujean, M., Goybet, P., and Jacquemin, A., 1988, *The Economics of 1992: The E.C. Commission's Assessment of the Economic Effects of Completing the Single Market*, Oxford University Press, Oxford

Emerson, M., Gros, D., Italianer, A., Pisani-Ferry, J., and Reichenbach, H., 1992, *One Market One Money: An Evaluation of the Potential Benefits and Costs of Forming an Economic and Monetary Union*, Oxford University Press, Oxford

Ernst and Young, 2014, *EY's Attractiveness Survey: Europe 2014 Back in the Game*, www.ey.com/attractiveness.

European Commission, 2010a, *Citizens' Awareness and Perceptions of EU Regional Policy*, Directorate-General for Regional Policy and the Directorate-General Communication, Brussels

European Commission, 2010b, *Europe 2020: A European Strategy for Smart, Sustainable and Inclusive Growth*, [COM (2010) 2020] 3.3.2010, Brussels

European Commission, 2010c, *Lisbon Strategy Evaluation Document*, Commission Staff Working Document, [SEC (2010) 114 Final] 2.2.2010, Brussels

European Commission, 2010d, *Investing in Europe's Future: Fifth Report on Economics, Social and Territorial Cohesion*, Publications Office, Brussels

European Commission, 2011a, *Results of the Public Consultation on the Conclusions of the Fifth Report on Economic, Social and Territorial Cohesion*, SEC (2011) 590 Final, 13.5.2011. See http://ec.europa.eu/regional_policy/consultation/5cr/index_en.cfm

European Commission, 2011b, *Europe 2020 Annual Growth Survey 2011: Advancing the EU's Comprehensive Response to the Crisis*, Brussels

European Commission, 2012, *Employment and Social Development in Europe 2012*, Directorate-General for Employment, Social Affairs and Inclusion, Brussels

European Commission, 2014a, "Cohesion Policy 2014-2020 Momentum Builds", *Panorama: Inforegio*, 48, Winter, Brussels

European Commission, 2014b, *Communication from the Commission to the European Parliament, the Council, the European Economic and Social Committee and the Committee of the Regions: Taking Stock of the Europe 2020 Strategy for Smart, Sustainable and Inclusive Growth*, COM (2014) 130 Final, 5.3.2014, Brussels

European Union, 2011, *The Urban and Regional Dimension of Europe 2020: Seventh Progress Report on Economic, Social and Territorial Cohesion*, Publications Office, Brussels

European Union, 2012, *The European Union Explained: How the European Union Works*, Directorate-General for Communication, Brussels

European Union, 2013a, *European Competitiveness Report 2013: Towards Knowledge Driven Reindustrialisation*, Publications Office, Brussels

European Union, 2013b, *The Urban and Regional Dimension of the Crisis: Eighth Report on Economic, Social and Territorial Cohesion*, Publications Office, Brussels

Ezcurra, R., 2007, "Is Income Inequality Harmful for Growth? Evidence from the European Union", *Urban Studies*, 44.10, 1953–1971

Faludi, A., 2008, *European Spatial Research and Planning*, Lincoln Institute of Land Policy, Cambridge MA

Fingleton, B., 2003, (ed.), *European Regional Growth*, Springer, Heidelberg

Fitoussi, J.-P, and Le Cacheaux, J., 2010, *Report on the State of the Union Volume 3: Crisis in the EU Economic Governance*, Palgrave Macmillan, Basingstoke

Florio, M., 2011, (ed.), *Public Investment, Growth and Fiscal Constraints: Challenges for the New EU Member States*, Edward Elgar, Cheltenham, UK and Northampton, MA, USA

Fogel, R.W., 1964, *Railroads and American Economic Growth: Essays in Econometric History*, Johns Hopkins Press, Baltimore

Ghamawat, P., and Altman, S.A., 2012, *DHL Global Connectedness Index 2012: Analysing Global Flows and their Power to Increase Prosperity*, IESE Business School, Barcelona, Spain

Hall, P., and Pain, K., 2006, *The Polycentric Metropolis: Learning from Mega-City Regions in Europe*, Earthscan, London

Iammarino S., and McCann, P., 2013, *Multinationals and Economic Geography: Location, Technology and Innovation*, Edward Elgar, Cheltenham, UK and Northampton, MA, USA

Jaegers, T., Lipp-Lingua, C., and Amil, D., 2013, "High-Technology and Medium-High Technology Industries Main Drivers of EU-27's Industrial Growth", *Eurostat Statistics in Focus 1/2013*, European Commission

João Rodrigues, M., 2009, *Europe, Globalization and the Lisbon Agenda*, Edward Elgar, Cheltenham, UK and Northampton, MA, USA

Jovanović, M., 2005, *The Economics of European Integration: Limits and Prospects*, Edward Elgar, Cheltenham

Jovanović, M., 2009, *Evolutionary Economic Geography: Location of Production and the European Union*, Routledge, London

Kahanec, M., and Zimmerman, K., 2011, (eds.), *Ethnic Diversity in European Labor Markets: Challenges and Solutions*, Edward Elgar, Cheltenham, UK and Northampton, MA, USA

Le Galès, P., 2002, *European Cities: Social Conflicts and Governance*, Oxford University Press, Oxford

Leonardi, R., 2005, *Cohesion Policy in the European Union: The Building of Europe*, Palgrave Macmillan, Basingstoke

Marsh, D., 2009, *The Euro: The Politics of the New Global Currency*, Yale University Press, New Haven

Martin, R., 1999, *The Regional Dimension in European Public Policy: Convergence or Divergence?*, St Martin's Press, Macmillan, New York

Mayhew, A., 1998, *Recreating Europe: The European Union's Policy Towards Central and Eastern Europe*, Cambridge University Press, Cambridge

McCann, P., 2008, "Globalization and Economic Geography: The World is Curved, Not Flat", *Cambridge Journal of Regions, Economy and Society*, 1.3, 351–370

McCann, P., 2009, "Globalisation, Multinationals and the BRIICS Countries", in Lattimore, R., and Safadi, R., (eds.), *Globalisation and Emerging Economies*, OECD Organisation for Economic Cooperation and Development, Paris

McCann, P., 2013, *Modern Urban and Regional Economics*, Oxford University Press, Oxford

MGI, 2013, *A New Dawn: Reigniting Growth in Central and Eastern Europe*, McKinsey Global Institute, December

MGI, 2014, *Global Flows in a Digital Age: How Trade, Finance, People and Data Connect the World Economy*, McKinsey Global Institute, April

Molle, W., 2007, *European Cohesion Policy*, Routledge, London

NIC, 2012, *Alternative Worlds 2030: Global Trends 2030*, National Intelligence Council, Office of the Director of National Intelligence, Washington DC

OECD, 2009a, *OECD "Global Charter"/"Legal Standard" An Inventory of Possible Policy Actions*, ILO International Labor Organization, the IMF International Monetary Fund, the OECD Organisation for Economic Cooperation and Development, the World Bank and the World Trade Organization, Organisation for Economic Cooperation and Development, Paris

OECD, 2009b, *How Regions Grow*, Organisation for Economic Growth and Development, Paris

OECD, 2009c, *Regions Matter: Economic Recovery, Innovation and Sustainable Growth*, Organisation for Economic Growth and Development, Paris

OECD, 2011a, *OECD Regional Outlook 2011: Building Resilient Regions for Stronger Economies*, Organisation for Economic Cooperation and Development, Paris

OECD, 2011b, *Regions at a Glance 2013*, Organisation for Economic Cooperation and Development, Paris

OECD, 2013a, *Investing Together: Working Effectively Across Levels of Government*, Organisation for Economic Cooperation and Development, Paris

OECD, 2013b, *Government at a Glance 2013*, Organisation for Economic Cooperation and Development, Paris

OECD, 2014, *OECD Factbook 2014: Economic, Environmental and Social Statistics*, Organisation for Economic Cooperation and Development, Paris

Padoa-Schioppa, T., Emerson, M., King, M., Milleron, J.-C., Paelinck, J., Papademos, L., Pastor, A., and Scharpf, 1987, *Efficiency, Stability and Equity: A Strategy for the Evolution of the Economic System of the European Community*, Oxford University Press, Oxford

Piketty, T., 2014, *Capital in the Twenty-First Century*, Harvard University Press, Cambridge MA, Translated from French by Arthur Goldhammer

Pinder, J., and Usherwood, S., 2007, *The European Union: A Very Short Introduction*, Oxford University Press, Oxford

Pisani-Ferry, J., 2014, *The Euro Crisis and its Aftermath*, Oxford University Press, Oxford

Rodriguez-Pose, A., 1998, *Dynamics of Regional Growth in Europe: Social and Political Factors*, Clarendon Press, Oxford

Rodriguez-Pose, A., 2002, *The European Union: Economy, Society, and Polity*, Oxford University Press, Oxford

Rogowski, R., Salais, R., and Whiteside, N., 2011, *Transforming European Employment Policy: Labour Market Transitions and the Promotion of Capability*, Edward Elgar, Cheltenham, UK and Northampton, MA, USA

Rosamond, B., 2000, *Theories of European Integration*, Palgrave Macmillan, Basingstoke

Rugman, A., 2000, *The End of Globalization*, Random House, New York

Sardadvar, S., 2011, *Economic Growth in the Regions of Europe: Theory and Empirical Evidence from a Spatial Growth Model*, Springer-Verlag, Heidelberg

Stierle-Von Schütz, U., Stierle, M.H., Jennings Jr, F.B., and Kuah, A.T.H., 2008, (eds.), *Regional Economic Policy in Europe: New Challenges for Theory, Empirics and Normative Interventions*, Edward Elgar, Cheltenham

Stiglitz, J.E., Sen, A., and Fitoussi, J.-P., 2009, *Report by the Commission on the Measurement of Economic and Social Progress*, see http://www.stiglitz-sen-fitoussi.fr/en/index.htm

Summers, A., Cheshire, P.C., and Senn, L., 1999, (eds.), *Urban Change in the United States and Western Europe: Comparative Analysis and Policy*, The Urban Institute Press, Washington DC

Sweet, M.L., 1999, *Regional Economic Development in the European Union and North America*, Praeger, Westport, CT

The Economist, 2014a, "Free Exchange: Inequality is Bad for Growth", 01 March

The Economist, 2014b, "A Troubled Union", 17 May

Thissen, M., Diodato, D., and Van Oort, F.G., 2013, *Integration and Convergence in Regional Europe: European Regional Trade Flows from 2000 to 2010*, PBL Netherlands Environmental Assessment Agency, The Hague. See http://www.pbl.nl/sites/default/files/cms/publicaties/PBL_2013_European%20Regional%20Trade%20Flows%20from%202000-2010_1036.pdf

Timmer, M.P., Inklaar, R., O'Mahoney, M., and van Ark, B., 2011, *Economic Growth in Europe: A Comparative Industry Perspective*, Cambridge University Press, Cambridge

Timmer, M.P., Los, B., Stehrer, R., and de Vries, G.J., 2013, "Fragmentation, Incomes and Jobs: An Analysis of European Competitiveness", *Economic Policy*, 613–661

UNCTAD, 2012, *World Investment Report 2012: Towards a New Generation of Investment Policies*, United Nations Conference on Trade and Development, Geneva

Van Ark, B., O'Mahony, M., and Timmer, M.P., 2012, "Europe's Productivity Performance in Comparative Perspective: Trends, Causes and Recent Developments", in Mas, M., and Stehrer, R., (eds.), *Industrial Productivity in Europe: Growth and Crisis*, Edward Elgar, Cheltenham, UK and Northampton, MA, USA

Vanhove, N., 1999, *Regional Policy: A European Approach* (3rd edition), Ashgate, Aldershot

Vaughan-Whitehead, D., 2013, (ed.), *Public Sector Shock: The Impact of Policy Retrenchment in Europe*, Edward Elgar, Cheltenham, UK and Northampton, MA, USA

World Bank, 2008, *Growth Report: Strategies for Sustained Growth and Inclusive Development*, World Bank, Commission on Growth and Development, Washington DC

World Bank, 2010a, *Post-Crisis Growth in Developing Countries: A Special Report of the Commission on Growth and Development on the Implications of the 2008 Financial Crisis*, Commission on Growth and Development, Washington DC

World Bank, 2010b, *Globalization and Growth: Implications for a Post-Crisis World*, Commission on Growth and Development, Spence, M., and Leipziger, D., (eds.), Washington DC

World Bank, 2012, *Golden Growth: Restoring the Lustre of the European Economic Model*, Washington DC

Zientara, P., 2009, *New Europe's Old Regions*, Institute of Economic Affairs, London

CHAPTER 2

Arita, T., and McCann, P., 2000, "Industrial Alliances and Firm Location Behaviour: Some Evidence from the US Semiconductor Industry", *Applied Economics*, 32, 1391–1403

Autor, D.H., Katz, L.F., and Kreuger, A.B., 1998, "Computing Inequality: Have Computers Changed the Labor Market?", *Quarterly Journal of Economics*, 113.4, 1169–1213

Barro, R.J., and Sala-i-Martin, X., 1992, "Convergence", *Journal of Political Economy*, 100, 223–251

Barro, R.J., and Sala-i-Martin, X., 1995, *Economic Growth*, McGraw-Hill, New York

Beaudry, C., and Schiffauerova, A., 2009, "Who's Right, Marshall or Jacobs? The Localization versus Urbanization Debate", *Research Policy*, 38, 318–337

Bel, G., and Fageda, X., 2008, "Getting there Fast: Globalization, Intercontinental Flights and Location of Headquarters", *Journal of Economic Geography*, 8, 471–495

Belezon, S., and Schankerman, M., 2013, "Spreading the Word: Geography, Policy, and Knowledge Spillovers", *Review of Economics and Statistics*, 95.3, 884–903

Bettencourt, L.M.A., 2013, "The Origins of Scaling in Cities", *Science*, 340, 6139, 1438–1441

Bettencourt, L.M.A., and West, G.B., 2011, "Bigger Cities do More with Less", *Scientific American*, 305, 52–53

Bettencourt, L.M.A., and West, G.B., 2014, *Scientific American MIND*; *Special Edition Creativity*, 23.1, 106–107, Winter

Bosma, N., and Sternberg, R., 2014, "Entrepreneurship as an Urban Event? Empirical Evidence from European Cities ", *Regional Studies*, 48.6, 1016–1033

Bottazzi, L., and Peri, G., 2003, "Innovation and Spillovers in European Regions: Evidence from European Patent Data", *European Economic Review*, 47.4, 687–710

Brakman, S., and van Marrewijk, C., 2013, "Reflections on Cluster Policies, *Cambridge Journal of Regions Economy and Society*, 6.2, 217–231

Brakman, S., Garretsen, H., and van Marrewijk, C., 2009, "Economic Geography Within and Between European Nations: The Role of Market Potential and Density Across Space", *Journal of Regional Science*, 49, 777–800

Brezzi, M., and Veneri, P., 2014, "Assessing Polycentric Urban Systems in the OECD: Country, Regional and Metropolitan Perspectives", OECD Regional Development Working Papers 2014/01, Organisation for Economic Cooperation and Development, Paris

Brülhart, M., and Mathys, N.A., 2008, "Sectoral Agglomeration Economies in a Panel of European Regions", *Regional Science and Urban Economics*, 38.4, 348–362

Brülhart, M., and Sbergami, F., 2009, "Agglomeration and Growth: Cross-Country Evidence", *Journal of Urban Economics*, 65, 48–63

Brülhart, M., and Traeger, R., 2005, "An Account of Geographic Concentration Patterns in Europe", *Regional Science and Urban Economics*, 35.6, 597–624

Bubbico, R., and Dijkstra, L, 2011, "The European Regional Human Development and Human Poverty Index", *Regional Focus No.02/2011*, European Commission Directorate-General for Regional Policy, Brussels

Charron, N., Lapuente, V., and Dijkstra, L., 2012, *Regional Governance Matters: A Study on Regional Variation in Quality of Government within the EU*, WP 01/2012, European Commission Directorate General for Regional Policy, Brussels

Charron, N., Lapuente, V., and Rothstein, B., 2013, *Quality of Government and Corruption from a European Perspective*, Edward Elgar, Cheltenham

Charron, N., Lapuente, V., and Dijkstra, L., 2014, "Regional Governance Matters: Quality of Government within European Union Member States", *Regional Studies*, forthcoming

Cheshire, P.C. and Magrini, S., 2006, "Population Growth in European Cities: Weather Matters – but Only Nationally", *Regional Studies*, 40.1, 23–37

Cheshire, P.C. and Magrini, S., 2009, "Urban Growth Drivers in a Europe of Sticky People and Implicit Boundaries", *Journal of Economic Geography*, 9.1, 85–115

Ciccone, A., 2002, "Agglomeration Effects in Europe", *European Economic Review*, 46, 213–227

Ciccone, A., and Hall, R.E., 1996, "Productivity and the Density of Economic Activity", *American Economic Review*, 86, 54–70

Combes, P.-P., Duranton, G., and Gobillon, L., 2008, "Spatial Wage Disparities: Sorting Matters!", *Journal of Urban Economics*, 63.2, 723–742

Coutard, O., Finnveden, G., Kabisch, S., Kitchin, R., Matos, R., Nijkamp, P., Pronello, C., and Robinson, D., 2014, *Urban Megatrends: Towards a European Research Agenda*, Report by the Scientific Advisory Board of the Joint Programming Initiative Urban Europe, March

Crescenzi, R., and Rodriguez-Pose, A., 2011, *Innovation and Regional Growth in the European Union*, Springer, Heidelberg

Criscuolo, P., and Verspagen, B., 2008, "Does It Matter Where Patent Citations Come From? Inventor vs Examiner Citations in European Patents", *Research Policy*, 37, 1892–1908

Davis, M.A., Fisher, J.D.M., and Whited, T.M., 2014, "Macroeconomic Implications of Agglomeration", *Econometrica*, 82.2, 731–764

De Groot, H.L.F., Poot, J., and Smit, M., 2009, "Agglomeration Externalities, Innovation and Regional Growth: Theoretical Perspectives and

Meta-Analysis", in Cappello, R., and Nijkamp, P., *Handbook of Regional Growth and Development Theories*, Edward Elgar, Cheltenham

De Melo, P., Graham, D., and Noland, R., 2009, "A Meta-Analysis of Estimates of Urban Agglomeration Economies", *Regional Science and Urban Economics*, 39.3, 332–342

Dennett, A., 2014, "Quantifying the Effects of Economic and Labour Market Inequalities on Inter-Regional Migration in Europe – Policy Perspective", *Applied Spatial Analysis and Policy*, 7, 97–117

D.G. Regio, 2008, *Regions 2020: Demographic Challenges for European Regions*, EU Directorate General for Regional Policy, Brussels

Dijkstra, L., 2009, "Metropolitan Regions in the EU", *Regional Focus, No.1/2009*, Directorate General for Regional Policy, European Commission, Brussels

Dijkstra, L., 2013, "Why Investing More in the Capital Can Lead to Less Growth", *Cambridge Journal of Regions, Economy and Society*, 6.2, 251–268

Dijkstra, L., Garcilazo, E., and McCann, P., 2013, "The Economic Performance of European Cities and City-Regions: Myths and Realities", *European Planning Studies*, 21.3, 334–354

Duranton, G., 2011, "California Dreamin': The Feeble Case for Cluster Policies", *Review of Economic Analysis*, 3.1, 3–45

EEA, 2010, *The European Environment State and Outlook 2010: Land Use*, European Environment Agency, Copenhagen

EEA, 2012a, *Climate Change, Impacts and Vulnerability in Europe 2012: An Indicator-Based Report*, European Environment Agency, Copenhagen

EEA, 2012b, *Greenhouse Gas Emission Trends and Projections in Europe 2012: Tracking Progress towards Kyoto and 2020 Targets*, European Environment Agency, Copenhagen

Ertur, C., LeGallo, J., and Beaumont, C., 2006, "The European Convergence Process, 1980-1995: Do Spatial Regimes and Spatial Dependence Matter?", *International Regional Science Review*, 29.1, 3–34

ESPON, 2013, *New Evidence on Smart, Sustainable and Inclusive: First ESPON 2013 Synthesis Report*, Luxembourg, http://www.espon.eu

ESPON DEMIFER, 2010, *Demographic and Migratory Flows Affecting Europe's Regions and Cities: Final Report*, Luxembourg, http://www.espon.eu

European Commission, 2004, *Urban Audit Perception Survey: Local Perceptions of Quality of Life in 31 European Cities*, Brussels

European Commission, 2007, *State of European Cities Report: Adding Value to the European Audit*, Directorate-General for Regional Policy, Brussels

European Commission, 2010, *Second State of European Cities Report: Adding Value to the European Audit*, Directorate-General for Regional Policy, Brussels

European Commission, 2013, *Report from the Commission to the Council and the European Parliament: Anti-Corruption Report*, COM (2014) 38 Final, 03.02.2014, Brussels

European Commission, 2014a, *Innovation Union Scoreboard 2014*, Directorate-General for Enterprise and Industry, Brussels

European Commission, 2014b, *Regional Innovation Scoreboard 2014*, Directorate-General for Enterprise and Industry, Brussels

European Union, 2011, *The Urban and Regional Dimension of Europe 2020: Seventh Progress Report on Economic, Social and Territorial Cohesion*, Publications Office, Brussels

European Union, 2013a, *EU Cohesion Policy Contributing to Employment and Growth in Europe*, Joint Paper from the Directorates-General for Regional and Urban Policy and Employment, Social Affairs and Inclusion, Publications Office, Brussels

European Union, 2013b, *The Urban and Regional Dimension of the Crisis: Eighth Report on Economic, Social and Territorial Cohesion*, Publications Office, Brussels

European Union, 2013c, *Quality of Life in Cities: Perception Survey in 79 European Cities*, Directorate General for Regional and Urban Policy Publications Office, Brussels

European Union, 2014, *Investment for Jobs and Growth – Promoting Development and Good Governance in EU Regions and Cities: Sixth Report on Economic, Social and Territorial Cohesion*, European Commission Directorate-General for Regional and Urban Policy, Publications Office, Brussels

Eurostat, 2013, "Regional GDP Per Capita in the EU in 2010: Eight Capital Regions in the First Ten Places", Eurostat News Release, 46/2013, 21 March

Faggian, A., and McCann, P., 2009, "Human Capital and Regional Development", in Capello, R., and Nijkamp, P., (eds.), *Regional Dynamics and Growth: Advances in Regional Economics*, Edward Elgar, Cheltenham, UK and Northampton, MA, USA

Fassman, H., Haller, M., and Lane, D., 2009, *Migration and Mobility in Europe: Trends, Patterns and Control*, Edward Elgar, Chetltenham, UK and Northampton, MA, USA

Florida, R., 2005, *Cities and the Creative Class*, Routledge, London

Garcilazo, E., and Rodriguez-Pose, A., 2013, Quality of Government and the Returns of Investment: Examining the Impact of Cohesion Expenditure in the European Regions", OECD Regional Development Working Papers, No.2013/12, Paris

Glaeser, E.L., 2011, *Triumph of the City: How Our Greatest Invention Makes Us Richer, Smarter, Greener, Healthier, and Happier*, Penguin Press, New York

Glaeser, E.L., 2014, "Engines of Innovation", *Scientific American MIND; Special Edition Creativity*, 23.1, 102–105, Winter

Goos, M., Manning, A., and Salomons, A., 2009, "Job Polarization in Europe", *American Economic Review*, 99.2, 58–63

Gordon, I.R., and Kaplanis, I., 2014, "Accounting for Big-City Growth in Low-Paid Occupations: Immigration and/or Service-Class Consumption", *Economic Geography*, 90.1, 67–90

Hall, P., and Pain, K., 2006, *The Polycentric Metropolis: Learning from Mega-City Regions in Europe*, Earthscan, London

Iammarino, S., and McCann, P., 2013, *Multinationals and Economic Geography: Location, Technology and Innovation*, Edward Elgar, Cheltenham, UK and Northampton, MA, USA

ILO International Labor Office, 2012, *Global Employment Trends 2012: Preventing a Deeper Jobs Crisis*, Geneva

Jonker, J.-J., 2012, (ed.), *Countries Compared on Public Performance*, SCP The Netherlands Institute for Social Research, The Hague

Mameli, F., Faggian, A., and McCann, P., 2008, "Employment Growth in Italian Local Labour Systems: Issues of Model Specification and Sectoral Aggregation", *Spatial Economic Analysis*, 3.3, 343–359

Mameli, F., Faggian, A., and McCann, P., 2014, "The Estimation of Local Employment Growth: Do Sectoral Aggregation and Industry Definition Matter?", *Regional Studies*, DOI: 10.1080/00343404.2012.756578, forthcoming

McCann, P., 2007, "Sketching out a Model of Innovation, Face-to-Face Interaction and Economic Geography", *Spatial Economic Analysis*, 2.2, 117–134

McCann, P., 2013, *Modern Urban and Regional Economics*, Oxford University Press, Oxford

McCann, P., and Acs, Z.J., 2011, "Globalisation: Countries, Cities and Multinationals", *Regional Studies*, 45.1, 17–32

McCann, P., and Ortega-Argilés, R., 2013a, "Redesigning and Reforming European Regional Policy: The Reasons, the Logic and the Outcomes", *International Regional Science Review*, 36.3, 424–445

McCann, P., and Ortega-Argilés, R., 2013b, "Transforming European Regional Policy: A Results-Driven Agenda and Smart Specialisation", *Oxford Review of Economic Policy*, 29.2, 405–431

MGI, 2011, *Urban World: Mapping the Economic Power of Cities*, McKinsey Global Institute

MGI, 2012a, *Urban World: Cities and the Rise of the Consuming Class*, McKinsey Global Institute

MGI, 2012b, *Urban America: US Cities in the Global Economy*, McKinsey Global Institute

MGI, 2013, *Urban World: The Shifting Global Business Landscape*, McKinsey Global Institute

Midelfahrt-Knarvik, H., and Overman, H.G., 2002, "Delocation and European Integration: Is Structural Spending Justified", *Economic Policy*, 17, 322–369

Monasteriotis, V., 2014, "Regional Growth and National Development: Transition in Central and Eastern Europe and the Regional Kuznets Curve in the East and the West", *Spatial Economic Analysis*, 9.2, 142–161

Monfort, P., and Nicolini, R., 2000, "Regional Convergence and International Integration", *Journal of Urban Economics*, 48, 286–306

Neven, D., and Gouyette, C., 1995, 'Regional Convergence in the European Community', *Journal of Common Market Studies*, 33.1, 47–65

NIESR, 2013, *Geographic Labour Mobility in the Context of the Crisis*, Ad Hoc Request by the European Employment Observatory, Holland, D., and Paluchowski, P., National Institute of Economic and Social Research, London

Nijkamp, P., Poot, J., and Sahin, M., 2012, *Migration Impact Assessment: New Horizons*, Edward Elgar, Cheltenham, UK and Northampton, MA, USA

OECD, 2006, *Competitive Cities in the Global Economy*, Organisation for Economic Cooperation and Development, Paris

OECD, 2008, *OECD Environmental Outlook to 2030*, Organisation for Economic Cooperation and Development, Paris

OECD, 2009a, *Regions Matter: Economic Recovery, Innovation and Sustainable Growth*, Organisation for Economic Cooperation and Development, Paris

OECD, 2009b, *How Regions Grow*, Organisation for Economic Cooperation and Development, Paris

OECD, 2009c, *Integrating Climate Change Adaptation into Development Co-Operation*, Organisation for Economic Cooperation and Development, Paris

OECD, 2010a, *Cities and Climate Change*, Organisation for Economic Cooperation and Development, Paris

OECD, 2010b, *Regional Development Policies in OECD Countries*, Organisation for Economic Cooperation and Development, Paris

OECD, 2010c, *Organising Local Economic Development: The Role of Development Agencies and Companies*, Organisation for Economic Cooperation and Development, Paris

OECD, 2011a, *OECD Regions and Innovation Policy*, Organisation for Economic Cooperation and Development, Paris

OECD, 2011b, *OECD Regional Outlook 2011: Building Resilient Regions for Stronger Economies*, Organisation for Economic Cooperation and Development, Paris

OECD, 2012a, *Redefining 'Urban': A New Way to Measure Metropolitan Regions*, Organisation for Economic Cooperation and Development, Paris

OECD, 2012b, *International Migration Outlook 2012*, Organisation for Economic Cooperation and Development, Paris

OECD, 2012c, *OECD Environmental Outlook to 2050: The Consequences of Inaction*, Organisation for Economic Cooperation and Development, Paris

OECD, 2012d, *Compact City Policies: A Comparative Assessment*, Organisation for Economic Cooperation and Development, Paris

OECD, 2012e, *Promoting Growth in All Regions*, Organisation for Economic Cooperation and Development, Paris

OECD, 2012f, *Linking Renewable Energy to Rural Development*, Organisation for Economic Cooperation and Development, Paris

OECD, 2013a, *OECD Regions at a Glance 2013*, Organisation for Economic Cooperation and Development, Paris

OECD, 2013b, *Regions and Innovation*, Organisation for Economic Cooperation and Development, Paris

OECD, 2013c, *Rural–Urban Partnerships: An Integrated Approach to Economic Development*, Organisation for Economic Cooperation and Development, Paris

OECD, 2013d, *Investing Together: Working Effectively Across Levels of Government*, Organisation for Economic Cooperation and Development, Paris

OECD, 2013e, *Government at a Glance 2013*, Organisation for Economic Cooperation and Development, Paris

OECD, 2014a, "What Makes Cities More Productive? Evidence on the Role of Urban Governance from OECD Countries", Ahrend, R., Farchy, E., Kaplanis, I., and Lembcke, A., *OECD Regional Development Working Papers 2014/05*, Organisation for Economic Cooperation and Development, Paris

OECD, 2014b, *OECD Territorial Reviews: The Netherlands*, Organisation for Economic Cooperation and Development, Paris

Overman, H.G., Puga, D., and Vandenbussche, H., 2002, "Unemployment Clusters Across Europe's Regions and Countries", *Economic Policy*, 34, 115–148

Partridge, M.D., 2010, "The Duelling Models: NEG vs Amenity Migration in Explaining US Engines of Growth", *Papers in Regional Science*, 89.3, 513–536

PBL, 2013, *The European Landscape of Knowledge-Intensive Foreign-Owned Firms and the Attractiveness of Dutch Regions*, The Netherlands Environmental Assessment Agency, The Hague

Percoco, M., 2013, "Strategies of Regional Development in European Regions: Are They Efficient?", *Cambridge Journal of Regions, Economy and Society*, 303–318

Poelman, H., 2013, "Measuring Accessibility to Passenger Flights in Europe: Towards Harmonised Indicators and the Regional Level", *Regional Focus 01/2013*, September, Directorate-General for Regional and Urban Policy, Brussels

PWC, 2012, *Cities of Opportunity*, Price Waterhouse Coopers

Quah, D., 1996, "Regional Convergence Clusters Across Europe", *European Economic Review*, 40.3-5, 951–958

Rodriguez-Pose, A., and Gill, N., 2003, "The Global Trend Towards Devolution and Its Implications", *Environment and Planning C*, 21.3, 333–351

Rodriguez-Pose, A., and Gill, N., 2004, "Is There a Global Link Between Regional Disparities and Devolution?", *Environment and Planning A*, 36.12, 2097–2117

Rosenthal, S.S., and Strange, W.C., 2004, "Evidence on the Nature and Sources of Agglomeration Economics", in Henderson, V., and Thisse, J-F., (eds.), *Handbook of Urban and Regional Economics Vol. 4*, North-Holland, Amsterdam

Shucksmith, M., Cameron, S., Merridew, T., and Pichler, F., 2009, "Urban-Rural Differences in Quality of Life across the European Union", *Regional Studies*, 43.10, 1275–1289

Sorensen, J.F.L., 2014, "Rural-Urban Differences in Life Satisfaction: Evidence from the European Union", *Regional Studies*, forthcoming

Spence, M., 2011, "The Impact of Globalization on Income and Employment: The Downside of Integrating Markets", *Foreign Affairs*, 90.4, 28–41, July/August

Sternberg, R., 2011, "Regional Determinants of Entrepreneurial Activities – Theories and Empirical Evidence", in Fritsch, M., (ed.), *Handbook of Research on Entrepreneurship and Regional Development: National and Regional Perspectives*, Edward Elgar, Cheltenham, UK and Northampton, MA, USA

Storper, M., 2013, *Keys to the City: How Economics, Institutions, Social Interaction, and Politics Shape Development*, Princeton University Press, Princeton

Thissen, M., Diodato, D., and Van Oort, F.G., 2013a, *Integration and Convergence in Regional Europe: European Regional Trade Flows from 2000 to 2010*, PBL Netherlands Environmental Assessment Agency, The Hague. See http://www.pbl.nl/sites/default/files/cms/publicaties/PBL_2013_European%20Regional%20Trade%20Flows%20from%202000-2010_1036.pdf

Thissen, M., Diodato, D., and Van Oort, F.G., 2013b, *Integrated Regional Europe: European Regional Trade Flows in 2000*, PBL Netherlands Environmental Assessment Agency, The Hague. See http://www.pbl.nl/sites/default/files/cms/publicaties/PBL_2013_European%20Regional%20Trade%20Flows%20in%202000_1035.pdf

UN-Habitat, 2012, *State of the World's Cities 2012/2013. Prosperity of Cities*, United Nations Human Settlements Programme, Nairobi

United Nations, 2012, *World Urbanization Prospects 2011: The 2011 Revision*, Department of Economic and Social Affairs: Population Division, ST/ESA/SER.A/322, New York

Van Dijk, J., 2014, "Local Multipliers in OECD Regions", OECD Working Paper, forthcoming

Wilson, S.G., Plane, D.A., Mackun, P.J., Fischetti, T.R., Goworowska, J., Cohen, D., Perry, M.J., and Hatchard, G.W., 2010, *Patterns of Metropolitan and Micropolitan Population Change: 2000 to 2010: 2010 Census Special Reports*, United States Census Bureau, Washington DC

World Bank, 2009, *World Development Report 2009: Reshaping Economic Geography*, Washington DC

CHAPTER 3

Aiello, F., and Pupo, V., 2012, "Structural Funds and the Economic Divide in Italy", *Journal of Policy Modeling*, 34, 403–418

Arcalean, C., Glomm, G., and Schiopu, I., 2012, "Growth Effects of Spatial Redistribution Policies", *Journal of Economic Dynamics and Control*, 36.7, 988–1008

Artis, M., and Nixson, F., 2001, *The Economics of the European Union: Policy and Analysis*, Oxford University Press, Oxford

Bachtler, J., and Mendez, C., 2013, "EU Cohesion Policy 2007–2013: Are the Goals of the 2006 Reform Being Achieved?", *European Structural and Investment Funds Journal*, 1.1, 15–19

Bachtler, J., and Turok, I., 1997, (eds.), *The Coherence of EU Regional Policy: Contrasting Perspectives on the Structural Funds*, Jessica Kingsley, London

Bachtler, J., and Wren, C., 2006, "Evaluation of European Union Cohesion Policy: Research Questions and Policy Challenges", *Regional Studies*, 40.2, 143–153

Bachtler, J., Mendez, C., and Wishlade, F., 2013, *EU Cohesion Policy and European Integration: The Dynamics of EU Budget and Regional Policy Reform*, Ashgate, Aldershot

Bähr, C., 2008, "How Does Sub-National Autonomy Affect the Effectiveness of Structural Funds?", *Kyklos*, 61.1, 3–18

Baldwin, R., and Wyplosz, C., 2004, *The Economics of European Integration*, McGraw-Hill, New York

Barca, F., 2009, *An Agenda for A Reformed Cohesion Policy: A Place-Based Approach to Meeting European Union Challenges and Expectations*, Independent Report Prepared at the Request of the European Commissioner for Regional Policy, Danuta Hübner, European Commission, Brussels

Barro, R.J., and Sala-i-Martin, X., 1992, "Convergence", *Journal of Political Economy*, 100, 223–251

Barro, R.J., and Sala-i-Martin, X., 1995, *Economic Growth*, McGraw-Hill

Bayar, A., 2007, *Simulation of R&D Investment Scenarios and Calibration of the Impact on a Set of Multi-Country Models*, IPTS Institute for Prospective Technological Studies, Joint Research Centre of the European Commission, Seville

Becker, S.O., Egger, P.H., and von Ehrlich, M., 2010, "Going NUTS: The Effect of EU Structural Funds on Regional Performance", *Journal of Public Economics* 94, 578–590

Becker, S.O., Egger, P.H., and von Ehrlich, M., 2012a, "Too Much of a Good Thing? On the Growth Effects of the EU's Regional Policy", *European Economic Review*, 56, 648–668

Becker, S.O., Egger, P.H., and von Ehrlich, M., 2012b, "Absorptive Capacity and the Growth and Investment Effects of Regional Transfers: Regression Discontinuity Design and with Heterogeneous Treatment Effects", CAGE Working Paper No.89, University of Warwick and ESRC Centre for Competitive Advantage in the Global Economy, June

Begg, I., 2009, "The Future of Cohesion Policy in Richer Regions", Working Paper No.03/2009, Directorate-General for Regional Policy, Brussels

Begg, I., 2010, "Cohesion or Confusion: A Policy Searching for Objectives", *Journal of European Integration*, 32.1, 77–96

Beugelsdijk, M., and Eijffinger, S., 2005, "The Effectiveness of Structural Policy in the European Union: An Empirical Analysis for the EU-15 in 1995–2001", *Journal of Common Market Studies*, 43, 37–51

Boldrin, M., and Canova, F., 2001, "Europe's Regions – Income Disparities and Regional Policies", *Economic Policy*, 32, 207–253

Bouayad-Agha, S., Turpin, N., and Védrine, L., 2014, "Fostering the Development of European Regions: A Spatial Dynamic Panel Data Analysis of the Impact of Cohesion Policy", *Regional Studies*, forthcoming. DOI: 10.1080/00343404.2012.628930

Bouvet, F., and Dall'erba, S., 2010, "European Regional Structural Funds: How Large is the Influence of Politics on the Allocation Process?", *Journal of Common Market Studies*, 48.3, 501–528

Bradley, J., Herce, J.-A., and Modesto, L., 1995, "The HERMIN Project, *Economic Modelling*, 12.3, 219–220

Bradley, J., Untiedt, G., and Mitze, T., 2007, "Analysis of the Impact of Cohesion Policy: A Note Explaining the HERMIN-Based Simulations", Technical Note. See: http://www.herminonline.net/images/downloads/pub/2007-BradelyUntiedtMitze.pdf

Brandsma, A., Kancs, d'A., Monfort, P., and Rillaers, A., 2013, "RHOMOLO: A Dynamic Spatial General Equilbrium Model for Assessing the Impact of Cohesion Policy", Working Paper No.01/2013, Directorate General for Regional and Urban Policy, Brussels

Bubbico, R., and de Michelis, N., 2011, "The Financial Execution of Structural Funds", Working Paper No.03/2011, Directorate-General for Regional Policy, Brussels

Burnside, C., and Dollar, D., 2000, "Aid, Policies, and Growth", *American Economic Review*, 90.4, 847–868

Cappelen, A., Castellacci, F., Fagerberg, J., and Verspagen, B., 2003, "The Impact of EU Regional Support on Growth and Convergence in the European Union", *Journal of Common Market Studies*, 41, 621–644

Chambon, N., and Rubio, E., 2011, "In Search of the 'Best Value for Money' Analysing Current Ideas and Proposals to Enhance the Performance of CAP and Cohesion Policy", Working Paper, Notre Europe, Paris. See: http://www.notre-europe.eu/media/nadege_chambon_-_eulalia_rubio_final_version.pdf?pdf=ok

Charron, N., Lapuente, V., and Dijkstra, L., 2012, *Regional Governance Matters: A Study on Regional Variation in Quality of Government within the EU*, Working Paper No.01/2012, European Commission Directorate General for Regional Policy, Brussels

Charron, N., Lapuente, V., and Rothstein, B., 2013, *Quality of Government and Corruption from a European Perspective*, Edward Elgar, Cheltenham, UK and Northampton, MA, USA

Charron, N., Lapuente, V., and Dijkstra, L., 2014, "Regional Governance Matters: Quality of Government within European Union Member States", *Regional Studies*, forthcoming

Checcherita, C., Nickel, C., and Rother, P., 2009, "The Role of Fiscal Transfers for Regional Economic Convergence in Europe", ECB Working Paper Series No.1029, Frankfurt. See: http://www.ecb.int/pub/pdf/scpwps/ecbwp1029.pdf

Corrado, L., Martin, R., and Weeks, M., 2005, "Identifying and Interpreting Regional Convergence Clusters Across Europe", *Economic Journal*, 115, C133–C160

Dall'erba, S., 2005, "Distribution of Regional Income and Regional Funds in Europe 1989-1999: An Exploratory Spatial Data Analysis", *Annals of Regional Science*, 39, 121–148

Dall'erba, S., and Hewings, G.J.D., 2003, "European Regional Development Policies: The Trade-Off Between Efficiency-Equity Revisited", REAL Working Paper No.03-T-2, Regional Economics Applications Laboratory, University of Illinois at Urban-Champaign. See: www.real.illinois.edu/d-paper/03/03-t-2.pdf

Dall'Erba, S., and LeGallo, J., 2007, "The Impact of EU Regional Support on Growth and Employment", *Czech Journal of Economics and Finance*, 57.7–8, 325–340

Dall'Erba, S., and LeGallo, J., 2008, "Regional Convergence and the Impact of European Structural Funds over 1989-1999: A Spatial Econometric Analysis", *Papers in Regional Science*, 87, 219–244

Dall'erba, S., Guillain, R., and LeGallo, J., 2009, "Impact of Structural Funds on Regional Growth: How to Reconsider a 9 Year-Old Black Box", *Région et Développement*, 30, 77–99

De Freitas, M.L., Pereira, F., and Torres, F., 2003, "Convergence among EU Regions 1990–2001: Quality of National Institutions and 'Objective 1' Status", *Intereconomics*, 38.5, 270–275

De la Fuente, A., and Vives, X., 1995, "Infrastructure and Education as Instruments of Regional Policy: Evidence from Spain", *Economic Policy*, 10.20, 13–51

Delors, J., 1989, *Report on Economic and Monetary Union in the European Community*, Report prepared by the Committee for the Study of Economic and Monetary Union in response to the mandate of the European Council "to study and propose concrete stages leading towards economic and monetary union", Presented April 17, Brussels

Dijkstra, L., and Poelman, H., 2011, "Regional Typologies: A Compilation", *Regional Focus No.01/2011*, European Commission Directorate-General for Regional Policy, Brussels

Dijkstra, L., and Poelman, H., 2012, "Cities in Europe: The New OECD-EC Definition", *Regional Focus RF 01/2012*, European Commission Directorate-General for Regional and Urban Policy, Brussels

Drabenstott, M., 2005, *A Review of the Federal Role in Regional Economic Development*, Federal Reserve Bank of Kansas City, First Quarter

Ederveen, S., Gorter, J., de Mooij, R., and Nahuis, R., 2002, *Funds and Games: The Economics of European Cohesion Policy*, CRB and Koninklijke De Swart, Amsterdam. See: http://www.enepri.org/files/CPBstudy.pdf

Ederveen, S., de Groot, H.L.F., Nahuis, R., 2006, "Fertile Soil for Structural Funds? A Panel Data Analysis of the Conditional Effectiveness of European Cohesion Policy", *Kyklos*, 59, 17–42

El-Agraa, A.M., 2001, *The European Union: Economies and Policies* (6th edition), Financial Times and Prentice-Hall, Pearson Education, London and New York

EPRC, 2013, *EPRC Policy Briefing. Cohesion Policy 2014–20: National Allocations. Who are the Winners and Losers from the 7–8 February European Council?* 25 February 2013. See: http://www.eprc.strath.ac.uk/news/COHESION_POLICY_ALLOCATIONS_2014-20_EPRC_Policy_Briefing_Feb_2013.pdf

EPRC and LSE, 2013, *Evaluation of the Main Achievements of Cohesion Policy Programmes and Projects over the Longer Term in 15 Selected Regions (from 1989–1993 Programme Period to the Present), Final Report to the European Commission DG Regio*, European Policies Research Centre, University of Strathclyde and the London School of Economics, 13 September

Espositi, R., and Bussoletti, S., 2008, "Impact of Objective 1 Funds on Regional Growth Convergence in the European Union: A Panel-Data Approach", *Regional Studies*, 42.2, 159–173

European Commission, 1994a, *Europe 2000+: Cooperation for European Territorial Development*, Directorate-General for Regional Policy, Publications Office of the European Communities, Luxembourg

European Commission, 1994b, *Fifth Periodic Report on the Social and Economic Situation and Development of the Regions in the Community*, Directorate-General for Regional Policy, Publications Office of the European Communities, Luxembourg

European Commission, 1996a, *Structural Funds and Cohesion Fund 1994–99: Regulations and Commentary*, Directorate-General for Regional Policy, Publications Office of the European Communities, Luxembourg

European Commission, 1996b, *First Report on Economic and Social Cohesion 1996*, Directorate-General for Regional Policy, Publications Office of the European Communities, Luxembourg

European Commission, 1998, *Guide to the Community Initiatives 1994–99 Volume 2*, Directorate-General for Regional Policy, Publications Office of the European Communities, Luxembourg

European Commission, 1999, *Sixth Periodic Report on the Social and Economic Situation and Development of the Regions of the European Community*, Directorate-General for Regional Policy, Publications Office of the European Communities, Luxembourg

European Commission, 2000, *Structural Actions 2000–2006: Commentary and Regulations*, Directorate-General for Regional Policy, Publications Office of the European Communities, Luxembourg

European Commission, 2001, *Unity, Solidarity, Diversity for Europe, its People and its Territory: Second Report on Economic and Social Cohesion Vols. 1–2*, Directorate-General for Regional Policy, Publications Office of the European Communities, Luxembourg

European Commission, 2004, *A New Partnership for Cohesion: Third Report on Economic and Social Cohesion*, Directorate-General for Regional Policy, Publications Office of the European Communities, Luxembourg

European Commission, 2007a, *Cohesion Policy 2007–13. Commentaries and Official Texts*, January, Directorate-General for Regional Policy, Publications Office of the European Union, Luxembourg

European Commission, 2007b, *Growing Regions, Growing Europe: Fourth Report on Economic and Social Cohesion*, Directorate-General for Regional Policy, Publications Office of the European Communities, Luxembourg

European Commission, 2008, *Guide to Cost Benefit Analysis of Investment Projects*, Directorate-General for Regional Policy, Brussels

European Commission, 2009, *Cohesion Policy 2009, The Control System for Cohesion Policy. How it Works in the 2007–13 Budget Period*, Directorate-General for Regional Policy, Publications Office of the European Union, Luxembourg

European Commission, 2010a, *Investing in Europe's Future: Fifth Report on Economics, Social and Territorial Cohesion*, Publications Office, Brussels

European Commission, 2010b, *Ex Post Evaluation of Cohesion Policy Programmes 2000–06 Co-Financed by the ERDF (Objective 1&2): Synthesis Report*, Publications Office, Brussels

European Commission, 2010c, *Ex Post Evaluation of Cohesion Policy Programmes 2000–06: The URBAN Community Initiative: Evaluation Report*, Publications Office, Brussels

European Commission, 2010d, *Ex Post Evaluation of INTERREG III 2000–06: Evaluation Report*, Publications Office, Brussels

European Court of Auditors, 2013, *2012 EU Audit in Brief: Information Note on the 2012 Annual Reports*, Luxembourg

European Parliament, 2009, *Vade Mecum on Cohesion Policy and the Committee on Regional Development*, Directorate-General for Internal Policies, The Secretariat, DV\786352EN.doc, 15.06.2009, Brussels

European Union, 2013a, *The Urban and Regional Dimension of the Crisis: Eighth Report on Economic, Social and territorial Cohesion*, Publications Office, Brussels

European Union, 2014, *Investment for Jobs and Growth – Promoting Development and Good Governance in EU Regions and Cities: Sixth Report on Economic, Social and Territorial Cohesion*, European Commission Directorate-General for Regional and Urban Policy, Publications Office, Brussels

Fagerberg, J., and Verspagen, B., 1996, "Heading for Divergence? Regional Growth in Europe Reconsidered", *Journal of Common Market Studies*, 34, 431–438

Falk, M., and Sinabell, F., 2008, "The Effectiveness of Objective 1 Structural Funds in the EU15: New Empirical Evidence from NUTS3 Regions", WIFO Working Paper 310/2008, February, Austrian Institute of Economic Research, Vienna

Ferrara, A., Ivanova, O., and Kancs, d'A., 2010, "Modelling the Policy Instruments of the EU Cohesion Policy", Working Paper No.02/2010, Directorate-General for Regional Policy, Brussels

Filippetti, A., and Peyrache, A., 2014, "Labour Productivity and Technology Gap in European Regions: A Conditional Frontier Approach", *Regional Studies*, forthcoming DOI: 10.1080/00343404.2013.799768

Gáková, Z., Grigonytė, D., and Montfort, P., 2009, "A Cross-Country Impact Assessment of EU Cohesion Policy", Working Paper No.01/2009, Directorate-General for Regional Policy, Brussels

Garcia-Milà, T., and McGuire, T.J., 2001, "Do Interregional Transfers Improve the Economic Performance of Poor Regions? The Case of Spain", *International Tax and Public Finance*, 8, 281–295

Garcilazo, E., and Rodriguez-Pose, A., 2013, "Quality of Government and the Returns of Investment: Examining the Impact of Cohesion Expenditure in the European Regions", *OECD Regional Development Working Papers, No.2013/12*, Paris

Gibbons, S., and Overman, H.G., 2012, "Mostly Pointless Spatial Econometrics", *Journal of Regional Science*, 52, 172–191

Hagen, T., and Mohl, P., 2008, "Which is the Right Dose of EU Cohesion Policy for Economic Growth?", Discussion Paper No.08-104, ZEW, Mannheim

Hagen, T., and Mohl, P., 2009, "Econometric Evaluation of EU Cohesion Policy: A Survey", Discussion Paper No.09-052, ZEW, Mannheim

Hansen, J.D., 2001, (ed.), *European Integration: An Economic Perspective*, Oxford University Press, Oxford

Hervé, Y., and Holtzmann, R., 1998, *Fiscal Transfers and Economic Convergence in the EU: An Analysis of Absorption Problems and an Evaluation of the Literature*, Nomos Verlagsgesellschaft, Baden-Baden

HM Treasury, 2013, *Budget 2013*, The Stationery Office, London

Honohan, P., 1997, (ed.), "EU Structural Funds in Ireland: A Mid-Term Evaluation of the CSF 1994-99", ESRI Policy Research Series Paper No.31, Economic and Social Research Institute, Dublin

In't Veld, J., 2007, "The Potential Impact of the Fiscal Transfers under the EU Cohesion Policy Programme", *European Economy Economic Papers No.283*, European Commission Directorate-General for Economic and Financial Affairs, June. See: http://ec.europa.eu/regional_policy/sources/docgener/evaluation/pdf/impact_transfer.pdf

LeGallo, J., Dall'erba, S., and Guillain, R., 2011, "The Local versus Global Dilemma of the Effects of Structural Funds", *Growth and Change*, 42.4, 466–490

Leonardi, R., 2005, *Cohesion Policy in the European Union: The Building of Europe*, Palgrave Macmillan, Basingstoke

LSE Enterprise, 2011, *Study on the Impact of the Single Market on Cohesion: Implications for Cohesion Policy, Growth and Competitiveness*, Final Report to the European Commission Directorate-General for Regional Policy, Brussels, December

Martin, R., and Tyler, P., 2006, "Evaluating the Impact of the Structural Funds on Objective 1 Regions: An Exploratory Analysis", *Regional Studies*, 40.2, 201–210

McCann, P., and Ortega-Argilés, R., 2013a, "Redesigning and Reforming European Regional Policy: The Reasons, the Logic and the Outcomes", *International Regional Science Review*, 36.3, 424–445

McCann, P., and Ortega-Argilés, R., 2013b, "Transforming European Regional Policy: A Results-Driven Agenda and Smart Specialisation", *Oxford Review of Economic Policy*, 29.2, 405–431

Midelfart-Knarvik, K.H., and Overman, H.G., 2002, "Delocation and European Integration – is Structural Spending Justfified?", *Economic Policy*, 17, 323–359

Mohl, P., and Hagen, T., 2011, "Do Structural Funds Promote Regional Employment? Evidence from Dynamic Panel Data Models", Working Paper Series, 1403, European Central Bank

Molle, W., 2007, *European Cohesion Policy*, Routledge, London

Monfort, P., 2012, "The Role of International Transfers in Public Investment in CESEE: The European Commission's Experience with Structural Funds", Regional Policy Working Paper No.02/2012, Directorate-General for Regional Policy, Brussels

Monti, M., 2010, *A New Strategy for the Single Market*, Report to the President of the European Commission, José Manuel Barroso

Moretti, E., 2011, "Local Labour Markets", in Ashenfelter, O., and Card, D., (eds), *Handbook of Labor Economics Volume 4B*, North Holland, Amsterdam

OECD, 2001a, *Cities for Citizens: Improving Metropolitan Governance*, Organisation for Economic Cooperation and Development, Paris

OECD, 2001b, *Citizens as Partners: OECD Handbook on Information, Consultation and Public Participation in Policy-Making*, Organisation for Economic Cooperation and Development, Paris

OECD, 2004, *New Forms of Governance for Economic Development*, Organisation for Economic Cooperation and Development, Paris

OECD, 2005, *Building Competitive Regions: Strategies and Governance*, Organisation for Economic Cooperation and Development, Paris

OECD, 2007, *Linking Regions and Central Government: Contracts for Regional Development*, Organisation for Economic Cooperation and Development, Paris

OECD, 2009, *Community Capacity Building: Creating a Better Future Together*, Organisation for Economic Cooperation and Development, Paris

OECD, 2011, *OECD Regional Outlook 2011: Building Resilient Regions for Stronger Economies*, Organisation for Economic Cooperation and Development, Paris

OECD, 2012, *Redefining "Urban": A New Way to Measure Metropolitan Regions*, Organisation for Economic Cooperation and Development, Paris

OECD, 2013a, *Investing Together: Working Effectively Across Levels of Government*, Organisation for Economic Cooperation and Development, Paris

OECD, 2013b, *Government at a Glance 2013*, Organisation for Economic Cooperation and Development, Paris

OECD, 2013c, *Regions at a Glance 2013*, Organisation for Economic Cooperation and Development, Paris

OECD, 2014, "What Makes Cities More Productive? Evidence on the Role of Urban Governance from OECD Countries", Ahrend, R., Farchy, E., Kaplanis, I., and Lembcke, A., *OECD Regional Development Working Papers 2014/05*, Organisation for Economic Cooperation and Development, Paris

Overman, H.G., 2013, "Geographical Economics and Policy", in Fisher, M.M., and Nijkamp, P., (eds), *Handbook of Regional Science, Volume 2*, Springer, Berlin

Padoa-Schioppa, T., Emerson, M., King, M., Milleron, J.-C., Paelinck, J., Papademos, L., Pastor, A., and Scharpf, 1987, *Efficiency, Stability and*

Equity: A Strategy for the Evolution of the Economic System of the European Community, Oxford University Press, Oxford

Pellegrini, G., Terribile, F., Tarola, O., Muccigrosso, T., and Busillo, F., 2013, "Measuring the Effects of European Regional Policy on Economic Growth: A Regression Discontinuity Approach", *Papers in Regional Science*, 92.1, 217–233

Percoco, M., 2005, "The Impact of Structural Funds on the Italian Mezzogiorno, 1994–1999", *Région et Développement*, 21, 141–153

Percoco, M., 2013, "Strategies of Regional Development in European Regions: Are They Efficient?", *Cambridge Journal of Regions, Economy and Society*, 303–318

Porter, M.E., 1990, *The Competitive Advantage of Nations*, Free Press, New York

Puigcerver-Peñalver, M.-C., 2007, "The Impact of Structural Funds Policy on European Regions' Growth. A Theoretical and Empirical Approach", *European Journal of Comparative Economics*, 4.2, 179–208

Ramajo, J., Márquez, M.A., Hewings, G.J.D., and Salinas, M., 2008, "Spatial Heterogeneity and Interregional Spillovers in the European union: Do Cohesion Policies Encourage Convergence Across Regions?", *European Economic Review*, 52, 551–567

Rodriguez-Pose, A., and Fratesi, U., 2004, "Between Development and Social Policies: The Impact of European Structural Funds in Objective 1 Regions", *Regional Studies*, 38.1, 97–113

Rodrik, D., 2007, *One Economics Many Recipes: Globalization, Institutions and Economic Growth*, Princeton University Press, Princeton

Sala-i-Martin, X., 1996, "Regional Cohesion: Evidence and Theories of Regional Growth and Convergence", *European Economic Review*, 1325–1352

Sapir, A., Aghion, P., Bertola, G., Hellwig, M., Pisani-Ferry, J., Rosati, D., Viñals, J., and Wallace, H., 2004, *An Agenda for a Growing Europe: The Sapir Report*, Oxford: Oxford University Press.

Senior Nello, S., 2005, *The European Union: Economics, Politics and History*, McGraw-Hill, New York

Sosvilla-Rivero, S., Bajo-Rubio, O., and Diaz-Roldán, C., 2006, "Assessing the Effectiveness of the EU's Regional Policies on Real Convergence: An Analysis Based on the HERMIN Model", *European Planning Studies*, 14, 383–396

Soukiazis, E., and Antunes, M., 2006, "Two Speed Regional Convergence in Portugal and the Importance of Structural Funds on Growth", *Ekonomia*, 9.2, 222–241

Varga, J., and In 't Veld, J., 2010, "The Potential Impact of EU Cohesion Policy Spending in the 2007-13 Programming Period: A Model-Based

Analysis", ECFIN *European Economy Economic Paper 422*, European Commission Directorate-General for Economic and Financial Affairs, Brussels

Varga, J., and In 't Veld, J., 2011, "A Model-Based Analysis of the Impact of Cohesion Policy Expenditure 2000–06: Simulations with the QUEST III Endogenous R&D Model", *Economic Modelling*, 28, 647–663

Ward, T., Greunz, L., and Botti, S., 2012, *Ex Post Evaluation of the Cohesion Fund (Including Former ISPA) in the 2000-2006 Period: Work Package E, Synthesis Report*, Applica sprl. See: http://ec.europa. eu/regional_policy/sources/docgener/evaluation/pdf/expost2006/wpe_ exec_sum.pdf

Wostner, P., and Slander, S., 2009, *The Effectiveness of EU Cohesion Policy Re-visited: Are EU Funds Really Additional?*, EPRC Paper 69, European Policies Research Centre, University of Strathclyde, November

CHAPTER 4

Acemoglu, D., and Robinson, J.A., 2000, "Political Losers as a Barrier to Economic Development", *American Economic Review*, 90.2, 126–130

Acemoglu, D., and Johnson, S.H., 2006a, "De Facto Political Power and Institutional Persistence", *American Economic Review*, 96.2, 325–330

Acemoglu, D., and Johnson, S.H., 2006b, "Unbundling Institutions", *Journal of Political Economy*,113.5, 949-995

Atkinson, A., Cantillon, B., Marlier, E., and Nolan, B., 2002, *Social Indicators, the EU and Social Inclusion*, Oxford University Press, Oxford

Bachtler, J., and Mendez, C., 2013, "EU Cohesion Policy 2007–2013: Are the Goals of the 2006 Reform Being Achieved?", *European Structural and Investment Funds Journal*, 1.1, 15–19

Bachtler, J., and Turok, I., 1997, (eds.), *The Coherence of Regional Policy: Contrasting Perspectives on the Structural Funds*, Jessica Kingsley, London

Bachtler, J., Mendez, C., and Wishlade, F., 2013, *EU Cohesion Policy and European Integration: The Dynamics of EU Budget and Regional Policy Reform*, Ashgate, Aldershot

Barca, F., 2009, *An Agenda for A Reformed Cohesion Policy: A Place-Based Approach to Meeting European Union Challenges and Expectations*, Independent Report Prepared at the Request of the European Commissioner for Regional Policy, Danuta Hübner, European Commission, Brussels

Barca, F., 2011, "Alternative Approaches to Development Policy: Intersections and Divergences", in OECD 2011c, *OECD Regional Outlook 2011: Building Resilient Regions for Stronger Economies*, Organisation for Economic Cooperation and Development, Paris

Barca, F., and McCann, P., 2010, "The Place-Based Approach: A Response to Mr Gill" available at the website: http://www.voxeu.org/index.php?q=node/5644

Barca, F., and McCann, P., 2011, *Methodological Note: Outcome Indicators and Targets – Towards a Performance Oriented EU Cohesion Policy* and examples of such indicators are contained in the two complementary notes on outcome indicators for EU2020 entitled *Meeting Climate Change and Energy Objectives* and *Improving the Conditions for Innovation, Research and Development*. See: http://ec.europa.eu/regional_policy/sources/docgener/evaluation/performance_en.htm

Barca, F., McCann, P., and Rodriguez-Pose, A., 2012, "The Case for Regional Development Intervention: Place-Based versus Place-Neutral Approaches", *Journal of Regional Science*, 52.1, 134–152

Barro, R.J., and Sala-i-Martin, X., 1995, *Economic Growth*, McGraw-Hill

Bauer, C., 2014, "A Macro-Regional Strategy for the Alpine Region", *European Structural and Investment Funds Journal*, 1.2, 47–53

Begg, I., 2009, "The Future of Cohesion Policy in Richer Regions", Working Paper No.03/2009, Directorate-General for Regional Policy, Brussels

Begg, I., 2010, "Cohesion or Confusion: A Policy Searching for Objectives", *Journal of European Integration*, 32.1, 77–96

Berg, A.G., and Ostry, J.D., 2011, "Inequality and Unsustainable Growth: Two Sides of the Same Coin", IMF Staff Discussion Note, SDN/11/08, International Monetary Fund, Washington DC

Borts, G.H., and Stein, J.L., 1964, *Economic Growth in a Free Market*, Columbia University Press, New York

Braga de Macedo, J., and Oliveira-Martins, J., 2008, "Growth, Reform Indicators and Policy Complementarities", *Economics of Transition*, 16, 141–164

Braga de Macedo, J., and Oliveira-Martins, J., 2010, "Policy Complementarities and Growth", 1–37, *OECD/CESifo/Ifo Workshop Regulation: Political Economy, Measurement and Effects on Performance*, 29–30 January, Munich

Braga de Macedo, J., Oliveira-Martins, J., and Rocha, B., 2013, "Are Complementary Reforms a 'Luxury' for Developing Countries", *Journal of Comparative Economics*, doi: 10.1016.j.jce.2013.06.003

Bryson, A., Dorsett, R., and Portes, J., 2012, "Policy Evaluation in a Time of Austerity: Introduction", *National Institute Economic Review*, 219, R1–R3

CAF, 2010, *Desarrollo local: hacia un Nuevo protagonismo de las ciudades y regiones*, Corporación Andina de Fomento, Caracas

Cash, D.W., and Buizer, J., 2005, *Knowledge-Action Systems for Seasonal to Interannual Climate Forecasting*, Report to the Roundtable on Science and Technology for Sustainability, National Academy of Sciences, National Academies Press, Washington DC, www.nap.edu

Cash, D.W., Clark, W.C., Alcock, F., Dickson, N.M., Echley, N., Guston, D.H., Jäger, J., and Mitchell, R.B., 2003, "Knowledge Systems for Sustainable Development", *Proceedings of the National Academy of Sciences*, 100.14, 8086–8091

Charlot, S., Gaigné, C., Robert-Nicoud, F., and Thisse, J.-F., 2006, "Agglomeration and Welfare: The Core–Periphery Model in the Light of Bentham, Kaldor and Rawls", *Journal of Public Economics*, 90, 325–347

Charron, N., Lapuente, V., and Dijkstra, L., 2012, "Regional Governance Matters: A Study on Regional Variation in Quality of Government within the EU", Working Paper No.01/2012, European Commission Directorate General for Regional Policy, Brussels

Charron, N., Lapuente, V., and Rothstein, B., 2013, *Quality of Government and Corruption from a European Perspective*, Edward Elgar, Cheltenham, UK and Northampton, MA, USA

Charron, N., Lapuente, V., and Dijkstra, L., 2014, "Regional Governance Matters: Quality of Government within European Union Member States", *Regional Studies*, forthcoming

Committee of the Regions, 2012a, *Draft Opinion of the Commission for Territorial Cohesion Policy: Proposal for a General Regulation on the Funds Covered by the Common Strategic Framework*, 11 Commission Meeting, 5 March 2012, CoR 4/2012 IT/CD/MW/ht, Committee of the Regions, Brussels

Committee of the Regions, 2012b, *Draft Opinion of the Committee of the Regions, Building a European Culture of Multilevel Governance: Follow-Up to the Committee of the Regions' White Paper*, CdR 273/2011 rev.2, 94th Plenary Session of the Committee of the Regions, 15–16 February 2012, Brussels

Council of the European Union, 2012, Draft Opinion 7/2011 of the Court of Auditors, 26 December, 2012, Interinstitutional File 2011/0276 (COD), The Council of the European Union, 5798/12, 27 January 2012, Brussels

Crafts, N., 2010, "Overview and Policy Implication", in *BIS Economics Paper No.6, Learning from Some of Britain's Successful Sectors: An*

Historical Analysis of the Role of Government, Department for Business, Innovation and Skills, London, March

Crafts, N., 2012, "Creating Competitive Advantage: Policy Lessons from History", in Greenaway, D., (ed.), *The UK in a Global World: How Can the UK Focus on Steps in Global Value Chains that Really Add Value?*, CEPR, Centre for Economic Policy Research, London

Cultplan, 2007, Cultural Differences in European Cooperation: Learning from INTERREG Practice. See http://www.cultplan.org/downloads/RAPPORT%20DEF%202%20LR.pdf

Davies, H.T.O., Nutley, S.M., and Smith, P.C., 2000, *What Works? Evidence-Based Policy and Practice in Public Services*, Policy Press, Bristol

De Michelis, N., and Monfort, P., 2008, "Some Reflections Concerning GDP, Convergence and European Cohesion Policy", *Regional Science: Policy and Practice*, 1.1, 15–22

Dijkstra, L., Garcilazo, E., and McCann, P., 2013, "The Economic Performance of European Cities and City-Regions: Myths and Realities", *European Planning Studies*, 21.3, 334–354

Dreher, A., 2009, "IMF Conditionality: Theory and Evidence", *Public Choice*, 141, 233–267

EEA, 2010, *The Territorial Dimension of Environmental Sustainability: Potential Territorial Indicators to Support the Environment Dimension of Territorial Cohesion*, EEA Technical Report No.9/2010, Environment Agency, Copenhagen

EEA, 2012, *Environmental Indicator Report 2012: Ecosystem Resilience and Resource Efficiency in a Green Economy in Europe*, Environment Agency, Copenhagen

EPRC, 2013, *EPRC Policy Briefing. Cohesion Policy 2014–20: National Allocations. Who are the Winners and Losers from the 7–8 February European Council?* 25 February 2013. See: http://www.eprc.strath.ac.uk/news/COHESION_POLICY_ALLOCATIONS_2014-20_EPRC_Policy_Briefing_Feb_2013.pdf

Estache, A., and Fay, M., 2010, "Current Debates on Infrastructure Policy", in Spence, M., and Leipziger, D., (eds.), *Globalization and Growth: Implications for a Post-Crisis World*, Commission on Growth and Development, World Bank, Washington DC

European Commission, 2007, *State of the European Cities Report: Adding Value to the European Urban Audit*, Brussels

European Commission, 2008, *Regions 2020: An Assessment of Future Challenges for EU Regions*, Commission Staff Working Document, European Commission, Directorate-General for Regional Policy, Brussels, November 2008, SEC(2008) 2868 Final

European Commission, 2010a, *Europe 2020: A European Strategy for Smart, Sustainable and Inclusive Growth*, [COM (2010) 2020] 3.3.2010, Brussels

European Commission, 2010b, *Second State of European Cities Report: Adding Value to the European Audit*, Directorate-General for Regional Policy, Brussels

European Commission, 2010c, *The European Union Strategy for the Baltic Sea Region. Background and Analysis*, May 2010, Directorate-General for Regional Policy, Publications Office of the European Union, Luxembourg:

European Commission, 2010d, *Ex Post Evaluation of Cohesion Policy Programmes 2000–06: The URBAN Community Initiative: Evaluation Report*, Publications Office, Brussels

European Commission, 2010e, *Ex Post Evaluation of INTERREG III 2000–06: Evaluation Report*, Publications Office, Brussels

European Commission, 2011a, *Proposal for a regulation of the European Parliament and of the Council laying down common provisions on the European Regional Development Fund, the European Social Fund, the Cohesion Fund, the European Agricultural Fund for Rural Development and the European Maritime and Fisheries Fund covered by the Common Strategic Framework and laying down general provisions on the European Regional Development Fund, the European Social Fund and the Cohesion Fund and repealing Regulation (EC) No 1083/2006 [COM(2011) 615 final of 6.10.2011]*, European Commission, Brussels

European Commission, 2011b, *Cities of Tomorrow. Challenges, Visions, Ways Forward*, Directorate-General for Regional Policy, Publications Office of the European Union, Luxembourg

European Commission, 2011c, "The EU Strategy for the Danube Region. A United Response to Common Challenges", *Panorama Inforegio*, 37, Spring, Directorate-General for Regional Policy, Publications Office of the European Union, Luxembourg

European Commission, 2012a, *Elements for a Common Strategic Framework 2014 to 2020: the European Regional Development Fund, the European Social Fund, the Cohesion Fund, the European Agricultural Fund for Rural Development and the European Maritime and Fisheries Fund*, Commission Staff Working Document, Brussels, 14.3.2012, SWD (2012) 61 Final Part I and II

European Commission, 2012b, *The Partnership Principle in the Implementation of the Common Strategic Framework Funds – Elements for a European Code of Conduct on Partnership*, Commission Staff Working Document, Brussels, 24.4.2012, SWD (2012) 106 Final

European Commission, 2012c, *Integrated Sustainable Urban Develop-ment: Cohesion Policy 2014–2020*, Factsheet, Directorate-General for Regional Policy, Brussels

European Commission, 2014, "Cohesion Policy 2014–2020 Momentum Builds", *Panorama: Inforegio*, 48, Winter, Brussels

European Parliament, 2012a, *Comparative Study on the Visions and Options for Cohesion Policy after 2013: Study*, Directorate-General for Internal Policies, Policy Department B: Structural and Cohesion Policies, European Parliament, Brussels

European Parliament, 2012b, *Moving Towards a More Result/ Performance-Based Delivery System in Cohesion Policy: Study*, Directorate-General for Internal Policies, Policy Department B: Structural and Cohesion Policies, European Parliament, Brussels

European Union, 2007, *Cohesion Policy 2007–2013 Commentaries and Official Texts*, Publications Office, Brussels

European Union, 2010a, *Ex-Post Evaluation of Cohesion Policy Programmes 2000–2006 Co-Financed by the ERDF (Objective 1 & 2)*, Publications Office, Brussels

European Union, 2010b, *Ex-Post Evaluation of INTERREG III 2000–2006*, Publications Office, Brussels

European Union, 2011, *European Territorial Cooperation: Building Bridges Between People*, Publications Office, Brussels

European Union, 2012a, *The European Union Explained: How the European Union Works*, Directorate-General for Communication, Brussels

European Union, 2012b, "Partnership in Cohesion Policy: Reinforcing the Implementation of this Key Principle", *Panorama Inforegio*, 42, Directorate-General for Regional Policy, Publications Office, Brussels

European Union, 2012c, "Investing in Regions: Using Financial Instruments to Leverage Support for Regional Policy", *Panorama Inforegio*, 43, Directorate-General for Regional Policy, Publications Office, Brussels

European Union, 2013a, *Urban Development in the EU: 50 Projects Supported by the European Regional Development Fund During the 2007–2013 Period*, Directorate General for Regional and Urban Policy Brussels

European Union, 2013b, *The Urban and Regional Dimension of the Crisis: Eighth Report on Economic, Social and Territorial Cohesion*, Publications Office, Brussels

European Union, 2014, *Investment for Jobs and Growth Promoting Development and Good Governance in EU Regions and Cities: Sixth*

Report on Economic, Social and Territorial Cohesion, European Commission Directorate-General for Regional and Urban Policy, Publications Office, Brussels

Farole, T., Rodriguez-Pose, A., and Storper, M., 2011, "Cohesion Policy in the European Union: Growth, Geography and Institutions", *Journal of Common Market Studies*, 49.5, 1089–1111

Farrow, S., and Zerbe, R.O., Jr., (eds.), 2013, *Principles and Standards for Benefit–Cost Analysis*, Edward Elgar, Cheltenham, UK and Northampton, MA, USA

Ferrara, A., 2010, *Cost–Benefit Analysis of Multi-Level Government: The Case of EU Cohesion Policy and of US Federal Investment Policies*, Routledge, London

Frazer, H., Marlier, E., and Nicaise, I., 2010, *A Social Inclusion Roadmap for Europe 2020*, Garant, Antwerpen-Apeldoorn

Gaffey, V., 2013a, "A Fresh Look at the Intervention Logic of Structural Funds", *Evaluation*, 19.2, 195–203

Gaffey, V., 2013b, "Methods for Evaluating Cohesion Policy Programmes", *European Structural and Investment Funds Journal*, 1.1, 31–34

Garretsen, J.H., McCann, P., Martin, R., and Tyler, P., 2013, "The Future of Regional Policy", *Cambridge Journal of Regions, Economy and Society*, 6.2, 179–186

Gill, I., 2010, "Regional Development Policies: Place-Based or People-Centred?" available at the website: http://www.voxeu.org/index.php?q=node/5644

Glennerster, R., 2012, "The Power of Evidence: Improving the Effectiveness of Government by Investing in More Rigorous Evaluation", *National Institute Economic Review*, 219, R4–R14

Hall, R., 2005, "The Future of European Regional Policy: Issues Surrounding an Agenda for a Growing Europe", *Regional Studies*, 39.7, 966–971

Hausmann, R., and Rodrik, D., 2003, "Economic Development as Self-Discovery", *Journal of Development Economics*, 72.2, 603–633

Hughes, A., 2012, "Choosing Races and Placing Bets: UK National Innovation Policy and the Globalisation of Innovation Systems", in Greenaway, D., (ed.), *The UK in a Global World. How Can the UK Focus on Steps in Global Value Chains that Really Add Value?*, BIS e-book, CEPR and Department for Business, Innovation and Skills See: http://www.cepr.org/pubs/books/cepr/BIS_eBook.pdf

Link, A.N., and Vonortas, N.S, 2013, (eds.), *Handbook on the Theory and Practice of Program Evaluation*, Edward Elgar, Cheltenham, UK and Northampton, MA, USA

Marlier, E., Natali, D., and Van Dam, R., 2008, *Europe 2020: Towards a More Social EU? Work and Society*, Vol. 69, P.I.E. Peter Lang, Brussels

Martin, P., 2005, "The Geography of Inequalities in Europe", *Swedish Economic Policy Review*, 12, 83–108

Martin, R., 2008, "National Growth versus Spatial Equality? A Cautionary Note on the New 'Trade-Off' Thinking in Regional Policy Discourse", *Regional Science: Policy and Practice*, 1.1, 2–13

Martin, R., and Tyler, P., 2006, "Evaluating the Impact of the Structural Funds on Objective 1 Regions: An Exploratory Analysis", *Regional Studies*, 40.2, 201–210

McCann, P., 2011, "Notes on the Major Practical Elements of Commencing the Design of an Integrated and Territorial Place-Based Approach to Cohesion Policy", in *Territorial Dimension of Development Policies: Post Seminar Publication of the High Level Conference on Territorial Cohesion hosted by the Polish Presidency of the EU*, Ministry of Regional Development, Warsaw, July 2011

McCann, P., 2013, *Modern Urban and Regional Economics*, Oxford University Press, Oxford

McCann, P., and Ortega-Argilés, 2013a, "Redesigning and Reforming European Regional Policy: The Reasons, the Logic and the Outcomes", *International Regional Science Review*, 36.3, 424–445

McCann, P., and Ortega-Argilés, 2013b, "Transforming European Regional Policy: A Results-Driven Agenda and Smart Specialisation", 2013, *Oxford Review of Economic Policy*, 29.2, 405–431

McCann, P., and Rodriguez-Pose, A., 2011, "Why and When Development Policy Should be Place-Based", *OECD Regional Outlook 2011*, Organisation for Economic Cooperation and Development, Paris

Menzes, C., 2013, "The Post 2013 Reform of EU Cohesion Policy and the Place-Based Narrative", *Journal of European Public Policy*, 20.5, 639–659

MGI, 2011, *Urban World: Mapping the Economic Power of Cities*, McKinsey Global Institute

MGI, 2013, *A New Dawn: Reigniting Growth in Central and Eastern Europe*, McKinsey Global Institute, December

Moretti, E., 2012, *The New Geography of Jobs*, Houghton Mifflin Harcourt, New York

Mouqué, D., 2012, "What are Counterfactual Impact Evaluations Teaching us About Enterprise and Innovation Support?", *Regional Focus, 02/2012*, European Commission Directorate-General, for Regional and Urban Policy, Brussels, December

Moore, B., and Rhodes, J., 1973, "Evaluating the Effects of British Regional Economic Policy", *Economic Journal*, 83, 87–110

OECD, 2001a, *Cities for Citizens: Improving Metropolitan Governance*, Organisation for Economic Cooperation and Development, Paris

OECD, 2001b, *Citizens as Partners: OECD Handbook on Information, Consultation and Public Participation in Policy-Making*, Organisation for Economic Cooperation and Development, Paris

OECD, 2003, *The Future of Rural Policy: From Sectoral to Place-Based Policies in Rural Areas*, Organisation for Economic Cooperation and Development, Paris

OECD, 2004, *New Forms of Governance for Economic Development*, Organisation for Economic Cooperation and Development, Paris

OECD, 2005a, *Building Competitive Regions: Strategies and Governance*, Organisation for Economic Cooperation and Development, Paris

OECD, 2005b, *New Approaches to Rural Policy: Evidence from Around the World*, Organisation for Economic Cooperation and Development, Paris

OECD, 2007a, *Linking Regions and Central Government: Contracts for Regional Development*, Organisation for Economic Cooperation and Development, Paris

OECD 2007b, *Investment Strategies and Financial Tools for Local Development,* Organisation for Economic Cooperation and Development, Paris

OECD, 2008, *Making Local Strategies Work: Building the Evidence Base*, Organisation for Economic Cooperation and Development, Paris

OECD, 2009a, *Community Capacity Building: Creating a Better Future Together,* Organisation for Economic Cooperation and Development, Paris

OECD, 2009b, *How Regions Grow*, Organisation for Economic Growth and Development, Paris

OECD, 2009c, *Regions Matter: Economic Recovery, Innovation and Sustainable Growth*, Organisation for Economic Growth and Development, Paris

OECD, 2009d, *Governing Regional Development Policy: The Use of Performance Indicators*, Organisation for Economic Growth and Development, Paris

OECD, 2010, *Cities and Climate Change*, Organisation for Economic Growth and Development, Paris

OECD 2011a, *Making the Most of Public Investment in a Tight Fiscal Environment: Multi-Level Governance Lessons from the Crisis*, Organisation for Economic Cooperation and Development, Paris

OECD 2011b, *Together for Better Public Services: Partnering with Citizens and Civil Society*, Organisation for Economic Cooperation and Development, Paris

OECD, 2011c, *OECD Regional Outlook 2011: Building Resilient Regions for Stronger Economies*, Organisation for Economic Cooperation and Development, Paris

OECD, 2011d, *How's Life? Measuring Well-Being*, Organisation for Economic Cooperation and Development, Paris

OECD, 2012a, *Promoting Growth in All Regions*, Organisation for Economic Cooperation and Development, Paris

OECD, 2012b, *Compact City Policies: A Comparative Perspective*, Organisation for Economic Cooperation and Development, Paris

OECD, 2012c, *Linking Renewable Energy to Rural Development*, Organisation for Economic Cooperation and Development, Paris

OECD, 2013a, *Investing Together*, Organisation for Economic Cooperation and Development, Paris

OECD, 2013b, *Regions and Innovation*, Organisation for Economic Cooperation and Development, Paris

OECD, 2014a, "What Makes Cities More Productive? Evidence on the Role of Urban Governance from OECD Countries", Ahrend, R., Farchy, E., Kaplanis, I., and Lembcke, A., *OECD Regional Development Working Papers 2014/05*, Organisation for Economic Cooperation and Development, Paris

OECD, 2014b, "Approaches to Metropolitan Governance: A Country Overview", Ahrend, R., and Schumann, A., *OECD Regional Development Working Papers 2014/03*, Organisation for Economic Cooperation and Development, Paris

OECD, 2014c, "The OECD Metropolitan Governance Survey: A Quantitative Description of Governance Structures in Large Urban Agglomerations", Ahrend, R., Gamper, C., and Schumann, A., *OECD Regional Development Working Papers 2014/04*, Organisation for Economic Cooperation and Development, Paris

Ostrom, E., 1990, *Governing the Commons. The Evolution of Institutions for Collective Action*, Cambridge University Press, New York

Ostrom, E., 1998, "A Behavioural Approach to the Rational Choice Theory of Collective Action", *American Political Science Review*, 92.1, 1–22

Ostrom, E., 2005, *Understanding Institutional Diversity*, Princeton University Press, Princeton

Ostrom, E., 2007, "A Diagnostic Approach for Going Beyond Panaceas", *Proceedings of the National Academy of Sciences*, 104, 15181–15187

Pawson, R., 2006, *Evidence-Based Policy: A Realist Perspective*, Sage, London

Petzold, W., 2013, "Conditionality, Flexibility, Unanimity: The Embedded 2013 Reform of EU Cohesion Policy", *European Structural and Investment Funds Journal*, 1.1, 7–14

Piacentini, M., and Rosina, K., 2012, "Measuring the Environmental Performance of Metropolitian Areas with Geographic Information Sources", *OECD Regional Development Working Papers, 2012/05*, Organisation for Economic Cooperation and Development, Paris

Priemus, H., Flyvbjerg, and van Wee, 2008, (eds.), *Decision-Making on Mega-Projects: Cost–Benefit Analysis, Planning and Innovation*, Edward Elgar, Cheltenham, UK and Northampton, MA, USA

Prager, J.-C, and Thisse, J.-F., 2012, *Economic Geography and the Unequal Development of Regions*, Routledge, London

Puga, D., 2002, "European Regional Policies in the Light of Recent Location Theories", *Journal of Economic Geography*, 2, 373–406

Rodrik, D., 1999, "Institutions for High Quality Growth: What They Are and How to Acquire Them", Lecture Presented at the IMF Conference on Second Generation Reforms. See http://www.imf.org/external/pubs/ft/seminar/1999/reforms/rodrik.htm and published as Rodrik, D., 2000, NBER Working Paper 7540 and in Roy, K.C. and Sideras, J., 2006, (eds.) *Institutions, Globalisation and Empowerment*, Edward Elgar, Cheltenham UK and Northampton, MA, USA

Rodrik, D., 2004, "Industrial Policy for the Twenty-First Century", Working Paper, Kennedy School of Government, Harvard University, Cambridge MA

Rodrik, D., 2007, *One Economics, Many Recipes: Globalization, Institutions and Economic Growth*, Princeton University Press, Princeton

Sachs, J.D., 2003, "Institutions Don't Rule: Direct Effects of Geography on Per Capita Income", WP 9490, NBER, Cambridge, MA

Sachs, J.D., 2012, "Government, Geography, and Jobs: The True Drivers of Economic Development", *Foreign Affairs*, September/October

Sapir, A., Aghion, P., Bertola, G., Hellwig, M., Pisani-Ferry, J., Rosati, D., Viñals, J., and Wallace, H., 2004, *An Agenda for a Growing Europe: The Sapir Report*, Oxford: Oxford University Press.

Sedlacko, M., and Martinuzzi, A., 2012, *Governance by Evaluation for Sustainable Development,: Institutional Capacities and Learning*, Edward Elgar, Cheltenham, UK and Northampton, MA, USA

Sen, A., 1988, *The Concept of Development*, in Chenery, H. and Srinivasan, T.N., (eds.), *Handbook of Development Economics*, Vol. 1, 2–23, Elsevier: North-Holland

Sen, A., 1989, "Development as Capability Expansion", *Journal of Development Planning*, 19, 41–58, reprinted in Fukuda-Parr, S., and Shiva Kumar, A.K., (eds.), 2003, *Readings in Human Development*, 3–16, Oxford University Press, New York

Sen, A., 1993, "Capability and Well-Being", in Nussbaum, M., and Sen, A., (eds.), *The Quality of Life*, 30–53, Clarendon Press, Oxford

Stiglitz, J.E., Sen, A., and Fitoussi, J.-P., 2009, *Report by the Commission on the Measurement of Economic and Social Progress*. See: http://www.stiglitz-sen-fitoussi.fr/en/index.htm

Stockmann, R., 2011, *A Practitioner Handbook on Evaluation*, Edward Elgar, Cheltenham, UK and Northampton, MA, USA

Storper, M., 2013, *Keys to the City: How Economics, Institutions, Social Interaction, and Politics Shape Development*, Princeton University Press, Princeton

Swales, J.K., 1997, "A Cost–Benefit Approach to the Evaluation of Regional Selective Assistance", *Fiscal Studies*, 18, 73–85

Swales, J.K., 2009, "A Cost–Benefit Approach to the Assessment of Regional Policy", in Farshchi, M.A., Janne, O.E.M., and McCann, P., (eds.), *Technological Change and Mature Regions: Firms, Knowledge and Policy*, Edward Elgar, Cheltenham, UK and Northampton, MA, USA

Technopolis Group and MIOIR, 2012, *Evaluation of Innovation Activities: Guidance on Methods and Practices*, Study Funded by the European Commission Directorate-General for Regional Policy, Brussels

Tell Cremades, M., 2014, "Review of the European Parliament's Role in the Interinstitutional Negotiations for the EU Cohesion Policy Legislative Package 2014–2020", *European Structural and Investment Funds Journal*, forthcoming

The Economist, 2013, "Life after Doha", 14 December

World Bank, 2003, *World Development Report: 2003: Transforming Institutions, Growth and Quality of Life*, Washington DC

World Bank, 2005, *Conditionality Revisited: Concepts, Experiences and Lessons*, World Bank, Washington DC

World Bank, 2006, *Local Economic Development: A Primer. Developing and Implementing Local Economic Development Strategies and Action Plans*, World Bank, Washington DC

World Bank, 2009, *World Development Report 2009: Reshaping Economic Geography*, Washington DC

World Bank, 2010, *Innovation Policy: A Guide for Developing Countries*, World Bank, Washington DC

World Bank, 2012, *Golden Growth: Restoring the Lustre of the European Economic Model*, Washington DC

Zoellick, R.F., 2012, "Why We Still Need the World Bank: Looking Beyond Aid", *Foreign Affairs*, March/April, 91.2, 66–78

CHAPTER 5

Acs, Z.J., 2002, *Innovation and the Growth of Cites*, Edward Elgar, Cheltenham, UK and Northampton, MA, USA

Acs, Z.J., and Audretsch, D.B., 1988, "Innovation in Large and Small Firms: An Empirical Analysis", *American Economic Review*, 78.4, September, 678–690

Acs, Z.J., and Audretsch, D.B., 1990, *Innovation and Small Firms*, MIT Press, Cambridge, MA

Aghion, P., and Howitt, P., 1992, "A Model of Growth Through Creative Destruction", *Econometrica*, 60, 323–351.

Anselin, L., Varga, A., and Z. Acs, 1997, "Local Geographic Spillovers Between University Research and High Technology Innovations", *Journal of Urban Economics*, 42, 422–448

Arita, T., and McCann, P., 2000, "Industrial Alliances and Firm Location Behaviour: Some Evidence from the US Semiconductor Industry", *Applied Economics*, 32, 1391–1403

Arrow, K.J., 1962, "The Economic Implications of Learning by Doing", *Review of Economic Studies*, 29, 155–173

Audretsch, D.B. and Feldman, M., 1996, "R&D Spillovers and the Geography of Innovation and Production", *American Economic Review*, 86.3, 630–640

Bachtler, J., Mendez, C., and Wishlade, F., 2013, *EU Cohesion Policy and European Integration: The Dynamics of EU Budget and Regional Policy Reform*, Ashgate, Aldershot

Baláž, V., 2007, "Regional Polarization under Transition: The Case of Slovakia", *European Planning Studies*, 15.5, 587–602

Baldwin, R., and Evenett, S.J., 2012, "Value Creation and Trade in 21st Century Manufacturing: What Policies for UK Manufacturing?", in Greenaway, D., (ed.), *The UK in a Global World. How can the UK Focus on Steps in Global Value Chains that Really Add Value?*, BIS e-book, CEPR, ESRC and Department for Business, Innovation and Skills. See: http://www.nottingham.ac.uk/gep/documents/reports/dge bookcomplete.pdf

Barca, F., 2009, *An Agenda for A Reformed Cohesion Policy: A Place-Based Approach to Meeting European Union Challenges and Expectations*, Independent Report Prepared at the Request of the European Commissioner for Regional Policy, Danuta Hübner, European Commission, Brussels

Barca, F., McCann, P., and Rodriguez-Pose, A., 2012, "The Case for Regional Development Intervention: Place-Based versus Place-Neutral Approaches", *Journal of Regional Science*, 52.1, 134–152

Best, M.H., 1990, *The New Competition: Institution of Industrial Restructuring*, Harvard University Press

Borrás, S., and Tsagdis, D., 2008, *Cluster Policies in Europe: Firms, Institutions and Governance*, Edward Elgar, Cheltenham, UK and Northampton, MA, USA

Boschma, R.A., 2005, "Proximity and Innovation. A Critical Assessment", *Regional Studies*, 39.1, 61–74

Boschma, R.A., and Frenken, K., 2011, "Technological Relatedness and Regional Branching, in Bathelt, H., Feldman, M.P., and Kogler, D.F., (eds.), *Dynamic Geographies of Knowledge Creation and Innovation*, Taylor and Francis, Routledge, London

Boschma, R.A., and Iammarino, S., 2009, "Related Variety, Trade Linkages and Regional Growth", *Economic Geography*, 85.3, 289–311

Boschma, R.A., and Martin, R.L., 2010, (eds.), *Handbook of Evolutionary Economic Geography*, Edward Elgar, Cheltenham, UK and Northampton, MA, USA

Boschma, R.A., Minondo, A., and Navarro, M., 2012, "Related Variety and Regional Growth in Spain", *Papers in Regional Science*, 91.2, 241–256

Brakman, S., and van Marrewijk, C., 2013, "Reflections on Cluster Policies", *Cambridge Journal of Regions Economy and Society*, 6.2, 217–231

Breschi, S., and Malerba, F., 2005, (eds.), *Clusters, Networks, and Innovation*, Oxford University Press, Oxford

Carlaw, K.I., and Lipsey, R.G., 2006, "GPT-Driven Endogenous Growth", *Economic Journal*, 116, 155–174

Carlino, G.A., Chatterjee, S., and Hunt, R.M., 2007, "Urban Density and the Rate of Invention", *Journal of Urban Economics*, 61.3, 389–419

Casson, M.C., 1982, *The Entrepreneur: An Economic Theory*, Martin Robertson, Oxford

Casson, M., Yeung, B., and Basu, A., and Wadeson, N., 2006, (eds.), *The Oxford Handbook of Entrepreneurship*, Oxford University Press, Oxford

Ciccone, A., and, R.E. Hall, 1996, "Productivity and the Density of Economic Activity", *American Economic Review*, 86.1, 54–70

Cooke, P.N., and Morgan, K.J., 1998, *The Associational Economy: Firms, Regions and Innovation*, Oxford University Press, Oxford

Cooke, P., Asheim, B., Annerstedt, J., Blažec, J., Boschma, R., Brzica, D., Dahlstrand Lindholm, A., Del Castillo Hermosa, J., Laredo, P., Moula, M., and Piccaluga, A., 2006, *Constructing Regional Advantage: Principles, Perspectives, Policies*, Report to European Commission Directorate-General for Research, Brussels

Cozza, C., Ortega-Argilés, R., Piva, M., and Baptista, R., 2012, "Productivity Gaps Among EU regions", in Audretsch, D.B., Lehmann, E.E., Link, A.N., and Starnecker, A., (eds.), *Technology Transfer in a Global Economy*, International Studies on Entrepreneurship, vol 28. Springer, Berlin

Crafts, N., 2010, "Overview and Policy Implication", in *BIS Economics Paper No.6, Learning from Some of Britain's Successful Sectors: An Historical Analysis of the Role of Government*, Department for Business, Innovation and Skills, London, March

Crafts, N., 2012, "Creating Competitive Advantage: Policy Lessons from History", in Greenaway, D., (ed.), *The UK in a Global World: How Can the UK Focus on Steps in Global Value Chains that Really Add Value?*, CEPR, Centre for Economic Policy Research, London

Crépon, B., Duguet, E., and Mairesse, J., 1998, "Research, Innovation and Productivity: An Econometric Analysis at the Firm Level", *Economics of Innovation and New Technology*, 7, 115–158

Crescenzi, R., and Rodriguez-Pose, A., 2011, *Innovation and Regional Growth in the European Union*, Springer, Heidelberg

CST, 2007, "Strategic Decision-Making for Technology Policy", UK Council for Science and Technology, November. See: http://web archive.nationalarchives.gov.uk/+/http://www2.cst.gov.uk/cst/reports/# Strategic

David, P.A., 1985, "Clio and the Economics of QWERTY", *American Economic Review: Papers and Proceedings*, 75.2, 332–337

Dosi, G., Marsili, O., Orsenigo, L., and Salvatore, R., 1995, "Learning, Market Selection and the Evolution of Industrial Structures", *Small Business Economics*, 7, 411–436

Dosi G., Malerba, F., Marsili, O. and L. Orsenigo, 1997, "Industrial Structures and Dynamics: Evidence, Interpretations and Puzzles", *Industrial and Corporate Change*, 6(1), 3–24.

Drabenstott, M., 2005, *A Review of the Federal Role in Regional Economic Development*, Federal Reserve Bank of Kansas City, First Quarter

Duranton, G., 2011, "California Dreamin': The Feeble Case for Cluster Policies", *Review of Economic Analysis*, 3.1, 3–45

ESPON, 2012, *KIT Territorial Dimension of Innovation and Knowledge Economy*, Luxembourg

European Commission, 2012, *Industrial Performance Scoreboard and Member States' Competitiveness Performance and Policies*, European Commission, Directorate-General for Enterprise and Industry, Brussels

European Commission, 2014a, *Innovation Union Scoreboard 2014*, Directorate-General for Enterprise and Industry, Brussels

European Commission, 2014b, *Regional Innovation Scoreboard 2014*, Directorate-General for Enterprise and Industry, Brussels

Fagerberg, J., Mowery, D.C., and Nelson, R.R., 2005, (eds.), *The Oxford Handbook of Innovation*, Oxford University Press, Oxford

Faggian, A., and McCann, P., 2006, "Human Capital Flows and Regional Knowledge Assets: A Simultaneous Equation Approach", *Oxford Economic Papers*, 58.3, 475–500

Faggian, A., and McCann, P., 2009a, "Human Capital, Graduate Migration and Innovation in British Regions", *Cambridge Journal of Economics*, 33.2, 317–333

Faggian, A., and McCann, P., 2009b, "Human Capital and Regional Development", in Capello, R., and Nijkamp, P., (eds.), *Regional Dynamics and Growth: Advances in Regional Economics*, Edward Elgar, Cheltenham, UK and Northampton, MA, USA

Feldman, M.P., 1994, *The Geography of. Innovation. Economics of Science, Technology and Innovation*, Dordrecht; Kluwer Academic

Foray, D., 2004, *The Economics of Knowledge*, MIT Press, Cambridge MA

Foray, D., 2009, (ed.), *The New Economics of Technology Policy*, Edward Elgar, Cheltenham, UK and Northampton, MA, USA

Foray, D., and Freeman, C., 1993, (eds.), *Technology and the Wealth of Nations*, Pinter, London

Freeman, C., 1995, "The 'National System of Innovation' in Historical Perspective", *Cambridge Journal of Economics*, 19, 5–24

Frenken, K., Van Oort, F.G., and Verburg, T., 2007, "Related Variety, Unrelated Variety and Regional Economic Growth," *Regional Studies*, 41.5, 685–697

Gaspar, J., and Glaeser, E.L., 1998, "Information Technology and the Future of Cities", *Journal of Urban Economics*, 43, 136–156

Gertler. M., 2003, "Tacit Knowledge and the Economic Geography of Context, or Undefinable Tacitness of Being (There)", *Journal of Economic Geography*, 3, 75–99

Glaeser, E.L., 2011, *Triumph of the City: How Our Greatest Invention Makes Us Richer, Smarter, Greener, Healthier, and Happier*, Penguin Press, New York

Glaeser, E.L., Rosenthal, S.S., and Strange, W.C., 2010, "Urban Economics and Entrepreneurship", *Journal of Urban Economics*, 67.1, 1–14

Gordon, I.R., and McCann, P., 2005, "Innovation, Agglomeration and Regional Development", *Journal of Economic Geography*, 5.5, 523–543

Grindley, P.C. and Teece, D.J., 1997, "Managing Intellectual Capital: Licensing and Cross-Licensing in Semiconductors and Electronics", *California Management Review*, 29, 8–41

Haltiwanger, J.C., Jarmin, R.S., and Miranda, J., 2010, "Who Creates Jobs? Small vs. Large vs. Young", NBER Working Paper Series, 16300

Hausmann, R., Hidalgo, C.A., Bustos, S., Coscia, M., Chung, S., Jiminez, J., Somoes, A., and Yildirim, M., 2013, *The Atlas of Economci Complexity: Mapping Paths to Prosperity*, Center for International Development and Kennedy School of Government, Harvard University, Cambridge MA See: http://www.hks.harvard.edu/centers/cid/publications/featured-books/atlas

Hong, S., McCann, P., and Oxley, L., 2012, "A Survey of the Innovation Surveys", *Journal of Economic Surveys*, 26.3, 420–444

Hughes, A., 2012, "Choosing Races and Placing Bets: UK National Innovation Policy and the Globalisation of Innovation Systems", in Greenaway, D., (ed.), *The UK in a Global World. How Can the UK Focus on Steps in Global Value Chains that Really Add Value?*, BIS e-book, CEPR, ESRC and Department for Business, Innovation and Skills See: http://www.nottingham.ac.uk/gep/documents/reports/dge bookcomplete.pdf

Hulten, C., 2013, "Stimulating Economic Growth Through Knowledge-Based Investments", *OECD Science, Technology and Industry Working Papers 2013/02*, Organisation for Economic Cooperation and Development, Paris

Iammarino, S., and McCann, P., 2006, "The Structure and Evolution of Industrial Clusters: Transactions, Technology and Knowledge Spillovers", 2006, *Research Policy*, 35, 1018–1036

Iammarino, S., and McCann, P., 2013, *Multinationals and Economic Geography: Location, Technology and Innovation*, 2013, McCann, P., Edward Elgar, Cheltenham, UK and Northampton, MA, USA

Jaffe, A.B., 1986, "Technological Opportunity and Spillovers of R&D: Evidence from Firms' Patents, Profits and Market Value", *American Economic Review*, 76.5, 984-1001

Jaffe, A.B., Trajtenberg, M., and Henderson, R., 1993, "Geographic Localization of Knowledge Flows as Evidenced by Patent Citations", *Quarterly Journal of Economics*, 108, 577–598

Jorgenson, D.W., Ho, M.S., and Stiroh, K.J., 2008, "A Retrospective Look at the U.S. Productivity Growth Resurgence", *Journal of Economic Perspectives*, 22.1, 3–24

Kaldor, N., 1975, "Economic Growth and the Verdoorn Law", *Economic Journal*, 85, 891–896

Ketels, C., 2013, "Recent Research on Competitiveness and Clusters: What Are the Implications for Regional Policy?", *Cambridge Journal of Regions, Economy and Society*, 6.2, 269–284

Kline, S.J., and Rosenberg, N., 1986, "An Overview of Innovation", in Landau, R., and Rosenberg, N., (eds.), *The Positive Sum Strategy: Harnessing Technology for Economic Growth*, National Academy Press, Washington

Kumbhakar, S., Ortega-Argilés, R., Potters, L., Vivarelli, M., and Voigt, P., 2012, "Corporate R&D and Firm's Distance to the Frontier: Evidence from Europe's Top-R&D Investors", *Journal of Productivity Analysis*, 37.2, 125–140, April

Lagendijk, A., and Oinas, P., 2005, "Proximity, External Relations, and Local Economic Development", in Lagendijk, A., and Oinas, P, (eds.), *Proximity, Distance and Diversity: Issues on Economic Interaction and Local Development*, Ashgate, Burlington VT

Landabaso, M., and Rosenfeld, S., 2009, "Public Policies for Industrial Districts and Clusters", in Becattini, G., Bellandi, M., and de Propris, L., (eds.), *A Handbook of Industrial Districts*, Edward Elgar, Cheltenham, UK and Northampton, MA, USA

Lee, N., and Rodriguez-Pose, 2013, "Original Innovation, Learnt Innovation and Cities: Evidence from UK SMEs", *Urban Studies*, 50.9, 1742–1759

Levin, R.C., Klevorick, A.K., Nelson, R.R., and Winter, S.G., 1987, "Appropriating the Returns from Industrial Research and Development", *Brookings Papers on Economic Activity*, 3.0, 783–820

Lipsey, R.G., Carlaw, K.I, and Bekar, C.T, 2006, *Economic Transformations: General Purpose Technologies and Long Term Economic Growth*, Oxford University Press, Oxford

Lucas, R.E., 1988, "On the Mechanics of Economic Development", *Journal of Monetary Economics*, 22, 3–42

Lundvall, B.A., 1992, *National Systems of Innovation: Towards a Theory of Innovation and Interactive Learning*, Pinter, London

Macpherson, A., 2008, "Producer Services Linkage and Industrial Innovation: Results of a Twelve Tear Tracking Study of New York Stake Manufacturers", *Growth and Change*, 39.1, 1–23

Malerba, F. and Orsenigo, L., 1997, "Technological Regimes and Sectoral Patterns of Innovative Activities", *Industrial and Corporate Change*, 6, 83–117

Malerba, F., Nelson, R.R., Orsenigo, L., and Winter, S.G., 1999, "History-friendly Models of Industry Evolution: The Computer Industry", *Industrial Dynamics and Corporate Change*, 8, 1–36

Mansfield, E., Schwartz, M., and Wagner, S., 1981, "Imitation Costs and Patents: An Empirical Study", *Economic Journal*, 91.364, 907–918

Martin, R.L., and Sunley, P., 2003, "Deconstructing Clusters: Chaotic Concept or Policy Panacea?", *Journal of Economic Geography*, 3.1, 5–35

Martin, P., Mayer, T., and Mayneris, F., 2011, "Public Support to Clusters: A Firm Level Study of French 'Local Productive Systems'", *Regional Science and Urban Economics*, 41, 108–123

McCann, P., 2007, "Sketching out a Model of Innovation, Face-to-Face Interaction and Economic Geography", *Spatial Economic Analysis*, 2.2, 117–134

McCann, P., 2008, "Globalization and Economic Geography: The World is Curved, Not Flat", 2008, *Cambridge Journal of Regions, Economy and Society*, 1.3, 351–370

McCann, P., 2011, "International Business and Economic Geography: Knowledge, Time and Transactions", *Journal of Economic Geography*, 11.2, 309–317

McCann, P., and Acs, Z.J., 2011, "Globalisation: Countries, Cities and Multinationals", 2011, *Regional Studies*, 45.1, 17–32

McCann, P., and Arita, T., 2006, "Clusters and Regional Development: Some Cautionary Observations from the Semiconductor Industry", *Information Economics and Policy*, 18.2, 157–180

McCann, P., and Mudambi, R., 2004, "The Location Decision of the Multinational Enterprise: Some Theoretical and Empirical Issues", *Growth & Change*, 35.4, 491–524

McCann, P., and Mudambi, R., 2005, "Analytical Differences in the Economics of Geography: The Case of the Multinational Firm", *Environment and Planning A*, 37.10, 1857–1876

McCann, P., and Ortega-Argilés, R., 2013, "Modern Regional Innovation Policy", *Cambridge Journal of Regions, Economy and Society*, 6.2, 187–216

Mian, S.A., 2011, (ed.), *Science and Technology Based Entrepreneurship: Global Experience in Policy and Program Development*, Edward Elgar, Cheltenham, UK and Northampton, MA, USA

Morgan, K.J., 1997, "The Learning Region: Institutions, Innovation and Regional Renewal", *Regional Studies*, 31.5, 491–503

Moretti, E., 2012, *The New Geography of Jobs*, Houghton Mifflin Harcourt, New York

Morroni, M., 1992, *Production Process and Technical Change*, Cambridge University Press, Cambridge

Moulaert, F., and Sekia, F., 2003, "Territorial Innovation Models: A Critical Survey", *Regional Studies*, 37.3, 289–302

Nathan, M., and Lee, N., 2013, "Cultural Diversity, Innovation, and Entrepreneurship: Firm-Level from London", *Economic Geography*, 367–394

Neffke, F., Henning, M., and Boschma, R., 2011, "How do Regions Diversify over Time? Industry Relatedness and the Development of New Growth Paths in Regions", *Economic Geography*, 87.3, 237–265

Nelson, R.R., 1993, *National Systems of Innovation: A Comparative Analysis*, Oxford University Press, Oxford

Nelson, R.R. and Winter, S.G., 1982, *An Evolutionary Theory of Economic Change*, Harvard University Press, Cambridge MA

NESTA, 2009, *The Vital Six Per Cent: How High-Growth Innovative Businesses Generate Prosperity and Jobs*, NESTA, London

OECD, 2002, *Frascati Manual: Proposed Standard Practice for Surveys on Research and Experimental Development*, Organisation for Economic Growth and Development, Paris

OECD, 2004, *The Economic Impacts of ICT: Measurement, Evidence and Implications*, Organisation for Economic Growth and Development, Paris

OECD, 2005, *Oslo Manual: Guide for Collecting and Interpreting Innovation Data*, Organisation for Economic Growth and Development, Paris

OECD, 2010, *The OECD Innovation Strategy: Getting A Head Start on Tomorrow*, Organisation for Economic Cooperation and Development, Paris

OECD, 2011, *Regions and Innovation Policy*, Organisation for Economic Cooperation and Development, Paris

OECD, 2012, *Promoting Growth in All Regions*, Organisation for Economic Cooperation and Development, Paris

OECD, 2013a, *Interconnected Economies: Benefiting from Global Value Chains*, Organisation for Economic Cooperation and Development, Paris

OECD, 2013b, *Regions and Innovation: Collaborating Across Borders*, Organisation for Economic Cooperation and Development, Paris

Ortega-Argilés, R., 2012, "The Transatlantic Productivity Gap: A Survey of the Main Causes", *Journal of Economic Surveys*, 26.3, 395–419

Ortega-Argilés, R., Moreno, R., and J. Suriñach, 2005, "Ownership Structure and Innovation: Is there a Real Link?", *Annals of Regional Science*, 39.4, 637–662

Ortega-Argilés, R. and Moreno, R., 2007, "Product and Process Innovations and the Likelihood of Survival", in Arauzo-Carod, J.M. and Manjon-Antolín, M.C., (eds.), *Entrepreneurship, Industrial Location and Economic Growth*, Edward Elgar, Cheltenham, UK and Northampton, MA, USA

Ortega-Argilés, R. and Moreno, R., 2009, "Differences in Survivor Functions According to Different Competitive Strategies", in Karlsson,

C., Johansson, B., and Stough, R. (eds.), *Innovations and Entrepreneurship in Functional Regions*, Edward Elgar, Cheltenham, UK and Northampton, MA, USA

Ortega-Argilés, R., Piva, M.C., and Vivarelli, M., 2011, "Productivity Gains from R&D Investment: Are High-tech Sectors Still Ahead?", IZA Discussion Paper 5975, Institute for the Study of Labor (IZA)

Pavitt, K., 1984, "Sectoral Patterns of Technical Change: Towards a Taxonomy and a Theory", *Research Policy*, 13, 343–373

Pavitt, K., 2000, *Technology, Management and Systems of Innovation*, Edward Elgar, Cheltenham, UK and Northampton, MA, USA

Paunov, C., 2013, "Innovation and Inclusive Development: A Discussion of the Main Policy Issues", *OECD Science, Technology and Industry Working Papers 2013/01*, Organisation for Economic Cooperation and Development, Paris

Piore, M.J., and Sabel, C.F., 1984, *The Second Industrial Divide: Possibilities for Prosperity*, Basic Books, New York

Polenske, K., 2007, (ed.), *The Economic Geography of Innovation*, Cambridge University Press, Cambridge

Porter, M.E., 1985, *Competitive Advantage: Creating and Sustaining Superior Performance*, Free Press, New York

Porter, M.E., 1990, *The Competitive Advantage of Nations*, Free Press, New York

Porter, M.E., 1998, "Clusters and the New Economics of Competition", *Harvard Business Review*, 76.6, 77

Porter, M.E., 1998b, "Competing Across Locations", in Porter, M.E., (ed.), *On Competition*, Harvard Business School Press, Cambridge, MA

Prager, J.-C, and Thisse, J.-F., 2012, *Economic Geography and the Unequal Development of Regions*, Routledge, London

Quah, D., 2001, "The Weightless Economy in Economic Development", in Pohoja, M., (ed.), *Information Technology, Productivity, and Economic Growth*, Oxford University Press, Oxford

Rodrik, D., 2007, *One Economics Many Recipes: Globalization, Institutions and Economic Growth*, Princeton University Press, Princeton

Romer, P.M., 1986, "Increasing Returns and Long-Run Growth", *Journal of Political Economy*, 94, 1002–1037

Romer, P.M., 1990, "Endogenous Technological Change", *Journal of Political Economy*, 98, S71–S102

Scherer, F.M., 1965, "Firm Size, Market Structure, Opportunity, and the Output of Patented Inventions", *American Economic Review*, 55, 1097–1125

Schonberger, R.J., 1981, *World Class Manufacturing: The Next Decade*, Free Press, New York

Schumpeter, J.A., 1934, *The Theory of Economic Development*, Harvard University Press, Cambridge MA

Scotchmer, S., 2004, *Innovation and Incentives*, MIT Press, Cambridge MA

Shearmur, R., 2011, "Innovation, Regions and Proximity: From Neo-Regionalism to Spatial Analysis", *Regional Studies*, 45.9, 1225–1244

Shearmur, R., 2012, "Are Cities at the Forefront of Innovation? A Critical Review of the Literature on Cities and Innovation", *Cities*, 29 (S2), S9–S18

Shearmur, R., and Doloreux, D., 2008, "Urban Hierarchy or Local Buzz? High-Order Producer Service and (or) Knowledge-Intensive Business Service Location in Canada, 1991-2001", *Professional Geographer*, 60.3, 333–355

Shearmur, R., and Doloreux, D., 2013, "Innovation and Knowledge-Intensive Business Service: The Contribution of Knowledge Intensive Business Service to Innovation in Manufacturing Establishments", *Economics of Innovation and New Technology*, 22.8, 751–774

Simonen, J., and McCann, P., 2008, "Firm Innovation: The Influence of R&D Cooperation and the Geography of Human Capital Inputs", *Journal of Urban Economics*, 64.1, 146–154

Simonen, J., and McCann, P., 2010, "Knowledge Transfers and Innovation: The Role of Labour Markets and R&D Cooperation between Agents and Institutions", *Papers in Regional Science*, 89.2, 295–309

Solow, R., 1987, "We'd Better Watch Out", *New York Times Book Review*, July 12, p. 36

Sonobe, T., and Keijiro, O., 2006, (eds.), *Cluster-Based Industrial Development: An East Asian Model*, Palgrave Macmillan, London

Sternberg, R., 2011, "Regional Determinants of Entrepreneurial Activities – Theories and Empirical Evidence", in Fritsch, M., (ed.), *Handbook of Research on Entrepreneurship and Regional Development: National and Regional Perspectives*, Edward Elgar, Cheltenham, UK and Northampton, MA, USA

Stiglitz, J.E., Sen, A., and Fitoussi, J.-P., 2009, *Report by the Commission on the Measurement of Economic and Social Progress*. See http://www.stiglitz-sen-fitoussi.fr/en/index.htm

Swann, G.M., 2009, *The Economics of Innovation: An Introduction*, Edward Elgar, Cheltenham, UK and Northampton, MA, USA

Teece, D.J., 1986, "Profiting from Technological Innovation", *Research Policy*, 15.6, 285–305

Teece, D.J., 2011, *Dynamic Capabilities and Strategic Management: Organizing for Innovation and Growth*, Oxford University Press, Oxford

Tether, B.S., Smith, I.J., Thwaites, A.T., 1997, "Smaller Enterprises and Innovation in the UK: The SPRU Innovations Database Revisited", *Research Policy*, 26, 19–32

Tidd, J., Bessant, J., and Pavitt, K., 1997, *Managing Innovation: Integrating Technological, Market and Organizational Change*, John Wiley & Sons, Chichester

Timmer, M.P., Los, B., Stehrer, R., and de Vries, G.J., 2013, "Fragmentation, Incomes and Jobs: An Analysis of European Competitiveness", *Economic Policy*, 613–661

Torre, A., and Rallet, A., 2005, "Proximity and Localization", *Regional Studies*, 39.1, 47–59

Van der Linde, C., 2003, "The Demography of Clusters – Findings from the Cluster Meta-Study", in Bröcker, J., Dohse, D., and Soltwedel, R., (eds.), *Innovation Clusters and Interregional Competition*, Springer, Heidelberg

Van Oort, F.G., 2004, *Urban Growth and Innovation: Spatially Bounded Externalities in The Netherlands*, Ashgate, Aldershot

Viladecans-Marsal, E., and Arauzo-Carod, J.-M., 2012, "Can a Knowledge-Based Cluster be Created? The Case of Barcelona 22@ District", *Papers in Regional Science*, 91.2, 377–400

World Bank, 2010, *Innovation Policy: A Guide for Developing Countries*, World Bank, Washington DC

World Bank, 2011, *Igniting Innovation: Rethinking the Role of Government in Emerging Europe and Central Asia*, Goldberg, I., Goddard, J.G., Kuriakose, S., and Racine, J.-L., World Bank, Washington DC

CHAPTER 6

Abreu, M., Grinevich, V., Hughes, A., and Kitson, M., 2009, *Knowledge Exchanges between Academics and the Business, Public and Third Sectors*, Centre for Business Research, University of Cambridge

Acs, Z.J., Szerb, L., Ortega-Argilés, R., Aidis, R., and Coduras, A., 2014, "The Regional Application of the Global Entrepreneurship and Development Index (GEDI): The Case of Spain", *Regional Studies*, forthcoming, DOI:10.1080/00343404.2014.888712

Annoni, P., and Dijkstra, L., 2013, *EU Regional Competitiveness Index RCI 2013*, http://ec.europa.eu/regional_policy/sources/docgener/studies/pdf/6th_report/rci_2013_report_final.pdf

Autor, D.H., Katz, L.F., and Kreuger, A.B., 1998, "Computing Inequality: Have Computers Changed the Labor Market?", *Quarterly Journal of Economics*, 113.4, 1169–1213

Bachtler, J., Mendez, C., and Wishlade, F., 2013, *EU Cohesion Policy and European Integration: The Dynamics of EU Budget and Regional Policy Reform*, Ashgate, Aldershot

Barca, F., 2009, *An Agenda for A Reformed Cohesion Policy: A Place-Based Approach to Meeting European Union Challenges and Expectations*, Independent Report Prepared at the Request of the European Commissioner for Regional Policy, Danuta Hübner, European Commission, Brussels

Best, M.H., 1990, *The New Competition: Institutions of Industrial Restructuring*, Polity Press, Cambridge

Boschma, R.A., 2014, "Constructing Regional Advantage and Smart Specialisation: Comparison of two European Policy Concepts", *Italian Journal of Regional Science*, 13.1, 51–68

Boschma, R.A., and Frenken, K., 2011, "Technological Relatedness and Regional Branching", in Bathelt, H., Feldman, M.P., and Kogler, D.F., (eds.), *Dynamic Geographies of Knowledge Creation and Innovation*, Taylor and Francis, Routledge, London

Boschma, R.A., and Iammarino, S., 2009, "Related Variety, Trade Linkages and Regional Growth", *Economic Geography*, 85.3, 289–311

Boschma, R.A., Minondo, A., and Navarro, M., 2012, "Related Variety and Regional Growth in Spain", *Papers in Regional Science*, 91.2, 241–256

Borrás, S., and Tsagdis, D., 2008, *Cluster Policies in Europe: Firms, Institutions and Governance*, Edward Elgar, Cheltenham, UK and Northampton, MA, USA

Braga de Macedo, J., and Oliveira-Martins, J., 2010, "Policy Complementarities and Growth", 1–37, *OECD/CESifo/Ifo Workshop Regulation: Political Economy, Measurement and Effects on Performance*, 29–30 January, Munich

Camagni, R., Capello, R., and Lenzi, C., 2014, "A Territorial Taxonomy of Innovative Regions and the European Regional Policy Reform: Smart Innovation Policies", *Italian Journal of Regional Science*, 13.1, 69–106

Coffano, M., and Foray, D., 2014, "The Centrality of Entrepreneurial Discovery in Building and Implementing a Smart Specialisation Strategy", *Italian Journal of Regional Science*, 13.1, 33–50

Cooke, P., 2012, *Complex Adaptive Innovation Systems: Relatedness and Transversality in the Evolving Region*, Routledge, London

Cooke, P., Asheim, B., Annerstedt, J., Blažec, J., Boschma, R., Brzica, D., Dahlstrand Lindholm, A., Del Castillo Hermosa, J., Laredo, P., Moula, M., and Piccaluga, A., 2006, *Constructing Regional Advantage: Principles, Perspectives, Policies*, Report to European Commission Directorate-General for Research, Brussels

Cozza, C., Ortega-Argilés, R., Piva, M., and Baptista, R., 2012, "Productivity gaps among EU regions", in Audretsch, D.B., Lehmann, E.E., Link, A.N., and Starnecker, A., (eds.), *Technology Transfer in a Global Economy*, International Studies on Entrepreneurship, Vol. 28, Springer, Berlin

Crescenzi, R., and Rodriguez-Pose, A., 2012, "An 'Integrated' Framework for the Comparative Analysis of the Territorial Innovation Dynamics of Developed and Developing Countries", *Journal of Economic Surveys*, 26.3, 517–533

CST, 2007, "Strategic Decision-Making for Technology Policy", UK Council for Science and Technology, November See: http://web archive.nationalarchives.gov.uk/+/http://www2.cst.gov.uk/cst/reports/# Strategic

David, P.A., 1985, "Clio and the Economics of QWERTY", *American Economic Review: Papers and Proceedings*, 75.2, 332–337

David, P., Foray, D., and Hall, B., 2009, *Measuring Smart Specialisation: The Concept and the Need for Indicators,* Knowledge for Growth Expert Group, See: http://cemi.epfl.ch/files/content/sites/cemi/files/users/178044/public/Measuring%20smart%20specialisation.doc

Davies, H.T.O., Nutley, S.M., and Smith, P.C., 2000, *What Works? Evidence-Based Policy and Practice in Public Services*, Policy Press, Bristol

Dijkstra, L., and Poelman, H., 2012, "Cities in Europe: The New OECD-EC Definition", *Regional Focus RF 01/2012*, Directorate-General for Regional and Urban Policy, Brussels

Dijkstra, L., Garcilazo, E., and McCann, P., 2013, "The Economic Performance of European Cities and City-Regions: Myths and Realities", *European Planning Studies*, 21.3, 334–354

Duranton, G., 2011, "California Dreamin': The Feeble Case for Cluster Policies", *Review of Economic Analysis*, 3.1, 3–45

Duranton, G., and Puga, D., 2004, "Micro-Foundations of Urban Agglomeration Economies", in Henderson, J.V., and Thisse, J.-F., (eds.), *Handbook of Regional and Urban Economics, Vol IV: Economic Geography*, Elsevier, Amsterdam

ERAWATCH, 2011, *Development of a Methodology for the Profiling of Regional Economies*, Erawatch Network ASBL, Fraunhofer ISI UNU-MERIT IAIF Logotech, Brussels

ESPON, 2012, *KIT Territorial Dimension of Innovation and Knowledge Economy*, Luxembourg

European Commission, 2010, *Investing in Europe's Future: Fifth Report on Economics, Social and Territorial Cohesion*, Brussels

European Commission, 2011a, *Connecting Universities to Regional Growth: A Practical Guide*, Smart Specialisation Platform, IPTS Seville

European Commission, 2011b, *High-Level Expert Group on Key Enabling Technologies: Final Report*, Brussels

European Union, 2013a, *The Urban and Regional Dimension of the Crisis: Eighth Report on Economic, Social and Territorial Cohesion*, Publications Office, Brussels

European Union, 2013b, *Regional Policy for Smart Growth of SMEs: Guide for Managing Authorities and Bodies in Charge of the Development and Implementation of Research and Innovation Strategies for Smart Specialisation*, Directorate General for Regional and Urban Policy, Publications Office, Brussels

European Union, 2013c, *The Guide to Multi-Benefit Cohesion Policy Investments in Nature and Green Infrastructure*, Directorate General for Regional and Urban Policy Publications Office, Brussels

European Union, 2013d, *European Public Sector Innovation Scoreboard 2013*, Directorate-General for Enterprise and Industry, Publications Office, Brussels

European Union, 2013e, *Lessons from Decades of Innovation Policy: What can be Learned from the INNO Policy TrendChart and The Innovation Union Scoreboard*, Directorate-General for Enterprise and Industry, Publications Office, Brussels

Fagerberg. J., Feldmann, M.P., and Srholec, M., 2014, "Technological Dynamics and Social Capability: US States and European Nations", *Journal of Economic Geography*, 14.2, 313–337

Faggian, A., and McCann, P., 2006, "Human Capital Flows and Regional Knowledge Assets: A Simultaneous Equation Approach", *Oxford Economic Papers*, 58.3, 475–500

Faggian, A., and McCann, P., 2009a, "Human Capital, Graduate Migration and Innovation in British Regions", *Cambridge Journal of Economics*, 33.2, 317–333

Faggian, A., and McCann, P., 2009b, "Human Capital and Regional Development", in Capello, R., and Nijkamp, P., (eds.), *Regional Dynamics and Growth: Advances in Regional Economics*, Edward Elgar, Cheltenham, UK and Northampton, MA, USA

Foray, D., 2004, *The Economics of Knowledge*, MIT Press, Cambridge MA

Foray, D., and Goenaga, X., 2013, "The Goals of Smart Specialisation", *S3 Policy Brief Series No.01/2013*, European Commission Joint Research Centre IPTS, Seville

Foray, D., and Rainaldi, A., 2013, "Smart Specialisation Programmes and Implementation", *S3 Policy Brief Series No.02/2013*, European Commission Joint Research Centre IPTS, Seville

Foray, D., David, P., and Hall, B., 2009, "Smart Specialisation – The Concept", Knowledge Economists Policy Brief No.9, June

Foray, D., David, P., and Hall, B., 2011, "Smart Specialization: From Academic Idea to Political Instrument, the Surprising Career of a Concept and the Difficulties involved in its Implementation", MTEI Working Paper, École Polytechnique Fédérale de Lausanne

Foray, D., Goddard, J., Goenaga Beldarrain, X., Landabaso, M., McCann, P., Morgan, K., Neuwelaars, C., and Ortega-Argilés, R., 2012, *Guide to Research and Innovation Strategies for Smart Specialisation (RIS 3)*, S3 Smart Specialisation Platform, IPTS Institute for Prospective Technological Studies, Joint Research Centre of the European Commission, Seville. See http://ec.europa.eu/regional_policy/sources/docgener/presenta/smart_specialisation/smart_ris3_2012.pdf

Fraunhofer ISI, 2013, *Smart Specialisation Approaches: A New Policy Paradigm on its Way from Policy to Practice*, See http://www.isi.fraunhofer.de/isi-media/docs/p/de/vortragsfolien/regionen_cluster/S3_Projekt_final.pdf

Frenken, K., and Boschma, R.A., 2007, "A Theoretical Framework for Evolutionary Economic Geography: Industrial Dynamics and Urban Growth as a Branching Process", *Journal of Economic Geography*, 7.5, 635–649

Frenken, K., Van Oort, F.G., and Verburg, T., 2007, "Related Variety, Unrelated Variety and Regional Economic Growth", *Regional Studies*, 41.5, 685–697

Fujita, M., Krugman, P., and Venables, A.J., 1999, *The Spatial Economy: Cities, Regions and International Trade*, MIT Press, Cambridge MA

Gault, F., 2013, (ed.), *Handbook of Innovation Indicators and Measurement*, Edward Elgar, Cheltenham, UK and Northampton, MA, USA

Goos, M., Manning, A., and Salomons, A., 2009, "Job Polarization in Europe", *American Economic Review*, 99.2, 58–63

Gordon, I.R., and Kaplanis, I., 2014, "Accounting for Big-City Growth in Low-Paid Occupations: Immigration and/or Service-Class Consumption", *Economic Geography*, 90.1, 67–90

Hausmann, R., and Rodrik, D., 2003, "Economic Development as Self-Discovery", *Journal of Development Economics*, 72.2, 603–633

Hausmann, R., Hidalgo, C.A., Bustos, S., Coscia, M., Chung, S., Jiminez, J., Somoes, A., and Yildirim, M., 2013, *The Atlas of Economic Complexity: Mapping Paths to Prosperity*, Center for International Development and Kennedy School of Government, Harvard

University, Cambridge MA. See http://www.hks.harvard.edu/centers/cid/publications/featured-books/atlas

House of Commons, 2013, "Bridging the Valley of Death: Improving the Commercialisation of Research", *Eighth Report of Session 2012–13*, The Stationery Office, London

Hughes, A., 2012, "Choosing Races and Placing Bets: UK National Innovation Policy and the Globalisation of Innovation Systems", in Greenaway, D., (ed.), *The UK in a Global World. How Can the UK Focus on Steps in Global Value Chains that Really Add Value?*, BIS e-book, CEPR and Department for Business, Innovation and Skills. See http://www.cepr.org/pubs/books/cepr/BIS_eBook.pdf

Hughes, A., and Kitson, M., 2013, *Connecting with the Ivory Tower: Business Perspectives on Knowledge Exchange in the UK*, Centre for Business Research, University of Cambridge

Hughes, A., Moore, K., and Kataria, N., 2011, *Innovation in Public Sector Organisations: A Pilot Survey for Measuring Innovation Across the Public Sector*, NESTA, London

Iacobucci, D., 2014, "Designing and Implementing a Smart Specialisation Strategy at Regional Level: Some Open Questions", *Italian Journal of Regional Science*, 13.1, 107–126

Iammarino, S., and McCann, P., 2006, "The Structure and Evolution of Industrial Clusters: Transactions, Technology and Knowledge Spillovers", *Research Policy*, 35, 1018–1036

Ketels, C., 2013, "Recent Research on Competitiveness and Clusters: What Are the Implications for Regional Policy?", *Cambridge Journal of Regions, Economy and Society*, 6.2, 269–284

Landabaso, M., 1997, "The Promotion of Innovation in Regional Policy: Proposals for a Regional Innovation Strategy", *Entrepreneurship and Regional Development*, 9.1, 1–24

Landabaso, M., 2014, "Time for the Real Economy: The Need for New Forms of Public Entrepreneurship", *Italian Journal of Regional Science*, 13.1, 127–140

Landabaso, M., and Mouton, B., 2005, "Towards a Different Regional Innovation Policy: 8 Years of European Experience Through the European Regional Development Fund Innovative Actions", in Heitor, M., (ed.), *Regional Development and Conditions for Innovation in the Network Society*, pp. 209–240, Purdue University Press, West Lafayette, IN

Landabaso, M., and Reid, A., 1999, "Developing Regional Innovation Strategies: the European Commission as Animator", in Morgan. K., and Nauwelaars, C., (eds.), *Regional Innovation Strategies: Key Challenge for Europe's Less Favoured Regions*, pp. 19–39, The Stationery

Office, London (published in association with the Regional Studies Association)

Landabaso, M., Oughton, C., and Morgan, K., 2001, "Learning Regions in Europe: Theory, Policy and Practice Through the RIS experience", in Conceição, P., Gibson, D.V., Heitor, M.V., and Stolp, C., (eds.), *Systems and Policies for the Globalized Learning Economy*, QUORUM Books Series on Technology Policy and Innovation, Volume 3, Greenwood Publishing Inc, Westport, CT

Lee, N., and Rodriguez-Pose, 2013, "Original Innovation, Learnt Innovation and Cities: Evidence from UK SMEs", *Urban Studies*, 50.9, 1742–1759

McCann, P., 2007, "Sketching out a Model of Innovation, Face-to-Face Interaction and Economic Geography", *Spatial Economic Analysis*, 2.2, 117–134

McCann, P., 2008, "Globalization and Economic Geography: The World is Curved, Not Flat", *Cambridge Journal of Regions, Economy and Society*, 1.3, 351–370

McCann, P. and Acs, Z. J., 2011, "Globalisation: Countries, Cities and Multinationals", *Regional Studies*, 45

McCann, P., and Ortega-Argilés, R., 2013a, "Redesigning and Reforming European Regional Policy: The Reasons, the Logic and the Outcomes", *International Regional Science Review*, 36.3, 424–445

McCann and Ortega-Argilés 2013b, "Transforming European Regional Policy: A Results-Driven Agenda and Smart Specialisation", *Oxford Review of Economic Policy*, 29.2, 405–431

McCann, P., and Ortega-Argilés, R., 2013c, "Modern Regional Innovation Policy", *Cambridge Journal of Regions, Economy and Society*, 6.2, 187–216

McCann and Ortega-Argilés 2014a, "Smart Specialisation, Regional Growth and Applications to EU Cohesion Policy", *Regional Studies*, DOI: 10.1080/00343404.2013.799769, forthcoming

McCann and Ortega-Argilés 2014b, "The Role of the Smart Specialisation Agenda in a Reformed EU Cohesion Policy", *Italian Journal of Regional Science*, 13.1, 15–32

MGI, 2013, *A New Dawn: Reigniting Growth in Central and Eastern Europe*, McKinsey Global Institute, December

MGI, 2014, *Education to Employment: Getting Europe's Youth into Work*, McKinsey Global Institute. See: http://www.mckinsey.com/Insights/Social_Sector/Converting_education_to_employment_in_Europe?cid=other-eml-alt-mip-mck-oth-1401

Moretti, E., 2012, *The New Geography of Jobs*, Houghton Mifflin Harcourt, New York

Nathan, M., and Overman, M., 2013, "Agglomeration, Clusters and Industrial Policy", *Oxford Review of Economic Policy*, 29.2, 383–404

Neffke, F., Henning, M., and Boschma, R., 2011, "How do Regions Diversify over Time? Industry Relatedness and the Development of New Growth Paths in Regions", *Economic Geography*, 87.3, 237–265

NRC National Research Council, 2009, *An Assessment of the Small Business Innovation Research Program*, Wessner, C.W., (ed.), National Academies Press, Washington DC

OECD, 2007, *Higher Education and Regions: Globally Competitive, Locally Engaged*, Organisation for Economic Growth and Development, Paris

OECD, 2009a, *How Regions Grow*, Organisation for Economic Growth and Development, Paris

OECD, 2009b, *Regions Matter: Economic Recovery, Innovation and Sustainable Growth*, Organisation for Economic Growth and Development, Paris

OECD, 2011a, *Regions and Innovation Policy*, Organisation for Economic Growth and Development, Paris

OECD, 2011b, *OECD Regional Outlook 2011: Building Resilient Regions for Stronger Economies*, Organisation for Economic Cooperation and Development, Paris

OECD, 2011c, *The OECD Innovation Strategy: Getting A Head Start on Tomorrow*, Organisation for Economic Cooperation and Development, Paris

OECD, 2012a, *Draft Synthesis Report on Innovation-Driven Growth in Regions: The Role of Smart Specialisation*, Organisation for Economic Growth and Development, December

OECD, 2012b, *Promoting Growth in All Regions*, Organisation for Economic Cooperation and Development, Paris

OECD, 2012c, *Redefining "Urban": A New Way to Measure Metropolitan Regions*, Organisation for Economic Cooperation and Development, Paris

OECD, 2013a, *Regions at a Glance 2013*, Organisation for Economic Growth and Development, Paris

OECD, 2013b, *Interconnected Economies: Benefiting from Global Value Chains*, Organisation for Economic Cooperation and Development, Paris

OECD, 2013c, *Rural–Urban Partnerships: An Integrated Approach to Economic Development*, Organisation for Economic Cooperation and Development, Paris

OECD, 2013d, *Regions and Innovation: Collaborating Across Borders*, Organisation for Economic Cooperation and Development, Paris

OECD, 2013e, *Innovation-Driven Growth in Regions: The Role of Smart Specialisation*, Organisation for Economic Growth and Development, December. See http://www.oecd.org/sti/inno/smartspecialisation.htm

Ortega-Argilés, R., 2012, "The Transatlantic Productivity Gap: A Survey of the Main Causes", *Journal of Economic Surveys*, 26.3, 395–419

Ortega-Argilés, R., 2013, "R&D, Knowledge, Economic Growth and the Transatlantic Productivity Gap", in Giarratani, F., Hewings, G.J.D., and McCann, P., (eds.), *Handbook of Industry Studies and Economic Geography*, Edward Elgar, Cheltenham, UK and Northampton, MA, USA

Ortega-Argilés R., Piva, M., Potters, L., and Vivarelli, M., 2010, "Is Corporate R&D Investment in High-Tech Sectors More Effective?", *Contemporary Economic Policy*, 28, 353–365

Ortega-Argilés, R., Piva, M., and Vivarelli, M., 2014, "The Transatlantic Productivity Gap: Is R&D the Main Culprit?", *Canadian Journal of Economics*, forthcoming

Osborne, S.P., and Brown, L., 2013, (eds.), *Handbook of Innovation in Public Services*, Edward Elgar, Cheltenham, UK and Northampton, MA, USA

Paunov, C., 2013, "Innovation and Inclusive Development: A Discussion of the Main Policy Issues", *OECD Science, Technology and Industry Working Papers 2013/01*, Organisation for Economic Cooperation and Development, Paris

Pavitt, K., 1984, "Sectoral Patterns of Technical Change: Towards a Taxonomy and a Theory", *Research Policy*, 13, 343–373

Pawson, R., 2006, *Evidence-Based Policy: A Realist Perspective*, Sage, London

Prager, J.-C., and Thisse, J.-F., 2012, *Economic Geography and the Unequal Development of Regions*, Routledge, London

Putnam. R., 1996, *Bowling Alone: The Collapse and Revival of American Community*, Simon and Schuster, New York

Quah, D., 2001, "The Weightless Economy in Economic Development", in Pohoja, M., (ed.), *Information Technology, Productivity, and Economic Growth*, Oxford University Press, Oxford

Rodrik, D., 2004, "Industrial Policy for the Twenty-First Century", Working Paper, Kennedy School of Government, Harvard University, Cambridge MA

Rodrik, D., 2007, *One Economics Many Recipes: Globalization, Institutions and Economic Growth*, Princeton University Press, Princeton

Sassen, S., 2002, (ed.), *Global Networks: Linked Cities*, Routledge, London

Soete, L., 2009a, "The European Research Area as Industrial Policy Tool", in Delanghe, H., Muldur, U., and Soete, L., (eds.), *European*

Science and Technology Policy: Towards Integration and Fragmentation?, Edward Elgar, Cheltenham, UK and Northampton, MA, USA

Soete, L., 2009b, "Research without Frontiers", in Foray, D., (ed.), *The New Economics of Technology Policy*, Edward Elgar, Cheltenham, UK and Northampton, MA, USA

Sternberg, R., 2011, "Regional Determinants of Entrepreneurial Activities – Theories and Empirical Evidence", in Fritsch, M., (ed.), *Handbook of Research on Entrepreneurship and Regional Development: National and Regional Perspectives*, Edward Elgar, Cheltenham, UK and Northampton, MA, USA

Stiglitz, J.E., Sen, A., and Fitoussi, J.-P., 2009, *Report by the Commission on the Measurement of Economic and Social Progress*. See http://www.stiglitz-sen-fitoussi.fr/en/index.htm

Storper, M., 2013, *Keys to the City: How Economics, Institutions, Social Interaction, and Politics Shape Development*, Princeton University Press, Princeton

Swann, G.M., 2009, *The Economics of Innovation: An Introduction*, Edward Elgar, Cheltenham, UK and Northampton, MA, USA

Taylor, P.J., 2004, *World City Network: A Global Urban Analysis*, Routledge, London

Technopolis, 2012, *Public Sector Innovation: Case Study on the Red Tape Challenge in the United Kingdom*. See http://www.technopolis-group.com

Technopolis Group and MIOIR, 2012, *Evaluation of Innovation Activities: Guidance on Methods and Practices*, Study Funded by the European Commission Directorate-General for Regional Policy, Brussels

The Economist, 2013, "The New Interventionism", 21st September

Thissen, M., van Oort, F.G., Diodato, D., and Ruijs, A., 2013, *Regional Competitiveness and Smart Specialization in Europe: Place-Based Development in International Economic Networks*, Edward Elgar, Cheltenham, UK and Northampton, MA, USA

Timmer, M.P., Inklaar, R., O'Mahony, M., and van Ark, B., 2011, *Economic Growth in Europe: A Comparative Industry Perspective*, Cambridge University Press, Cambridge

Timmer, M.P., Los, B., Stehrer, R., de Vries, G.J., 2013, "Fragmentation, Incomes and Jobs: An Analysis of European Competitiveness", *Economic Policy*, 613–661

Tödtling, F., and Trippl, M., 2005, "One Size Fits All? Towards a Differentiated Regional Innovation Policy Approach", *Research Policy*, 34, 1203–1219

Trajtenberg, M., 2009, "The Rumblings of a Paradigm Shift: Concluding Comments", in Foray, D., (ed.), *The New Economics of Technology Policy*, Edward Elgar, Cheltenham, UK and Northampton, MA, USA

UNCTAD, 2012, *World Investment Report 2012: Towards a New Generation of Investment Policies*, United Nations Conference on Trade and Development, United Nations, Geneva

Von Tunzelmann, N., 2009, "Regional Capabilities and Industrial Regeneration", in Farshchi, M., Janne, O.E.M., and McCann, P., (eds.), *Technological Change and Mature Industrial Regions: Firms, Knowledge and Policy*, Edward Elgar, Cheltenham, UK and Northampton, MA, USA

World Bank, 2009, *2009 World Development Report: Reshaping Economic Geography*, World Bank, Washington DC

World Bank, 2010, *Innovation Policy: A Guide for Developing Countries*, World Bank, Washington DC

World Bank, 2011, *Igniting Innovation: Rethinking the Role of Government in Emerging Europe and Central Asia*, Goldberg, I., Goddard, J.G., Kuriakose, S., and Racine, J.-L., World Bank, Washington DC

World Bank, 2012, *Golden Growth: Restoring the Lustre of the European Economic Model*, Washington DC

CHAPTER 7

Bachtler, J., and Turok, I., 1997, (eds.), *The Coherence of Regional Policy,: Contrasting Perspectives on the Structural Funds*, Jessica Kingsley, London

Bachtler, J., Mendez, C., and Oraže, H., 2014, "From Conditionality to Europeanization in Central and Eastern Europe: Administrative Performance and Capacity in Cohesion Policy", *European Planning Studies*, 22.4, 735–757

CoR, 2014, *A Mid-Term Assessment of Europe 2020 from the Standpoint of EU Regions and Cities*, Committee of the Regions, Brussels

European Commission, 2010, *Investing in Europe's Future: Fifth Report on Economic, Social and Territorial Cohesion*, Brussels

European Union, 2011, *The Urban and Regional Dimension of Europe 2020: Seventh Progress Report on Economic, Social and Territorial Cohesion*, Publications Office, Brussels

European Union, 2013, *The Urban and Regional Dimension of the Crisis: Eighth Report on Economic, Social and Territorial Cohesion*, Publications Office, Brussels

European Union, 2014, *Investment for Jobs and Growth – Promoting Development and Good Governance in EU Regions and Cities: Sixth*

Report on Economic, Social and Territorial Cohesion, European Commission Directorate-General for Regional and Urban Policy, Publications Office, Luxembourg

Foray, D., 2015, *Smart Specialisation: Opportunities and Challenges for Regional Innovation Policy*, Routledge, London.

Gordon, I.R., and McCann, P., 2005, "Innovation, Agglomeration and Regional Development", 2005, *Journal of Economic Geography*, 5.5, 523–543

Lindbeck, A., and Snower, D.J., 1988, *The Insider–Outsider Theory of Employment and Unemployment*, MIT Press, Cambridge MA

Petzold, W., 2013, "Conditionality, Flexibility, Unanimity: The Embedded 2013 Reform of EU Cohesion Policy", *European Structural and Investment Funds Journal*, 1.1, 7–14

Rodrik, D., 2007, *One Economics Many Recipes: Globalization, Institutions and Economic Growth*, Princeton University Press, Princeton

Rodrik, D., 2014, "When Ideas Trump Interests: Preferences, Worldviews, and Policy Innovations", *Journal of Economic Perspectives*, 28.1, 189–208

Storper, M., 2013, *Keys to the City: How Economics, Institutions, Social Interaction, and Politics Shape Development*, Princeton University Press, Princeton

Index